DATE DUE

			PRINTED IN U.S.A.

Children's
Literature
Review

Guide to Gale Literary Criticism Series

For criticism on	Consult these Gale series
Authors now living or who died after December 31, 1959	*CONTEMPORARY LITERARY CRITICISM (CLC)*
Authors who died between 1900 and 1959	*TWENTIETH-CENTURY LITERARY CRITICISM (TCLC)*
Authors who died between 1800 and 1899	*NINETEENTH-CENTURY LITERATURE CRITICISM (NCLC)*
Authors who died between 1400 and 1799	*LITERATURE CRITICISM FROM 1400 TO 1800 (LC)* *SHAKESPEAREAN CRITICISM (SC)*
Authors who died before 1400	*CLASSICAL AND MEDIEVAL LITERATURE CRITICISM (CMLC)*
Black writers of the past two hundred years	*BLACK LITERATURE CRITICISM (BLC)*
Authors of books for children and young adults	*CHILDREN'S LITERATURE REVIEW (CLR)*
Dramatists	*DRAMA CRITICISM (DC)*
Hispanic writers of the late nineteenth and twentieth centuries	*HISPANIC LITERATURE CRITICISM (HLC)*
Native North American writers and orators of the eighteenth, nineteenth, and twentieth centuries	*NATIVE NORTH AMERICAN LITERATURE (NNAL)*
Poets	*POETRY CRITICISM (PC)*
Short story writers	*SHORT STORY CRITICISM (SSC)*
Major authors from the Renaissance to the present	*WORLD LITERATURE CRITICISM, 1500 TO THE PRESENT (WLC)*

ISSN 0362-4145

volume 38

Children's Literature Review

Excerpts from Reviews,
Criticism, and Commentary
on Books for Children
and Young People

Alan Hedblad
Editor

Sharon R. Gunton
Associate Editor

Gale Research

An ITP Information/Reference Group Company

Changing the Way the World Learns

NEW YORK • LONDON • BONN • BOSTON • DETROIT
MADRID • MELBOURNE • MEXICO CITY • PARIS
SINGAPORE • TOKYO • TORONTO • WASHINGTON
ALBANY NY • BELMONT CA • CINCINNATI OH

STAFF

Alan Hedblad, *Editor*

Sharon R. Gunton, *Associate Editor*

Linda R. Andres, Shelly Andrews, Joanna Brod, Elizabeth A. Des Chenes, Tina Grant, Motoko Huthwaite, Julie K. Karmazin, Sean McCready, Thomas F. McMahon, Gerard J. Senick, Diane Telgen, *Contributing Editors*

Marilyn Allen, Paul Zyskowski, *Assistant Editors*

Marlene S. Hurst, *Permissions Manager*
Margaret A. Chamberlain, *Permissions Specialist*
Susan Brohman, Diane Cooper, Maria Franklin, Arlene Johnson, Michele Lonoconus, Maureen Puhl, Shalice Shah, Kimberly F. Smilay, Barbara A. Wallace, *Permissions Associates*
Sarah Chesney, Edna M. Hedblad, Margaret McAvoy-Amato, Tyra Y. Phillips, Lori Schoenenberger, Rita Velazquez, *Permissions Assistants*

Victoria B. Cariappa, *Research Manager*
Donna Melnychenko, *Project Coordinator*
Tamara C. Nott, Norma Sawaya, *Research Associates*
Eva Felts, Amy Wieczorek, *Research Assistants*

Mary Beth Trimper, *Production Director*
Deborah Milliken, *Production Assistant*

Barbara J. Yarrow, *Graphic Services Manager*
Erin Martin, *Desktop Publisher*
Randy Bassett, *Image Database Supervisor*
Pamela A. Hayes, *Photography Coordinator*

∞ This book is printed on acid-free paper that meets the minimum requirements of American National Standard for Information Sciences—Permanence Paper for Printed Library Materials, ANSI Z39.48-1984.

Library of Congress Catalog Card Number 76-643301
ISBN 0-8103-9285-2
ISSN 0362-4145
Printed in the United States of America

ITP Gale Research, an International Thomson Publishing Company.
ITP logo is a trademark under license.

10 9 8 7 6 5 4 3 2 1

Contents

Preface   vii
Acknowledgments   xi

Preface

Literature for children and young adults has evolved into both a respected branch of creative writing and a successful industry. Currently, books for young readers are considered among the most popular segments of publishing. Criticism of juvenile literature is instrumental in recording the literary or artistic development of the creators of children's books as well as the trends and controversies that result from changing values or attitudes about young people and their literature. Designed to provide a permanent, accessible record of this ongoing scholarship, *Children's Literature Review (CLR)* presents parents, teachers, and librarians—those responsible for bringing children and books together—with the opportunity to make informed choices when selecting reading materials for the young. In addition, *CLR* provides researchers of children's literature with easy access to a wide variety of critical information from English-language sources in the field. Users will find balanced overviews of the careers of the authors and illustrators of the books that children and young adults are reading; these entries, which contain excerpts from published criticism in books and periodicals, assist users by sparking ideas for papers and assignments and suggesting supplementary and classroom reading. Ann L. Kalkhoff, president and editor of *Children's Book Review Service Inc.,* writes that "*CLR* has filled a gap in the field of children's books, and it is one series that will never lose its validity or importance."

Scope of the Series

Each volume of *CLR* profiles the careers of a selection of authors and illustrators of books for children and young adults from preschool through high school. Author lists in each volume reflect:

- an international scope.

- representation of authors of all eras.

- the variety of genres covered by children's and/or YA literature: picture books, fiction, nonfiction, poetry, folklore, and drama.

Although the focus of the series is on authors new to *CLR*, entries will be updated as the need arises.

Organization of This Book

An entry consists of the following elements: author heading, author portrait, author introduction, excerpts of criticism (each preceded by a bibliographical citation), and illustrations, when available.

- The **Author Heading** consists of the author's name followed by birth and death dates. The portion of the name outside the parentheses denotes the form under which the author is most frequently published. If the majority of the author's works for children were written under a pseudonym, the pseudonym will be listed in the author heading and the real name given on the first line of the author introduction. Also located at the beginning of the introduction are any other pseudonyms used by the author in writing for children and any name variations, including transliterated forms for authors whose languages use nonroman alphabets. Uncertainty as to a birth or death date is indicated by question marks.

- An **Author Portrait** is included when available.

- The **Author Introduction** contains information designed to introduce an author to *CLR* users by presenting an overview of the author's themes and styles, biographical facts that relate to the author's literary career or critical responses to the author's works, and information about major awards and prizes the author has received. The introduction begins by identifying the nationality of the author and by listing the genres in which s/he has written for children and young adults. Introductions also list a group of representative titles for which the author or illustrator being profiled is best known; this section, which begins with the words "major works include," follows the genre line of the introduction. For seminal figures, a listing of major works about the author follows when appropriate, highlighting important biographies about the author or illustrator that are not excerpted in the entry. The centered heading "Introduction" announces the body of the text. Where applicable, introductions conclude with references to additional entries in biographical and critical reference series published by Gale Research Inc.

- **Criticism** is located in three sections: **Author's Commentary** (when available), **General Commentary** (when available), and **Title Commentary** (commentary on specific titles).

  - The **Author's Commentary** presents background material written by the author or by an interviewer. This commentary may cover a specific work or several works. Author's commentary on more than one work appears after the author introduction, while commentary on an individual book follows the title entry heading.

  - The **General Commentary** consists of critical excerpts that consider more than one work by the author or illustrator being profiled. General commentary is preceded by the critic's name in boldface type or, in the case of unsigned criticism, by the title of the journal. *CLR* also features entries that emphasize general criticism on the oeuvre of an author or illustrator. When appropriate, a selection of reviews is included to supplement the general commentary.

  - The **Title Commentary** begins with the title entry headings, which precede the criticism on a title and cite publication information on the work being reviewed. Title headings list the title of the work as it appeared in its first English-language edition. The first English-language publication date of each work (unless otherwise noted) is listed in parentheses following the title. Differing U. S. and British titles follow the publication date within the parentheses. When a work is written by an individual other than the one being profiled, as is the case when illustrators are featured, the parenthetical material following the title cites the author of the work before listing its publication date.

    Entries in each title commentary section consist of critical excerpts on the author's individual works, arranged chronologically by publication date. The entries generally contain two to seven reviews per title, depending on the stature of the book and the amount of criticism it has generated. The editors select titles that reflect the entire scope of the author's literary contribution, covering each genre and subject. An effort is made to reprint criticism that represents the full range of each title's reception, from the year of its initial publication to current assessments. Thus, the reader is provided with a record of the author's critical history. Publication information (such as publisher names and book prices) and parenthetical numerical references (such as footnotes or page and line references to specific editions of works) have been deleted at the discretion of the editors to provide smoother reading of the text.

- Centered headings introduce each section, in which criticism is arranged chronologically; beginning with Volume 35, each excerpt is preceded by a boldface source heading for easier access by readers. Within the text, titles by authors being profiled are also highlighted in boldface type.

- Selected excerpts are preceded by **Explanatory Annotations,** which provide information on the critic or work of criticism to enhance the reader's understanding of the excerpt.

- A complete **Bibliographical Citation** designed to facilitate the location of the original book or article precedes each piece of criticism.

- Numerous **Illustrations** are featured in *CLR*. For entries on illustrators, an effort has been made to include illustrations that reflect the characteristics discussed in the criticism. Entries on authors who do not illustrate their own works may also include photographs and other illustrative material pertinent to their careers.

Special Features: Entries on Illustrators

Entries on authors who are also illustrators will occasionally feature commentary on selected works illustrated but not written by the author being profiled. These works are strongly associated with the illustrator and have received critical acclaim for their art. By including critical comment on works of this type, the editors wish to provide a more complete representation of the author's career. Criticism on these works has been chosen to stress artistic, rather than literary, contributions. Title entry headings for works illustrated by the author being profiled are arranged chronologically within the entry by date of publication and include notes identifying the author of the illustrated work. In order to provide easier access for users, all titles illustrated by the subject of the entry are boldfaced.

CLR also includes entries on prominent illustrators who have contributed to the field of children's literature. These entries are designed to represent the development of the illustrator as an artist rather than as a literary stylist. The illustrator's section is organized like that of an author, with two exceptions: the introduction presents an overview of the illustrator's styles and techniques rather than outlining his or her literary background, and the commentary written by the illustrator on his or her works is called "illustrator's commentary" rather than "author's commentary." All titles of books containing illustrations by the artist being profiled as well as individual illustrations from these books are highlighted in boldface type.

Other Features: Acknowledgments, Indexes

- The **Acknowledgments** section, which immediately follows the preface, lists the sources from which material has been reprinted in the volume. It does not, however, list every book or periodical consulted for the volume.

- The **Cumulative Index to Authors** lists all of the authors who have appeared in *CLR* with cross-references to the biographical, autobiographical, and literary criticism series published by Gale Research Inc. A full listing of the series titles appears before the first page of the indexes of this volume.

- The **Cumulative Index to Nationalities** lists authors alphabetically under their respective nationalities. Author names are followed by the volume number(s) in which they appear.

- The **Cumulative Index to Titles** lists titles covered in *CLR* followed by the volume and page number where criticism begins.

A Note to the Reader

CLR is one of several critical references sources in the Literature Criticism Series published by Gale Research Inc. When writing papers, students who quote directly from any volume in the Literature Criticism Series may use the following general forms to footnote reprinted criticism. The first example pertains to material drawn from periodicals, the second to material reprinted from books.

[1]T. S. Eliot, "John Donne," *The Nation and the Athenaeum,* 33 (9 June 1923), 321-32; excerpted and reprinted in *Literature Criticism from 1400 to 1800,* Vol. 10, ed. James E. Person, Jr. (Detroit: Gale Research, 1989), pp. 28-9.

[1]Henry Brooke, *Leslie Brooke and Johnny Crow* (Frederick Warne, 1982); excerpted and reprinted in *Children's Literature Review,* Vol. 20, ed. Gerard J. Senick (Detroit: Gale Research, 1990), p. 47.

Suggestions Are Welcome

In response to various suggestions, several features have been added to *CLR* since the beginning of the series, including author entries on retellers of traditional literature as well as those who have been the first to record oral tales and other folklore; entries on prominent illustrators featuring commentary on their styles and techniques; entries on authors whose works are considered controversial; occasional entries devoted to criticism on a single work or a series of works; sections in author introductions that list major works by and about the author or illustrator being profiled; explanatory notes that provide information on the critic or work of criticism to enhance the usefulness of the excerpt; more extensive illustrative material, such as holographs of manuscript pages and photographs of people and places pertinent to the careers of the authors and artists; a cumulative nationality index for easy access to authors by nationality; and occasional guest essays written specifically for *CLR* by prominent critics on subjects of their choice.

Readers who wish to suggest authors to appear in future volumes, or who have other suggestions, are cordially invited to write the editor.

Acknowledgments

The editors wish to thank the copyright holders of the excerpted criticism included in this volume and the permissions managers of many books and magazine publishing companies for assisting us in securing reprint rights. We are also grateful to the staffs of the Detroit Public Library, the Library of Congress, the University of Detroit Library, Wayne State University Purdy/Kresge Library Complex, and the University of Michigan Libraries for making their resources available to us. Following is a list of the copyright holders who have granted us permission to reprint material in this volume of *CLR*. Every effort has been made to trace copyright, but if omissions have occurred, please let us know.

COPYRIGHTED EXCERPTS IN *CLR*, VOLUME 38, WERE REPRINTED FROM THE FOLLOWING PERIODICALS:

Appraisal: Children's Science Books, v. 2, Fall, 1969; v. 3, Winter, 1970; v. 4, Spring, 1971; v. 7, Winter, 1974; v. 7, Fall, 1974; v. 8, Spring, 1975; v. 9, Winter, 1976; v. 9, Spring, 1976; v. 10, Winter, 1977; v. 10, Spring, 1977; v. 13, Fall, 1980; v. 14, Spring, 1981; v. 15, Fall, 1982; v. 17, Winter, 1984. Copyright © 1969, 1970, 1971, 1974, 1975, 1976, 1977, 1980, 1981, 1982, 1984 by the Children's Science Book Review Committee. All reprinted by permission of the publisher.—*Best Sellers,* v. 22, 1963. Copyright 1963, 1965, by the University of Scranton. Reprinted by permission of the publisher.—*Bookbird,* v. IV, 1966; v. V, 1967; v. IX, December, 1971; v. 33, Spring, 1995. Reprinted by permission of the publisher.—*Booklist,* v. 73, May, 1, 1977; v. 74, January 1, 1978; v. 75, December 15, 1978; v. 75, March 1, 1979; v. 76, April 1, 1980; v. 77, September 1, 1980; v. 77, December 1, 1980; v. 78, February 1, 1982; v. 80, September 1, 1983; v. 80, January 1, 1984; v. 80, April 1, 1984; v. 80, June 15, 1984; v. 81, June 1, 1985; v. 81, August, 1985; v. 82, March 15, 1986; v. 85, November 15, 1988; v. 85, June 1, 1989; v. 86, December 15, 1989; v. 86, March 1, 1990; v. 87, August, 1991; v. 88, December 1, 1991; v. 88, December 15, 1991; v. 88, February 15, 1992; v. 88, April 1, 1992; v. 89, November 1, 1992; v. 89, February 1, 1993; v. 89, April 15, 1993; v. 90, September 15, 1993. Copyright © 1978, 1979, 1980, 1982, 1983, 1984, 1985, 1988, 1990, 1991, 1992, 1993 by the American Library Association. All reprinted by permission of the publisher.—*The Booklist,* v. 69, March 1, 1973; v. 70, June 15, 1974; v. 71, March 1, 1975; v. 72, December 15, 1975; v. 72, June 1, 1976. Copyright © 1973, 1974, 1975, 1976 by the American Library Association. Reprinted by permission of the publisher.—*The Booklist and Subscription Books Bulletin*, v. 62, January 1, 1966; v. 62, April 15, 1966; v. 64, February 15, 1968; v. 65, March 15, 1969. Copyright © 1966, 1968, 1969 by the American Library Association. All reprinted by permission of the publisher.—*Books for Keeps,* n. 35, November, 1985; n. 40, September, 1986; n. 44, May, 1987; n. 47, November, 1987; n. 49, March, 1988; n. 52, September, 1988; n. 55, March, 1989; n. 56, May, 1989; n. 70, September, 1991; n. 84, January, 1994. © School Bookshop Association 1985, 1986, 1987, 1988, 1989, 1991, 1994. All reprinted by permission of the publisher.—*Books For Your Children,* v. 17, Autumn/Winter, 1982; v. 22, Autumn/Winter, 1987; v. 22, Summer, 1987; v. 24, Spring, 1989; v. 29, Spring, 1994. © Books For Your Children 1982, 1987, 1989, 1994. All reprinted by permission of the publisher.—*British Book News Children's Books,* March, 1986; September, 1987. © The British Council, 1987. Reprinted by permission of the publisher.—*British Book News Children's Supplement,* Autumn, 1980. © The British Council, 1987. Reprinted by permission of the publisher.—*Bulletin of the Center for Children's Books,* v. XV, May, 1962. Copyright © 1962, renewed 1990; v. XVI, December, 1962. Copyright © 1962, renewed 1990 by the University of Chicago. Both reprinted by permission of University of Illinois Press./ v. 20, June, 1967; v. 21, October, 1967; v. 23, November, 1969; v. 23, March, 1970; v. 24, May, 1971; v. 27, September, 1973; v. 28, May, 1975; v. 34, October, 1980; v. 35, January, 1982; v. 35, March, 1982; v. 37, September, 1983; v. 41, April, 1988; v. 42, December, 1988; v. 43, December, 1989; v. 43, April, 1990; v. 45, October, 1991; v. 45, November, 1991; v. 45, February, 1992; v. 45, March, 1992; v. 46, October, 1992; v. 46 December, 1992; v. 47, October, 1993; v. 47, July/August, 1994. Copyright © 1967, 1969, 1971, 1975, 1980, 1982, 1983, 1988, 1989, 1990, 1991,1992, 1993, 1994 by The University of Chicago. All reprinted by permission of University of Illinois Press.—*Catholic Library*

Children's Literature Review

Louisa May Alcott

1832-1888

American author of fiction, nonfiction, and poetry.

Major works include *Little Women; Or, Meg, Jo, Beth and Amy* (2 vols., 1868-69), *Little Men: Life at Plumfield with Jo's Boys* (1871), *Aunt Jo's Scrap-Bag* (6 vols., 1872-82), *Eight Cousins; Or, The Aunt-Hill* (1875), *Rose in Bloom: A Sequel to "Eight Cousins"* (1876), *Jo's Boys, and How They Turned Out* (1886).

Major works about the author include *Louisa May Alcott: Her Life, Letters, and Journals* (edited by Ednah D. Cheney, 1889), *Louisa May Alcott* (by Madeleine B. Stern, 1950), *Louisa May: A Modern Biography of Louisa May Alcott* (by Martha Saxton, 1977).

The following entry presents criticism on *Little Women; Or, Meg, Jo, Beth and Amy*.

INTRODUCTION

The author of novels and short stories for readers of all ages, Alcott is best known for *Little Women,* a book written for girls based largely on Alcott's own family life. Widely recognized as an early example of American realism, *Little Women* celebrates everyday occurrences in the lives of an American family during the Civil War years. The story centers on the four young women of the March family, siblings Meg, Jo, Beth, and Amy, whose ages range from ten through sixteen at the beginning of the novel. In describing the lives of each of these primary characters, Alcott championed self-improvement through both introspection and hard work; as each of the March girls matures, she learns to recognize her strengths and work toward correcting such faults as temper, selfishness, and vanity. Perhaps the first story for young people to portray such flaws in its central protagonists, *Little Women* was also Alcott's first critical success, gaining a wide readership in the late nineteenth century and remaining popular with readers of all ages today.

Biographical Information

Having achieved moderate success with earlier stories and essays for adults, Alcott attempted to write children's literature at her publisher's request in 1868, producing the first volume of *Little Women* in just six weeks. Her idea for the story came from her own family life, having grown up the second of four daughters born to Amos Bronson Alcott, a New England Transcendentalist philosopher, and his wife, Abigail May Alcott. Alcott and her sisters were educated at home, where they were taught by their mother to cook and sew and were encouraged by their father, who often entertained such friends and fellow philoso-

phers as Henry David Thoreau and Ralph Waldo Emerson, to study literature and art. Frequently without money, particularly after their father invested heavily in a failed attempt to establish a utopian community in Massachusetts, the Alcott children were inspired to develop skills and work hard to support themselves. Like her character Jo, Alcott pursued a career as a writer. As she worked on *Little Women,* however, she remained skeptical about the appeal of her autobiographical story, noting in her journal, "I plod away, though I don't enjoy this sort of thing. Never liked girls or knew many, except my sisters; but our queer plays and experiences may prove interesting, though I doubt it." Nevertheless, the novel proved a popular success; Alcott completed the second part the following year and was thereafter able to support herself financially by writing more works for children, including sequels to *Little Women* and *Little Men* for boys. In her later years, Alcott received large amounts of mail from young girls wanting to know about the real women on which she had based her characters. In an open letter to *Little Women* fans published in *St. Nicholas* magazine in 1903, Alcott's sister, Annie Alcott Pratt (pictured by Meg in the novel), explained that she and Louisa were now "sober old women, nearly forty years of age, full of cares and troubles like other people; and that although nearly every event in the book is true, of course things did not happen exactly as they are set down."

Plot and Major Characteristics

Chronicling several years in the lives of the March family, *Little Women* traces the growth of Meg, Jo, Beth, and Amy. As the novel opens, the girls complain of a seemingly bleak Christmas season: their family is poor, and their father, serving as a chaplain in the Union Army, is unable to return home. The siblings are moved to shame, however, when their mother, Marmee, reads them a letter from their father, who writes: "I know that when I come back . . . I may be fonder and prouder than ever of my little women." Resolving to be good and happy, the girls act upon Marmee's suggestion that they pattern their lives after Christian in John Bunyan's *Pilgrim's Progress,* who must face and overcome several obstacles and burdens on his journey to heaven. Thus, they make lists of their burdens, or faults, and resolve to better themselves.

Critics have noted that each chapter of *Little Women* forms a short, complete story in itself, featuring conflict and resolution. For example, in the chapter entitled "Meg Goes to Vanity Fair," Meg's experience at a society ball helps her to recognize her tendency to place too great an emphasis on her physical appearance. In another chapter, Amy receives a lesson in humility following an episode in which she shows off for her friends at school. Jo, whom many commentators cite among the most memorable characters of children's literature, is a tomboy who strives to learn patience, curb her temper, and become a proper lady. According to Elizabeth Janeway, "Jo is a unique creation: the one young woman in 19th-century fiction who maintains her individual independence, who gives up no part of her autonomy as payment for being born a woman—and gets away with it." Over the years, Meg is the first to marry and leave home; Amy studies art, travels in Europe, and marries Laurie, the boy who lived next door; and Jo embarks on a writing career, eventually marrying Dr. Bhaer, a German professor. Beth, the shy and sensitive sister, dies after a bout with scarlet fever, as had Alcott's sister Elizabeth (Lizzie). Describing the appeal of the characters in *Little Women*, Madeleine B. Stern has observed that Alcott's "knowledge of adolescent psychology reveals itself in twofold form throughout the work, for it consisted first of an appeal to adolescents, the skill of making them laugh or cry, and secondly of an ability to describe adolescents, to catch and transfix the varied emotions and thoughts of the young."

Awards

A 1968 edition of *Little Women,* illustrated by Jessie Willcox Smith, won the Lewis Carroll Shelf Award in 1969.

COMMENTARY

The Nation, New York

SOURCE: A review of *Little Women,* in *The Nation,* New York, Vol. VIII, No. 203, May 20, 1869, p. 400.

Miss Alcott's literary success seems to be very like that achieved by her favorite, "Jo," in this pleasant little story. She has not endangered her popularity by any excessive refinement, nor by too hard a struggle after ideal excellence in her work. Her book is just such a hearty, unaffected, and "genial" description of family life as will appeal to the majority of average readers, and is as certain to attain a kind of success which is apt enough fatally to endanger its author's pretensions to do better work in future. Meantime, **Little Women** is entertaining reading, and, as far as its moral lesson goes, may safely be put into the hands of young people, and will be likely, too, to give their elders a certain pleasure.

Annie Alcott Pratt

SOURCE: "A Letter from Miss Alcott's Sister about *Little Women,*" in *St. Nicholas',* Vol. XXX, Part II, May, 1903, p. 631.

Doubtless many of the girl readers of *St. Nicholas,* who have also read and enjoyed **Little Women,** will be interested in the following letter, written thirty years ago to two young girls of that day, who had sent a letter to Miss Alcott herself, asking if the characters in **Little Women** were real persons, and if the story were true. In due time they received the following letter in reply.—Editor.

CONCORD, January 20, 1871.

Dear Julia And Alice: From your note to Miss Alcott I infer that you are not aware that she is at present in Italy, having gone abroad in April last, with the intention of remaining a year or more, trying to get well. But knowing how pleased she would be with your friendly note, I think perhaps a word from sister "Meg" will be better than leaving it unanswered, and far better than that any "little woman" should feel that "Jo" was unkind or ungrateful.

Of course you know that neither "Meg" nor "Jo" are young and pretty girls now, but sober old women, nearly forty years of age, full of cares and troubles like other people; and that although nearly every event in the book is true, of course things did not happen exactly as they are there set down.

You ask if "Amy" is not May Alcott, and I can truly say she is her very self, and she is the only one of the "Little Women" who would, I think, realize your ideal drawn from the story. She is, indeed, "Lady Amy," and a fair and noble woman, full of graces and accomplishments, and, what is better far, a pure and generous heart. "Jo," "Beth," and "Amy" are all drawn from life, and are entirely truthful pictures of the three dear sisters who played and worked, loved and sorrowed together so many years ago. Dear "Beth"—or Louie, as we called her—died, after long suffering, twelve years since. She was a sweet and gentle creature, and her death was so great a sorrow to poor "Jo" that she has never been quite happy since her "conscience" was laid away under the pines of Sleepy Hollow. "Meg" was never the pretty vain little maiden, who coquetted and made herself so charming. But "Jo" always admired poor, plain "Meg," and when she came to put her into the story, she beautified her to suit the occasion, saying, "Dear me, girls, we must have one beauty in the book!" So "Meg," with her big mouth and homely nose, shines forth quite a darling, and no doubt all the "little women" who read of her admire her just as loving old "Jo" does, and think her quite splendid. But, for all that, she is nothing but homely, busy, and, I hope, useful "Annie" who writes this letter to you.

As for dear old "Jo" herself, she was just the romping, naughty, topsy-turvy tomboy that all you little girls have learned to love; and even now, when care and sickness have made her early old, she is at heart the same loving, generous girl. In *Little Women* she has given a very truthful story of her haps and mishaps, her literary struggles and successes, and she is now enjoying her well-earned honors and regaining her health in travel with her sister "Amy." They are spending the winter in Rome, in a delightful circle of artists, receiving attentions and honors that make proud the heart of the sister left behind. "Amy" is in the studio of a well-known painter, working hard to perfect herself in her chosen art, while "Jo" is resting and gaining strength and courage for her promised *Little Men*, of which I imagine "Meg's" boys, Freddie and Johnnie, are to be the heroes.

You inquire about "Laurie." The character was drawn partly from imagination, but more perhaps from a very nice boy Louisa once knew, whose good looks and "wheedlesome" ways first suggested to her the idea of putting him into a book. She has therefore put upon him the love-making and behavior of various adorers of her youthful days.

Dear little friends, if I have told you all you wish to know, and shown that you need have no fear of being thought "intrusive," perhaps sometime you will honor "Meg" herself with a letter.

Be assured she will be glad to hear from any of the "little women."

Sincerely yours,
Annie Alcott Pratt.

G. K. Chesterton

SOURCE: "Louisa Alcott," in *A Handful of Authors: Essays on Books & Writers,* Sheed and Ward, 1953, pp. 163-67.

[The following excerpt was originally published in The Nation *in 1907.]*

It is very good for a man to talk about what he does not understand; as long as he understands that he does not understand it. Agnosticism (which has, I am sorry to say, almost entirely disappeared from the modern world) is always an admirable thing, so long as it admits that the thing which it does not understand may be much superior to the mind which does not understand it. Thus if you say that the cosmos is incomprehensible, and really mean (as most moderns do) that it is not worth comprehending; then it would be much better for your Greek agnosticism if it were called by its Latin name of ignorance. But there is one thing that any man can fairly consider incomprehensible, and yet in some ways superior. There is one thing that any man may worry about, and still respect; I mean any woman. The deadly and divine cleavage between the sexes has compelled every woman and every man, age after age, to believe without understanding; to have faith without any knowledge.

Upon the same principle it is a good thing for any man to have to review a book which he cannot review. It is a good thing for his agnosticism and his humility to consider a book which may be much better than he can ever understand. It is good for a man who has seen many books which he could not review because they were so silly, to review one book which he cannot review because it is so wise. For wisdom, first and last, is the characteristic of women. They are often silly, they are always wise. Commonsense is uncommon among men; but commonsense is really and literally a common sense among women. And the sagacity of women, like the sagacity of saints, or that of donkeys, is something outside all questions of ordinary cleverness and ambition. The whole truth of the matter was revealed to Mr. Rudyard Kipling when the spirit of truth suddenly descended on him and he said: "Any woman can manage a clever man; but it requires a rather clever woman to manage a fool."

The wisdom of women is different; and this alone makes the review of such books by a man difficult. But the case is stronger. I for one will willingly confess that the only thing on earth I am frightfully afraid of is a little girl. Female children, she babies, girls up to the age of five are perfectly reasonable; but then all babies are reasonable. Grown girls and women give us at least glimpses of their meaning. But the whole of the period between a girl who is six years old and a girl who is sixteen is to me an abyss not only of mystery, but of terror. If the Prussians were invading England, and I were holding a solitary outpost, the best thing they could do would be to send a long rank or regiment of Prussian girls of twelve, from which I should fly, screaming.

Now the famous books of Miss Alcott are all about little girls. Therefore, my first impulse was to fly screaming. But I resisted this impulse, and I read the books; and I discovered, to my immeasurable astonishment, that they were extremely good. *Little Women* was written by a woman for women—for little women. Consequently it anticipated realism by twenty or thirty years; just as Jane Austen anticipated it by at least a hundred years. For women are the only realists; their whole object in life is to pit their realism against the extravagant, excessive, and occasionally drunken idealism of men. I do not hesitate. I am not ashamed to name Miss Alcott and Miss Austen. There is, indeed, a vast division in the matter of literature (an unimportant matter), but there is the same silent and unexplained assumption of the feminine point of view. There is no pretence, as most unfortunately occurred in the case of another woman of genius, George Eliot, that the writer is anything else but a woman, writing to amuse other women, with her awful womanly irony. Jane Austen did not call herself George Austen; nor Louisa Alcott call herself George Alcott. These women refrained from that abject submission to the male sex which we have since been distressed to see; the weak demand for masculine names and for a part in merely masculine frivolities; parliaments, for instance. These were strong women; they classed parliament with the public-house. But for another and better reason, I do not hesitate to name Miss Alcott by the side of Jane Austen; because her talent, though doubtless inferior, was of exactly the same kind. There is an unmistakable material truth about the thing; if that material truth were not the chief female characteristic, we should most of us find our houses burnt down when we went back to them. To take but one instance out of many, and an instance that a man can understand, because a man was involved, the account of the quite sudden and quite blundering proposal, acceptance, and engagement between Jo and the German professor under the umbrella, with parcels falling off them, so to speak, every minute, is one of the really human things in human literature; when you read it you feel sure that human beings have experienced it often; you almost feel that you have experienced it yourself. There is something true to all our own private diaries in the fact that our happiest moments have happened in the rain, or under some absurd impediment of absurd luggage. The same is true of a hundred other elements in the story. The whole affair of the children acting the different parts in *Pickwick,* forming a childish club under strict restrictions, in order to do so; all that is really life, even where it is not literature. And as a final touch of human truth, nothing could be better than the way in which Miss Alcott suggests the borders and the sensitive privacy of such an experiment. All the little girls have become interested, as they would in real life, in the lonely little boy next door; but when one of them introduces him into their private club in imitation of *Pickwick,* there is a general stir of resistance; these family fictions do not endure being considered from the outside.

All that is profoundly true; and something more than that is profoundly true. For just as the boy was an intruder in that club of girls, so any masculine reader is really an intruder among this pile of books. There runs through the whole series a certain moral philosophy, which a man can never really get the hang of. For instance, the girls are always doing something, pleasant or unpleasant. In fact, when they have not to do something unpleasant, they deliberately do something else. A great part, perhaps the more godlike part, of a boy's life, is passed in doing nothing at all. Real selfishness, which is the simplest thing in the world to a boy or man, is practically left out of the calculation. The girls may conceivably oppress and torture each other; but they will not indulge or even enjoy

themselves—not, at least, as men understand indulgence or enjoyment. The strangest things are taken for granted; as that it is wrong in itself to drink champagne. But two things are quite certain; first, that even from a masculine standpoint, the books are very good; and second, that from a feminine standpoint they are so good that their admirers have really lost sight even of their goodness. I have never known, or hardly ever known, a really admirable woman who did not confess to having read these books. Haughty ladies confessed (under torture) that they liked them still. Stately Suffragettes rose rustling from the sofa and dropped *Little Women* on the floor, covering them with public shame. At learned ladies' colleges, it is, I firmly believe, handed about secretly, like a dangerous drug. I cannot understand this strange and simple world, in which unselfishness is natural, in which spite is easier than self-indulgence. I am the male intruder, like poor Mr. Laurence and I withdraw. I back out hastily, bowing. But I am sure that I leave a very interesting world behind me.

Ednah D. Cheney

SOURCE: "Europe, and *Little Women,*" in *Louisa May Alcott: Her Life, Letters, and Journals,* edited by Ednah D. Cheney, Little, Brown, and Company, 1907, pp. 170-203.

Miss Alcott's fancy had always been for depicting the life of boys rather than girls; but she fortunately took the suggestion of the publisher, and said, like Col. Miller, "I'll try, sir." The old idea of "The Pathetic Family" recurred to her mind; and she set herself to describe the early life of her home. The book was finished in July, named *Little Women,* and sent to the publishers, who promptly accepted it, making Miss Alcott an outright offer for the copyright, but at the same time advising her not to part with it. It was published in October, and the result is well known. She was quite unconscious of the unusual merit of the book, thinking, as she says, the first chapters dull, and so was quite surprised at her success. "It reads better than I expected," she says; and she truly adds, "We really lived most of it, and if it succeeds, that will be the reason of it."

But that is not the whole secret of its success. Through many trials and many failures Louisa had learned her literary art. By her experience in melodrama she had proved the emptiness of sensational writing, and knew how to present the simple and true,—seemingly without art, but really with the nicest art of discrimination and emphasis. All her previous training and experience were needed to fit her for the production of her masterpiece; for in spite of all the good work she did later, this remains her masterpiece, by which she will be remembered and loved. Already twenty-one years have passed, and another generation has come up since she published this book, yet it still commands a steady sale; and the mothers who read it in their childhood renew their enjoyment as they watch the faces of their little girls brighten with smiles over the theatricals in the barn, or moisten with tears at the death of the beloved sister. One of the greatest charms of the book is its perfect truth to New England life. But it is not merely local; it touches the universal heart deeply.

Madeleine B. Stern

SOURCE: "Louisa M. Alcott: An Appraisal," in *The New England Quarterly,* Vol. 22, No. 4, December, 1949, pp. 475-98.

In 1868, when, at the request of Thomas Niles of Roberts Brothers, Louisa Alcott sat down to write a household story for girls, the domestic novel, as evolved by Susan Warner, Maria Cummins, Ann Stephens, and Mrs. E. D. E. N. South-worth, consisted of commonplace episodes worked into a trite plot involving pious and insipid characters. Bronson Alcott's opinion of juvenile literature, recorded in his diary for 1839, had, in the generation that followed, been given no reason for alteration. In 1868 it was still true that the "literature of childhood" had not been written. A youngster eager for picture books must content himself with *Missionary Stories* or *The Holy Land,* while a child thumbing expectantly through the pages of the Juvenile Library would find nothing more satisfying than *Paper Preachers* or *Always Do Right.* If such extraordinarily moral tales as *The Wide, Wide World,* the Rollo books, the Lucy books, and the first of the Elsie books became unbearable, there was compensation for a youthful reader only in grave-and-horror stories, Hawthorne's legendary tales, or "Peter Parley's" edifying descriptions of natural wonders.

The times were ripe for Louisa Alcott, and she was well equipped to fill the gap in domestic literature. During a period of twenty years, she had attempted one form of writing after another, from the melodramatic *Comic Tragedies* concocted for performance in the Concord barn in 1848 to the fairy *Flower Fables* (1855) she had unfolded for the delight of Ellen Emerson. In the *Saturday Evening Gazette,* her early tales of cloying sweetness and cloudless light had appeared, and in *Frank Leslie's Illustrated Newspaper* and *The Flag of Our Union* she had found an eager market for her sensational stories. Combining the plot of the thriller with the timely theme of abolition, she had reached the readers of *The Atlantic Monthly* and *The Commonwealth,* and at length she had taken the important step of eliminating melodrama and depicting simple scenes of the Rebellion in her *Hospital Sketches* (1863). Once having discovered the salability of truthful war stories, Louisa Alcott had returned to Concord ready to use the techniques of realism in portrayals of her neighbors and her sisters. Her travels abroad increased her ability for journalistic reporting, and by the time that Thomas Niles asked her for a girls' story, she was ready to write the "tale embodying the simple facts and persons and scenery of the family" for which her father had long ago felt the need.

Bronson Alcott's realization that a tale, domestic in nature, would fill the gap in the literature of childhood, had been astute. It was by combining the incidents of a household story with a technique appealing to juvenile readers that Louisa Alcott created in *Little Women* (1868) a pioneer work not only in the literature of childhood but in the history of the domestic novel. Her muse was, first and foremost, domestic. She unlatched the door to one house, and her readers speedily discovered that it was their own house that they entered. She unroofed every dwelling in the land by unroofing the home of the four March girls. *Little Women* is great because it is a book on the American home, and hence universal in its appeal. As long as human beings delight in "the blessings that alone can make life happy," as long as they believe, with Jo March, that "families are the most beautiful things in all the world," the book will be treasured. It is a domestic drama, indeed, and Louisa Alcott knew, as her representative did, that when she wrote of her own home "something got into that story that went straight to the hearts of those who read it." Like Jo, the author had "found her style at last." The jolly larks, the plays and tableaux, the sleigh rides and skating frolics are enjoyed not by an isolated heroine, but by a family. The poverty, the domestic trials, including Beth's illness and death, Mrs. March's arrival from Washington, the father's Christmas homecoming, are the troubles and the joys of family life. The omissions indicate as notably as the actual content the writer's contributions to the domestic novel. The father remains a muffled figure throughout, for the close depiction of Bronson Alcott would have resulted in an atypical family portrait. The fads, the vegetarianism, the speculations after the unknowable are purposely excluded. The March family indulges in an occasional sip of coffee, and a fat turkey graces their table. With a clear insight the author not only delineated but glorified domesticity, and by lighting the fire in one home on Concord's Lexington Road kindled the American hearthstone. Long before she wrote her own literary credo, Louisa Alcott had practised it, hunting up "some homely, happy folks to write about; folks that don't borrer trouble and go lookin' for holes in their neighbors' coats, but take their lives brave and cheerful." These folks were the March family of Concord, the universal family of mankind.

To the domestic novel the author made still another contribution in *Little Women.* While her glorification of family life is universal in its appeal, her details offer a local flavor that gives the work a documentary value. The atmosphere of mid-century New England is preserved in *Little Women,* from the garret life of a Concord home to the preoccupations of the villagers. The interest in Dickens, the advocation of temperance, the arrival of the Prince of Wales, the fair for freedmen were timely episodes and afford a new insight into life and letters in Massachusetts. By its documentary value alone, *Little Women,* as an index of New England manners in the midcentury, would be accorded a place in literary history. It is the great merit of the book that it is at once a documentary account of a given locality and a universal delineation of any American home. By those two contributions, the one local, the other universal, the author raised the domestic novel from the state of trite insipidity in which it had remained so long, and carved for herself a niche in American letters.

Louisa Alcott added no less to juvenile literature than to

Alcott's parents, Amos Bronson and Marmee Alcott.

the domestic novel. *Little Women* is far more than a "picture of a happy childhood" [Lewis Mumford, *The Golden Day*]. It is far more even than a story "suited to the early days of youth, and at the same time conformable to the complicated relations of modern society" [Maria Edgeworth, *Moral Tales*]. The author's knowledge of adolescent psychology reveals itself in twofold form throughout the work, for it consisted first of an appeal to adolescents, the skill of making them laugh or cry, and secondly of an ability to describe adolescents, to catch and transfix the varied emotions and thoughts of the young. Juvenile readers stated with the Lucy books and *Paper Preachers* reveled in the celebration of birthdays at the March home, in the room-to-room notes and the family post office, in the sofa with a haircloth cushion, in the rides on "Ellen Tree." They wept when Beth lay dying, and they laughed when the tower collapsed during the performance of "The Witch's Curse," and they sighed deeply when Laurie murmured in response to Amy's "How well we pull together," "So well that I wish we might always pull in the same boat."

The salability of a work may be insured when its writer knows how to appeal to her public. A more lasting value is attained when the author practises the higher art of describing her public, setting down their characteristics, translating for more adult readers the thoughts and hopes of the young. Louisa Alcott remembered her adolescence and recorded it before the memory faded. For all times she painted Amy, afflicted with a nose that was not "nice,"

quirking her little finger and simpering over her plate, inditing her own will when Beth lay dying. Jo's gallantry, when she allowed Laurie to win at chess, is as perennial a characteristic of adolescence as her odd, blunt ways and her fiery spirit. The delightful account of Amy and the pickled limes, the pinching of Meg's papered locks before the ball, the dramatic incident in which Amy burns Jo's manuscript when she is denied permission to see "The Seven Castles of the Diamond Lake," and her subsequent fall through the ice—these episodes indeed transfix forever the varied emotions of the adolescent heart. *Little Women* is rich in its record of adolescent psychology. From Meg's experience at Annie Moffat's home to Laurie's demand for an apology from his grandfather, from Amy's plaster cast of her foot to her Frenchified letters, from the description of the tempestuous Jo "in a vortex" of creative effort to the girls' desire to know what will have happened "ten years hence," from Laurie's boyish infatuation with Jo to Amy's unfortunate fête attended by a single guest—*Little Women* runs the gamut of the adolescent heart and mind, and supplies a case book of adolescent psychology far surpassing any text on the subject.

By combining her local and universal contributions to the domestic novel with her knowledge of adolescent psychology, Louisa Alcott cleared the ground of juvenile literature and wrote a best-seller for the generations. The means whereby she arrived at such an end are less apparent than the end itself. She forgot none of the varied techniques she had tried when she sat down to produce a girls' book for Thomas Niles. She remembered her apprenticeship in the short story, and the method she evolved in *Little Women* is therefore episodic. Each chapter in turn is granted almost invariably to one of the sisters, so that Meg's married life alternates with Amy's experiences abroad or Jo's tussles with herself at home. This segmental structure results in a mighty architecture when it houses human beings, for the author knew that "our lives are patchwork." For all the defects in such an "amalgam of the novel and the story book," the episodic technique requires a short attention span for young readers and at the same time gives the effect of verisimilitude in the lives of human beings which do indeed resemble patchwork.

Though the author laid aside the blood-and-thunder thrillers of her salad days, she had learned from writing sensational stories the art emphasis, the ability to heighten a dramatic scene, and subordinate the less dramatic. She had not forgotten the penny dreadfuls or the troupers of the Hillside barn. In her account of "The Witch's Curse" in *Little Women* she remembered the melodramatic interests of her earlier days, taking Hagar from "The Unloved Wife," Hugo from "Norna," Zara from "The Captive of Castile," and miraculous potions from "Bianca" to evolve her operatic tragedy. She had not forgotten the Hillside troupers, but she had learned to look at them with tongue in cheek. For the amusement of thousands of readers throughout the country, rather than for the fulfillment of her own theatrical desires, incantations were chanted over a steaming kettle and the stamp of boots was heard in a gloomy wood.

Even the sentimentality of her effusions for the *Saturday Evening Gazette* was applied in *Little Women.* Without that apprenticeship she could never have made of the family poverty an experience that enriched those who lived above it, nor painted in Beth the glorified cricket on the hearth who became Jo's conscience.

Of all the techniques she had attempted, that of realism, the latest learned, provided the finest grist for her mill. In *Little Women* Louisa Alcott recorded her own observations and her actual experiences, from the Silling School that flourished at Vevey to "Ellen Tree," from Meg's wedding to Jo's literary career. The journalist who had served as a nurse during the Civil War at Georgetown had learned to report events as they were, people as they ever will be.

The style that a hack-writer had had, perforce, to employ stood the author in good stead when she wrote *Little Women* The use of "good strong words, that mean something," the grammar that is as natural as it is unpolished aided her in producing that "mannerless manner" by which verisimilitude is achieved. She was well aware of the value of never using a long word when a short one would do as well. Her defenses of impure English were not written until later, but they were practised in *Little Women.* It is better to "let children write their own natural letters . . . than to make them copy the Grandisonian style" [Alcott,

Aunt Jo's Scrap Bag]. Let children talk as real children do. "I deeply regret being obliged to shock the eyes and ears of such of my readers as have a prejudice in favor of pure English, . . . but, having rashly undertaken to write a little story about Young America, for Young America, I feel bound to depict my honored patrons as faithfully as my limited powers permit" [Alcott, *An Old-Fashioned Girl*]. So she did depict them in *Little Women,* with all the flaws in their grammar intact.

All these devices, garnered from a varied apprenticeship in short-story writing, in the fields of melodrama, sentimentality and realism, were stirred now in a new crucible. By a composite method whereby she combined much fact with a little fiction, the author expanded the preliminary sketches of "The Sisters' Trial," "A Modern Cinderella," and "The King of Clubs" and supplied an example for Emerson's precept: "The essential ground of a new book . . . is a new spirit." The new spirit was here, in this amalgam of the domestic novel and the juvenile tale. Family life was integrated with adolescent psychology. A local interest was offered at the same time with a universal appeal. When the book was completed the literature of childhood had been written.

Plied by the uncritical paeans of reviewers and the insatiable demands of publisher and public for "more," Louisa Alcott after her first success produced seven books in what has been called the *Little Women* Series. Though none of them quite rose to the level of *Little Women,* the author, aware of the reasons for her popularity, followed the patterns she had set and simply offered variations on the themes of domesticity and adolescent psychology. *An Old-Fashioned Girl* (1870) is a domestic drama in reverse, exposing the fashionable absurdities of the Shaw home by contrast with Polly, the wholesome representative of domesticity. The Campbell clan of *Eight Cousins* (1875) exalts the family hearth once again, and Rose's education is not complete until she has made a study of house-keeping and baked "the perfect loaf" under Aunt Plenty's supervision. In *Jack and Jill* (1880) the author enlarged upon the theme of domesticity, offering to her public the home life of a village rather than of single household. The Cold Water Army, the Debating and Dramatic Clubs, the May Day festivities, the yearly apple picking, the cattle show, the "forbidden" store are details in the domestic life of a New England village, and have the same documentary and universal value as the details of family life in *Little Women.* As the March tribe represents the families of the country, Harmony represents its villages, and for that reason *Jack and Jill* rises more nearly to the high water mark of *Little Women* than any other volume in the series.

The author was less successful in her attempts at repeating her characterizations of adolescence. By reason of her hearty good will and honest realism, Polly, of *An Old-Fashioned Girl,* narrowly escapes being a "little prig in a goody story-book." She is at once a symbol of the old-fashioned virtues and a genuine little girl who heartily enjoys a coast down the mall, dolls' dresses, and Grandma Shaw's stories. The March girls were individuals who never deteriorated into symbols. Once the writer converted Polly into "Sweet P.," "Polly Peacemaker," she ran the risk of weakening the verisimilitude of her character. An individual treated as a symbol is likely to degenerate into a stereotype. The boys of *Little Men* (1871) lack the three-dimensional qualities of the March girls for that very reason. To each the author endowed one glaring fault awaiting correction by the Plumfield methods; hence the reader is likely to think of Ned as the braggart, Stuffy as the glutton, Tommy as the mischievous youth, and Dan as the wild boy rather than as fully rounded individuals. Nan, transforming her doll Poppydilla into an Indian chief and making Silas tattoo an anchor on her arm, was modeled from the mold of Jo March, but she lacks Jo's completeness and becomes a mere symbol of the tomboy. The symbols continue to pursue the readers of *Eight Cousins,* where the characterizations were touched off boldly with broad strokes, each of the dramatis personae possessing one distinguishing trait adumbrated in the beginning and continually stressed—Mac his bookishness, Charlie his princeliness, Steve his dandyism, Archie his leadership. Though Mac was better developed in the sequel, *Rose in Bloom* (1876), Louisa Alcott was never to repeat the more minute characterizations of *Little Women.* Bab of *Under the Lilacs* (1878) is simply another Nan, the tomboy who inherits Jo March's gallantry and allows Ben to win the archery contest. Jack of *Jack and Jill* is a symbol of pluck rather than a plucky adolescent; Merry Grant is a representative of household art rather than an artistic girl. Jo's Boys continue to be the stereotypes of *Little Men,* for Stuffy still deserves his name, Tom is still a scapegrace, and Dan a wild young man. In Josie, the last of the Marches, the author came closest to a detailed portrayal of adolescence, and the picture of the stage-struck youngster laboring under the delusion that the course of her whole life would depend upon her interview with Miss Cameron is almost as satisfying as the delineation of Jo in the office of the "Weekly Volcano." But Josie was, unfortunately, the last of the Marches. The author had no time to add full-length portraits to her gallery of adolescents or to complete with minute touches the sketches too broadly painted in her *Little Women* Series.

Louisa Alcott was more successful in appealing to adolescents than in describing them. The Plumfield theatricals, the camp of the Campbell clan, the cousins' Christmas party, Ben's equestrian performance astride Lita, Sancho working his nose, quivering his tail, and slyly devouring a tart, the "Great International Telegraph" that stretched between the homes of Jack and Jill, the interroom telephone rigged up by Frank—these were as certain of appealing to youthful readers as any of Jo March's escapades. So aware was the author of the means of titillating the minds of her readers that when she could no longer invent fresh incidents she repeated the old to delight them. Where Amy March had nearly met her death after a fall through the ice, Rob of *Jo's Boys* (1886) narrowly escapes hydrophobia because of Ted's wilfulness. Where Laurie had asked to pull forever in the same boat with his beloved, Tom expresses the wish to go on cycling with his angel. Like Meg, who had visited at "Vanity Fair," Meg's daughter, arrayed in "sweeping

flounces," resists the allurements of society in the play at Plumfield. As the years drew on, the author found it impossible to resist the temptation of repeating her themes with or without variation. She knew her public and she catered to their demands. "For the amusement of certain little persons" her tales "gently rambled along," evoking from her readers tears and laughter. Children, she believed, were "good critics . . . , and to suit them was an accomplishment that any one might be proud of" [Alcott, *Little Men*]. Suit them she did, and she will continue to suit them as long as their tastes remain unchanged.

Since Louisa Alcott was more interested, apparently, in appealing to her young public than in describing in detail the domestic life of America, she made a third contribution to juvenile literature. It was a dubious contribution, whereby she ran the risk of kicking over a milk pail filled with the wholesome fare of domesticity and adolescent psychology, and converting herself into "a literary nursery-maid who provided moral pap for the young" [Alcott, *Jo's Boys*]. Forgetting the future, thinking only of the demands of the present, she interlarded her tales with the timely propagandist themes of one who believed in "reforms of all kinds." Since those themes are all but absent in *Little Women,* it seems clear that with Louisa Alcott preaching was "an acquired habit and discipline" rather than "an inherited, divine impulse" [Gamaliel Bradford, "Portrait of Louisa May Alcott"]. The royalty reports of Roberts Brothers taught her to pander to the adolescent passion of her day for seeing virtue rewarded and vice punished. The virtues and vices which she chose for moral reward and punishment were those of her own age rather than those of all time, and the author was tireless in "stirring her bit of leaven, and waiting, . . . for the fermentation" which she believed would slowly but surely occur. In the seven full-length stories that followed *Little Women,* and in one hundred and twenty of the one hundred and seventy-six tales and articles published from 1868 on, Louisa Alcott continued to stir her moral leaven and offer a plea for "reforms of all kinds." She either championed a cause or crusaded against it. The reforms she selected for her propaganda are of interest today only as they cast light upon the social history of the latter half of the nineteenth century. By yielding to the demands for timely themes, Louisa Alcott almost lost her place among writers for all times. By converting herself voluntarily into a preacher, she almost wandered away from the timeless fields of the story-teller. *Little Women,* devoid for the most part of pointed morals and reforms, saved her, as did the domesticity and adolescent psychology of the works that followed. By those two contributions the author built for herself a bulwark strong enough to stand against the third. Against that bulwark the *do's* and *do not's* of her ethical decalogue fall like rain upon a granite roof.

Alvina Treut Burrows

SOURCE: "A Critical Study of *Little Women,*" in *Elementary English,* Vol. XXXVII, No. 5, May, 1960, pp. 285-92.

Can the faithful March family survive the skepticism of the Atomic Age? Will Invincible Louisa triumph in the Cold War after surviving two World Wars as well as the Reconstruction Period in which it was written? Is Miss Alcott's artistry valid for today, or has veneration grown habitual as the residuum of oft-heard praise? Is the story's idealism merely a phony "togetherness" or is it an expression of some of the universals of human life?

Some of these questions can be answered only by the passing of time. At the moment *Little Women* remains a ranking favorite among girl readers as it has for well-nigh a hundred years. It is strange that the editor, Mr. Thomas Niles, who requested Miss Alcott to write the book, had various misgivings about it, and might not have published it but for the enthusiastic approval of a niece and of several other young girls. Fortunately for the publishing firm of Roberts Brothers the doubting editor was wise enough to consult these girls, who were at the very age for whom Louisa wrote. It must be admitted that she, too, had some reluctance to write for girls. Only the stimulus of poverty finally started her on the task. An old idea of telling about her family's ups and downs and real adventures came back to her, and with the addition of certain other persons, both real and imagined, the story began to take shape. The author actually began the book in May, 1868, and finished the first twelve chapters in June; she wrote the remaining eleven chapters of Part I in July. In October, 1868, this first part was published. So warm was its reception that in November Miss Alcott embarked upon Part II of what was to be a best seller.

Attempting to see *Little Women* critically from an adult viewpoint after having lived with its influence since childhood may be impossible; nonetheless, the effort to analyze a revered "classic" may be useful. Among all the books that young women remember even in the year 1960, *Little Women* still dominates. An analysis of its literary excellence or lack of it may clarify at least a part of this popularity.

Re-reading the story after many years is itself a curious experience, very much like returning to a home once lived in. A certain timidity occurs—fear that Jo and her family may not emerge as remembered, fear that one may be bitterly disillusioned. Even more curious is the discovery that certain phrases, indeed whole sentences, were held in memory over the years. Characters and their names had been retained with the exception of peripheral ones, such as the fashionable Moffats and the indigent Hummels. All the others—Mr. Lawrence, Larry, John Brooke, Mr. Bhaer, along with the March family—did not need even to be reintroduced. The re-reading was closely akin to that of meeting a rare old friend with whom one can pick up threads of communication as though there had been no separation over the years.

What are some of the characteristics, seen by one adult reader at least, of a book that has so strongly imprinted itself upon its readers? The March family has become a stronger influence on American family life than many a serious preachment or scientific presentation. "We know

these girls as well as we know any living people," says Mrs. May Hill Arbuthnot about the famous sisters. Some portion of this pervasive influence may be traced to the literary quality of *Little Women.* An attempt will be made first to examine the book critically as biography. Consideration will be given to literary form and technique. Attention will be given last to its concern with the universal themes of literature.

One can not analyze *Little Women* critically without first assessing it as biography. Parallelism between the story of Meg, Jo, Beth, and Amy, and the Alcotts has been pointed out frequently. Miss Alcott herself reported that she told her family's story. There were four living children in the March family at the time they lived in Hillside House in Concord, the locale of a large part of the story. Their talents were considerable and varied. Anna, the oldest, was a teacher who married John Bridge Pratt. She was a gentle person skilled in homemaking, and an eager listener for Louisa's plays and stories. She, of course, became Meg in the book. Louisa, one year younger than Anna, was mirrored in Jo, who loved theatricals, and writing, and jokes and laughter—Jo, who was impetuous and devoted, almost literally worked herself to death for her beloved family. Perhaps Jo emerges best of all as a real person because her biographer best understood herself. Elizabeth did not even have a change of name in the book. From the famous journals kept by all the Alcott family it seems that Beth was the unobtrusive affectionate little girl whose death made such a deep impression upon Louisa both as person and as writer. The youngest daughter was May Alcott, better known as Amy, and an artist of real talent. Actually, May Alcott married a Swiss businessman named Ernest Nieriker, whom she met in London. She died there as quite a young woman and sent her only child home for Louisa to bring up. One of Louisa's saddest moments occurred when their good friend and neighbor, Ralph Waldo Emerson, brought her the telegram telling of May's death.

"Marmee," born Abba May, the daughter of Colonel May of Connecticut, came from famous family connections. Fortunately for her children she was warm and loving, but also efficient and practical, with a buoyant sense of humor.

Louisa's father, Bronson Alcott, appears less vividly in the story, which is baffling since he was a philosopher of distinction, frequently the center of movements and ideas deemed radical at the time. Schools he founded were closed because his teaching principles and procedures were far ahead of the times. Parents were frightened at Alcott's frank discussions with children and aghast at his taking a little Negro girl into his famous Temple School in Boston. And many of these parents were Abolitionists! Most of his ideas are accepted now, though far from common practice in all quarters: helping each child to unfold his own powers, surrounding children with beautiful books, paintings, statuary, with comfortable and appropriate furniture; treating them with kindness along with firmness. Friend of Emerson and Thoreau and of many another of the New England intellectuals in that period deemed New

England's "flowering," Alcott achieved his greatest apparent success in the Summer School of Philosophy which he conducted in his latter days when Louisa's success made compensation less necessary. Perhaps his supreme achievement, however, lay in the education of his own family. Through Louisa's writing his ideas reached out to a world audience, and affected untold thousands of families and entire schools.

In many respects *Little Women* is biographical only within the spirit of the teachings of Bronson and Abba May Alcott and in its cast of characters. The story is laid in the Civil War period, with Father serving as chaplain to the armed forces and stationed in Washington. In the book, Jo is a girl of fifteen while Father is away. Actually Louisa herself served as an army nurse when she was twenty nine years old, working heroically for the Union soldiers in a filthy, understaffed, mismanaged hospital set up in a hotel in Washington, D. C. Her letters home told vividly of her efforts to bring fresh air and cleanliness to a building where windows were nailed down, and soap and water scarce. They told equally dramatically of her apparently successful attempts to bring cheer to suffering men and to at least one young drummer boy only twelve years old. These letters were published under the title *Hospital Sketches,* preceding the epoch-making *Little Women* by five years. Louisa contracted typhoid, which was raging in the hospital, and was rescued from almost certain death by her father, who went to Washington to nurse her and to take her back to Concord as soon as she could travel. But Bronson himself did not serve as a chaplain, according to the several Alcott biographers. In real life, Jo never married. Aunt March was a composite of several of Mrs. Alcott's relatives; Laurie was the protagonist of Ladislaz Wisniewski, a Polish friend to whom Louisa was greatly attracted while she was in Paris serving as a traveling companion for a young invalid girl.

Even more important departures from the facts of Louisa Alcott's life are to be noted. The Alcotts were abysmally poor. Before Louisa became the mainstay of her family's finances, their deprivations were many and serious. In seeking employment Bronson Alcott moved his family some thirty times. In a stretch of twenty-two years they lived in twenty-four different houses. The saddest of these homes was *Fruitlands,* the communal enterprise in which Mr. Alcott became a leader. In this planned Utopia everyone was to share the toil and the rewards; animal products were not to be eaten or used; part of the day was to be spent in spiritual cultivation. Here the children experienced near-starvation. The fierce loyalty to her family and the compelling urge to protect and support them may well have sprung in part from this experience. One of the English residents at Fruitlands, Mr. Lane, foreseeing the imminent failure of the colony, proposed that he and Bronson Alcott forsake the oppressive family commitments and join the nearby Shaker colony where family ties were abandoned. A family council was called, for Bronson believed in the equal rights of men and women and in the wisdom of children's helping to make decisions. Bronson decided to remain with his family although he was broken in health for a considerable period after this Utopian failure. The shadow of this threatened separation seems to have remained with Louisa.

One reads in *Little Women* of Jo's resentment against Meg's marriage. Louisa herself put off marriage all her life. According to her journals, she preferred the independence of single life and was reluctant to break up her own family circle.

In spite of poverty and many movings from house to house, there was apparently a rich fabric of secure family life, of delight in personal triumphs, in hard work, in simple festivities. Mrs. Alcott's motto was "Hope and keep busy." Mr. Alcott set a good example for combining intellectual and physical work by taking jobs—such as cutting wood or gardening, in an effort to support his family. The children, when living in or near Concord, were the companions of the Emerson children, joining them in Maypole dances and other celebrations. At home there were many amateur theatricals, and much reading, and keeping the personal journals which Bronson Alcott looked upon as means to character development as well as a sound procedure for learning to write. All these activities appear in *Little Women*; indeed, the theatricals and the journal writing were carried directly into the story.

A number of persons have questioned the dominance of Marmee as a character in *Little Women.* After all, Bronson Alcott was a person of dignity and importance, even though almost always financially insolvent. His influence among the intellectual leaders of his day was considerable. He achieved some measure of popular acceptance through a successful term as superintendent of schools in Concord some years before the publication of *Little Women.* Yet, unmistakably, the March household revolves around Marmee.

In the light of modern understanding of unconscious motivation, it may well be that Louisa thus shaped her story in pursuit of the home she would have liked hers to be. Bronson Alcott was reported to be the kind of conversationalist who expected others to listen rather than to join in. Removing him from a central role in the story gave free rein to the conversation of the rest of the family. Louisa's biographers assert that she intended to write her father's story as a separate volume. Her early death, only two days after her father's, when she was fifty six years old, prevented this fulfillment. Perhaps she would really have done it; no one can be sure.

Other instances of wish fulfillment rather than clear biography also appear. One of these is that of the finances. The March family's house, though poor, is infinitely less so than those the Alcotts actually lived in. In *Little Women* there was always plenty of wood for warmth, there were flowers and comfortable old furniture left over from the days when "papa was rich," a condition that never had existed among the Alcotts. There was Hannah reigning over the kitchen and foods that were expensive in the 1860's. By contrast the Alcotts sometimes lacked wood for fires, and their vegetarian diet was often reduced to bread and water. Finances were actually so shattered that

Louisa dedicated herself to supporting her family with an intensity that she never gave up. She paid off the old debts eventually and poured out her generosity upon the family with little hint at self-indulgence in spite of comparative affluence in her later years.

Biographically, then, *Little Women* seems a genteel reflection of the spiritual teachings of Bronson Alcott, the image blurred and softened by Louisa's defensive desires, and tenderly dramatized by the Alcott sisters and their parents.

An adult is concerned with form as well as substance in his reading. Here, too, Louisa's yearning for the stage had a strong influence upon the style of her writing. She wrote many plays as a young girl which her sisters and friends joined her in producing. The Alcott dining room was often a stage; so too was the barn in pleasant summer weather. While in Boston, Louisa almost succeeded in having a play successfully produced. The author, herself, spoke of *Little Women* as a domestic drama, and drama it is. The characters live and act. At least three quarters of the lineage is given over to direct discourse, much of it to discourse crowded with action. Some of it is contemplative, a little of it is moralizing and tiresomely dutiful, though based upon an honest acceptance of human frailty. It is the combination of dialogue and action that projects a vitality so galvanic as to make the story last in memory for many years.

One technique Miss Alcott fell into, however, can only be viewed with regret; the frequent intrusion of the author in the first person between the reader and the characters, although the story is not a first-person narrative. Two instances are sufficient for illustration:

"You?" cried Meg, dropping her work.

"It's very good," said Amy critically.

"I knew it! I knew it! O my Jo, I am so proud!" and Beth ran to hug her sister, and exult over this splendid success.

Dear me, how delighted they all were, to be sure! how Meg wouldn't believe it till she saw the words, "Miss Josephine March" actually printed—

"I don't believe fine young ladies enjoy themselves a bit more than we do, in spite of burnt hair, old gowns, one glove apiece, and tight slippers that sprain our ankles when we are silly enough to wear them." And I think Jo was quite right.

It is curious that anyone so well read as was Louisa Alcott could fall quite often into this inconsistency and intrusion. One must remember, of course, that her reading included a great deal besides the classics; that she was largely self-taught as a writer, that her earliest writing both of plays and stories was largely of a melodramatic sort. Much of it is now unavailable, having fallen into disuse because of its artificiality and lack of realism.

Louisa's early ambitions were to write about "splendid" people, about knights and ladies in great castles, about the world of wealth and fortune she dreamed of but did not know. It is not surprising that a few popular tricks of "pot-boiler-writing" stayed with the indefatigable writer whose first production of stories was chiefly to meet the demands of the moment in style and characterization.

One element of style calls forth genuine admiration, even in a re-reader attempting to be critical. One can scarcely resist being impressed by the sense of immediacy that Miss Alcott projects upon nearly every page. Characters act and talk; they are not sketched in cutline nor generalized about. If Bronson taught most successfully through his famous conversations so, too, did his famous daughter. That some of this talk seems pedantic if not downright "preachy" to a twentieth century reader is not surprising. Nearly a century has elapsed since the story was written. At the time it was revolutionary in its inclusion of homely detail and its revealing of characters as good and bad, awkward and graceful, angry and loving. Alcott's characters are many-dimensioned persons and they live in her pages. Home life is revealed in its trials and tempests as well as in its smoother moments. A wholesome realism was realized. Few modern writers for young people have achieved so vivid a realism and in stories of family life the number is even smaller. The vividness of most characters is memorable. To the critical eye, Hannah the faithful house servant seems shadowy and questionable, particularly in her letter written to Marmee. Anyone who used Hannah's dialect could scarcely have spelled with such efficiency as she did, even to placing apostrophes in *col'k'late!* Obviously, too, Mr. Bhaer is never quite clearly realized, even though formulated as the husband for Jo. Undoubtedly he is an amalgam of several persons known to the family; the synthesis is logical but never quite alive.

One other characterization seems somewhat exaggerated. In the X-Ray probing of today, doubt must be cast upon some of Mrs. March's sermons. Even more doubt must be held that children to whom these admonitions were addressed would chorus "We will! We will!" no matter how charmingly those sermons were administered.

One important thread runs through the beloved tale that may well explain its lasting hold upon young people, particularly upon little girls whose social sensitivity and interest in family life is believed to mature much earlier than do these attitudes in little boys. This thread is the universal struggle between the inner and the outer world, between subjective and objective phases of experience.

Bronson Alcott has been called the most transcendental of the Transcendentalists. But, even though tempted, he did not retreat from life. His several schools failed, the Fruitlands communal experiment crashed, yet he returned to all sorts of jobs while continuing his pursuit of "indwelling," of cultivation of mind and spirit. "I set out from the wide ground of spirit. This is, all else is its manifestation." Such conviction was as common as bread and butter, indeed, sometimes more common, in the Alcott household. This conviction, or some reflection of it, is woven into the story.

With no self-consciousness the author projects family life around the subjective values of individual integrity, of artistic fulfillment, of continuing growth toward personal ideals. She could do this with so little painful introspection because of the spirit that animated the entire family. It was a commonplace to keep a journal about one's feelings and one's moral-intellectual development as well as to record externals of experience. It was as natural to compliment a sister for triumph over temper as for a new dress or a pleasant invitation. Discussion of inner experience pours out quite naturally on the pages of *Little Women* because it occurred quite naturally in the author's household. In spite of discomfort and poverty, there was no compromise between individuality and the world's standards. For Bronson Alcott, what one believed was reality. Where this reality could harmonize with the community, through neighbors, friends, and organizations, one worked and struggled. Physical comfort was incidental. Such a belief was not retreat. Inner life had to be realized in the environment. Courage was not merely admired; it was put into action. Beth was overwhelmingly timid, but she went over to see the forbidding Mr. Lawrence, and her family rejoiced in her new-found strength. Meg hated poverty and discomfort; she disliked her job as governess, yet she persisted. She even grew in grace to the point of loving a poor man who represented the ideals she and her family held in high esteem. Thus did the Alcotts' dedication to integrity come into the drama of *Little Women.*

Perhaps the strongest hold of *Little Women* over the years lies in this struggle between the inner world of personal values, of individual expression, reflection, and creativity and the outer world of material and social values, and at times of stolid conformity. For the Marches, as for the Alcotts, there was no escape from the world. There was only resolute life welling out from the centers of personal and inner life. Great literature deals constantly with this theme. Modern critics as well as older ones evaluate literature in part through its honest dealing with the dilemma of the individual in a material world with other men. Dramatizing this approach to adult verities in terms that are concrete and vital as well as understandable to children can be done by few authors. Louisa had the experience and the unique education that made it possible.

In spite of some saccharine moments and intrusions of an earlier undisciplined style of writing, Miss Alcott brings the warmth and triumph of a troubled family living in an age of conflict into the arena of another age. It may well be that her dramatization of a struggle for integrity and individuality will survive the change of pace from Civil War to Space Age.

Margery Fisher

SOURCE: "Growing Up: *Little Women,*" in *Intent upon Reading: A Critical Appraisal of Modern Fiction for Children,* Brockhampton Press, 1961, pp. 297-98.

It is, after all, a fair test of a book, whether it still has its dust-jacket on or not—unless it is a second or third copy bought for a family of obsessive readers. A reviewer wrote recently:

> In the bad old Victorian days children's books made (we are told now) not nearly enough concessions to their diminutive readers. Their authors crammed them with instruction and moral uplift. They used an uncompromising, polysyllabic, adult vocabulary. They bombarded the youthful mind with raw, if not unadulterated, heroic legend. They were not what is today known as 'entertainment', or anywhere near; and the denizens of the nursery undistracted by TV or the Pleasure Principle, read and re-read them till they fell to bits.

> —"Ulysses in Modern Dress," *The Times Literary Supplement,* 20 May, 1960.

Why do children still read *Little Women?* What does Louisa Alcott give them still which they do not always find in contemporary stories? Could it be that her gently humorous tales are nearer to reality than the more up-to-date versions children take, mint-new, from the library shelf?

From their first junior books onwards, children should be able to find something of what people and places are really like. The writer who studies his public too closely may well leave out, on some misguided principle, a good deal of adult comment that children really need. It is only too easy to underestimate the understanding of the young. What we give them must be strong and honest. Victorian story-books are criticized for their repressions and omissions. We would do well to ask whether writers of today give children any more of the truth, or indeed as much.

How many family stories there are in which the plot centers round poverty: how few in which you can really *smell* that poverty. *Little Women* has a permanent place on the bookshelves of the young because of its sterling honesty. The author herself described the book as 'Not a bit sensational, but simple and true, for we really lived most of it, and if it succeeds, that will be the reason for it.' Whoever doubted, when reading about the scorched breadth in Jo March's evening dress, that these girls were poor? And it is the same with every issue that touches the Marches. Love, social adventure, jobs, friction among themselves, illness and death—the author looks at everything squarely. Brought up in a liberal family, where children were treated as sensible individuals, it never occurred to her that her young readers would expect anything else.

Brigid Brophy

SOURCE: "Sentimentality and Louisa M. Alcott," in *Don't Never Forget: Collected Views and Reviews,* Holt, Rinehart and Winston, 1966, pp. 113-20.

Who's afraid of Louisa M. Alcott? Well, Louisa M. Alcott, for one; and, for another, me.

I'm afraid of her in a quite straightforward way—because she makes me cry. Being myself an almost wholly unsentimental writer, I'm not a bit afraid of her example, which doesn't tempt me. It's not as a writer but as a reader that I fear her.

Her own fear of herself was, however, more ambiguous. She is, I suppose, of all writers the one whose name *means* sentimentality: and yet sentimentality is what she and her characters most dread. Indeed, the very reason why Josephine March preferred to be known as Jo (and I would guess the nickname was the final simple stroke which turned her into one of the classic characters of popular-cum-nursery culture, up there with Sherlock Holmes and Little Miss Muffet) is that she found the name Josephine 'so sentimental'.

I was driven back to Louisa M. Alcott, whom I hadn't read since I was fourteen, by the recent revival on television of the old film of *Little Women.* By the old film I mean the one with the young Katharine Hepburn—and there I instantly caution myself not to render unto Alcott credit which belongs to Hepburn. The cinematic person-ality of Katharine Hepburn (for which I imagine the credit belongs to the real-life personality of Katharine Hepburn) is one of those purely poetic literary inventions like Rosalind or the very idea of a seraph. Tears shed over Hepburn are diamonds, cutting clean and deep lacerations into the cheeks they course down. They have no connexion at all with the synthetically pearled snail-track left by the tears of sentimentality. It was just Louisa M. Alcott's good posthumous luck that Hepburn played Jo and that the high ruffled necks of 'period' clothes (to use the word in its purely evocative or estate agent's sense) set off to perfection the essentially tragic sinewiness of the Hepburn throat.

And yet: one can't say Alcott did *nothing* to deserve her luck. Hepburn was never so ideally cast again. It's already something that Alcott created the character which most perfectly became her. And then—the clinching point—the film provoked tears even when Hepburn was not on the screen.

It also brought back enough memory of the text for me to think that it was sticking fairly reverently to Alcott situ-

Alcott (left) and her sister Annie, the models for the characters Jo and Meg in Little Women.

ations and dialogue—which I soon afterwards confirmed by getting hold of the book or, rather, books; the film is in fact taken from both *Little Women* and *Good Wives.* Buying them turned out to be an exercise in itself in nostalgia for a pre-war childhood. They are pretty well the last genuine *books,* with binding and dust wrapper, to be had for a paperback price. Presumably, therefore, they still sell in commercially worthwhile quantities (though as they are out of copyright there is no author's royalty to add its mite to the selling price). Indeed, perhaps they still sell as a going contemporary concern: for though the publishers admit, by the clothes on the pictorial wrappers, that the stories themselves are 'period', there is nothing to make it unequivocally clear that they weren't written yesterday. You have to consult a reference book to discover that *Little Women* was first published in 1868. The blurb of one edition still speaks of 'Miss Alcott'—which seems to surrender the advantages of suggesting she's immortal in favour of those of suggesting she's still alive.

Having re-read them, dried my eyes and blown my nose (it is itself a sentimentality that this less dignified aspect of weeping is so seldom mentioned: one day I shall go through the fiction in the public library and to every 'His eyes filled' add 'so did his nose'), I resolved that the only honourable course was to come out into the open and admit that the dreadful books are masterpieces. I do it, however, with some bad temper and hundreds of reservations.

For of course to admit sentimentality at all is to play with fire. Sentimentality is always doing something of which art can stand only very small and controlled amounts—bursting out of the conventions of art and making a direct appeal (all art makes an oblique one) to real life. Sentimentality is always playing on your experience of real drowned kittens and real lost mothers—or, worse still, playing on your real dread of losing kittens or mothers. The weepiest of trashy movies is the one which throws in a moment or two of genuine newsreel. And then, having invoked the reality of the real world, sentimentality does the one thing neither morality nor art can stand for—it is hypocritical.

The true artistic impulse is, largely, cruel—or at least relentless. To bring a novel, for instance, to a climax, the artist must drive the situation, and probably the characters, to extremes. He harries his *donnée* until it falls apart and its logical structure is pitilessly exposed. The sentimentalist, on the other hand, is a nonartist who won't take the responsibility of being ruthless. He won't drive his situations to the point of artistic inevitability. Instead, he appears to hold his hand in compunction. He resigns himself—much too soon—to the will of God; but covertly he is manipulating the will of God to suit what he is too hypocritical to admit is really his own taste.

Hundreds of fictional infants were so to speak raped on their deathbeds by Victorian anecdotalists—both novelists and painters—in order to procure for author and audience the pleasure of destroying an innocence but in such a way that the pleasure could pass for the quite innocent, the even creditable, enjoyment of feeling a spasm across the eyelids. Even now one cannot stand quite indifferent beside those deathbeds. I think Oscar Wilde said that no man of feeling could read the death of Little Nell without laughing. But the unwitty and much more terrible truth is that no one can read it without crying. Dickens has made the illegitimate appeal to real life and, no matter what ludicrous nonsense he makes of the death of Little Nell, the death of children *is* sad.

The sentimentalist always breaks the rules of art and frequently those of morality. The most unforgivable of all the occasions when sentimentality has burst through the artistic conventions is the one when Peter Pan bursts through the proscenium and invites the audience to keep Tinker Bell alive by affirming that they believe in fairies. That the audience consists of children is the ultimate sentimental immorality. Christendom's inveterate habit of telling its children fairy tales and then breaking the convention by assuring them that the tale is true and they must feel obliged to its hero, who died for *them,* is, if not justified, mitigated by the fact that most of the adults concerned really believed the story themselves and certainly believed it would do the children good to believe it. But I will not accept for a moment that J. M. Barrie had any more belief in fairies than—well, than the children in his audiences had.

When Theseus calls the lovers' account of what took place in that wood near Athens 'antique fables' and 'fairy toys', Hippolyta objects that their story 'More witnesseth than fancy's images, And grows to something of great constancy'. So it does: to a fairy tale genuinely imagined (and therefore genuinely and poetically moving), which is to be believed utterly—but strictly in the realm of the imagination. But Peter Pan's telling the audience that Tinker Bell 'thinks she could get well again if the children believed in fairies . . . If you believe, clap your hands!' is moral torture inflicted by a wanton—but highly skilled—sentimentalist. Ours is a paradoxical society which dreads that one of its children might come on that charming, sentimentality-free little tale *Fanny Hill* and yet for decades put on *Peter Pan* at the very times of day and year when it was most likely to be seen by children. (Unless our winter holiday is in fact built round not the 25th December but the 28th—which commemorates the Slaughter of the Innocents?)

Not that I am supporting censorship, even for *Peter Pan,* though if I could see any sense in censorship at all *Peter Pan* would be my first and probably only candidate. I just think we ought to treat *Peter Pan* as a play for adults, as we already sensibly do its runners-up as sentimental masterpieces for the theatre, *Private Lives* and *Who's Afraid Of Virginia Woolf?*

It would certainly be unkind to deprive adults of *Peter Pan,* because as a piece of craftsmanship it is perhaps the most highly skilled job in the repertory, and is therefore capable of giving pleasure to two groups which more usually fail to agree on anything. For, incongruously enough, it is on works of literary craftsmanship that highbrow and lowbrow can often meet. Really, of course, they are at cross purposes. The lowbrow cares nothing for technique as technique, and probably doesn't even notice it as such. All he wants is a good read at or a good cry over a good story; and he wants to have that without subjecting himself to the subversive effect—whether of society or of individual emotions—which is inherent in all good works of art. The highbrow, on the other hand, studies technique in order to pick up tips, which he intends to put to use in better appreciating or even better practising the subversiveness of art. But though they are at cross purposes and the lowbrow wouldn't approve of the highbrow's purpose if he knew of it, both highbrow and lowbrow (the two cultures which we really are divided into) are glad, through simple good will, of any meeting place. They could go further and find worse rendezvous than Louisa M. Alcott.

You can measure Alcott's technical skill by asking any professional novelist how he would care to have to differentiate the characters of four adolescent girls—particularly if he were confined to a domestic setting, more-or-less naturalism and the things which were mentionable when Alcott wrote. Greater scope in at least the first and last of those departments has not prevented more than one recent novel from making a hash of almost the identical technical problem. Alcott, of course, triumphed at it (that is why we have heard of her), incidentally turning out for one of her four, Meg, a brilliant portrait of the sort of girl whose character consists of having no character. Girls of this sort are the commonest to meet in life and the rarest in literature, because they are so hard to depict (the problem is a variant of the old one about depicting a bore without being boring): usually it takes the genius of a Tolstoy (who specialised in them) to bring them off.

Whereas Meg was a commonplace of Alcott's own—or any—time, in Amy Alcott actually shewed sociological prescience. Or, rather, I think, it shewed despite her. Try as she will to prettify and moralise, she cannot help making Amy the prototype of a model which did not become numerous in the United States until the twentieth century—the peroxided, girl-doll gold-digger. Of course it's Amy who gets Laurie in the end (he's rich, isn't he?): she's had 'Good pull-in for Laurie' emblazoned on her chest from the moment her chest began to bud.

With Beth, I admit, Alcott went altogether too far. Beth's patience, humility and gentle sunniness are a quite monstrous imposition on the rest of the family—especially when you consider at what close, even cramped, quarters they live (two bedrooms to four girls): no one in the household could escape the blight of feeling unworthy which was imposed by Beth. I concur in the judgment of the person with whom I watched the film (and who wept even more than I did) in naming her the Black Beth. (I also concur in his naming Marmee Smarmee.) I think Louisa Alcott may herself have had an inkling that in designing a fate for Beth she was inspired by revenge. She seems, perhaps through suspicion of her own motives, to have faltered, with the result that she committed the sort of blunder only a very naïve technician would

fall into and only a very self-assured one could, as she does, step out of in her stride. She brings Beth to the point of dying in *Little Women,* and then lets her recover; whereupon, instead of washing her hands—as not ruthless enough to do it—of the whole enterprise, she whips the situation up again in *Good Wives* and this time does ('As Beth had hoped, "the tide went out easily"') kill her off.

As for Laurie: well, of course, Laurie is awful, tossing those awful curls (though in *Good Wives* he has them cropped and is told off for it): yet though I will go to my death (may the tide go out easily) denying that Laurie has a millionth part of the attractions he thinks he has and the girls think he has, I cannot deny that he is lifelike. If you want to see the romanticised implausibility which even an intelligent woman of the world (and great novelist into the bargain) could make of a curly-haired young man, look at George Eliot's Will Ladislaw. Laurie by contrast is—if awfully—probable.

In the most important event affecting Laurie, the fact that Jo refuses him, Alcott goes beyond verisimilitude and almost into artistic honesty. No doubt she found the courage for this, which meant cutting across the cliché-lines of the popular novel and defying her readers' matchmaking hopes, in the personality of Jo. Jo is one of the most blatantly autobiographical yet most fairly treated heroines in print. All that stands between her and Emma Woodhouse is her creator's lack of intellect. Alcott is not up to devising situations which analyse and develop, as distinct from merely illustrating, her characters.

And in fact absence of intellectual content is the mark of the sentimental genre; conversely it is because of her intellect that Jane Austen is never sentimental. I think, incidentally, that the word 'sentimental' may have been in bad repute with Louisa Alcott because in 1868 it still wore eighteenth-century dress. And the reason, of course, why the eighteenth-century sentimental mode, unlike the nineteenth-century one, no longer works on us (the death of Virginie in *Paul et Virginie* really can't be read without laughing) is that the eighteenth century was so double-dyed intellectual that it *couldn't* put aside intellect when it took out its handkerchief: its many attempts to be affectingly simple were made self-conscious and absurd by its (perfectly correct) suspicion that it was being a simpleton.

As sentimentalists go, Louisa M. Alcott is of the gentler and less immoral sort. Beth's is the only really lushed-over death (the canary who dies in Chapter Eleven of *Little Women* is virtually a throw-away): on the whole, Alcott prefers to wreak her revenges on her characters by making them unhappy in their moments of happiness. (They make it easy for her to do so, through their own proneness to sentimentality.) Even here, one can morally if not aesthetically justify her. It's all, so to speak, between consenting adolescents. All four girls are quite masochists enough to enjoy what she does to them.

I rest on Louisa M. Alcott my plea—hedged about with

provisos, reduced, indeed, to a mere strangled sob—that we should recognise that, though sentimentality mars art, craftsmanship in sentimentality is to be as legitimately enjoyed as in any of those genres (thrillers, pornography, ghost stories, yarns, science fiction—whichever way your taste lies) which, because they suppress some relevant strand in artistic logic, are a little less than literature. The spasm across the eyelids is not inherently more despicable than the *frisson* of the supernatural or the muted erotic thrill imparted by a brilliant sado-erotic literary craftsman like Raymond Chandler. It is, however, more dangerous. One should take to heart this stray little fable by Kierkegaard (whose personality is, indeed, to be taken to heart in all contexts): 'In itself, salmon is a great delicacy; but too much of it is harmful, since it taxes the digestion. At one time when a very large catch of salmon had been brought to Hamburg, the police ordered that a householder should give his servants only one meal a week of salmon. One could wish for a similar police order against sentimentality.'

Elizabeth Janeway

SOURCE: "Meg, Jo, Beth, Amy and Louisa," in *The New York Times Book Review,* September 29, 1968, pp. 42, 44, 46.

Meg, Jo, Beth and Amy are 100 years old on Oct. 3 [1968] and except for Natasha Rostova, who is almost exactly their contemporary (*War and Peace* appeared over the years 1865 to 1869), the Marches must be the most read about and cried over young women of their years. In my time we read *Little Women* of course, but we liked to think it was because our sentimental mothers had loved the book so and urged it on us. For all I know, this is still the cover story today, but just the same, the answer to "Have you read *Little Women*?" is still "Of course." In the last week I've heard it from three Americans, an Italian and an English girl, all in their twenties—the English girl quoted the whole opening: "Christmas won't be Christmas without any presents," it begins, in case you've forgotten—and a mother of teen-agers assured me that her daughters were even now devouring the works of Miss Alcott. Read *Little Women*? Of course.

Why? It is dated and sentimental and full of preaching and moralizing, and some snobbery about the lower classes that is positively breathtaking in its horror: that moment, for instance, when old Mr. Laurence is improbably discovered in a fishmarket, and bestows his charity on a starving Irish woman by hooking a large fish on the end of his cane, and depositing it, to her gasping gratitude, in her arms. It is as often smug as it is snug, and its high-mindedness tends to be that peculiar sort that pays. Brigid Brophy, writing in *The New York Times Book Review* a few years ago, called it a dreadful masterpiece, and the judgment stands (though not, I think, quite on Miss Brophy's grounds). And yet, here it is in a new and handsome centennial edition, as compulsively readable as it was a century ago when publisher Thomas Niles's nieces overrode their uncle's doubts and urged him to bring it out.

Its faults we can see in a moment. They cry to heaven, and when Miss Brophy dwelt at length on the literary sin of sentimentality which falsifies emotion and manipulates the process of life, she hardly had to cite evidence. *Little Women* does harp on our nerves, does play on our feelings, does stack the cards to bring about undeserved happy outcomes here and undeserved come-uppance there. But that is not the whole story, and couldn't be, or there wouldn't be all those girls with their noses in the book right now, and all those women who remember the supreme shock of the moment when Jo sold her hair; when Beth was discovered on the medicine chest in the closet with scarlet fever coming on; when Meg let the Moffats dress her up; when Amy was packed off, protesting and bargaining, to Aunt March's stiff house.

No, *Little Women* does manipulate life, but it is also *about* life, and life that is recognizable in human terms today. Miss Alcott preached, and the conclusions she came to are frequently too good to be true; but the facts of emotion that she started with were real. She might end by softening the ways to deal with them, but she began by looking them in the eye. Her girls were jealous, mean,

Frontispiece sketched by Alcott's sister May for the first volume of Little Women.

silly and lazy; and for 100 years jealous, mean, silly and lazy girls have been ardently grateful for the chance to read about themselves. If Miss Alcott's prescriptions for curing their sins are too simple, it doesn't alter the fact that her diagnoses are clear, unequivocal and humanly right. When her girls are good, they are apt to be painful; but when they are bad, they are bad just the way we all are, and over the same things. It must have been a heavenly relief 100 years ago to learn that one's faults were not unique. Today I suspect that it is a relief to be told to take them seriously and struggle with them; that it is important to be good.

This general background of human interest makes *Little Women* still plausible, but it is hardly enough to keep it a perennial classic. The real attraction is not the book as a whole, but its heroine, Jo, and Jo is a unique creation: the one young woman in 19th-century fiction who maintains her individual independence, who gives up no part of her autonomy as payment for being born a woman—and who gets away with it. Jo is the tomboy dream come true, the dream of growing up into full humanity with all its potentialities instead of into limited femininity: of looking after oneself and paying one's way and doing effective work in the real world instead of learning how to please a man who will look after you, as Meg and Amy both do with pious pleasure. (So, by the way, does Natasha). It's no secret that Jo's story is the heart of *Little Women,* but just what that story represents has not, to my knowledge, been explored, and I think it is worth looking at.

We shall have to work back and forth from Louisa May Alcott's life to her book, but no one has ever denied that Jo is Louisa and that a great deal of her story is autobiographical. The very fact that *Little Women* was written so quickly makes that conclusion inescapable: two and a half months for the first part and two months for the second. More clearly in life, but clearly enough in her book, Louisa-Jo wanted to become the head of the family. In part, this was necessity. Bronson Alcott suffered from a kind of obsessional generosity that appears at times to have verged on *folie de grandeus;* and his wife and daughters learned early to shift for themselves, for Papa's plans not only went astray, they were apt to ignore the existence of his family completely.

Then there came a time—Louisa was 11—when Bronson Alcott all but deserted his wife and daughters and went off to join a Shaker colony with his English friend, Charles Lane, who (as his wife put it) had almost hypnotic power over him. In the end he did not go, but suffered so powerfully from the crisis that he did in fact abdicate the father's role in the family. In that frequent 19th-century gesture of despair, he took to his bed and turned his face to the wall. None of this was hidden from Louisa. She and her older sister Anna made part of the family council which discussed Mr. Alcott's decision to go off with his friend to the celibate Shakers or to stay.

This clumsy agony is glossed over in *Little Women,* where absent Mr. March is away as a chaplain during the Civil War. But the pressure on Jo to hold her family together by working and earning is all there, and so is the emotion of the one who aspires to play the role of responsibility when it has become vacant. When Meg is falling in love, Jo blurts out in fury, "I just wish I could marry Meg myself, and keep her safe in the family." This is, of course, treated as a joke, though sociologist students of the incest taboo in the nuclear family would find it of interest. It is, at any rate, indicative of Jo's desire to become the responsible head of the household, and the last half of the book is devoted to her effort to achieve this end, which, in her life, she did achieve.

This aim explains her refusal to marry handsome Laurie, the next-door hero. Their relationship has always been that of two equals, which in 19th-century America (and in some places today) implies two equals of the same sex. Twice at least Laurie suggests that they run off together, not for love-making, but for adventure; very much in the manner and mood in which Tom Sawyer and Huck Finn plan to run away from comfort and civilization. Again when Jo speaks to her mother about the possibility of marriage to Laurie, Mrs. March is against it "because you two are too much alike." So they are, and so—with no explanations ever given—Jo refuses Laurie, and the reader knows she is right, for Jo and Laurie are dear friends, competitors and not in the least a couple. It is worth nothing that the two other adored 19th-century heroines who say "No" to the hero's proposal give way in the end, when circumstances and the hero have changed: Elizabeth Bennet and Jane Eyre. But Jo says "No" and does not shift.

The subtlety of Miss Alcott's character drawing (or self knowledge, if you will) comes through here, for Jo is a tomboy, but never a masculinized or Lesbian figure. She is, somehow, an idealized "New Woman," capable of male virtues but not, as the Victorians would have said, "unsexed." Or perhaps she is really archaic woman, re-created out of some New-World-frontier necessity when patriarchy breaks down. For Jo marries (as we all know! Who can forget that last great self-indulgent burst of tears when Professor Bhaer stops, under the umbrella, and asks "Heart's dearest, why do you cry?"). Yes, Jo marries and becomes, please note, not a sweet little wife but a matriarch: mistress of the professor's school, mother of healthy sons (while Amy and Laurie have only one sickly daughter), and cheerful active manager of events and people. For this Victorian moral tract, sentimental and preachy, was written by a secret rebel against the order of the world and woman's place in it, and all the girls who ever read it know it.

Lavinia Russ

SOURCE: "Not to Be Read on Sunday," in *The Horn Book Magazine,* Vol. XLIV, No. 5, October, 1968, pp. 521-26.

Not everybody loves *Little Women.* Brigid Brophy didn't love it—she took six full columns in the *New York Times*

Book Review to say why, ending her blast against sentimentality by calling it "a masterpiece, and dreadful," a blast which shot her readers straight to their bookshelves to reread their copies of *Little Women.*

Ernest Hemingway did not love the idea of it—in Paris, when he and this century were young, Hadley and he once asked me up to their flat. When I walked in with a copy of Ibsen's plays under my arm, Ernest put me down with "You're so full of young sweetness and light you ought to be carrying *Little Women.*" (He had never read it.)

The unknown critic who wrote one of its first reviews didn't dislike *Little Women,* but did not announce the birth of a masterpiece with any ruffle of drums. "Louisa Alcott is a very spritely and fascinating writer, and her sister, May Alcott, always makes beautiful pictures to illustrate the books. Their books and stories are always interesting and instructive about everyday life. They are not religious books, should not be read on Sunday, and are not appropriate for the Sunday School. This is the character of the book before us. It is lively, entertaining, and not harmful."

Why did *I* love it? Why did all the millions of girls who have read it in the last hundred years love it? Why do all the girls who are reading it all around the world today love it? To find out, I reached for my copy of *Little Women* with its title page "Little Women or Meg, Jo, Beth and Amy, by Louisa M. Alcott, with illustrations in color by Jessie Willcox Smith, Boston, Little Brown and Company, 1915," with its inscription on the fly leaf from the most important person in my life—"Lavinia Faxon— To a Little Woman—Father." And for the first time in fifty years, I read it straight through, from the very beginning—"'Christmas won't be Christmas without any presents,' grumbled Jo, lying on the rug"—to the very end, to the sunny afternoon at Plumfield, where all the Marches had gathered to celebrate Marmee's sixtieth birthday with presents and songs—"Touched to the heart, Mrs. March could only stretch out her arms as if to gather children and grandchildren to herself, and say, with face and voice full of motherly love, gratitude, and humility, 'Oh my girls, however long you may live, I never can wish you a greater happiness than this!'"

I read it all, and I found out, I found out why I loved it. I had a strong hunch I had found out why when I read earlier Cornelia Meigs's splendid biography of Miss Alcott, *Invincible Louisa,* and when I read *Louisa M. Alcott: Her Life, Letters and Journals,* edited by Ednah D. Cheney. I found out for sure when I reread *Little Women.* I loved it because Louisa M. Alcott was a rebel, with rebels for parents. I found out why other girls loved it—because Jo was a rebel, with rebels for parents. Not the rebels of destruction—they never threw a brick—but rebels who looked at the world as it was, saw the poverty, the inequality, the ignorance, the fear, and said, "It isn't good enough" and went to work to change it. . . .

Brigid Brophy was wrong about *Little Women.* A girl in Russia cries over Beth's death, not because it is sentimental, but because it is brave. And a girl in India cries when Jo refuses Laurie, because she realizes suddenly that life is not going to hold a neat, happy ending for her.

Ernest Hemingway was wrong about *Little Women.* If he had read *Little Women,* he would have realized that it is not "sweetness and light," it is stalwart proof of his definition of courage: grace under pressure.

Its early reviewer was wrong about *Little Women,* because if religion is living Faith, Hope and Charity every minute of your life, the Alcott-Marches were a truly religious family.

Above all, girls are right to love *Little Women,* every word of it, because it is a story about *good* people. And if there is one generality that is true (and it is the only generality I will ever make about them), it is that young people love goodness. And if there is one hope for us in 1968, the only one, it is that the young recognize the power of goodness, and the responsibility that goodness demands of men and women of good will—the responsibility to their brothers, the responsibility to look at the world as it is—at the poverty, the inequality, the ignorance, the fear—and to say "It isn't good enough" and go to work to change it.

Cornelia Meigs

SOURCE: "Introduction to the Centennial Edition of *Little Women,*" in *The Horn Book Magazine,* Vol. XLIV, No. 5, October, 1968, pp. 527-35.

In September, 1867, [Alcott] mentions in her diary that Mr. Thomas Niles of Roberts Brothers had asked her for a book for girls. It seems to have been somewhat of a shot in the dark even for him; for her it was even more unpromising than that. She agreed to try, but linked the task so little that she did not go on with it. Other and easier-seeming undertakings were allowed to come in the way and in May, 1867, she sent her father to Mr. Niles to ask him if he would not be interested in a fairy book. Thomas Niles answered firmly that he wanted a book for girls.

She had no confidence that she could carry out such a project. She protested that she was not interested in girls and did not understand them. But necessity can take the place of confidence when it must, and necessity was pressing hard upon her now. Necessity again dictated that she take for her subjects the girls who were at hand, namely herself and her three sisters, and make the most of her intimate knowledge of them. Some families seem to know rather little of one another, but this was not true of the Alcotts, particularly not of Louisa. Her capacity for understanding others, her deep affection for her parents and her sisters, was combined with the determination that she was going to win security and happiness for this beloved circle. A profound belief that true happiness lay in the perfecting of family life joined in her with a stoutness of heart with which she approached any task to which she had definitely set herself. All this brought its own results and produced *Little Women.*

She contributed not only sympathy and understanding to her characters but also a complete and generous honesty which gave the book its strong sense of reality. She pretended nothing and concealed nothing; all of her persons were fully and frankly themselves. People who read the book could see reflected their own failings, their own small and secret temptations, and be reassured by the account of other people trying to get the better of their shortcomings. Particularly in relation to herself, Miss Alcott showed Jo in all her hasty-tempered errors, all her doubts and hesitations and her many failures in trying to avoid them. With her instinctive keenness of observation she was able to describe how people could and did change, could develop and make the most of themselves as they went forward. Louisa, whose father was a philosopher, whose intimate family friend was Ralph Waldo Emerson, one of the greatest thinkers of his time, had unconsciously learned the full importance and meaning in the progress of daily life.

In certain ways the book inevitably shows that it was written in another age, one in which people felt free to express their feelings and their spiritual and inner thoughts more fully than they would today. In spite of that, the book showed a long step forward for its time. In books for young people it was then the custom to weigh down the narrative with moral platitudes, strewn with an all too heavy hand. Louisa was fully aware of the dangers of too much preaching. She says of Jo at one point when things were not going happily for her: "Now if she had been the heroine of a moral storybook, she ought at this period of her life to have become quite saintly, renounced the world and gone about doing good in a mortified bonnet with tracts in her pocket." Miss Alcott makes it plain that such was not the case and that Jo was "sad, cross, listless or energetic, as the mood suggested."

Mrs. March's occasional little lectures have their own solid worth; they are, actually, only made up of matters that all parents would like to put before their children. Jo's mother, when the two consult together over Jo's impulsive difficulties in the conduct of her life, does not hesitate to meet her troubled daughter on her own ground and exposes all of her own failures in learning to control a hot and explosive temper.

The natural progress of events which is involved in the growing up of four lively girls and the boy who lives next door would make plot enough, but the course of the story follows a more distinctive pattern which should not be overlooked. There is an illuminating scene in the earlier part of the book which ought not to be too hastily passed over. On a certain summer afternoon Laurie sees the girls going up the hill behind the house, wearing big hats, with bags hanging on their shoulders and with staffs in their hands. When he joins them he finds that they are playing a game which they have been fond of since they were small children, that of being people in *Pilgrim's Progress,* the book to which every one of the Alcotts was so devot-

ed. Sitting on the grass the girls and Laurie fall to talking of the future and each one voices his or her ambition, telling of the thing that is at the back of every growing young person's mind, "What would I like to be?"

Meg has arrived somewhere near the fulfillment of her wish, although she only speaks of it cautiously as "To have a lovely house, full of luxurious things" and containing "pleasant people." Jo is also somewhat indefinite. "I want to do something splendid . . . something heroic and wonderful that won't be forgotten after I'm dead. I don't know what, but I'm on the watch for it and mean to astonish you all some day. I think I shall write books and get rich and famous: that would suit me, so that is *my* favorite dream." Beth is too shy to tell what is her real desire, although we learn of it later. All that she will own to now is the wish "that we may all keep well and be together; nothing else."

Amy has "ever so many wishes; but the pet one is . . . to go to Rome and do fine pictures and be the best artist in the whole world." Laurie is not far behind her. "I'm to be a famous musician myself and all creation is to rush to hear me; and I'm never to be bothered about money or business, but just enjoy myself and live for what I like." He adds reflectively, "We're an ambitious set, aren't we? Every one of us but Beth wants to be rich and famous, and gorgeous in every respect. I do wonder if any of us will ever get our wishes."

While the reader is not aware of it, one of the things that holds the story together is the fact that all these cherished schemes do, in actual fact, come to their desired ends but only after each person has accepted the modification and compromise that circumstances and his or her own character have made inevitable. The happy and irresponsible materialism and youthful vanity that clothe these ambitious plans are shed away and replaced by something far more valuable. It is the highest proof of Louisa Alcott's mastery of storytelling that none of us realize this until we look back long after we have read the book.

David Curtis

SOURCE: "Little Women: A Reconsideration," in *Elementary English,* Vol. XLV, No. 7, November, 1968, pp. 878-80.

Modern readers are inclined to dismiss Louisa May Alcott's *Little Women* as hardly more than a sentimental novel of nineteenth century idealism; a novel with little to say to us in the twentieth century—except as a curiosity piece for American schoolgirls interested in the customs and manners of the Civil War era. It is now a hundred years since *Little Women* first appeared, and few American novels, indeed, can claim continued success for a century. It immediately attracted an enthusiastic audience when it initially appeared in 1868, at first as adult fiction. Shortly thereafter, it became more of a women's novel, then an adolescent girls' book, and finally what it is now: a notable piece of children's literature, specifically perhaps, a work for seventh and eighth grade girls. A great many parents still encourage their daughters to read *Little Women,* under the impression that every intelligent American schoolgirl ought to be acquainted with Meg, Jo, Beth and Amy March—not only for the familiar metaphor in the title, but for a reading experience that is, in itself, a symbol of innocence. To a certain extent, it is the last reading experience of childhood: after *Little Women,* a story that is only slightly more sentimental than *Marjory Morningstar,* an American girl grows up to *The Heart Is a Lonely Hunter* and *A Tree Grows in Brooklyn.*

On the surface, *Little Women* portrays a courageous quartet of growing girls, left with their mother to struggle uncomplainingly during the absence of their father, an army chaplain, away at the front. Most modern parents would like to uphold its apparent philosophical statement that a bright group of healthy girls, guided by a patient and understanding mother, can bear any hardship with reasonable equinimity. Subtilely, *Little Women* suggests that fathers are not altogether necessary for survival; on Louisa May Alcott's terms, fathers are almost inhibiting. Parents, recognizing the uncertainties of contemporary life, might like to feel that their children possess some innate capacity to succeed; yet, they know that such attributes are found only in the fairytale world of Hansel and Gretel. Like the fairytale fantasies of all children's stories, *Little Women* is partly a kind of dream—an illusionary picture of life as we wish it might be, relatively certain that it never was really like this.

The popularity of *Little Women,* however, is more than a matter of its märchenlike qualities. History and the American experience have favored the novel. It found a most responsive reading public in the post-Civil War period among thousands of families, who, like the March women, had survived the struggle and were beginning to look back at the war with less bitter recollections. And, too, it expressed an optimism about the future that was free of rancor. In this respect, *Little Women* resembles its greater contemporary, *Huckleberry Finn,* in their underlying agreement that we emerge spiritually chastened, better humans, for the hardships we endure and the obstacles we persevere in overcoming. Like *Huckleberry Finn,* it realistically adds that money is the measure of success in a materialistic society. Both use the windfall, unexpected good fortune, as a means of attaining an objective, and both scorn money, *per se,* except for the good it will do. In a sense, this reflects the dichotomy in the American spirit, which is at once materialistic and idealistic; acquisitive and self-sacrificing.

We find this tension between idealism and financial demands demonstrated very early in *Little Women,* when Jo sells her hair in order to send Marmee to their stricken father in Washington. The irony of the sacrifice lies in the tears Jo sheds, not for her sick father, but for her lost hair. We know that she has been cheated, but we know, too, as Louisa May Alcott so clearly demonstrates, that the innocent and the desperate are often the victims of the unscrupulous. To be poor is to be in no position to bargain—not even for one's own hair.

Jo, we are always reminded, works entirely on the level of reason and practicality. She writes and sells her stories with an eye on popular tastes and editorial demands. Her rewards are ultimately quite durable. Beth is the figure of Victorian goodness; she can crochet a pair of slippers for a kindly old man, and receive a piano in return. In 1968, we can only smile at such patent naivety. Yet, though our credulity is stretched, our good judgment is never violated. Death takes our pristine figure in a scene reminiscent of Little Eva and Little Nell, but Louisa May Alcott, with a good sense of proportion, hangs on to literary restraint.

The truly modern figure is essentially demonstrated by Amy, who is something of a stylish Rosa Bonheur and a close prototype of Mary Cassatt. Amy is an independently talented woman, a more meaningful literary type than the independently wealthy woman. She is also a woman of taste, and if she is not particularly intelligent, she is well-schooled in social graces. As an American woman abroad, she is an early and emerging type that leads to Isable Archer and Daisy Miller. Amy's marriage to young Laurie is a conventional union of the deserving girl with charm and natural attributes, to the scion of an old aristocratic family.

Little Women is, in this respect, a reflection of the post-Civil War era, when tastes and interests were broadening from a parochial view of regional themes to an awakening awareness of Europe. At home, it was primarily a novel about a family that struggled through the war and survived into a number of well-deserved rewards. It is the first important American novel to appear after the Civil War and is in juxtaposition to *Uncle Tom's Cabin.* Assuredly, Louisa May Alcott did as much to heal the breach in the Reconstruction Era as Harriet Beecher Stowe did to precipitate it in the pre-war era. The background of political conflict in *Little Women* is carefully underwritten. We sense the war, aware of the demands it makes on courageous women while their men are absent at the front. It is to her credit that Louisa May Alcott touches on one of the universalities of war by avoiding the horror. It is not unlikely that a great many Southern women, following the defeat and the bitter aftermath, came to feel in Louisa May Alcott's novel, a reassuring tone of hope and reconciliation.

Yet, in still another way, *Little Women* helped to build a better understanding for the American ideal. Almost immediately after its appearance in America in 1868, it achieved an enormous popularity in England. With the success of this novel among English readers, it became difficult for English-speaking critics abroad to think of the American family as crass, crude and uncultured. Few of the ordinary readers in England regarded *Little Women* as an autobiographical work involving a prominent New England family. We are the ones who keep reading the Alcott family into the pages, as though our primary concern with the novel is to lift it out of the commonplace and assign it some kind of documentary role that sheds light on the later Transcendentalists. This is our mistake, and one that is not likely to be corrected.

It is primarily when we see our modern attitudes expressed in *Little Women*: that money is a valuable asset; that intellect is extremely important; that good health and talents must be exercised; that women can succeed—sometimes more than their men, and sometimes despite their men—and, that most difficulties have a chastening effect, we can find in the novel an honest attempt to break away from pure sentiment. It does not always succeed, nor could it, in 1868. And, although it is by no means a realistic novel, the incipient elements of realism begin to emerge. No doubt, as *Little Women* begins a second century, it will become more and more a chestnut of the nineteenth century with its many unrealistic attributes. Yet, it will probably stay in print another full century, and somehow through the patina of sentiment, the underlying core of realism, dim though it is, will continually emerge. The perceptive reader, even as an elementary school child, will sense the honesty in *Little Women,* and appreciate its candor, despite its more obvious sentimentality. On this account, Little Women is not soon likely to be relegated to the shelf of obscure novels, along with *Uncle Tom's Cabin* and any number of other American works more researched than read. A century of popularity—an enviable record in itself—justifies the term: children's classic, although in other respects, *Little Women* deserves more at the hands of the American reader.

Sean O'Faolain

SOURCE: "This Is Your Life . . . Louisa May Alcott," in *Holiday,* Vol. 44, No. 5, November, 1968, pp. 18, 22-6.

A lot of novels besides *Little Women* are still read a hundred years after they were written. I doubt that any is read as widely, remembered as fondly and preserved as loyally, often in a much-thumbed copy that has been around the house since long before one was born. The centennial of its appearance this year will see a special edition in celebration of its long life, and doubtless many essays. Though not as good, by a long chalk, as *Treasure Island* or *Robinson Crusoe* or *The Three Musketeers,* it must rank beside them in popularity. And I think the reason for the popularity of those four books, and of a few others of the same order, is that we escape with them honorably. I would not much like to be caught in my study deep in *Beau Geste* or *The Beloved Vagabond* or Vicki Baum's *Grand Hotel;* if I were surprised with *Little Women,* I could hold it up with, at most, a self-deprecating smile or an At-My-Age shrug and go on escaping, unabashed.

Miss Alcott's formula for escape was, however, a little more complicated than most. The formula of most escapist novels is anything from five to twenty-five grains of truth, and the rest plain water. No sugar required. Omission is, of its nature, saccharine. But the reader knows or can guess what has been left out of such novels. In fact, he has to, because it is what is left out that validates what is left in. I am, say, reading a novel about Hong Kong's spies, pirates, sampans, Oriental junks, drugs, brave men, kind whores, true lovers, graft, filth and magnificent sunsets. I can believe every word of it simply by saying to myself, "Well, yes, *all* this—and all the rest that he has left out and that I don't want to consider for the time being." The essential that is left out, however, is not more facts—it is the personality of the writer. This has to be left out, because if the author put it in, his nonsense would become real, his book would no longer be escapist; it would, in fact, if the fellow could write at all, become a good book. In the personality of a writer lies the sole reality of his life and the quality of his work.

Miss Alcott's technique of escape was quite different. Her personality is all over *Little Women.* She fibbed about almost all the facts. She had lived for years the life of a galley slave, toiled in the utmost poverty, humiliation and hardship, looked on hopelessly while her impractical father brought his family to the ground, wept over the misery of her mother and sisters. Being as honest a woman as was ever shaped by the best Puritan traditions of New England, she did not want to obliterate that sadder side of her life or of life at large. At the same time, being also a very gallant young woman, without an iota of self-pity in her composition, she wanted to present life in a heroic glow. She solved her problem by sheer force of character. She exorcised her miserable past by recording it with more gaiety and gusto than she can possibly have felt while living it.

To have done this was, it must be agreed, in the nature of, bordering on or actually a fib; but whichever it was—and her degree of fibbery varies enormously throughout her book—no modern, hard-boiled novelist has the right to take a lofty attitude about it. Gusto and disgust come from the same root. If any reader feels that he should lay aside *Little Women* because there is too much happiness in it, he should also think how little happiness there is in *Ulysses, The Sound and the Fury* or *The Group.* I will not quarrel with any reader's right to lay her book aside because there is too much sweetness and light in it, but I do feel that the balance she strikes between the dark and bright sides of life is more true to common experience than the opposite imbalance of our so-called realists. And she did, despite all her regrettable factual reticences, lift those genteel muslin curtains of Boston just enough, in hints and clues scattered through every chapter, to let us guess the whole truth about her period—one of the least attractive in the history of America.

We are in deep water. Critical storms loom. Is not all art a form of artifice? Fiction is surely not fact? A novel is not a police report? How far may one writer embellish, how far may another debellish, without going too far? To such questions there can be no answer in principle; it is all a matter of practice. The Whatness of any novel depends in the end on a *Why?* We can only ask why, to what end, does a novelist do whatever he does, and then tentatively balance loss and gain.

What was the whole, sad, sometimes horrid life story that Louisa May Alcott did not dare tell Boston?

Her mother, the "Marmee" of the novel, was a true Bostonian, Abigail May, the daughter of a colonel who had been for many years one of the wardens of Kings College Chapel. She was a thoroughly practical, hardheaded, long-suffering woman. The papa of the novel, Bronson Alcott, was of another class—the thoroughly impractical, warm-hearted, wildly idealistic, self-educated son of a farmer in Connecticut. After wandering around various states as a tinsmith's peddler and teaching school in a number of towns and villages, he started his final and fatal career as preacher, prophet and messiah in what we would now call a private school in Boston. Through his wife's connections Bronson collected a number of well-brought-up pupils, and he might have made a success of the venture had he not been the sort of man who was doomed never to make a success of anything.

As it was, that city of high ideals and noble religious traditions soon found that Mr. Alcott entertained the most outrageous ideas about how to teach children. He was mad enough to think that children at school should be happy, have pretty schoolrooms, learn gymnastics, prac-tice the honor system, have their own juvenile library, and not think of education as a means to a material end. He believed in human goodness. He maintained that man can reach heaven without the aid of priestly mediators. He also believed, in his own way, in reincarnation. That his school lasted as long as it did is a tribute to his tenac-ity, his charm and his few loyal friends.

When the school was closed, Mrs. Alcott counted her own small, private pittance, sold whatever possessions she could and, generously helped by a gift of five hun-dred dollars from Ralph Waldo Emerson, bought a small house near Concord, where there began what Louisa, at that time seven years old, would refer to in her novel as those times "when home was beautiful, life full of ease and pleasure and want of any kind unknown."

They rose daily at cockcrow, ate a sparse breakfast of unleavened bread, water and porridge, and then began their day's study, perhaps reading the New Testament about unclean appetites and evil passions or undergoing Papa's combination course in gymnastics and spelling—he would make a compass of his legs and throw his hands in the air, and that was X; stand straight as a ramrod, and that was I; hoop himself like a worm, and that was S; lie on his back and raise his long legs, and that was V. (This also is in *Little Women*.) For their main meal they would eat squash and potatoes, boiled rice or bread of unsifted flour.

And yet, perhaps, being children, they really did have lovely times? They sometimes had that nice man Henry Thoreau to talk to them, telling them about the drops he saw sliding down the stubble, or about the squirrel that had the key to the pitch-pine cone, or about all the fairies' handkerchiefs out to dry with the cobwebs shining in dew. Mr. Emerson visited them.

This Concord phase lasted a little over a year. Then Pa-pa's really happy, if brief, day began. People elsewhere had heard of him, and he was invited to go to England to meet some kindred souls with similar ideas; he returned

with a Mr. Wright, a Mr. Lane and his son, to start with their financial aid a splendid "consocation" that would show the world how practicable their noble ideals were—a New Eden in New England's gray and hardy land. This new farm, Fruitlands, was thirty miles south of Boston, near Harvard Village. Marmee said the house was like a refined pigsty. There were at one point eleven people living here, for whom this unbelieving but loyal woman slaved day and night without a murmur.

The lunatic scheme did not last a year. The snows fell. The farm produce was invisible. Hunger faced them. The disciples scattered. Bronson's health gave way. He went to bed to die. For weeks he hardly ate, and nothing but the tender passion of his wife for him, and his for her, helped him to rally. (He lived to be 88.) They rented four rooms in a nearby village, and there Marmee had to sew and he chop wood to earn even a bare subsistence.

Louisa was then thirteen. They went back to poverty in Boston—and to lives of sacrifice and generosity. Three evenings a week Louisa, with her mamma and her sister Anna (the Meg of *Little Women*), taught adult Negroes to read and write. Mamma at one stage kept lodgers. Louisa scribbled—she was always scribbling from this time on. She went out to work as a servant girl. She kept house in Dedham Street, toiling in a basement kitchen, seeing little all day but muddy boots passing on the pavement level with the basement window. Another time she worked in the Relief Room in Washington Street, helping destitute children. When cholera broke out in Boston that year, Lizzie (the Beth of the novel) caught scarlet fever, and the whole family caught smallpox. Louisa went out to work as companion to a clergyman—against all her mam-ma's warnings that companion she might be called, but servant she would be. She scrubbed the clergyman's floors, dug snow from his paths, sifted his ashes, and beat him off when he was too flirtatious. (This is not in the novel. There Jo March works instead as companion for rich, fussy, tedious, generous Aunt March.)

Why is none of this in *Little Women*? The answer is simple. Louisa wrote for money. It was a lasting compul-sion, and she never made any bones about it. She says it even in the novel. "Money is the end and aim of my mercenary existence!" Behind the Old Corner Bookshop, so beloved of tourists searching for Old Boston, was a Mr. Fields, who published a magazine. She wrote of him to a friend: "He says he has enough manuscripts on his hands for a dozen numbers, but has to choose war-stories, if he can, to suit the times. I will write Great Guns, Hail Columbia and the Concord Fight if he will only take it, for money is the staff of life and without it one falls flat no matter how much genius he may carry."

When she was twenty, she got her first author's fee—five dollars for a story called **"The Rival Painters."** When she was twenty-two, *The Saturday Evening Gazette* paid her ten dollars for a piece called **"The Rival Prima Donnas,"** about girls named Beatrice and Teresa who are rivals on the stage and in love; she made one singer murder the other by crushing her head with an iron ring, and

Alcott's childhood home in Concord, Massachusetts. She wrote: "Those Concord days were the happiest of my life. Plays in the barn were a favorite amusement."

brought all to a happy, moral end with the remorse of the desired man and the insanity of the wicked criminal. For years she poured out the sorry stuff, under the pen name Flora Fairfield.

So bit by bit—five bits, ten bits, a hundred bits—she slaved to lift the entire family from poverty and deprivation. It may be as much in revulsion as because such gestures were part of her nature that she went to Georgetown in 1862, when she was thirty, to nurse wounded soldiers, and fell ill with a fever during which all her lovely long hair (sold nobly in the novel to help Marmee) had to be cropped; on the basis of this she wrote *Hospital Sketches.* For the same reason, perhaps, she began to write stories for children under such names as Aunt Wee, Aunt Louisa and Aunt Ada.

Somewhere around this point in Louisa's life a certain Mr. Niles of the publishing firm of Roberts, Ltd., sniffed the air of Boston one morning and got an unfamiliar smell. It was the smell of steam. Publishers are like that, they catch on quickly. In America and elsewhere a lot of other people had been smelling steam for fifty years. Indeed, such prescient gentlemen as Jay Gould and Cornelius Vanderbilt had, by the 1860's, already made large for-

tunes out of it. Mr. Niles excelled in that he also smelled a new market by relating publishing to the large middle-class society he saw rising up all over the East as the old economy based on sails, plows, handicraft and Harvard gave way to the new economy based on coal, iron, manufacture and State Street. He saw a growing society, not yet sure of itself, still looking upward and backward to Beacon Hill, as conservative as the Brahmins in its values, as self-helpful as Samuel Smiles in its ambitions, as genteel in its image of The Desirable Life as the middle classes always are, and as sentimental in its memories as Boston always will be. Acting on his intuition, Mr. Niles said, in effect, to Miss Alcott: "The War is over. Home is the hunter home from the hill. We are sick of blood and thunder. Why not a pleasant book now, about ordinary domestic life—and, for a change, why not a book about *girls?*"

She seized her pen, and from the first word she conquered the hearts of millions. Her curtain rises on a cosy living room in Boston. It is Christmas Eve, wet, cold and slushy. It is still wartime. In this room we find a pleasant, average, middle-class family of four girls coping vivaciously with the problem, familiar to many at that period, of how to be festive without money. Their Christmas gifts will be of the simplest, since each girl has only one self-earned dollar to spend. One girl proposes to buy some music, one a box of drawing pencils and one a book.

Very quickly the dominant theme of the novel is struck: the conflict in these four young souls between self-love and self-sacrifice, between the poverty of the body and the riches of the heart, between courage and the challenges of life. So, having gloated over the presents they mean to buy themselves, the four suddenly think of mamma, who is out in the cold at that very moment packing boxes of quilts to be sent to the army in the South, and they at once agree to sacrifice their few coins to buy presents for her.

On Christmas morning they will go even farther. They will sacrifice their entire breakfast of buckwheat cakes, hot muffins and cream, gruel and tea to feed a starving German family in a nearby slum—six children in one bed, no fire, and a newborn baby crying with the cold. And as the five return home that cold morning through the dark back streets, there will not be "in all the city four merrier people than the hungry little girls who gave away their breakfasts and contented themselves with bread and milk on Christmas morning."

As we read on, we realize that all this is based on idealized recollections of that one happy if hard year in Concord before their unfortunate father. . . .

But here we stop. What has she done with papa? He is, apparently, the one character she could not deal with. She has packed Bronson off the scene to the war—as a chaplain; nor does she permit him to appear until the very end of the book, a mere shadow of reality.

Once we observe this obliteration—and we do so on page one—we realize that *Little Women* presents us with two considerations that help us measure its quality, both by the pleasure it gives us and the pain it denies us. The novel is patently and undeniably true to life insofar as we are delighted to accept, from the first page, that there really was such a family, at that time, in that place, close-knit, hard-pressed, loving and loyal. Having acknowledged this, in admiration and gratitude, we come up against the second consideration, possibly put into our heads by that passing glance at the starving German immigrants. It is that the background picture is regrettably incomplete in almost all the more interesting social aspects of the life of New England in her time.

I imagine that my experience of reading *Little Women* must be similar to that of most others. When I first read it, many years ago now, it made me feel an enormous increase of affection for the city in which it is placed. It was many more years before I delved into the memoirs and biographies of those scholars who, like Leona Rostenberg and Madeline Stern, have uncovered the cold facts about that happy family. Thereafter whenever I have re-read or remembered the novel, that appealing urban facade of ruby houses lining the green Common, and the society it symbolized for so many generations, have come back to me in a slightly darker, if not sinister, light. I think how effectively Boston imposed its own polite reticences and devious evasions on a novelist who, in her private life, hardly knew what those words meant.

The key to these reticences is, surely, that primal omission of the father. It was his hopeless, gallant struggle with Boston's (and, by inference, America's) philistinism and provincialism that started her whole life story. In leaving him out, she deflected the loyalty of the family from him to their mother. She simply had to leave him out, not so much—though that, no doubt, too—because the memory of his follies and his apparent indifference or blindness to the unhappiness of his wife had hurt her cruelly, but because if she had left him in, his accusing finger would have offended her readers on every page. (She could, of course, have put him in and softened all the oddity and humanity out of him, and where he does fleetingly come in at the end of the first part of the novel—and as fleetingly again in its sequel—that is precisely what she did.)

Unfortunately, by so idealizing the kindness of the mother she had to slide over the loyalty of the wife—a theme any serious writer would have wanted to depict in full. From this deflection we also get the watering down of the bitter wine of the actual poverty and dire misery the entire family suffered over many years. But what I, for one, regret most of all is that we only barely guess what we now know—the magnitude of Louisa Alcott's heroism in her chosen role as the spinster breadwinner and ultimate savior of what she once called The Pathetic Family.

She was wise to throw the book a little backward in time. It enabled her to invoke an older, sterner, simpler morality than that of the full-blast steam age, even if we must observe that it was a morality or theory of life with as many holes in its gleaming surface as melting ice. She constructed her novel on the principle that good girls always get on. So after these good girls give up their breakfast on Christmas morning to the raggedness of the unhappy German immigrants, what happens? Great rewarding dishes of ice cream, the daintiest French bonbons and four large bouquets of hothouse flowers appear that very Christmas night—the gift of a God-the-Father figure, old Mr. Lawrence in the big house next door. In the same way, when two of the girls bravely attend a big New Year's dance in their slightly tarnished dresses, with odd gloves and borrowed shoes, they pick up one of the nicest boys at the party and come home in a carriage attended by their "maid." Because Beth makes slippers for God-the-Father, she gets a present of a new piano. Because Amy is so sweet and generous at Mrs. Chester's fair, and Jo is haughty and rude, Aunt Carrol decides to take Amy abroad with her and leaves Jo behind. So far as I can recall, only one large incident in the novel occurs outside this convenient theory of Happy Causation: it occurs, that is, inexplicably or, in the real sense of the word, tragically: the death of Beth. We cannot, however, be too rigid about Louisa's (Boston's) morality. There are also many times when the prize to goodness is not material reward but inner happiness.

If I were asked what her gravest fib was, after her denial of her papa, I think it was her overworking of a theme that must have enchanted her publisher and given much pleasure to upper, lower and middle Boston—the theme of hardworking Respectability. It is not the hard work one dislikes; it is rather her attitude to Respectability, that universal obsession of the middle classes the world over. She has no reservations about it. Indeed, she again fibs about papa to advance its worthiness, explaining that the reason why "the two eldest girls begged to be allowed to do something for their own support at least" was that their father (in real life a society-scorning, rebellious, penniless, Owenite socialist) had once been rich, but had lost all his property in trying to help a friend. Not that Bronson might not have done such a thing, but that he did not—he had no property at all.

There were, however, some things that Louisa would not surrender, even to please the Boston Beast growling at her door. One of these self-assertions must have greatly worried Mr. Niles and given much satisfaction to her father. It is that all the "correct" things are done during the Christmas season except one—no member of the family goes to church. As one might expect of any of Bronson Alcott's children, Louisa did not believe in any from of organized religion whatever.

But the most fascinating of all her stubborn self-assertions was her firm refusal to marry her heroine, Jo March, to Laurie Lawrence, a decision which may well be one of the main reasons why the book has always appealed so much to young girls. Throughout most of *Little Women* Jo is at that familiar girlish stage that rejects girlishness. She several times wishes she were a boy. In my country, girls at this age frequently become what we call horsey: they long to possess a horse, wear jodhpurs, let their hair grow tangled and slosh around in stables. It is a form of sex-rejection. At one time, with a charming pre-Freudian innocence of what she is doing, Jo actually wanted to be a horse, and pranced and neighed like a horse as she ran. For Jo to marry like any other girl would have been the sort of fib Louisa simply could not tell. We remember how she hated it when Meg was found courting; and we remember (another unconscious Freudian symbol?) how offended she was when Mr. Brooke was found to have secreted Meg's glove in his pocket, and how much she hated all that soppy courting stuff, and how unromantically her own engagement to old (old to her), bearded, Jovelike Professor Bhaer is managed in that tender little scene under the umbrella in the rain. "Heart's dearest, why do you cry?" he asked, and Jo, too frank to dissemble, said weepingly, "Because you are going away," thus opening the way for his final declaration of his love.

Without Jo March *Little Women* would really be nothing at all. Countless young people, male as well as female, must have taken her to their hearts because she was so "unsoppy," so full of high boyish spirits, so hot-tempered, independent, unconventional, with plenty of grit and lots of go, her loose-limbed body always in movement, her lovely long hair either tumbling down or flowing in the wind. She gives us the impression of being boxed up in that house, of belonging more to the river and the fields. In a Boston suburb—though a Boston much smaller than ours, much nearer to the wild, open country—she gives us the impression of being at heart an open-air girl, matching the open-air men of the era before hers, whom Matthew Brady or Southward and Hawes photographed and Eakins and Mount painted as farmers, soldiers, fishermen, lumbermen, under the vast, cold, cloudless skies of a wider America. In her is centered the nostalgic appeal of an age passing away even while she lived, and today, ironically, as hard to find as a steam engine. Before *Little Women* there had been boys like Jo March; in her we meet for the first time a new kind of heroine, who, allowing for the changes of fashion and of morals since then, grins across the ages at many an American girl of today.

So it may not be entirely through folly or sentimentality or advancing senility that I sometimes see, through the masks of so many girls I meet in your streets, campuses and subways, at least the potential of another Jo March. An admirable, if idealized, Miss America?

Mary F. Thwaite

SOURCE: "The Story of Home and School," in *From Primer to Pleasure in Reading,* revised edition, The Horn Book, Inc., 1972, pp. 142-56.

Meg March one day found her sister Jo 'eating apples and crying over *The Heir of Redclyffe*', and Charlotte Yonge's books, as well as other literary influences from Europe, had much influence on Louisa M. Alcott and the writing of *Little Women* (1868). Innovations by American authors in the story for girls had already found much popularity [in Britain] when this famous publication arrived to win the hearts of girl readers. Life and manners in America were more democratic and free-and-easy than for Victorian young-ladyhood, although moral and religious fervour was just as widespread, as the stories of that very popular American author, 'Elizabeth Wetherell', make plain. This was the pen-name of Susan Warner (1819-1883), a native of New York. Her stories were much read by girls in Britain as well as in her own land, and the first to win success, *The Wide, Wide World* (New York, 1850), was one of the best and most characteristic. It is in the tradition of the pious and tearful tales of the mid-Victorian age, but it is less hampered by the conventions and stratification of that society. Ellen Montgomery, the young heroine, who soon becomes an orphan, is very intense in her feelings, and much pre-occupied with religion, but she has some natural traits. There is an interesting contrast shown in the early chapters between Ellen's sheltered existence with her mother in New York City, and the more primitive life she endures after she has reached the home of a Puritanical and unfeeling aunt in the backwoods of New York State. Farm life, cooking, country ways, and the beauty of an open landscape make this part of Ellen's story memorable and evidently the author was drawing upon her own knowledge. Later the heroine's vitality flags as she grows up into a young lady and becomes perfected in her Christian faith. *The Wide,*

Wide World, like other books of its kind, succeeded because the reader could identify herself with Ellen, and share her trials and experiences, and the many religious passages heightened its emotional appeal. . . . Other American writers were also producing stories for girls about this time, but none came anywhere near the standard of *Little Women.*

The author of this best-loved tale for girls, Louisa May Alcott (1832-1888), was the daughter of a New England teacher and philosopher, Amos Bronson Alcott, a progressive who admired Emerson. Her mother was no less cultured, and Louisa drew upon a spiritually rich if materially austere home background for her story. The March sisters and 'Marmee', their mother, are true-to-life portraits. 'We really lived most of it', the author wrote, 'and if it succeeds, that will be the reason for it'. It did succeed becoming known and loved all over the world, and its success has never faded. Its secret lay in Louisa Alcott's ability to present lovable characters, brimful of life and personality, and to weave around them a compelling story. The four sisters, Meg, Jo, Beth, and Amy, so close in affection, so different in temperament and character, are real beings. Most popular with many generations of readers is Jo—quick-tempered, clever, tomboyish, generous Jo who, like her creator, wants to be a writer. Moral and religious teaching of a liberal and basic nature is an integral part of the tale, made as necessary and natural in the lives of the young Marches as the air they breathe.

There is an unconfined and happy atmosphere in the home into which the reader is admitted. The friendship with Laurie, the boy next door, especially between him and Jo, is something which could scarcely have been depicted by the more conventional pen of Miss Yonge. This less self-conscious attitude to human relationships, outside class-ridden Victorian society, brought a welcome transatlantic vigour into books for girls at this period. *Little Women* was followed by a sequel, *Good Wives,* originally published in 1869 as *Little Women, Part 2,* and Louisa Alcott continued to chronicle the activities of the March family, as well as to invent other tales of domestic life. The first two books, however, were to become the acknowledged classics of their kind.

Stephanie Harrington

SOURCE: "Does *Little Women* Belittle Women," in *The New York Times,* June 10, 1973, pp. D19, D37.

The women's movement is several television seasons old now and each season more and more column inches are written protesting the medium's caricature of women as a gaggle of witless wonders endowed with the intelligence, independence and emotional maturity of retarded guppies. But, as Judy Klemesrud pointed out on this page a few weeks ago ("TV's Women Are Dingbats"), relief is not even in sight—unless, in the shadow of the television stereotype, we look in unlikely places and revise a few prejudices. For, in contrast to the weekly humiliation of Edith Bunker, whose victimization is a matter for therapy

not comedy, "Little Women" (the BBC production . . .) takes on the force of a feminist tract.

And that is really saying something about the way television writers, producers and directors treat women in the standard fare they serve up because, taken on its own and not compared with currently prevailing caricatures, Louisa May Alcott's story of the four March sisters of Concord, Mass., and how they grew, might understandably strike a contemporary woman with only fellow-traveling ties to the movement as a perfectly disgusting, banal, and craven service to male supremacy. For Alcott is at all times careful to keep the development of her characters safely hemmed in by comfortable moralisms that make it perfectly clear that even Jo, the most "unfeminine" and independent of the March sisters, will come eventually to rest in the snug harbour of "Kirche, Küche und Kinder."

Marriage is anointed as "the sweetest chapter in the romance of womanhood," motherhood as "the deepest and tenderest [experience] of a woman's life," and the combination of these two circumstances as "the sort of shelf on which young wives and mothers may consent to be laid, safe from the restless fret and fever of the world, finding loyal lovers in the little sons and daughters who cling to them, undaunted by sorrow, poverty, or age; walking side by side, through fair and stormy weather, with a faithful friend, who is, in the true sense of the good old Saxon word, the 'house-band'. . . ." Yuchhh! But as if that is not enough, Meg, the oldest March sister and the first to marry, having weathered the initiation to her role, also learns "that a woman's happiest kingdom is home, her highest honor the art of ruling it, not as a queen, but as a wise wife and mother."

Jo, the second oldest and most stoutly independent of the March sisters, who works hard at being a writer, insists she will never marry and speaks her mind no matter what the social cost, eventually comes to value the traditionally feminine determination of Amy to be agreeable, to please people. For Amy, the youngest, who wants to marry well (and she does) and move in elegant circles, agreeableness is at first a socially expedient tool, but as the young woman matures she develops her desire to please into what, in Louisa May Alcott's moral universe, is considered admirable selflessness.

Though Jo never attains Amy's state of grace, with slow, painful effort she does temper her willfulness with increasing patience and understanding. Eventually she even finds fulfillment as a wife and mother and proclaims her old dream of a solitary writer's life as "selfish, lonely and cold." She is helped to this conclusion by the death of her younger sister Beth, a saintly creature who seemed too fragile for this life and who devoted her existence to the loving care of others. On her deathbed Beth implored Jo to take her place as companion and comfort to their parents, assuring her older sister that she would be "happier in doing that than writing splendid books or seeing all the world; for love is the only thing that we can carry with us when we go. . . ."

These are, of course, precisely the kinds of sentiments (or sentimentality) and conclusions that today's feminists reject, illusions that have served the feminine mystique and kept women in their place. As early as page three of *Little Women* Jo's independence and ambition are passed off as unnatural for a girl: "I can't," says Jo, "get over my disappointment in not being a boy." But she does, and, we are told, she is much the happier for it.

But, although the March sisters wage their inner struggles and work out their designs for living within a moral framework that renders their conclusions foregone, though the questions of individual character that absorb them may seem banal diversions from the weighty matters reserved for men, and their acceptance of their "given" roles a disappointing capitulation, they are at least presented as representatives, and not caricatures, of the women of their time and place. They at least think. They at least, in their own terms, grow. By comparison to the heroines of TV Land, who are bounced back and forth between "situations" like Ping-Pong balls, rarely even capable of reflexes, let alone intelligent volition, the March sisters stand as moral actors in the context of their world. . . .

The BBC production was filmed in England in 1970, and though the social consciousness of the novel is attuned to the 1860's, this version does include lines in which the March sisters object to being considered men's playthings and insist that they will go on with their work, Jo with her writing and Amy with her painting, even if they do marry.

Hardly militant sentiments for our time. But *Little Women* was first published in 1869, and Jo March is a far more liberated woman for those days than Edith Bunker is for these. And if Marlo Thomas, who played a cuddly little eyelash-batting kewpie doll of a woman on "That Girl," can emerge in 1973 as a militant feminist, why not Louisa May Alcott, who at least refers to her characters as women? No, we have not come a long way, baby. Nobody ever called Jo March baby.

Mary Cadogan and Patricia Craig

SOURCE: "Pilgrims and Pioneers," in *You're A Brick, Angela! A New Look at Girls' Fiction from 1839-1975,* Victor Gollancz Ltd., 1976, pp. 30-43.

Louisa Alcott never married but in deference to readers' wishes she provides Jo, a fictional representation of herself, with a husband. Jo rejects Laurie, her childhood friend and first suitor: "'I don't believe I shall ever marry. I'm happy as I am, and love my liberty too well to be in any hurry to give it up for any mortal man.'" In spite of Miss Alcott's arguments about Jo and Laurie's strong wills and quick tempers making the match impossible, readers have never forgiven her for separating the enchanters, and allowing lively Jo eventually to settle for prosaic, middle-aged Professor Bhaer. The Bhaers establish a residential school for their own children and other people's unwanted or problem offspring, but Jo's transition from tomboy

to great-earth-mother is disappointing and unconvincing. In common with many later writers of girl's fiction, Miss Alcott was less able to create attractive adult characters than juveniles. Jo is best remembered as a coltish teenager with literary ambitions and a contempt for affectation, and she epitomizes the desire of many girls for participation in intellectual life. Louisa Alcott manages to make the March sisters seem natural, even in mawkish situations. Jo is always wholehearted, whether burning the skin off her nose by excessive boating in the sunshine, reading till her eyes give out, or selling her abundant chestnut hair to provide money for "Marmee" to visit her husband when he is in hospital, badly wounded in the Civil War. Luxury-starved Meg's preoccupation with fripperies, and spoiled Amy's vanity arouse readers' sympathy and amusement, while thousands of young girls have suffered with uncomplaining Beth as ". . . on the bosom where she had drawn her first breath, she quietly drew her last, with no farewell but one loving look, one little sigh." Apart from "Marmee" Beth is the character who has dated most but her gentleness is a perfect foil for Jo's vitality:

> "It's bad enough to be a girl, anyway, when I like boys' games, and work, and manners. I can't get over my disappointment in not being a boy, and it's worse than ever now for I'm dying to go and fight with papa, and I can only stay at home and knit like a poky old woman," and Jo shook the blue army-sock till the needles rattled like castanets, and her ball bounded across the room. . . .

Melvyn Bragg

SOURCE: "*Little Women,*" in *Children's literature in education,* Vol. 9, No. 2, 1978, pp. 95-100.

I read *Jo's Boys* first. It was a present from my father. We had gone to a seaside town in winter, one Sunday morning, on the bus, to see a man who owned a funfair. He had a shop in the town, too, and we met there. While he talked to my father and they smoked cigarettes at the counter, I found the books and started to read one of them. I was so reluctant to leave it that my father bought it for me. I read it countless times, and the pleasure I found in it must have been powerful, for it enabled me to hurdle the terrible barrier presented by *Little Women,* which I sought out at the library on the hunt for anything else by Louisa May Alcott (*Little Women* was first published in 1868). For *Little Women,* Miss Alcott announced, firmly, on the title page was *A story for Girls.* Yet I read it. And I think that this is a rare case of Miss Alcott being mistaken. As years went on I discovered that quite a few men had read it as boys—although most of them would qualify the admission by muttering on about sisters or cousins leaving it lying around or found books in the house or the teacher "forcing" them to read it at school. Perhaps such excuses are still necessary. Miss Alcott would have smiled slyly at all of them.

One of the most powerful aspects of the book is that we emerge with a very clear idea of the author. Even as a boy I'm sure I could have made up a fairly accurate picture of what she was *like*. She had strict rules of conduct based on the Ten Commandments, Sermon on the Mount, and a certain sensitive way of behaving in company. Later I discovered that her father was one of Emerson's circle; that she was educated at home by her father and H. D. Thoreau; that she served as a hospital nurse during the Civil War, and that although her first book (*Flower Fables*) published when she was a precocious twenty-two and her next (*Hospital Sketches*—consisting of her letters home from the Union hospital during the war) published nine years later—both brought her kindly critical attention, it was *Little Women,* published when she was thirty-seven that brought her a wide reputation. All of that fitted into place too. For over and above everything else, Louisa May Alcott creates a perfectly consistent and water-tight world—once you accept her beliefs and assumptions; they were perfectly plain to me as a child, and on rereading the book today, I find them exactly the same, just as clear.

But are they still acceptable?

In the most important way, the question does not apply. The novel is a work of the imagination and if it works, then the morality is appropriate.

On the other hand, there is rarely anything as clearcut as a simple response to a work of art, and Miss Alcott's morality, her constant insistence on taking part in her story, visiting the characters with her remarks like Florence Nightingale with a pen for a lamp checking up on those in her care—all this obtrudes so boldly that it cannot be ignored. And in many ways it is very hard nowadays to accept the crystal certainties of Louisa May Alcott's world as it appears in *Little Women.* God exists and he is a Friend: He has our interests at heart and looks after us always and all the more efficiently if we are obedient to a well-defined list of rules, in which social behavior and morality are often indistinguishable. Few people believe that now, I'd guess: even fewer believe it with the earnestness and simplicity of Miss Alcott. Indeed, we look back in awe at what can appear the naiveté of that most intelligent woman. And it is not only God the Friend who is hard to accept: it is poverty with a servant and rich friends and relations. Just as it would be too heavy here to invoke the meaningless carnage of Auschwitz and Hiroshima, etc. in order to draw attention to some of the forces which have undermined the idea of God the ever-comforting Friend, so it would be rather too severe to point out that the real poverty now seen in the world, in India, in Africa and all over the Third World makes something of a mockery of the constant cry of the Little Women that they are poor. They are well-fed, well-housed, well-enough clothed, well-educated, well-served by Hannah, without whom they are helpless (is she black or white, as a matter of interest? Black, I'd assume from her speech, although no indication is given in the book) and protected by a mother who is "never too proud to beg" as she herself says, when necessity demands it—and fortunate to have an immensely rich, generous neighbour and an immensely rich, though stingy aunt. No, the please of poverty are as hard to take as the prayers to Our

Friend—and yet we cannot ignore them: the former activates a lot of the plots and incidents; the latter wraps up the book like a cocoon. Similarly, though of much less importance, it is hard to swallow the little moral snobberies by which we are constantly made aware that the Little Women are much superior *really* to—well, anybody! The nouveau riche, the English, everybody.

The word "little" appears in this book as often as the word "property" in John Galsworthy's *Man of Property.* In part, it is used properly: in part, though, it is used to milk our sentiment, and I am sure such an author cannot have been unaware of the effect she intended to produce as her pen misted over and "little" was written to evoke our sympathy in preparation for the sentimental scene or sentence to follow. But then, like Galsworthy, Miss Alcott had a purpose. Hers was to teach morality to the young—both to those inside her book and to those who read it. She is a powerful advocate, convinced of the rightness of her cause; and to her, the softening use of "little" would have been totally defensible. She had to reach the hearts as well as the minds of these young girls for whom the story was written, and so she employed the techniques which had served other sentimental writers in that century very well indeed—particularly Dickens, for whom she clearly has an enormous veneration and affection. This is not to say that the book is a lesser book because it is sentimental, but merely to point out that even in the use of this word the teacher's hand and the moralist's rule-book were determinedly present.

The rulebook is everywhere. It could be a textbook of do's and don'ts, and it is certain that Miss Alcott intended it that way. Vanity is punished; bad temper is punished; selfishness is punished; laziness is punished—the seven deadly sins get the full treatment and are slain by the gentle-Jesus virtues. Although *Pilgrim's Progress* is repeatedly invoked in the novel, there is little of Christian's fierce fighting (except, a bit, in Jo) to regain possession of his soul and his mission. In *Little Women* a simple tale at mother's knee brings instant confession and, usually, the beginnings of a permanent improvement. Like many writers before her, though far fewer since, Miss Alcott considered it her plain duty to guide and teach, and although we may find this quaint or merely of that period, it gives the book its moral strength; and without that, *Little Women* would be no more than a cosy tale.

Though all that I have written above emphasises what I find difficult to digest, it must be stressed that the insistence on a Christian morality, on rules, on the author stepping in to teach and help along on the sentimental softening—all this is what gives the book its force: for beneath the conventional religion and morality of her day, the writer is dealing with good and evil and the perennial struggle between character and environment.

However, the strengths and virtues of the story itself as an act of imagination should not be underestimated. It is very much to the point that the three books referred to within *Little Women* are *Pilgrim's Progress, Pickwick Papers* and *The Bible,* for in three different but complementary ways, these deal with character which, I think, is Miss Alcott's primary concern. Character in its relation to the Christian struggle and the Christian virtues as in John Bunyan's book; character as a free and highly individualistic expression of a unique personality as in Charles Dickens's book; and character as an expression of the will and wish of God as described in the New Testament. As a work of *imagination,* however, it is in the creation of believable and memorable characters that the art consists, and Miss Alcott undeniedly emulates Dickens's sublime talent for doing just that.

Consider the first few spoken sentences on page 1. The character of each of the little women is displayed in a nutshell, and in each case a theme is set which is later mined and explored thoroughly throughout the book. "'Christmas won't be Christmas without any presents,' grumbled Jo, lying on the rug." Note that Jo is "grumbling," *not* complaining; worried *not* about the presents themselves but about the break with tradition and with the past, of which she is the most jealous guardian. She is "lying on the rug"—boyishly, we can assume, careless of her dress, or her appearance. "'It's so dreadful to be poor,' sighed Meg, looking down at her old dress." Meg is shown to be a worrier over trifles, and her progress throughout the book is concerned with overcoming this badly-thought-out sense of her own poverty. Note the concern with her appearance and the self-pity.

"'I don't think it's fair for some girls to have lots of pretty things and other girls nothing at all,' added little Amy with an injured sniff." This is perfect Amy. She is much more vain and self-obsessed than Meg and she rails against Natural Justice. She means that *she* wants "lots of pretty things" for herself: we know that if that were the case, Amy would not utter the sentence ever again. The dispossessed (such as she imagines herself to be) would be forgotten. This characteristic is emphasised by the "injured sniff." The world has done her wrong, she feels, and throughout the book she has to fight against that resentment. Also, it is interesting to note that none of the three girls so far have thoughts for anyone but themselves. Beth settles all that and squares the account.

"'We've Father and Mother and each other anyhow,' said Beth contentedly from her corner." And there is Beth in a *corner,* i.e., tucked away, mouse-like, withdrawn from the hurly-burly, seeking protection, but at the same time on to the central common-sense sentiment that is the central theme of the positive side of the book, which is to count your blessings.

In some ways, of course, the girls can be seen in a rather disagreeable light. Jo, after all, has murder in her heart towards Amy and almost wills and neglects her to death. Meg, for all her sixteen years, has her head turned and frizzed and spoiled after a mere couple of days at the Moffats'. Amy burns Jo's only prize possession in a fit of sulks and then plays up to rich, old Aunt March in order to gain the turquoise ring. And Beth's constant humility is both cloying and extremely effective in getting her exactly what she wants. So much for those who think

Little Women is a pageant of virtues played out by sweet little maidens.

What saves or, more accurately, makes these characters is that Louisa May Alcott is careful to give each of them a bright side too. Jo's boldness, Meg's thoughtfulness, Amy's efforts with herself, Beth's devotion. These are admirable and help form the roundness of character. And the plots, in true nineteenth century style, pull out all the stops to test these characters to their limits. Deaths in the past, threatened deaths in the present, loss, the switch from wealth to poverty, from the Hummels' to Laurie's luxuries, from Mr. Brooke's valiant consistency and discretion to those few touches which make of Ned Moffat a ne'er-do-well: there is a wealth of incident, and heroes and villains around—all of which pack the novel around with riches.

Most of all, though, the novel creates a world of unassailable domestic comfort which, it proclaims, is the highest mundane achievement of man. Nothing is more sacred, in Miss Alcott's novel, than Our Friend: but after Him comes the hearth. Home is where all proper and righteous people put their talents, and their virtue. The house is both a focus and a fortress; everything comes into it, and within it the members are safe against the world. It is this flat belief—even more powerful and fundamental, I think, than the convictions of the right of the Christian virtues, which gives the book its abiding attraction. For very few people, I would guess, have that utterly certain and sure centre of domestic harmony which Mother March symbolizes and expresses. Her homilies and the tests and tricks she practises on her children are of the utmost importance to her and perhaps to the didactic side of Louisa May Alcott. But what comes through even more strikingly is the notion of home.

It is something we all have a taste of, although in my experience few seem fortunate enough to find in it the possibilities and rewards discovered there by everyone in *Little Women.* It is Louisa May Alcott's particular talent and strength that she portrays both a working household and the golden image of a household; both a real place and an ideal place, somewhere which could exist and something which ought to exist.

For all the snobberies and self-deceptions, the prudish homilies and complaisant reflections, the world of the little women is a real one—i.e., we feel that there could be such people; whether or not we like them or admire them is another matter. On the other hand, for all the detail about the relationships between sisters and their mother, their aunts, their friends and neighbours, I feel, as perhaps others do, that this is a totally imagined, highly patterned, artificial fable which yet, through the art of the author, brings an authentic feeling of the ideal state of a family in harmony and harness such as rarely, if ever, existed in the real world.

Incidentally, I have come to the conclusion that Jo really stands in for a boy. She is certainly the character most boys identify with—beside her, Laurie, for example, is

Frontispiece of the Orchard House edition of Little Women, *picturing (clockwise from left) Meg, Jo, Beth, and Amy. Illustrated by Jessie Willcox Smith.*

but a sketch. And of all childhood heroes/heroines, Jo, with her three loves—reading alone while eating apples, looking after the past, and going out into the world to "find adventures" is the character I myself have most strongly identified with.

Judith Fetterley

SOURCE: "*Little Women:* Alcott's Civil War," in *Feminist Studies,* Vol. 5, No. 2, Summer, 1979, pp. 369-83.

When, toward the end of *Little Women,* Jo finds her "true style at last," her father blesses her with the prospect of inner peace and an end to all ambivalence: "You have had the bitter, now comes the sweet. Do your best and grow as happy as we are in your success." And Alcott adds her benediction: "So, taught by love and sorrow, Jo wrote her little stories and sent them away to make friends for themselves and her, finding it a very charitable world to such humble wanderers." Finding her true style at last was not, however, such a peaceful arrival in safe waters for Alcott herself. She responded with alacrity to the opportunity afforded by the anonymous "No-Name Series" to write something not in her style, declaring that she was "tired of providing moral pap for the young" and enjoying the fun of hearing people say, "I know you didn't write it, for you can't hide your peculiar style." She prayed more than once for time enough to write a "good" book and realized that without it she would do what was easiest and succumb to the pressure of the "dears" who "will cling to the 'Little Women' style." And at the end of *Jo's Boys,* the last of her books on the March family, she longs to close with an "earthquake which should engulf Plumfield and its environs so deeply in the bowels of the earth that no youthful Schliemann could ever find a vestige of it."

Alcott's commitment to her "true style" was evidently somewhat less a choice than a necessity, somewhat less generated from within than imposed from without. Her initial resistance to the proposal from Thomas Niles, a partner in Roberts Brothers Publishing Company, that she write a book for girls had its origins perhaps in an instinct for self-preservation; certainly the success of *Little Women* limited her artistic possibilities thereafter. Hard it was to deny the lucrative rewards attendant upon laying such golden eggs; hard to reconcile the authorial image inherent in *Little Women* with the personality capable of the sensational **"Behind a Mask"**; harder still to ignore the statement of what was acceptable from a woman writer implicit in the adulation accorded *Little Women.* Indeed, Alcott ceased to write sensation fiction after the publication of *Little Women.* In Madeline Stern's analysis, "The author who had dispatched thrillers to Frank Leslie and James R. Elliott had presumably found her style. The niche she had walked into with *Little Women* was too comfortable to abandon."

The work of Stern in identifying and recovering Alcott's sensation fiction provides an important context for the reading of *Little Women* and for an understanding of the implications of its style. In these stories, written primarily between 1862 and 1867, there is no hint of the *Little Women* ethic or ambience. Quite the contrary. In **"Pauline's Passion and Punishment,"** for example, the heroine consecrates herself to the exacting of revenge on a man who has loved her but married an heiress. In this carefully planned and well-relished project, she is assisted by another man, younger than herself, who becomes her willing ally and almost slave. In **"Behind a Mask,"** by far the most interesting of the materials which Stern has made available to us in her two volumes, *Behind a Mask* and *Plots and Counterplots,* the heroine, Jean Muir, uses the mask of femininity and the persona of a little woman to enact a devastatingly successful power struggle with a series of men who are clearly perceived as a single class and an enemy one at that. What these stories, taken as a group, make clear is the amount of rage and intelligence Alcott had to suppress in order to attain her "true style" and write *Little Women.* Alcott's sensation fiction provides an important gloss on the sexual politics involved in Jo's renunciation of the writing of such fiction and on the sexual politics of Jo's relation with Professor Bhaer under whose influence she gives it up.

Yet clearly both anger and political perception are present in *Little Women,* and, not surprisingly, there is evidence within *Little Women* of Alcott's ambivalence toward her true style. *Little Women* takes place during the Civil War and the first of Jo's many burdens on her pilgrim's progress toward little womanhood is her resentment at not being at the scene of action. Later, however, she reflects that "keeping her temper at home was a much harder task than facing a rebel or two down South." The Civil War is an obvious metaphor for internal conflict and its invocation as background to *Little Women* suggests the presence in the story of such conflict. There is tension in the book, attributable to the conflict between its overt messages and its covert messages. Set in subliminal counterpoint to the consciously intended messages is a series of alternate messages which provide evidence of Alcott's ambivalence. To a considerable extent, the continuing interest and power of *Little Women* is the result of this internal conflict. As Alcott got farther and farther away from the moment of discovery, as the true style became more and more the only style, this tension was lost and the result was the tedious sentimentality of *A Rose in Bloom* or the unrelieved flatness of *Under the Lilacs. Little Women* survives by subversion.

The overt messages of *Little Women* are clearly presented in the first two chapters, "Playing Pilgrims" and "A Merry Christmas." The book opens on Christmas eve with the four girls—Meg, Jo, Amy, and Beth—around the fire awaiting the return of "Marmee." Remembering the joys of Christmas past when they were rich, they grumble at their present lot: "Christmas won't be Christmas without any presents"; "It's so dreadful to be poor!"; "I don't think it's fair for some girls to have plenty of pretty things, and other girls nothing at all." Such discontent with what one has inevitably leads to the determination to get something more. They recall their mother's suggestion that they not be self-indulgent when others are suffering, but they rationalize their determination to please themselves by arguing that these "others" will not be helped by their sacrifice and by protesting that they have worked hard and deserve some fun. In the logic of the true style, such commitment to self can only lead to a querulous debate on the question of who works hardest and who suffers most. Their peevishness and grumbling is luckily averted by the realization that Marmee is about to arrive and as Beth gets out the old slippers to warm by the fire, the girls experience a change of heart and decide to devote their little money to presents for their mother. Such behavior is in imitation of the "tall, motherly lady, with a 'can-I-help-you' look about her," for unselfish devotion to others is the keynote to Marmee's character.

Marmee is the model little woman. Her first words are an implicit reproof to the girls' self-centered, "poor me" discontent: "Well, dearies, how have you got on today? . . . Has anyone called, Beth? How is your cold, Meg? Jo, you look tired to death." The little lesson by contrast is followed by a more extended sermon in the reading of a letter from father, away at the war, who urges his girls "to conquer themselves so beautifully that when I come back to them I may be fonder and prouder than ever of my little women." The paternal exhortation to conquer the self is happily facilitated by Marmee's proposal that they play again their childhood game of "Pilgrim's Progress," only this time in earnest. Discussion of this plan for self-improvement enables them to get through an evening of uninteresting sewing without grumbling. At nine, they put away their work and sing, a household custom begun by Marmee whose voice was "the first sound in the morning . . . and the last sound at night." It is not enough that little women be content with their condition; they must be positively cheery at the prospect.

The importance and value of renouncing the self and thinking of others is further dramatized in the second chapter. Armed with their presents to Marmee, evidence of their little effort to forget themselves, they arrive at the breakfast table only to find that Marmee has been visiting the Hummels, a poor family in the neighborhood, and wants her girls to give them their breakfast as a Christmas present. After a moment's hesitation before the new level of sacrifice required, the girls enter into the project wholeheartedly, deliver up their breakfast to the poor, and discover that bread and milk and the sense of having helped others make the best breakfast ever.

The rebels that the girls must fight are clearly identified in these first two chapters: discontent, selfishness, quarrelsomeness, bad temper, thinking too much of worldly things (money, appearance, food). The success of their campaign depends on their acquiring one central weapon: self-control. They must learn to control the self so as to ensure that the self does in fact renounce the self. "Conquer yourself," says Father, reminding them that their civil war must be fought at home. In the midst of domestic difficulties, Meg remembers "maternal counsels given long ago": "'Watch yourself, be the first to ask pardon if you both err, and guard against the little piques, misunderstandings, and hasty words that often pave the way for

bitter sorrow and regret'." To turbulent, restless, quick-tempered Jo, Marmee offers the consolation of her most precious secret: "'I am angry nearly every day of my life, Jo, but I have learned not to show it; and I still hope to learn not to feel it, though it may take me another forty years to do so'." Conquer oneself and live for others are indeed the watchwords of this women's world.

Equal to the concern in *Little Women* for defining the ideal womanly character is the concern for defining woman's proper sphere and proper work. Early in *Little Women* there is a chapter entitled "Castles in the Air" in which each girl describes her life's ambition. The final chapter of the book, called "Harvesttime," makes reference to this earlier chapter, comparing what each of them dreamed with what each is now doing, clearly to the advantage of the latter. Meg's dream is from the start domestic: "I should like a lovely house, full of all sorts of luxurious things—nice food, pretty clothes, handsome furniture, pleasant people, and heaps of money. I am to be mistress of it, and manage it as I like, with plenty of servants, so I never need work a bit." All that time and maturity need modify for Meg is her overvaluation of wealth and her desire to have a lot of servants. Meg must learn that love is better than luxury; she must learn to put a man in the center of her picture; and she must learn that without domestic chores to keep them busy, women will be idle, bored, and prone to folly. These are but minor adjustments, however, for Meg's dream, centered on home, is eminently acceptable. Thus she can say at the end, "My castle was the most nearly realized of all."

In contrast, the lives of Amy and Jo are very different from their castles in the air. Neither Amy's ambition nor Jo's is domestic. Amy wants "to be an artist, and go to Rome, and do fine pictures, and be the best artist in the whole world," and Jo wants to "write books, and get rich and famous." In Rome, however, where Amy makes a real bid to realize her ambition, she comes to see that there is a difference between talent and genius, and that she has only the former. In the future, she decides, her relationship to art will be primarily that of patroness, encouraging and supporting the work of others. Through her experience with Laurie, she learns the truth of her mother's dictum that "to be loved and chosen by a good man is the best and sweetest thing which can happen to a woman," far better than being a famous artist. Although Amy never completely gives up her art, she places it in the service of home and family. In the final chapter she remarks that she has "begun to model a figure of baby, and Laurie says it is the best thing I've ever done. I think so myself, and mean to do it in marble, so that, whatever happens, I may at least keep the image of my little angel." Amy's motivation has shifted ground. No longer working for fame or fortune, she is inspired by love for her child. Her figure is not intended for public exhibition, for Amy works not to produce great art or to define herself as an artist, but to create a private memorial to her dying child. Her artistic impulses have been harnessed and subordinated to her "maternal instinct" and thereby sanctioned.

Jo's history is similar to Amy's. In the final chapter she comments on her "castle in the air" by saying, "the life I wanted then seems selfish, lonely, and cold to me now. I haven't given up the hope that I may write a good book yet, but I can wait, and I'm sure it will be all the better for such experiences and illustrations as these," and she points to her husband, children, and the familial scene around her. Again, the connection is made between motherhood and "good" art; when Jo writes her good book if she ever does, it will be the product of her experiences as a wife and mother. Until then, like Amy, she is content to deploy her talents in the service of the domestic: "she told no stories except to her flock of enthusiastic believers and admirers" and "found the applause of her boys more satisfying than any praise of the world."

Earlier treatments of Jo's relation to writing have also served to identify the proper relation of women to art. When Jo at last finds her true style, the impetus to write has been provided by Marmee and the motivation is solace and comfort for the loss of Beth. In contrast is the picture we get when Jo determines to try for the $100 prize offered in the columns of a newspaper for a sensation story: "She said nothing of her plan at home, but fell to work next day, much to the disquiet of her mother, who always looked a little anxious when 'genius took to burning'." As Marmee's anxiety is a barometer for the quality of Jo's writing, there is evidently an inverse relationship between Jo's interest in what she is doing and its acceptability. The more energetic Jo is in pursuing her writing and getting it published, the worse it is and the more anxious Marmee gets. But when Jo is finally brought to the point of saying, "I've no heart to write, and if I had, nobody cares for my things," then Marmee is all encouragement: "We do. Write something for us, and never mind the rest of the world." So Jo does what her mother wishes and writes a story which her father sends, "much against her will," to a popular magazine and which becomes, "for a small thing," a great success. Understandably, Jo is bewildered by this turn of events and when her father explains it to her, she cries, "If there is anything good or true in what I write, it isn't mine; I owe it all to you and Mother and to Beth." Good writing for women is not the product of ambition or even enthusiasm, nor does it seek worldly recognition. Rather it is the product of a mind seeking solace for private pain, that scarcely knows what it is doing and that seeks only to please others and, more specifically, those few others who constitute the immediate family. Jo has gone from burning genius to a state where what she writes isn't even hers.

At the end of the first volume of **Little Women,** Alcott refers to her book as a "domestic drama." Much of the popularity of **Little Women,** then and now, derives from its embodiment of a cultural fantasy of the happy family—the domestic and feminine counterpart to the nostalgia in male American literature captured by Hemingway in the succinct "long time ago good, now no good." At the heart of the fantasy family is, of course, the fantasy Mom, the kind of Mom we all at some time or other are made to wish we could have had. The inherent contradictions in the patriarchal mythology of the family are present in **Little Women,** however; it is, after all, a girls' book written from the perspective of the child. Being Marmee's child is one thing; being Marmee herself is another, a point which Alcott dramatized in **"The Lay of a Golden Goose,"** her poem about what it means to be forever asked to lay more eggs. Resistances to growing up abound in **Little Women** and suggest attitudes in conflict with the overt messages on the joys of little womanhood.

There is a remark of Jo's which reveals an attitude toward "women's work" in conflict with the doctrinal attempts to ennoble the domestic sphere through the endless endearing diminutives of "the little mop and the old brush." When Jo discovers Professor Bhaer darning, she is horrified: "think of the poor man having to mend his own clothes. The German gentlemen embroider, I know; but darning hose is another thing and not so pretty." But more important than the revelation that women's work is ugly and degrading when done by men is the implication that women's work is not real work. Before their marriage, John says to Meg, "You have only to wait, I am to do the work." This opposition between working and waiting defines the brutal truth about woman's role. After marriage Meg is "on the shelf," still waiting. Only when she gets rid of her servants and makes work for herself can she settle down, give up the foolish expenditures which are as much the result of boredom as vanity, and become a good wife. "Making work" is the implicit subject of the chapter which deals with Meg's relation to her children. Much of what she does for them is unnecessary; the rest could be done in half the time and could indeed be done better by John: "Baby respected the man who conquered him, and loved the father whose grave 'No, no,' was more impressive than all Mamma's love pats"; thus, "the children throve under the paternal rule, for accurate, steadfast John brought order and obedience into Babydom."

The perception that women's work is made work generates the encounter between Meg and John over her dress and his coat. In protest against the limitations imposed by John's modest salary and desiring to impress a wealthy friend, Meg orders a fifty-dollar silk dress. Meg has been warned by her mother about John and here she discovers one of the sources of this warning. John "was very kind, forgave her readily, and did not utter one reproach." He simply cancels the order for his overcoat. In response to Meg's inquiry, he comments, "I can't afford it, my dear." Consumed with guilt, Meg swallows her pride and her desire, prevails upon her friend to buy her dress, and uses the money to get John's coat. "One can imagine . . . what a blissful state of things ensued." This blissful state, however, is based on the premise that John needs and deserves a coat because he has to go out in the world and work. Meg, on the contrary, neither needs nor deserves her dress because, with no real work to do in the world, she has no basis for attention to the self.

Implicit in **Little Women** is an understanding of the genesis of the ideal womanly character far different from that overtly stated through the pilgrim's progress metaphor of the first chapter. "Women," says Amy, "should learn to be agreeable." With no legitimate function in life, women will not be tolerated unless they are agreeable; only through a life of cheerful service to others can they justify their existence and assuage the guilt that derives from being useless. Women must watch themselves because they are economically dependent on men's income and emotionally dependent on their approval. Marmee's "maternal counsels" contain an implicit perception of the politics of marriage: "John is a good man, but he has his faults, and you must learn to see and bear with them, remembering your own. . . . He has a temper, not like ours—one flash and then all over—but the white, still anger that is seldom stirred, but once kindled is hard to quench. Be careful, very careful, not to wake his anger against yourself, for peace and happiness depend on keeping his respect." While Marmee schools Jo in the art of constricting her anger to a tightening of the lips, she admonishes Meg to accommodate herself to John's anger. Indeed, John's anger is "not like ours." It is male and must be attended to; Meg's, Jo's, Marmee's anger is female and must be suppressed. Little women must not be angry because they cannot afford it. Marmee's description of John is frightening for the veiled threat it conveys—men's love is contingent; be careful, very careful not to lose it, for then where will you be?

If the covert messages of **Little Women** suggest that the acquisition of the little woman character is less a matter of virtue than of necessity, so do they suggest that women's acceptance of the domestic sphere as the best and happiest place may be less a matter of wise choice than of harsh necessity. "To be loved and chosen by a good man is the best and sweetest thing which can happen to a woman," says Marmee to her girls; but she might as well have said it is the only thing that can happen. There are no other viable options. When Jo first meets Laurie, she describes herself to him as a "businessman—girl, I mean." The accuracy of this implicit presumption against her chance for economic independence is clearly supported by her subsequent experience. To earn money for her sick father, Jo can only sell her hair. Selling one's hair is a form of selling one's body and well buried within this minor detail is the perception that women's capital is their flesh and that they had better get the best price for it, which is, of course, marriage. Later Jo discovers a source of income in her stories but the economics of her relation to writing are revealing. At first, she gets nothing for her work; she is satisfied simply to have it published. When she finally does get paid, it is because Laurie acts in her behalf. Jo does not assume that she should or will be paid for her work; when payment comes, she treats it as a gift. Thus she is ripe for the exploitation she encounters in the office of the "Weekly Volcano": "Mr. Dashwood graciously permitted her to fill his columns at the lowest prices, not thinking it necessary to tell her that the real cause of his hospitality was the fact that one of his hacks, on being offered higher wages, had basely left him in the lurch." Eventually, even this minor source of income is denied because Jo comes to see that writing sensational fiction is a sordid and unwomanly activity and that good writing is not done for money. "Men have to work and women to marry for money," says Amy; and while her emphasis here is mistakenly on money, nothing in the

book contradicts her assessment of what women must do to live.

Little women marry, however, not only because they lack economic options, but because they lack emotional options as well. Old maidhood obliterates little womanhood and the fear of being an old maid is a motivating force in becoming a little woman. Fear is one of several unpleasant emotions simmering just below the sunny surface of Alcott's story and it plays a considerable role in determining the behavior of the "little women." Beth, for example, finds it necessary to invoke the fear of death in order to convince Jo of the primacy of loving service over writing "splendid books." Fear is always cropping up in Jo's relation to writing—fear of being selfish, fear of losing her womanliness, fear of becoming insensitive, fear of making money, fear of getting attention—requiring that she periodically renounce, in rather violent and self-punitive rituals, her literary ambitions. And fear plays an important role in the larger drama of Jo's conversion from disgruntled rebel to little woman. At the beginning of the book, Jo hates love, dislikes men and women in the romantic context, and has no desire to marry, unless it be to her sister. She finds Amy's flirting incomprehensible and Meg's capitulation to John disgraceful; she insists on viewing boys as equals and the only game she wishes to play with them is cricket. With Meg married, Beth dead, and Amy engaged, Jo begins to change her tune, for what has she to look forward to: "An old maid, that's what I'm to be. A literary spinster, with a pen for a spouse, a family of stories for children, and twenty years hence a morsel of fame, perhaps." Alcott emphasizes the unpleasantness of this prospect for Jo as much as is possible, given her commitment to the doctrine that every situation in life is full of beautiful opportunities. Jo is surrounded by evidence of Meg's "happy home" and inundated by glowing letters from Amy about how "it is so beautiful to be loved as Laurie loves me." On the evening when this happy couple arrives home, Jo is stricken with her worst fit of loneliness, for she sees that all the world is paired off but her: "a sudden sense of loneliness came over her so strongly that she looked about her with dim eyes, as if to find something to lean upon, for even Teddy [Laurie] had deserted her." Just at this moment Professor Bhaer arrives, Jo realizes that she is in love and capitulates to the description of herself as possessing a "tender, womanly half . . . like a chestnut burr, prickly outside, but silk-soft within, and a sweet kernel." Far from being the "best and sweetest thing which can happen to a woman," love is the court of last resort into which Jo is finally driven when all else fails and she must grow up.

The overt ideology of **Little Women** on the subject of marriage is undermined from still another direction. The reward for being "love-worthy," for acquiring the little womanly character of self-denial, self-control, accommodation, and concern for others, is not simply avoiding the fate of becoming an old maid; it is also getting the good man. As we have seen in the case of John, however, the good man is a somewhat mixed blessing. Indeed, while there is a lot of lip service paid in **Little Women** to the superior value of the "lords of creation," and to the importance of male reward, the emotional realities of the book move in a rather different direction. The figure of Mr. March is representative. At the beginning of part 2, Alcott assures us that while "to outsiders, the five energetic women seemed to rule the house," the truth is that "the quiet scholar, sitting among his books, was still the head of the family, the household conscience, anchor, and comforter; for to him the busy, anxious women always turned in troublous times, finding him, in the truest sense of those sacred words, husband and father." Yet this reputed center of power makes his first appearance "muffled up to his eyes," a broken man leaning on his wife's arm. While Beth's slow death takes place on center stage and occupies several chapters, the illness of Mr. March is consigned to the distant background and is only vaguely referred to. Literally absent during the first half of the book, during the second half he rarely emerges from his library and we are afforded brief glimpses into it to assure us that he is still there. If Marmee, on her departure to Washington, not knowing if her husband is alive or dead, comforts her girls by saying, "Hope and keep busy; and whatever happens, remember that you never can be fatherless," the true object of worship in *Little Women* is revealed in the description of Meg and Jo's vigil with Beth: "all day Jo and Meg hovered over her, watching, waiting, hoping, and trusting in God and Mother." It is Marmee who does all the things putatively ascribed to her husband; it is Marmee who always has the right word of comfort, love, and advice. Indeed, Beth's miraculous recovery is implicitly attributed to the fact that Marmee is merely on her way home. God may be a father but his agents on earth are women and the only worship we are privy to is that of Marmee and Beth. Similarly, in the question of love, the significance of men is essentially a matter of lip service. Despite Marmee's dictum about being loved by men, what we see and feel in reading *Little Women* is the love that exists between women: Marmee and her daughters; Jo and Beth. Thus while the events of Jo's life are determined by the book's overt message, her wish to resist the imperative to be a little woman and to instead marry her sister and remain forever with her mother is endorsed by the book's covert message.

The imaginative experience of *Little Women* is built on a paradox: the figure who most resists the pressure to become a little woman is the most attractive and the figure who most succumbs to it dies. Jo is the vital center of Alcott's book and she is so because she is least a little woman. Beth, on the other hand, is the least vital and the least interesting. She is also the character who most fully internalizes the overt values of *Little Women*; she is the daughter who comes closest to realizing the ideal of imitating mother. Like Marmee, Beth's devotion to her duty and her kindness toward others are never-failing and, like Marmee, she never expresses needs of her own. Beth is content with the role of house-keeping homebody; her castle in the air is "to stay at home safe with Father and Mother, and help take care of the family." In her content, her lack of ambition beyond broom and mop and feather duster, Beth is the perfect little woman. Yet she dies. Implicitly, a connection is made between the degree to which she fulfills the prescription for being a little wom-

an and the fact that she dies. The connection is reinforced by the plot since Beth gets the fatal scarlet fever from fulfilling Marmee's charge to the girls to take care of the Hummels while she is gone. Beth registers the cost of being a little woman; of suppressing so completely the expression of one's needs; of controlling so massively all selfishness, self-assertiveness, and anger. In Beth one sees the exhaustion of vitality in the effort to live as a little woman.

One also sees in Beth that negative self-image which is the real burden of the little woman. Such self-image is behind Beth's description of herself as "stupid little Beth, trotting about at home, of no use anywhere but there," and it is implicit in her identification with those broken dolls, cast off by her sisters, which she absorbs into her "infirmary" and makes her special care. Yet, if Beth identifies with these broken bits of outcast "dollanity" that constitute her imaginary world, her posture toward them expresses the hope that the world may treat her with the same kindness as she adopts toward them; and we are brought again to the connection between a life of loving service to others and the conviction of one's own worthlessness. Behind the paradox that Beth, the object of everyone's adoration, so thoroughly condemns herself, that Beth, so apparently content, cannot accept her right to live, rests the ultimate tension of Alcott's story. Beth's history carries out the implication of being a little woman to its logical conclusion: to be a little woman is to be dead.

Yet the drama of *Little Women* is the making of a little woman; and much of the book must be read as a series of lessons designed to teach Jo the value of a more submissive spirit and to reveal to her the wisdom of the doctrines of renunciation and adaptation announced so clearly in the opening pages. Jo is constantly shown the nasty consequences of not following Marmee's model of selflessness and self-control. While Marmee, though angry nearly every day of her life, has learned to control her anger, Jo at the opening of the story is "wild." When Amy burns her book, Jo refuses to forgive and forget; she sticks to her anger despite warning signals from Marmee. The results of her contumacy are nearly fatal: she fails to warn her sister of thin ice; Amy falls in and is only rescued by the timely, and manly, exertions of Laurie. The moral is clear. Jo's selfishness, followed by her anger, followed by her vindictiveness result in her sister's nearly dying. In the world of "little women" female anger is so unacceptable that there are no degrees to it; all anger leads to "murder." The consequence for Jo is horror at herself which in turn results in contrition, repression, and a firm vow to follow in the footsteps of Marmee and never to let her anger get beyond a tightening of the lips.

Jo pays for her quick temper and lack of self-control in a more tangible way later in the book. Amy has roped Jo into going with her to pay the family's social calls. Amy thrives on such activity; but Jo finds it intolerable and can only get through the experience by playing elaborate games at each place they stop. The final call is to their Aunt March. Both girls are tired, peevish, and anxious to go home; but when Jo suggests they skip the visit, Amy remonstrates that "it's a little thing to do, but it gives her pleasure." So Amy devotes herself to being nice to Aunt March and to Aunt Carroll who is with her, and to making the visit pleasant, while Jo gives vent to her peevishness and irritation in a series of decided remarks on the subject of patronage. Since Aunt March and Aunt Carroll are in the process of deciding which of the two girls should be offered the chance to accompany Aunt Carroll to Europe, Jo's testiness is costly indeed. Amy goes to Europe and Jo is left home to reflect on the fact that she has received a "timely lesson in the art of holding her tongue" and to draw the inevitable conclusion that in this world it is best to be a little woman like Amy.

An even more traumatic lesson is administered to Jo through her beloved sister Beth. Beth contracts scarlet fever because of the irresponsibility of Meg and Jo, but the burden falls primarily on Jo as she is the one particularly charged with responsibility for Beth. When Beth asks Jo to take over the job of seeing the Hummels, Jo is too busy, Jo is writing; and so Beth, who has never had scarlet fever, is exposed to the disease and catches it. Again there is the pattern of maximum possible consequences for a minimal degree of self-absorption and selfishness. It is a pattern well calculated to teach Jo a more submissive spirit. In fact, one can say that Beth's primary function in *Little Women* is to be a lesson to Jo; Beth's life is a constant reminder to Jo of her own inadequacies and failures and of what she ought to be, and her death is bitter testimony to the consequences of these failures. It is by no means accidental that Jo "falls in love" shortly after Beth's death. She gets scared, she gets good, she gets Professor Bhaer.

Obviously, one of the major problems Alcott faced in writing *Little Women* was making up someone for Jo to marry since, as we have seen, marry she must. She cannot marry, as she cannot "love," Laurie, not, as Marmee claims, because they are too alike in temperament, but because they are too alike in status; they are too equal. If anything, Laurie is Jo's inferior, as her constant reference to him as "the dear boy" implies. Unfortunately, perhaps, for Jo and Laurie, little women can only love up, not across or down; they must marry their fathers, not their brothers or sons. Thus Laurie gets Amy who is a fitting child for him and Jo gets her Papa Bhaer who, as the Germanic and ursine connotations of his name suggest, is the heavy authority figure necessary to offset Jo's own considerable talent and vitality. His age, his foreignness, his status as a professor, his possession of moral and philosophic wisdom all conspire to put him on a different plane from Laurie and John Brooke and to make him an appropriate suitor for Jo whose relationship to him is clearly that of pupil to teacher, child to parent, little woman to big man. In exchange for German lessons, she will darn his socks; at their school he will do all the teaching and she will do the housework; he has saved her soul by a timely warning against the effects of sensational literature and later we are told of Jo's future that she "made queer mistakes; but the wise professor steered her safely into calmer waters." It is clear, however, that such an

excessively heirarchical relationship is necessary to indicate Jo's ultimate acceptance of the doctrines of *Little Women*. In marrying Professor Bhaer, Jo's rebellion is neutralized and she proves once and for all that she is a good little woman who wishes for nothing more than the chance to realize herself in the service of some superior male. The process of getting her out of her boots and doublet and her misguided male-identification and into her role as a future Marmee is completed by placing her securely in the arms of Papa Bhaer.

We do not, of course, view this transformation with unqualified rejoicing. It is difficult not to see it as capitulation and difficult not to respond to it with regret. Our attitude, moreover, is not the result of feminist values imposed on Alcott's work but the result of ambivalence within the work on the subject of what it means to be a little woman. Certainly, this ambivalence is itself part of the message of *Little Women*. It accurately reflects the position of the woman writer in nineteenth-century America, confronted on all sides by forces pressuring her to compromise her vision. How conscious Alcott was of the conflict between the overt and covert messages of *Little Women*, how intentional on the one hand was her subversion of the book's "doctrine" and on the other hand her compromise with her culture's norms, it is impossible to say. What one can say, however, is that in failing to give Jo a fate other than that of the little woman, Alcott "altered her values in deference to the opinion of others" and obliterated her own identity as an economically independent single woman who much preferred to "paddle her own canoe" than to resign herself to the dependency of marriage. Clearly, her true style is rather less than true. When Professor Bhaer excoriates sensation fiction in an effort to set Jo on the road to attaining her true style, he exclaims, "They haf no right to put poison in the sugar plum, and let the small ones eat it." It is to Alcott's credit that at least covertly if not overtly she recognized the sugar plum was the poison.

Jill P. May

SOURCE: "Spirited Females of the Nineteenth Century: Liberated Moods in *Little Women*," in *Children's literature in education*, Vol. 11, No. 1, 1980, pp. 10-20.

When Miss Alcott's book *Little Women* was published in 1868, most reviewers described it as wholesome reading that depicted worthwhile models for young girls. Today's textbooks of children's literature discuss the characters with light descriptive phrases such as "flesh-and-blood girls, as different from each other as they could well be . . . never self-righteous, sometimes irritable but never failing in warm affection for each other." These generalized statements may be valid, but they fail to come to grips with Miss Alcott's knowledge of social attitudes in her era and of her use of children's literature to interpret the woman's role.

The female characters drawn by Louisa Alcott for *Little Women* represent a significant break from the typical late-

From Little Women, *by Louisa May Alcott.*
Illustrated by Jessie Willcox Smith.

nineteenth-century New England housewife image. They accept the notion that happiness comes in marriage, but each has strong opinions and a desire to satisfy her own goals within marriage. Far from being polite young women who engage in "proper" activities, Amy, Meg, and Jo are individuals who help define what women can do within the traditional wedded framework.

The continued popularity of **Little Women** is impressive. Young girls read with rapture the fictional story of another era, a genteel time when long skirts and netted hair were the fashion. Nevertheless, each reader is able to identify with at least one of the girls and to grow along with her. Even boys enjoy exposure to the book. Today's readers' reactions do reflect a change in values; most are disappointed that Jo chooses the professor over Laurie. One young man exclaimed: "I felt cheated! Jo and Laurie were the excitement of the book! How could they choose such placid mates?" Even to young men, the love interest is intriguing.

Understanding the social decorum of Miss Alcott's period will help point out Miss Alcott's use of a romance to describe the woman in society. Certainly, the book could

easily stimulate conversation with children about the subtle assertiveness of the women of its time. **Little Women** is more than a romanticized autobiography; it is a continually modern portrait of the young intellectual girl who grows up and faces the realities of marriage. Children need to know that Louisa May Alcott wrote about the importance of independence within marriage, and that Jo's personality is not in every way that of the author.

Louisa May Alcott's life cannot be considered typical. She was born into a highly intellectual family in 1832 and would know American philosophers throughout her life. Ralph Waldo Emerson was a frequent visitor to the Alcott household, and Henry Thoreau was a close family friend. Her father, Bronson Alcott, was an idealist, an educator, a man of causes and his daughter's chief educator; her mother was a strong, quiet woman who fostered Louisa's spirited growth into a capable, independent woman. Her father both encouraged and reproached her behavior; he was always aware of her high spirit and at times seemed bent upon breaking down her exuberance. Yet he marveled at her determination. When she was only two years old he wrote:

> Louisa is yet too young for the formation of just views of her character. She manifests uncommon activity and force of mind at present, and is much in advance of her sister when at the same age. Example has done much to call forth her nature. She is more active and practical than Anna, a different form of character essentially. Anna is ideal, sentimental. Louisa is practical, energetic . . . She finds no difficulty in devising ways and means to attain her purposes.

Louisa herself was always aware of her behavior and often complained of her bad temper or her moodiness. Her parents, although kind, were constantly reminding her that she should be submissive, sweet, cheerful, and quiet. Her mother read her diary and from time to time put in a comment. Most of the notes encouraged Louisa to watch her temper; these early cautions are found throughout Louisa's preteen diary. Although they were meant to comfort and guide her youthful spirit, they were strong reminders that good behavior meant being patient, obedient, and kind. At one point her mother wrote:

> My Louy—I was grieved at your selfish behavior this morning, but also greatly pleased to find you bore so meekly Father's reproof for it. That is the way, dear; if you find you are wrong, take the discipline sweetly, and do so no more. It is not to be expected that children should always do right; but oh, how lovely to see a child penitent and patient when the passion is over.

During her early years, Louisa was closely supervised by both parents. Her father demanded that his daughters rise early, work dutifully at household tasks, join morning worship services, and study hard. The family diet and lifestyle was stark; Bronson Alcott was never a monetary success, and poverty became a reality when his venture in communal farming failed. Yet the family unit was strong, and their faith in one another constant. Louisa never wrote strong criticism of either her mother or her father in her diaries. She always seemed able to understand that their unorthodox ways might later help her achieve her own goals. Years later, she wrote that the days spent in Concord as a child were her happiest days and that her father was the wisest of teachers.

At first glance, Miss Alcott always seemed most capable of criticizing herself and of overlooking the faults of her family. As she grew older, she was able to glance backward and fondly laugh at her family's reputation. At one point she wrote:

> People wondered at our frolics, but enjoyed them, and droll stories are still told of the adventures of those days. Mr. Emerson and Margaret Fuller were visiting my parents one afternoon, and the conversation having turned to the ever interesting subject of education, Miss Fuller said:—
>
> "Well, Mr. Alcott, you have been able to carry out your methods in your own family, and I should like to see your model children."
>
> She did in a few moments, for as the guests stood on the door-steps a wild uproar approached, and round the corner of the house came a wheelbarrow holding baby May arrayed as a queen; I was the horse, bitted and bridled, and driven by my elder sister Anna; while Lizzie played dog, and barked as loud as her gentle voice permitted . . . mother put a climax to the joke by saying, with a dramatic wave of the hand,—
>
> "Here are the model children, Miss Fuller."

In fact, it always bothered Louisa to see her mother in need, and it must have pained her to know that her intelligent father was incapable of managing his own affairs. Her adult life was a dichotomy appropriate for her time. She was a polite and unassuming female who abstained from radical public behavior. But she was also the family's private financier and guardian, and she devoted her life to her family. She measured personal success in her diary by her ability to pay the family debts. Louisa became the eldest son; she provided for her sisters' youthful needs and maintained her parents when they grew old.

It probably never occurred to Miss Alcott that any other behavior might be acceptable. As a child, she had always been reminded both of her high spirits and of her obligation to do the proper thing. By the time she was a woman, Louisa Alcott had taken both ideas to heart, and had accepted them as her own. When she was twenty-three years old she wrote in her diary:

> I was born with a boy's spirit under my bib and tucker, I *can't wait* when I *can* work . . . I don't often pray in words; but when I set out that day with all my worldly goods in the little old trunk, my own earnings ($25) in my pocket, and much hope and resolution in my soul, my heart was very full, and I said to the Lord, "Help us all and keep us for one another," as I never said it before, while I looked back at the dear faces watching me, so full of love and hope and faith.

Yet because she acknowledged her century's interpretation of the woman's role, Miss Alcott reacted to her accomplishments and her critical acclaim modestly. She quietly accepted praise and never allowed herself the luxury of taking seriously her possible literary abilities. Instead, she created stories that were considered sentimental, lively, lightweight, and very feminine. Her female characters openly and joyfully accepted traditional female roles. Most reviewers categorized them as wholesome, lovely creatures. *The Catholic World* ended its review of **Little Women** by saying: "Make their acquaintance; for Amy will be found delightful, Beth very lovely, Meg beautiful, and Jo splendid; that there is a real Jo somewhere we have not the slightest doubt."

Louisa never sought marriage with all of its trappings. Her parents had been a loving, happy couple, but their marriage had not given Mrs. Alcott any real social or economic freedom. She had actually had more social standing before her marriage; both her parents were members of well-known Massachusetts families. Louisa's father's family was respectable but modest, and his early life was a simple, rural one. The Alcott's married life was intellectually stimulating, but their devotion to idealistic causes and to one another could not erase their economic tribulations. Outwardly, their marriage could be considered ideal by most nineteenth century critics. Mrs. Alcott was an attractive woman with strong intellectual capabilities and a quick temper, who doted on her husband. He was a brilliant, if somewhat impractical, man of causes and principles, who never questioned that he was the best moral authority within the family. He was dominant; she was supportive. Louisa did not express an interest in having a similar relationship. She did not discuss a desire for wedded security. In reality, she was much more practical and realistic. The man she created for Jo would not have been acceptable for Louisa. When she was twenty-eight years old, Miss Alcott met a man similar to Jo's professor and wrote in her diary:

> Had a funny lover who met me in the cars and said he lost his heart at once. Handsome man of forty. A southerner, and very demonstrative and gushing, called and wished to pay his addresses; being told I didn't wish to see him, retired, to write letters and haunt the road with his hat off, while the girls laughed and had great fun over Jo's lover.

Thus, eight years before **Little Women** was published, Louisa May Alcott was privately denying her need for a lover, while asserting that her heroine would have one.

Just as it is inaccurate to regard Jo as a biographical sketch of Miss Alcott, it is equally inaccurate to consider Jo the only adventurous one of the sisters. Each of the sisters, except Beth, has strong opinions, which are usually held in rein publicly by social decorum. Jo, Amy and Meg all come to grips with their roles as wives and women by the end of the book, and each makes a subtle statement on the right of women to think and act as individuals. Each one develops a strong moral conscience and recognizes what is proper behavior for young women. But each one expresses a desire to satisfy her own goals, and all three are determined to be successful at their marriages without sacrificing these goals.

Beth is trapped in the role of a more traditional female. Her death indirectly shows that a woman cannot exist in a real sense unless she is willing to plan for her own personal fulfillment. When Beth tells Jo that she knows she will die she says,

> I only mean to say that I have a feeling that it was never intended I should live long. I'm not like the rest of you; I never made plans about what I'd do when I grew up; I never thought of being married, as you all did. I couldn't seem to imagine myself anything but stupid little Beth, trotting about at home, of no use anywhere but there.

Beth is the romanticized woman of the nineteenth century. Her intellect is not developed. She is sweet and child-like, happiest when she is helping others or playing the piano (both very feminine traits). She does not speak harsh words, considers herself dumb and useless in comparison to all around her, and constantly expresses her admiration of everyone in her family. Beth is the child woman: mature in body and spirit, but devoid of any personal goals or images. Her death demonstrates Miss Alcott's severance with the established mode for women.

Meg is the second-most-traditional character in the book. As a young girl, she is vain and simplistic. Her desire to be fashionable and to be properly married makes Meg the least modern sister by today's standards. But Meg is not a traditional romantic heroine. She chooses to break with the establishment and upsets her wealthy aunt (who represents the aristocracy) when she marries a poor young man. Her aunt arrives and is shocked to see Meg working on the wedding decorations with her bridegroom. Meg makes her break with decorum when she retorts,

> I'm not a show, aunty, and no one is coming to stare at me, to criticise my dress, or count the cost of my luncheon. I'm too happy to care what anyone says or thinks, and I'm going to have my little wedding just as I like it.

Through Meg, Miss Alcott is showing young girls that a young person should break with social attitudes and values if the result will be positive. Because Meg's transgression is minor—marrying a poor but honest young gentleman—she is immediately accepted by the society she has defied. Meg is never depicted as a young woman seeking real change within the traditional marriage pattern. Her romance is more idealistic than those of her sisters. She marries for love and is truly supportive of her husband. While she is adjusting to marriage, she does quarrel with her husband, but most of her anger is based upon her inability to completely run the household without help. She longs to be a good wife and a model mother, and she has no career goals outside the home. But in the beginning, she finds herself frustrated by her household duties and her desire to be the perfect housewife.

Mrs. March conveys to the reader Miss Alcott's belief that marriage should be a true partnership, and that the young woman who merely stays at home and cooks, cleans, and sews cannot be her husband's partner. The responsibility of sharing in marriage is pinpointed by Meg's mother as belonging to the woman. Thus, when talking to Meg about her frustrations, Mrs. March says,

> [Y]ou owe something to John as well as to the babies; don't neglect husband for children, don't shut him out of the nursery, but teach him how to help in it. His place is there as well as yours, and the children need him; let him feel that he has his part to do, and he will do it gladly and faithfully, and it will be better for you all . . . Then I'd take an interest in whatever John likes,—talk with him, let him read to you, exchange ideas, and help each other in that way. Don't shut yourself up in a bandbox because you are a woman, but understand what is going on, and educate yourself to take your part in the world's work, for it all affects you and yours.

Mrs. March's sound advice is given not only for the benefit of Meg, but also for the benefit of all romantic young women who want to be "just a housewife." Through Mrs. March, Louisa May Alcott is stressing her belief that the need for a cooperative relationship within marriage must be based on mutual respect, shared interests, and common goals. She takes a deliberate stance that a wife be given freedom to think and to intellectually discuss worldly affairs. Her own understanding of this is found in her diary when in December, 1877, after her mother's death she wrote: "She was so loyal, tender, and true; life was hard for her, and no one understood all she had to bear but we, her children."

By showing the reader Meg, Miss Alcott broke from the theory that a woman need only be cheerful, pleasant in appearance, capable of running a house and of raising her children. She created in Meg the prototype of the twentieth-century wife who *chooses* not to work, but to devote herself to her family. Miss Alcott's heroine knowingly makes that choice and actively plans for her social and intellectual growth. The author's use of Meg and her traditional values shows that even when the wife stays at home, the household responsibilities should be shared, that the woman should plan for the day when the children are grown, and that the couple should engage in amiable discussion.

On the surface, Amy is the spoiled, skittish youngest sister. She has determined not to marry someone poor, but to find someone who is well enough off to give her ample financial security. She is pretty and gay, so people are charmed by her. Amy is willing to accept all the conventions of society and is eager to enjoy life without poverty. Her natural popularity makes it easy for Amy to find willing suitors. But Amy's spirited soul will not be tamed by matrimony. While in Europe, Amy thinks her newest suitor will propose. In her letter home she says:

> I may be mercenary, but I hate poverty, and don't mean to bear it a minute longer than I can help. One

of us must marry well; Meg didn't, Jo won't, Beth can't yet, so I shall, and make everything cosey all around. I wouldn't marry a man I hated or despised. You may be sure of that; and, though Fred is not my model hero, he does very well, and, in time, I should get fond enough of him if he was very fond of me, and let me do just as I liked.

Amy is a practical young woman who determines to discover exactly how much artistic talent she has in order to arrange for her future. Like many artists, she is not adverse to having a rich benefactor, as long as she maintains control of her life's activities. It might have been considered unusual for a young woman to believe that she had great talents worth developing and pursuing. But Amy displays the self-assurance necessary for a woman living in a male-dominated century. Her thoughts are free from sexual stereotypes about the worth of anyone's talents. She is neither conceited nor is she a conniving female. But she does view marriage much as one views a business partnership; if the proposition is to be successful, she must be able to gracefully entertain and to maintain her artistic endeavors. Wedded bliss, Miss Alcott is saying, must be more than passionate ardor. The wise woman does not fall in love and then determine what she expects from a relationship. Instead she decides what qualities are essential for a good partnership and chooses to love someone who has the potential to help create a lasting marriage. Amy realizes that she has philanthropic desires that could not be carried out if she were poor, and so she chooses appropriate suitors. After she is lovingly married to someone who can help her obtain her goals she says,

> [A]nd there's another class who can't ask, and who suffer in silence. I know something of it, for I belonged to it before you made a princess of me, as the King does the beggarmaid in the old stories. Ambitious girls have a hard time, Laurie, and often have to see youth, health, and precious opportunities go by, just for want of a little help at the right minute. People have been very kind to me; and whenever I see girls struggling along, as we used to do, I want to put out my hand and help them, as I was helped.

But it is through Jo that Miss Alcott has illustrated the plight of the intelligent young woman with ambitions of her own. Jo does resemble the young Miss Alcott in her spirit counterbalanced by her concern over her own impetuous behavior. As a girl, Jo honestly speaks her thoughts but then feels guilty within minutes. Her desires only vaguely include marriage, and when she is confessing what she would like most in the future she says,

> I want to do something splendid before I go into my Castle,—something heroic or wonderful, that won't be forgotten after I'm dead. I don't know what, but I'm on the watch for it, and mean to astonish you all, some day. I think I shall write books, and get rich and famous: that would suit me, so that is my favorite dream.

Most of Jo's story concerns her change from a coltish young person with career drives to a blushing young woman who desires marriage to a dominant man. Her early exuberance brings rebukes from all her family, while her courtship behavior with the professor is lauded by all. The fact that marriage will completely change her lifestyle does not bother anyone. The professor she chooses to marry is much older and wiser. He is a father figure described in glowing terms. He is fifteen years older than Jo, and is far superior to her in scholarly knowledge. He is first her tutor, and second her lover. He treats Jo with gentle respect, but is not afraid to reproach her for her conduct. By the book's end, she exchanges her career frustrations for the traditional nineteenth-century view of a worthwhile woman—that of a wife and mother. When the professor finally proposes to her she says,

> I may be strong-minded, but no one can say I'm not of my sphere now, for woman's special mission is supposed to be drying tears and bearing burdens. I'm to carry my share, Friedrich, and help to earn the home. Make up your mind to that, or I'll never go.

Perhaps Miss Alcott sensed that her contemporary readers would accept the girls more willingly if they were all married. Each was portrayed as a light, wholesome creature, and all were loved and admired by young readers because of this character portrayal. They were capable at times of gushing sweetness, but they were independent girls who refused to be only wives and mothers. However, it is important to remember Miss Alcott's theme that women must find happiness and fulfillment within a conventional marriage. Because Louisa remained loyal to her family and supported them throughout her life, she could not have created a youthful heroine who rebelled against her family and eventually freed herself of family ties. Yet, although she stressed the importance of family security, nothing in her own life had shown her that marriage was the best of possible lifestyles. Instead she portrayed marriage as the best outward sign of security. At one point in *Little Women* she steps aside from the action and writes:

> At twenty-five, girls begin to talk about being old maids, but secretly resolve that they never will be; at thirty they say nothing about it, but quietly accept the fact, and, if sensible, console themselves by remembering that they have twenty more useful, happy years, in which they may be learning to grow old gracefully.

The Alcott family's attitude toward women was extremely liberal for the nineteenth century. Mrs. Alcott's opinion was generally respected, and all daughters were encouraged to pursue their artistic talents. Each girl was expected to keep a diary detailing her interests and readings. But family discussion did not encourage the girls to break with conventional behavior. Career success was to be measured quietly, without interfering with family pride and honor. Women could have talent and be admired, but they also had their proper social position.

Louisa's father attended the Woman's Convention in 1856 and characteristically made these observations of the women there in his diary.

Their ways, just now at the outset, may not be theirs always, but bad imitations of our worst ways— mistaking as they may, in their novitiate, the coarse instrumentalities as best, of convention, speech, resolution, petition, denunciation, the mob appeal, for the truer and more potent persuasions of the parlour, and conversation, prevailing manners, . . . the suggestions of literature, religion, and of pure art.

Nineteen years later Louisa May Alcott attended the Woman's Congress in Syracuse, and in 1878 she actively sought membership for the suffrage movement in Concord. In a letter to a friend she wrote:

Let us hear no more of "woman's sphere" from the State House or the pulpit—no more twaddle about sturdy oaks and clinging vines. Let woman find out her own limitations, but in heaven's name, give her a chance! Let the professions to be opened to her. Let fifty years of college education be hers. And then we shall see what she can do!

It is difficult to conjecture how much Louisa May Alcott consciously wrote into her book, and how much she portrayed about the needs of women without being thoroughly aware of her own attitudes. When she started writing her book, Louisa confessed in her diary:

Mr. N. wants a *girls' story,* and I begin "Little Women." I plot away, though I don't enjoy this sort of thing. Never liked girls or knew many, except my sisters; but our queer plays and experiences may prove interesting, though I doubt it.

Obviously uncomfortable with romantic endings, Miss Alcott married each woman to a man who counterbalanced her strengths. Her model for Jo's husband was probably based mostly on the relationship she had with her father. There is a calculated determination in each of the three heroines to marry someone intellectually suited for them.

The characters in *Little Women* do not make a vocal commitment to the early Women's Movement, but they do suggest that women have a right to express themselves freely in conversation, to choose roles for themselves, and to maintain their goals after marriage. Thus, they are the forerunners of their twentieth century sisters; their zest for life and ability to argue with men about social and economic theories make them much more free than the typical New England woman who lived in Louisa's region. While they appear to be seeking only the security of a loving family, Louisa's "little women" are quietly beginning the march toward freedom within a marriage.

Anne Hollander

SOURCE: "Reflections on *Little Women,*" in *Children's Literature: An Annual of the Modern Language Association Group on Children's Literature and the Children's Literature Association,* Vol. 9, 1981, pp. 28-39.

Little Women has been a justly famous children's classic for a century, even though none of the characters is really a child when the story begins. Amy, the youngest, is already twelve, well beyond the age at which girls first read the book. In consequence, this novel, like many great childhood books, must serve as a pattern and a model, a mold for goals and aspirations rather than an accurate mirror of known experience. The little girls who read *Little Women* can learn what it might be like to be older; but, most important, they can see with reassurance in Alcott's pages how the feelings familiar in childhood are preserved in later days, and how individual character abides through life.

A satisfying continuity informs all the lives in *Little Women.* Alcott creates a world where a deep "natural piety" indeed effortlessly binds the child to the woman she becomes. The novel shows that as a young girl grows up, she may rely with comfort on being the same person, whatever mysterious and difficult changes must be undergone in order to become an older and wiser one. Readers can turn again and again to Alcott's book solely for a gratifying taste of her simple, stable vision of feminine completeness.

Unscholarly but devoted readers of *Little Women* have often insisted that the book is good only because of the character of Jo. Most modern response to the novel consists of irritation at the death of Beth and annoyance at Amy's final marital success, accompanied by universal sympathy for Jo's impatience with ladylike decorum and her ambitions for a career. In current perception these last two of Jo's qualities have appeared to overshadow all the struggles undergone by the other sisters, in a narrative to which Alcott herself tried to give an even-handed symmetry.

The character of Jo is the one identified with Alcott, not only on the biographical evidence but through the more obvious interest the author takes and the keener liking she feels for this particular one of her four heroines. For many readers the memory of Jo's struggles remains the strongest later on. This enduring impression, along with dislike of Amy and impatience with bashful, dying Beth, may reflect the force of the author's own intractable preferences, not quite thoroughly transmuted into art.

But art there certainly is; and among those readers not themselves so averse to ladyhood as Jo or Alcott herself, or so literary in their own personal ambitions, there are other problems and conflicts in *Little Women* that vibrate in the memory. Alcott's acuteness and considerable talent were variously deployed among her heroines; and by using a whole family of sisters for her subject, she succeeded better than many authors have since in rendering some of the complex truth about American female consciousness.

It remains true that among the sisters Beth receives somewhat summary treatment and the least emotional attention. She is there to be hallowed by the others, and for that she is in fact better dead, since her actual personal experiences are not very interesting even to her creator.

Her goodness serves as a foil to the moral problems of the others; we really cannot care what her life is like for her. None of us, like none of them, is quite good enough. Beth's mortal illness, moreover, is accepted with no advice whatsoever from medical science. She seems to die a moral death, to retire voluntarily from life's scene so that the stage will be more spacious for the other actors.

The badness of the three other sisters, however, like their virtues, is more interestingly distributed than is usually remembered. If one can set aside the pervasive memory of impulsive tomboy Jo, whose only fault now seems to have been being ahead of her time, we can see Alcott's moral scheme more clearly. The novel is not just Jo's story; it is the tale of four Pilgrim's Progresses—admittedly with Beth fairly early out of the race, having won in advance. The three others have all got thoroughly realistic "bosom enemies," personal failings that each must try to conquer before their author can let them have their rewards. It is clear enough that certain of these failings privately seemed worse to Alcott than others, but she gives them all a serious look, keen enough to carry across generations into modern awareness.

Jo and Professor Baer. Illustration by Jessie Willcox Smith.

As the book transparently shows, Alcott cared a great deal about troublesome anger and rebelliousness and nothing whatever about shyness; but she does give a lot of thought to vanity, envy, selfishness, and pride. She likes literature and music much better than painting and sculpture; but she has a strong understanding of frustrated artistic ambition and the pain of not being very good at what you love best to do. Meg, for example, is the only sister with no talent, except a fleeting one for acting in childhood dramatics. Her chief struggle is with envy, and it is manifestly a harder one for a girl with no intrinsically satisfying and valuable gifts. She has only personal beauty, in a period of American cultural history when fine clothes really mattered.

In the second half of the nineteenth century feminine dress made strong visual demands, and the elements of conspicuous consumption had a vigorously gaudy flavor and an imposing social importance. Modest simplicity in dress and furnishing was unfashionable and socially degrading; and Meg is keenly aware that her own good looks would have more absolute current worth if they might always be framed and set off by the elaborate and costly appurtenances of contemporary taste. Fortunately, she is not only beautiful but also basically good and so able to respond spontaneously to true love in simple garb without any mercenary qualms when the moment arrives. Later, however, as a matron of slender means, she has some very instructive struggles with her unconquered demons. Alcott is careful to demonstrate that such inward problems are not solved by love, however true it may be.

Meg, in any case, has no trouble being "womanly"; her rebellion is entirely against not having the riches that she rightly believes would show her purely passive, feminine qualities to better advantage. Motherhood, wifehood, and daughterhood are her aptitudes, and she has to learn to accept the virtuous practice of them without the scope and visibility that money would make possible.

Jo is famous for hating feminine trappings and for wanting to get rich by her own efforts, and thus apparently has no real faults by modern standards. "Womanliness" is not for her, because she is afraid it will require idiotic small-talk and tight shoes. The roughness of manner for which Jo suffered was called "unladylike" at the time, and thus the character earns a deal of sympathy in the present, when "lady" is a derogatory word, and most nineteenth-century views of middle-class female behavior are under general condemnation. In fact, despite the red-flag term, Jo is never condemned by her family, or by her author, except for what we still believe is bad in either sex: quickness of temper and impatience, lack of consideration and rage. Otherwise, her physical gracelessness is lamented but not chastised, and the only prohibition that seems really strange is against her *running*. This requires explanation.

The nineteenth-century stricture against running for ladies seems to have been an aspect of sexual modesty, not simply a matter of general decorum. In an age before brassières, when corseting constricted only the thorax below the breasts, a well-behaved lady might not indulge in "any form of motion more rapid than walking," for fear of betraying somewhere below her neck the "portion of the general system which gives to woman her peculiar prerogative as well as her distinctive character." Bouncing breasts were apparently unacceptable to the respectable eye, and at the time only the restriction of bodily movement could ensure their stability.

Freedom-loving Jo is not loath to accept male instruction and domination; she is delighted to submit to her father, just as the others are. She is afraid only of sex, as she demonstrates whenever Laurie tries to approach her at all amorously. Jo's fear of sex, like her impatience, is one of the forms her immaturity takes, well past the age when an interest in sex might seem natural. Her fear erupts most noticeably during the period when Meg, who is only a year older, is tremulously succumbing to John Brooke's attractions. Jo, far from feeling any sympathetic excitement about this, or any envy of the delights of love, is filled with a fury and a misery born of terror. She is not just afraid of losing Meg; she fears Meg's emergent sexual being and, more deeply, her own. Later, she is shown as preferring literary romantic heroes to live ones, who might try to arouse her own responses. Very possibly many young girls who read about this particular aspect of Jo's late adolescence may find that this, too, is a sympathetic trait, along with Jo's hatred of the restrictive feminine "sphere."

The three older "little women" all have faults of a fairly minor character—feminine vanity, impulsiveness, shyness—which are often objectively endearing and are also apparently so to the author herself. These weaknesses are shown to be incidental to truly generous natures: Meg, Jo, and Beth are all unquestionably loving and good-hearted girls. Amy, the youngest, is basically different and (to this reader at least) much more interesting.

Amy is undoubtedly the Bad Sister throughout the early parts of the book. Alcott seems to have very little sympathy for her shortcomings, which are painted as both more irritating and more serious than those of the other girls. She is the one who is actually bad, whereas the others are only flawed, thus:

Meg—pleasure-loving and vain
Jo—quick-tempered and tomboyish } *generous*
Beth—shy and timid

Amy—conceited, affected, and *selfish*

One is tempted to believe that Alcott detests Amy for those same traits that George Eliot seems to hate in certain of her own characters: blond hair, blue eyes, physical grace, and personal charm. And Amy's faults are not at all endearing. This sister, judging from her behavior in the beginning, at least, is really both nasty and pretentious—a true brat; and not only that, she is the only one seriously committed to high standards of visual appearance, that well-known moral pitfall.

I have heard Amy described as "insipid," as if literary blondness must always guarantee a corresponding pallidness of character; but in fact her inward conflicts are harder than those of her sisters, since she has much graver faults to overcome. And she is successful, not only in conquering her selfishness but in turning her love of beauty to good spiritual account. It is not for nothing that Alcott has given her a "determined chin," wide mouth, and "keen blue eyes," along with the charm and blond curls that seem to blind all eyes to her real strength and to inhibit the interests of most readers. Amy has a hard time being good—all the harder because she has an easy time being pleasing—and gets hated for it into the bargain, even by her author. But Alcott is nothing if not fair, and she is scrupulous in her portrayal of Amy's trials, especially her efforts to be a serious artist, even though she writes of "artistic attempts" with considerable condescension. Alcott seems to find visual art somewhat ridiculous, whereas literature is *de facto* serious.

Unlike Jo, Amy aims for the highest with a pure ambition. Jo simply wants to be successful and to make money, but Amy says: "I want to be great or nothing." She refuses to be "a commonplace dauber." Her desire to be great is only finally and correctly deterred by the sight of true greatness during her visit to Rome; and so she gives up trying. This particular renunciation can also clearly be seen as part of Amy's refinement of character, a praiseworthy if symbolic subjugation of her overt sexuality. It may be pointed out, incidentally, that we hear nothing of any humility on the part of Jo in the face of great writing, since success, not creative excellence, is her standard.

On the face of it, Amy is a frivolous, failed artist, while Jo is a serious, successful one. But in fact Amy's creative talent can be seen as more authentic than Jo's, because Amy does recognize and accept and even enjoy her own sexuality, which is the core of the creative self. Alcott demonstrates this through the mature Amy's straightforward, uncoy ease in attracting men and her effortless skill at self-presentation, which are emblems of her commitment to the combined truths of sex and art. Her childhood selfishness and affectation are conquered quite early; she fights hard to grow up, so that her love of beauty, her personal allure, and her artistic talent may all be purely expressed, undistorted by vanity or hope of gain. Nevertheless, the too-explicit erotic drive in Amy must be suppressed, and this can be symbolically accomplished by the transmutation of her serious artistic aims into the endowments of a lady.

Jo's literary talent, on the other hand, is qualified in the earlier part of the book, even as her sexuality remains willfully neutralized. Her writing is not yet an authentic channel for the basic erotic force behind all art, as Amy's talent clearly is. Jo's writing rather is the agent of her retreat from sex—she uses it to make herself more like a man. Alcott expresses the slightly compromised quality of Jo's literary ambition (and of her sexuality) by having her primarily desire fame and financial gain, along publicly accepted lines of masculine accomplishment. She writes for newspapers in order to get paid, for instance, instead of struggling to write great poems, which might never sell. Jo can write as a true artist only later, when she finally comes to terms with her own sexual self and thus rather belatedly grows up in her own turn.

In the end, after Amy gives up art, Alcott permits her to use her taste and her esthetic skill for the embellishment of life with no loss of integrity or diminution in her strength of character. It is Amy, the lover of material beauty, not Jo, the lover of freedom, who gets to escape and go traveling in Europe, but only after she has earned the regard of all concerned for her successful conquering of self. Jo finally says, after Amy does the right thing in a compromising social situation: "You've a deal more principle and generosity and nobleness of character than I ever gave you credit for, Amy. You've behaved sweetly and I respect you with all my heart." And Amy repeats what she has already said a bit earlier in a different way: "You laugh at me when I say I want to be a lady, but I mean a true gentlewoman in mind and manners. . . . I want to be above the little meannesses and follies and faults that spoil so many women." Amy actively and painfully resists being spoiled, and so she wins—at first the trip to Europe and at last the one rich and handsome husband on the scene, not because of her blond beauty but rather in spite of it. She proves a true March daughter (and she, at least, is certainly not afraid of sex), and thus Laurie may love her at last.

Laurie, the neighboring, rich young man, finds his most important function in the novel not as a possible husband for any sister but as a student of The March Way of Life. Born to riches and idleness and personally neglected as a child, this youth is clearly destined for depravity, especially since he is half-Italian, and we must know what that means. Alcott lets this fact, plus a talent for music, stand (as she lets Amy's talent for art stand) for sexuality itself, the whole erotic and artistically creative dimension in life. Laurie, like Amy, seems always to be an acknowledged sexual being. Alcott shows this quality in him, as she shows it in Amy, by making him a lover of beauty who reveals his commitment to it through a natural, unsought creative talent—in his case, inherited directly from his Italian musical mother—and not in detached or cultivated appreciation. In both characters, their own physical beauty represents the fusion of art and sex.

This youthful and passionate male neighbor, an obvious candidate for the dissolute life, comes under the variously superior moral influences of all the females next door— Amy at this point, however, being still a nasty child of little account. We are given a good, old-fashioned demonstration of the redeeming power of love in the persons of virtuous women. But it is, of course, love minus sex, an American protestant love without unhealthy and uncomfortable Italian overtones, love which uses music to calm the fevered spirit of Saul and uplift the soul in German fashion, rather than to stir the senses or the passions in Italian operatic style. An energetic American lack of cynical European prurience, which Henry James often so tellingly describes, is emphasized by Alcott in her account of Laurie's relations with the Marches. Fellow-

ship, insisted on by Jo, appears here as an American ideal for governing the conduct between the sexes. Passion had better be quiet; and perhaps it will be if no one insists on it too much in advance. Later on, Laurie tears up the opera he had tried to write about Jo. In doing this, he seems to accept the incompatibility of sex and art with love and virtue; and, like Amy in Rome, he renounces the former and thus proves worthy to regain them—suitably transformed, of course, by the latter.

The passionate, creative element—frightening, powerful, and laden with danger—is set forth disapprovingly in both Amy and Laurie as an aspect of selfishness, laziness, and generally reprehensible narcissism entirely lacking in all the book's "good" characters, however imperfect they otherwise are. The action of the book in part consists in the taming of this dangerous force in both Amy and Laurie, a process which nevertheless then permits them to have one another and so cancel the threat they might otherwise represent to the rest of virtuous humanity. Amy, in an unusually explicit scene near the end of the book, after she is safely married to him, is shown stroking Laurie's nose and admiring his beauty, whereas Jo, during her long sway over him in the main part of the novel, had done nothing but tease and berate him and deflate his possible vanity and amorous temper. It is only after such harsh training for both these selfish and talented young beauties that they may marry; and it is also obvious that indeed they must. Laurie cannot marry Jo because he is immutably erotic, and she refuses to learn that lesson. Amy is saved from the "prostitution" of a wealthy, loveless marriage, Laurie is saved from "going to the devil" because the March morals have prevailed over them both, and they agree in unison to that domination.

But it is also very clear that they have been permitted to have no reciprocal influence, to teach nothing in return. In the course of *Little Women,* the creative strength and possible virtues of art and eroticism are gradually discredited, subdued and neutralized. Amy must give up art, Laurie must give up composing, and even Jo must abandon the sensational creations of her fantasy-life—her one such outlet—so that the negative and unworldly virtues may triumph: denial of the self; patience in suffering and, more important, in boredom; the willing abjuration of worldly pleasures. The two who have understood and acknowledged the creative, positive power of pleasure in physical beauty have got each other, and the rest can get on more comfortably without it and without wanting it.

At the core of all the interesting moral distributions in *Little Women* is not sex, however, but money. The riches of patience and self-denial are especially necessary to the self-respect of the women in this particular family because it has lost its material fortune, but not because it has always been poor. It is significant that the modest Marches are not "congenitally" poor at all, and they have very little understanding of the spiritual drain of that condition. Being really poor is very different from having lately become relatively poor, in an increasingly affluent society like that of later-nineteenth-century America. American wealth in Alcott's time was in the process of reaching the outrageous stage that was later to require antitrust legislation, income tax, and other basic socio-economic adjustments suitable to a democratic nation. The unworldly girls in **Little Women** must hold fast to what they hope are immutable values and to the capacity for inner steadfastness in a shifting and increasingly materialistic society. They are people with Old Money now vanished—a situation that could bring with it those advantages that leisure offers, such as education, reflection, the luxury of moral scruples, and the cultivation of the feelings. Indeed, these are the Marches' only legacy, and they must use and enjoy and hope to rely on them, always asserting their superiority over material riches newly, mindlessly, and soullessly acquired.

All this provides a foundation for an enduring American moral tale, one which continues to register as authentic even in a world changed out of all recognition. A notable absence in modern life of irksome rules for female decorum still cannot cancel the validity of the view that money may come and likewise go; that the status it quickly confers may be as quickly removed; and that some other sources of satisfaction and self-esteem had better be found.

When the March girls are first introduced, the two oldest are already following the first steps to modern American female success by earning money. But they are not pursuing careers, they are simply augmenting the family income; and a particular message comes through very clearly in every page of **Little Women.** Whereas impoverished American men may make use of drive, intellect, ambition, personal force, and the resources of public endeavor in order to gain the basic honor due to self-respecting males, poor women have only the resources of traditionally private female power and passive virtue. And these, as suggested in the case of Meg's enviousness, are best cultivated in circumstances of material ease. Poor middle-class women may not simply cut loose and try to make their way by their wits and strength of mind, as poor men may do, to preserve their self-esteem in degraded circumstances. Impoverished women have to bear not only poverty but the shame of poverty, because they may not wipe it out through positive action. As Amy admonishes Jo, poor women cannot even wield their moral power so successfully as rich women can, smiling and frowning according to their approval and disapproval, affecting the behavior and presumably elevating the souls of their male friends. As Amy explains it, poor and thus insignificant women who express moral scruples and judgments may risk being thought of as prudes and cranks, while rich women can perhaps do some good. Excellent goals for impoverished women seem to be to observe life closely but to keep their own counsel, to refine their own private judgments, and to develop an independence of mind that requires no reassuring responses. The female self may thus develop in its own esteem without requiring either male or material support.

Wealth—inherited, married, or earned—can thus be incidental to female personal satisfaction and sense of worth, and so can marriage. No attitude about money must be taken that might cloud the judgment: and so the judgment

must be continually strengthened, even while prudence may govern the scope of speech and action. Money may be thought of as an obviously desirable thing but clearly detachable from virtue, including one's own. One may marry a wealthy man or may inherit a fortune, or one may never do either; but one keeps one's personal integrity and freedom in all cases. Again, Alcott does not attempt to instruct the really poor, only the potentially impoverished. Being "a true gentlewoman" in this transcendent version of the American way is seen in part to consist of being supported only from within. Money and marriage are uncertain, especially for women: character lasts for life.

Alcott further demonstrates that to achieve a good character the practice of patience, kindness, discretion, and forbearance among one's fellows must totally absorb one's creative zeal. Such zeal may not be expended on the committed practice of any art, or any intellectual pursuit which might make the kind of demand that would promote the unseemly selfishness of the creative life. Alcott's little sermons against the seductions of serious art and abstract thought, at least for women, are peppered throughout **Little Women,** but she is most explicit in chapter thirty-four. Jo has been present at a serious philosophical discussion in the city; she feels fascinated and "pleasurably excited" until Professor Bhaer defends Truth, God, Religion, and all the Old Values. Then she is corrected: "She began to see that character is a better possession than money, rank, intellect, or beauty," or indeed, *talent,* one might believe Alcott privately added, in case it, too, should fail the severer tests of life.

Thus does Alcott excuse herself for not being a genius and justify the minorness of her own gifts. The linked faculties of erotic, artistic, and intellectual scope—again, especially for women—are sweepingly dismissed in favor of the cardinal virtues. These, she shows us, not only bring their own rewards but deserve and sweeten all other kinds of success. She is careful to offer her pilgrims no serious and interesting external temptations—no quick artistic triumphs, no plausible and exciting seducers, no possibilities of easy luxury, no compelling pressure of any kind toward the compromise of honor. Therefore we get no vivid image of the bitter costs virtue may exact, the very real losses entailed by those lasting gains she so eloquently describes and advocates. She may perhaps have felt them too keenly for words.

Humphrey Carpenter

SOURCE: "Louisa Alcott and the Happy Family," in *Secret Gardens: A Study of the Golden Age of Children's Literature,* Houghton Mifflin Company, 1985, pp. 86-99.

For the first ninety years of children's fiction in England and America, no one questioned the nature of the family. Home life was where the children were to get their religious and moral education. The rationalist authors of the moral tales which poured from the presses in the second half of the eighteenth century portrayed a home circle where the parents knew beyond doubt what was right and wrong, and passed on their certainties effortlessly to their offspring. Children often erred—thereby providing the authors with some sort of plot—but there was never any doubt as to where the path of righteousness lay. Such stories naturally accepted that family headship belonged to the father, and if he was not always much in evidence, that was simply because there were more important calls on his time than childish things. When he did appear, his authority was nothing less than God-like. Mr Fairchild in Mary Martha Sherwood's *The Fairchild Family* (1818), that most celebrated of hellfire evangelical novels for children, says to one of his sons: 'I stand in the place of God to you whilst you are a child', and he seems himself to have the power of deciding his children's salvation or damnation, as he warns them of the judgement that awaits sinners.

As it turned out, Mr Fairchild was one of the last of his species. The very evangelical fervour that had helped to create Mrs Sherwood's story undermined the notion of the family as the seat of moral and spiritual authority. Evangelical religion deals with the conversion of the individual, and writers of this persuasion soon discovered that children had plot-value not just as material for conversion but as the agents of that conversion. . . .

Quite apart from this, the old faith in the father-dominated family as the source of moral wisdom seems to have become shaky by about 1850, judging from the fact that the stream of moral tales for the young dried up in the 1830s. Its end was marked in 1830 by Catherine Sinclair's *Holiday House* (Lewis Carroll's 1861 Christmas present to the Liddells), a book which is about parentless children on the rampage, with the substitute parent (a jolly uncle) abdicating responsibility: the only piece of advice he gives the children is 'never crack nuts with your teeth'.

A few writers, notably Charlotte M. Yonge, continued to regard the family as the source of moral wisdom, and did not question this role. But elsewhere there were plenty of hints that a change of attitude was taking place. Lewis Carroll had nothing to say about parenthood, other than his depiction of the Duchess throwing her baby casually across the kitchen to Alice; but [Charles] Kingsley and [George] MacDonald are more explicit. Both have a striking interest in mothers or mother-figures, rather than fathers, as the moral arbiter Mrs Doasyouwouldbedoneby, North Wind, and so on—and both allow children to convert their elders: Tom the water-baby softens the hard heart of Grimes, and Diamond in *At the Back of the North Wind* reforms a drunken cabman. Kingsley has almost nothing to say about fathers, but MacDonald pays a good deal of attention to them, and though he generally paints them as kindly they are not the stern upholders of authority. Peter, Curdie's father, is his son's helper rather than his leader, ready to follow the boy's wisdom and judgement in matters of importance, and when the Princess Irene's 'king-papa' really comes on to the stage in *The Princess and Curdie,* we see an ailing old man, the dupe of his courtiers, who has to be nursed back to strength

and wisdom by his daughter and Curdie. Even when healthy again he remains childlike; his greatest pleasure is to let the housekeeper's small grand-daughter play with his crown, using it as a pretend porridge-pot.

This subversive attitude to the old structure of the family was not portrayed in any nineteenth-century 'realistic' novel for children written in England. But in the work of an American, Louisa M. Alcott, we see clearly the questioning of parental authority which is hinted at by the English fantasy writers. Alcott was driven to write in this fashion about home life because of the extraordinary nature of her own family.

We know that she was brought up, in her own nursery days, on the moral tales of Maria Edgeworth, the most accomplished of the old rational school of English lady writers for children. But the secure, placid world of Miss Edgeworth's *Harry and Lucy* stories must surely have highlighted for Louisa Alcott the instability of the home in which she found herself. She was the daughter of Bronson Alcott, who, depending on one's outlook, was either a major American thinker and educationalist, or a lazy good-for-nothing with a command of humbug equalling that of the Wizard of Oz. Amos Alcox (to give him his original name) had begun adult life as a travelling salesman, peddling fancy goods around his native Connecticut and further afield. He quickly developed a talent for making no money whatsoever and accumulating large debts—a characteristic that was to remain with him for the rest of his life, and was quite unaccompanied by bad conscience. He also changed his surname from Alcox to Alcott, apparently to avoid dirty jokes, and called himself by his second baptismal name. Under this new label, Bronson Alcott, he soon came to believe that he had a personal mission from God to set up schools on Transcendental principles. Quite what were those principles was hard to say, since a feature of Transcendentalism, as practised by Alcox/Alcott and other Americans of the same persuasion around the early 1830s, was a refusal to define ideas. Bronson Alcott's 'teaching method', if it can be called that, was to let idealistic talk pour from what one of his pupils called his 'dreamy brain', and hold Conversations with the children, so as to draw out of them talents which he believed were already there. Nothing was to be forced in—which was just as well, since Alcott's own store of education had been scanty, and he really had little *to* force in.

While trying to run a school on this basis in the city of Boston, he took on as 'female assistant' the sister of a preacher, a lady named Abigail May. The school was not much of a success, but he married her. Then they set off together to Philadelphia to run another, and it was there that she gave birth to their first two children. Anna, born in 1831, was a docile blonde whose gentle nature harmonised from the first with her father's dreaminess; Louisa May, born two years later, was quite different. Unlike her father and elder sister she was dark in hair and complexion (Alcott actually considered fair colouring a sign of grace); she had an angular, fretful personality, and was constantly chafing against the world.

Her father found it much harder to instil notions of right and wrong into her than into the placid Anna. On the other hand, Louisa was on much closer terms than Anna with their mother, whose rather pugnacious, masculine looks she had inherited. As an adult, her writing was to display both these characteristics—at one moment fretting against life for not allowing her to be as she wished, then turning with security to the protection and reassurance of maternal love.

The Philadelphia venture failed in due course, and Bronson Alcott opened his next school back in Boston, this time in the Masonic Temple, with a redoubtable spinster named Elizabeth Peabody (the original of Miss Birdseye in Henry James's *The Bostonians*) as his helper. The Alcotts named their third child Elizabeth (born in 1835) after her. But even Miss Peabody, who had a boundless appetite for good causes, found her patience and enthusiasm tried by Bronson, whom she said had a 'want of humility' and lacked a 'sober estimate of his own place among his fellows'. He published a volume of *Conversations on the Gospels,* based on talks he had with his pupils, but Boston society was offended by the way in which he had led the children on to ask, in connection with the birth of Christ, about such things as conception and circumcision. (One child remarked that babies were made 'out of the naughtiness of other people'.) Then he admitted a black child into his school—he was a committed Abolitionist—and this was too much for public opinion. The Temple School closed in 1840, and the Alcotts moved out to the small Massachusetts town of Concord, to be near Ralph Waldo Emerson, who liked and sympathised with Bronson and his ideas.

Concord was by now becoming a kind of Mecca of Transcendentalism, with writers and thinkers of like mind setting up home there. Alcott hopefully called it 'Concordia', and found a cottage at a low rent where he reckoned to be able to keep his family by growing vegetables for them. Meat, even if he could have afforded it, was in fact forbidden by the particular Transcendental code he had drawn up; a contemporary observed of him in verse:

> Give him carrots, potatoes, squash, turnips and
>   peas,
> And a handful of crackers without any cheese,
> And a cup of cold water to wash down all these,
> And he'd prate of the spirit as long as you please.

'Prating of the spirit' was about the only activity (other than growing vegetables) in which Bronson Alcott was now willing to engage, since the world had rejected his educational ideas. He was perfectly happy to accept fees for holding public Conversations to expound his thought, but that was as far as wage-earning went. After a while, he and a number of fellow-Transcendentalists began an experiment in communal living on a run-down farm near 'Concordia' that they named Fruitlands. The place was soon crammed with dietary reformers and assorted cranks, including a nudist. Most of the work was done by Alcott's wife Abigail, always known as 'Abba'—an appropriate name, considering its Aramaic meaning, 'father';

Photograph of Orchard House, the Alcott family home in Concord, Massachusetts.

for it was she who now carried the entire burden of providing for her family. She laboured at Fruitlands, doing all the chores and bringing up four children (the youngest, May, was born in 1840) while the men preoccupied themselves with idealism. Louisa, aged seven, observed the goings-on with a certain detached amusement—one member of the all-vegetarian community, she alleged, was sent packing for the sin of *eating a fish tail* at a neighbour's house.

The Fruitlands venture, unaptly named, collapsed after a few months, and there was nearly a break-up of the Alcott marriage, Abba having realised that her husband was no longer prepared to lift a finger for herself and the children. 'Anna and I cried in bed,' recorded Louisa in her journal, 'and I prayed to God to keep us all together.' She consoled herself by copying out the hymns from her favourite book, *The Pilgrim's Progress.* In fact the family stayed together, largely thanks to the charity of friends— Emerson would sometimes place a banknote under a book or behind a candlestick in the Alcott living room, 'when he thinks Father wants a little money, and no one will help him earn'. Abba was in a state of constant exhaustion and depression, but she managed to find the emotional energy to help and stimulate her second daughter— largely, no doubt, because she and Louisa were of the same physical and emotional type: dark, mannish-looking, full of nervous energy. When Louisa was in her early teens she wrote in her journal:

> I am old for my age, and don't care much for girls' things. People think I'm wild and queer; but Mother understands and helps me . . . Now I'm going to *work really,* for I feel a true desire to improve, and be a help and comfort, not a care, to my dear mother.

She soon had her chance to carry out this resolution, for the family moved into Boston to try to make some money. Bronson did nothing more than encourage people to pay him for the privilege of listening to him talk, but Abba earned a small wage by distributing charity to the poor (the activity which, like Marmee in *Little Women,* she liked best), and she, Anna, and Louisa held reading and writing classes for black adults. The moment the girls were old enough to undertake paid work by themselves, they did so; Louisa took jobs as a teacher, a lady's companion, and lower down the social scale, as a seamstress, maid, or even washerwoman. 'Father idle,' she wrote laconically in her journal. She began to earn a little by authorship, writing melodramatic little pieces of fiction for the newspapers and magazines. This sort of thing came naturally to her, for she and her sisters had long had the private amusement of performing plays, which Louisa wrote, with such titles as *The Captives of Castille, or the Moorish Maiden's Vow.* But she only received a few dollars from the newspaper editors, and life continued to be very hard. Her younger sister Elizabeth became ill with scarlet fever, caught from a neighbour whom Abba had been nursing; not surprisingly, considering her family's never-ending state of struggle, Elizabeth lost the will to live, became half-deranged, and died at the age of twenty-three. Anna, the placid sister, found herself a dull

but worthy insurance salesman named John Pratt as a husband; Louisa contemplated suicide, considering throwing herself off the Mill Dam into Boston's Back Bay, but she changed her mind, and soon afterwards started to make a lot more money, by pouring out dime-novel romances of an even more lurid kind.

Typical of these was **"Pauline's Passion and Punishment,"** one of many 'yellow-back' stories she produced pseudonymously or anonymously (her idealistic father was not let in on the secret) during the 1860s. Pauline is a sex-kitten (there is no other word for her) who has been jilted by her lover, and gets her revenge by marrying a handsome teenage Latin American and flaunting him in front of the lover and the woman he has wedded. The story ends with the jealous lover pushing Pauline's child-husband over a cliff, and the lover's wife (who has developed a passion for the boy) jumping after him.

Nothing could be further from *Little Women,* and one may be inclined to dismiss such stuff as merely a way to earn money fast—**"Pauline's Passion and Punishment"** got its creator a hundred dollar prize from a magazine. In fact this story, and others from what might be called the 'hidden years' of Louisa Alcott, says quite a lot about its author. For a start, the heroine is a protagonist and manipulator, whereas the stereotyped heroine of Gothic fiction is submissive and ultra-feminine, a victim. And there is something else that Pauline, creature of dime-novel as she may be, has in common with her creator.

Louisa Alcott's adolescence was marked by an almost complete absence of love-affairs. Her only romantic feelings seem to have been for a man fifteen years older than herself, no less than Henry David Thoreau, who with his brother John was running a school in Concord which the Alcott girls attended. Louisa wrote devoted letters to him, which she never sent. From this, and from the fact that in the sequel to *Little Women* she makes Jo marry a German professor of advanced years, we may infer that she was capable of being attracted by men old enough to be her father. (Was she actually looking for a substitute father, her real one having failed to perform his role?) Yet, like the passionate Pauline, she seems also to have been susceptible, by the time she reached maturity, to adolescent boys. She is known to have been very fond, if only in a maternal way, of one Ladislas Wisniewski, an eighteen-year-old Pole whom she met on a trip to Europe (as paid companion to an invalid) when she was thirty-three, shortly before she wrote *Little Women*; she said he was one of the originals of Laurie in that book. It is also recorded that, at the age of twenty-eight, she liked to spend the time with Ralph Waldo Emerson's sixteen-year-old son Julian, and there are hints of other attachments to teenagers. Pauline's choice of a boy of nineteen for her husband, in that lurid story, seems to reflect this inclination.

One may surmise that Louisa liked to be mother to young boys—and in the later part of the *Little Women* saga her heroine Jo does just that, mothering a crowd of young males at the school she and her Professor Bhaer are running (on vaguely Bronson Alcott principles). By the time of *Jo's Boys,* the final book in the series, Jo has become not just 'Aunty Jo' or 'Mrs Jo' but 'Mother Bhaer'. Yet if she was mother, and if she sought for a father in her yearnings for Thoreau, she also liked to *be* the father.

In the family plays she wrote and performed with her sisters, Louisa always took the male roles, just as Jo does on similar occasions in *Little Women.* It was natural: she had inherited her mother's masculine features. But one has the suspicion that the plays were written largely so that she could play these roles. Like Jo, she seems to have felt most true to her own nature when she could put on doublet and boots.

> No gentlemen were admitted; so Jo played male parts to her heart's content, and took immense satisfaction in a pair of russet-leather boots given her by a friend. These boots, an old foil, and a slashed doublet once used by an artist for some picture, were Jo's chief treasures, and appeared on all occasions. . . .

Louisa's elder sister Anna always played the leading ladies in these performances. Anna's counterpart in *Little Women* is Jo's sister Meg, and as the book progresses the reader is left in no doubt as to Jo's strength of feeling for her. 'She gets prettier each day, and I'm in love with her sometimes,' she tells her mother, in a letter signed 'Topsy-Turvey Jo'. When Meg gets engaged to John Brooke (who is almost as colourless as his real-life counterpart, Anna's husband John Pratt), Jo sighs: 'I just wish I could marry Meg myself, and keep her safe in the family.'

Anna Alcott's betrothal and marriage to John Pratt caused Louisa pain that seems, if anything, to have been deeper than that suffered by Jo. 'I moaned in private over my great loss, and said I'd never forgive J. for taking Anna from me,' she wrote in her journal. That entry, says one of her biographers, Martha Saxton, 'doesn't convey the violent anguish' the announcement of the engagement gave her. This was in the spring of 1858, when Louisa was twenty-six; her contemplation of suicide came about six months later. Was she really in love with her sister?

Not altogether surprisingly, she looked on the outbreak of the Civil War as offering, if not the solution to her difficulties, at least a break in the perpetual chain of her family's struggles to survive, and perhaps her private emotional-sexual sufferings too. She went as a nurse to a war hospital in Washington, found the conditions almost intolerable, caught typhoid, was heavily dosed with calomel, contracted mercury poisoning in consequence, and was sent home to her family in a broken-down state. Yet the experience seems to have been stimulating; she published a book about it, *Hospital Sketches* (1863), which made her a small reputation, and on the strength of this she found a publisher for a novel called *Moods* (1864), whose heroine has a romantic attachment to someone much like her beloved Thoreau. Its reception, however, was sufficiently poor for her to abandon any further plans for serious authorship for the time being, and turn back to 'rubbishy tales for they pay the best'. One of the pieces of hack-work she was asked to undertake was the editorship

of a Boston children's magazine called *Merry's Museum,* whose founder had been the celebrated popular pedagogue Peter Parley. Simultaneously a publisher asked her to write 'a *girls'* story', this being a newly discovered type of popular fiction. She agreed to begin work on both. 'Didn't like either,' she wrote in her journal.

The editorship soon faded out, and the book was done quickly—twelve chapters in a month or so, and the remaining eleven in a few weeks more. It was not easygoing, compared to the sensational dime-novel stuff—'I plod away', she said—and when the publisher (one Thomas Niles of Roberts Brothers in Boston) saw the first twelve chapters he was not enthusiastic. 'He thought it *dull*; so do I,' she wrote. 'But [I] work away and mean to try the experiment; for lively, simple books are very much needed for girls, and perhaps I can supply the need.'

Mr Niles and Louisa Alcott were not altogether wrong; *Little Women* really *is* dull, if read purely for narrative excitement. Almost nothing happens. The March girls (whose surname is a variant on that of Louisa's mother's surname, May, which Louisa herself bore as a second Christian name) manage to enjoy Christmas despite the absence of their father at the Civil War. They perform a play, meet a neighbour's grandson called Laurie, run a family magazine and a private post office, and have gentle flirtations. Beth nearly dies of scarlet fever, Meg becomes engaged to John Brooke, and Father comes home just in time to join the celebrations. The book seems at first glance to be no more than a series of sketches of life in a rather saccharinely portrayed but otherwise unremarkable family. The casual reader might suppose the Marches to be really quite conventional. Yet a second look shows that the story is a veiled account of all that Louisa had suffered, and at the same time a kind of celebration of the fact that she had survived. It castigates family life for imposing suffering, and yet asserts that only in the family can sanity be found.

She had a literary model, as well as her own experiences, to draw on. The genre of 'girls' stories' was new—indeed, had hardly established itself—but in England, Charlotte M. Yonge had already produced one notable book about a girl's experiences within her family circle, *The Daisy Chain* (1856). Since Louisa Alcott was devoted to Miss Yonge's tear-jerking bestseller *The Heir of Redclyffe* (Jo in *Little Women* is seen weeping over it), we may suspect that she had read *The Daisy Chain* too. In it she would have found, on the very first page, a character to attract her sympathy: Ethel, one of the daughters of the house, 'a thin, lank, angular, sallow girl, just fifteen, trembling from head to foot with restrained eagerness as she tried to curb her tone into the requisite civility'. The book describes Ethel's struggles with conventional sex-roles: she learns Latin and Greek from a brother's books, and is full of energetic plans for setting the world to rights, but she is eventually persuaded to suppress her boyishness and concentrate on ladylike pursuits. Not only does she anticipate Jo March in *Little Women;* her family's surname is May.

The Daisy Chain takes its title from Ethel's father's nick-name for his family; similarly *Little Women* is named after what Mr March would like his daughters to be. In the case of Jo, on whose personality *Little Women* hangs, the title is deeply ironic. She is neither little (she is 'very tall' and has 'big hands and feet'), nor womanly. She is 'rapidly shooting up into a woman' but 'didn't like it'. Masculinity is her guiding principle. 'I'm the man of the family now papa is away,' she tells her sisters at the beginning of the book, and the story is constructed to demonstrate the truth of this statement. She acts as broth-er, lover, and father to her sisters. She woos them in male costume during the Christmas play, earns money for them (by selling a story), and, in a revealing moment, has all her hair cut off:

> 'Your hair! Your beautiful hair!' 'Oh, Jo, how could you? Your one beauty.' 'My dear girl, there was no need of this.' 'She doesn't look like Jo any more, but I love her dearly for it!'

> As everyone exclaimed, and Beth hugged the cropped head tenderly, Jo assumed an indifferent air . . . 'It will do my brains good to have that mop taken off; my head feels deliciously light and cool, and the barber said I could soon have a curly crop, which will be boyish, becoming, and easy to keep in order. I'm satisfied; so please take the money, and let's have supper.'

She has done this ostensibly to get money (by selling the hair) to help her father, who is in hospital in Washington; but her action coincides with the departure from home of her mother, who up to then has been Jo's rival as father-figure. Meanwhile, the family's real father, Mr March, has to remain offstage for the entire drama, making his appearance only for the final tableau. It was not just that Louisa Alcott could not fit her own father into her utopi-an fictional household (which clearly she could not); Mr March's absence is essential to Jo's exploration of the male role.

When *Little Women* was published, in the late summer of 1868, Louisa Alcott began to receive letters about the sequel she had promised to write if the book should prove popular: 'Girls write to ask who the little women marry, as if that was the only end and aim of a woman's life. I *won't* marry Jo to Laurie to please any one.' This was not just cussedness towards her readers. A marriage of Jo to Laurie, the archetypal boy-next-door, would have been out of the question, for deep-seated reasons. Laurie in fact *is* Jo, in another manifestation; tall, dark and coltish, notably effeminate for his sex just as she is masculine for hers. He has 'small hands and feet', cuts flowers for her in a ladylike fashion, plays the piano beautifully, is 'not very strong', and, to top it all, is known by a female nickname: 'My first name is Theodore, but I don't like it, for the fellows called me Dora, so I made them say Lau-rie instead.' Other than these characteristics, Laurie has very little personality. He is in fact quite unnecessary to the story as a separate character: Jo herself is the real boy-next-door. In the sequel, he is supposed to be in love

with Jo, but this is scarcely convincing, and he is very quickly persuaded to change his mind and marry Jo's fluffily pretty little sister Amy instead—as Jo herself would surely have liked to do.

Although *Little Women* describes Jo's assumption of the masculine role, it is not an account of a battle won. The Jo-Louisa character loses out in the end, not so much to real men as to her own sex—to Marmee, her mother, who once fought the same battle herself, and lost it. Marmee, we are told, was once as impetuous and hasty-tempered (that is, as masculine) as Jo, but she finally subdued her real nature to convention:

> 'Yes, I've learned to check the hasty words that rise to my lips; and when I feel that they mean to break out against my will, I just go away a minute, and give myself a little shake for being so weak and wicked,' answered Mrs March . . . 'Your father, Jo, . . . helped and comforted me, and showed me that I must try to practise all the virtues I would have my little girls possess, for I was their example.'

The 'pilgrimage' which Marmee encourages the girls to make throughout the story—suggested by *The Pilgrim's Progress,* which they are rereading—is not (for Jo) the spiritual journey it appears to be, but a quest, undertaken reluctantly enough, for a conventionally feminine sex-role. By the end of the book, in spite of all her masculine role-playing, in spite even of her shorn head, Jo has reached that goal, and is recognised by her father as a true 'little women':

> 'In spite of the curly crop, I don't see the "son Jo" whom I left a year ago,' said Mr March. 'I see a young lady who pins her collar straight, laces her boots neatly, and neither whistles, talks slang, nor lies on the rug as she used to do . . . I rather miss my wild girl; but if I get a strong, helpful, tender-hearted woman in her place, I shall feel quite satisfied.'

And if we doubt whether Louisa Alcott herself had, like Jo, lost that particular battle, we need only turn to the pages of the Boston *Woman's Journal,* to which she con-tributed frequently after *Little Women* had made her fa-mous. She has been represented as a feminist, but her articles in this ladies' magazine are full of 'womanly' gush: 'The homemaking, the comfort, the sympathy, the grace and atmosphere that a true woman can provide is the noble part, and embraces all that is helpful for soul as well as body,' she writes in a piece about domestic arts. It is, she says, a woman's 'fate to be called upon to lead a quiet self-sacrificing life with peculiar trials, needs and joys, and it seems to me that a very simple one is fitted to us whose hearts are usually more alive than heads, and whose hands are tied in many ways.' Jo March has truly become Josephine.

Little Women, then, is a record of a struggle lost, and along the way it communicates something of the misery that Louisa had felt during her own battle. The turning-point in the novel comes when Amy, in revenge for being left out of an expedition, destroys the manuscript of a set of fairy stories which Jo has been working at for several years. Amy's behaviour seems to us quite outrageous, and Jo's anger—which allows her to let Amy ice-skate in a dangerous place, and so have a minor accident—is quite understandable, almost justifiable. But the accident causes Jo terrible remorse, and it is from this moment on that, with Marmee's encouragement, she tries to tame her masculine aggression and to cultivate feminine self-control. The incident seems to stand for something more than itself; Amy has, after all, symbolically destroyed Jo's capacity as a wage-earner, and has attacked her deep attachment to the life of the imagination, which throughout the book goes hand in hand with her masculinity—she is constantly found immersed in works of imaginative literature (*Undine, The Heir of Redclyffe,* Dickens) which seem to offer an escape from the family confines. Amy is cutting Jo off from all this, and bringing her back into the family fold.

The story is about Jo's struggles with the concept of 'family' just as much as it is about her sex-role battle. Near the beginning, she observes to herself 'that keeping her temper at home was a much harder task than facing a rebel or two down South', and for the first part of the book she is reluctant to put herself second to the needs of the family. As Meg says on the first page, 'we can make our little sacrifices, and ought to do it gladly. But I am afraid I don't.' These words must reflect Louisa Alcott's own feelings during the years when she had to be seamstress, washerwoman, hired domestic, and drudge of every kind, simply to support the family. But after Amy's destruction of her manuscript, Jo abandons any thoughts of independence, and instead conducts a battle to keep the family together; the final chapters are largely concerned with her hopes of frustrating Meg's romance with John Brooke, because a marriage is going to break up the family—Brooke's sin is that he is making 'a hole in the family'.

Louisa Alcott, like Jo in the early stages of her 'pilgrimage', at first hated the burden of supporting her family. But as the years passed she came to welcome that burden, and to make it her emotional preoccupation. She had done so much for the family that it *must* all have been worthwhile. And so Marmee in *Little Women* gives her daughters an exhortation to 'Make this home happy, so that you may be fit for homes of your own if they are offered you, and contented here if they are not'; and the voice that speaks this platitude is really that of Louisa, whose family home *had* to be happy, since it was all that she possessed. *Little Women* had originated as a piece of subversion against the family and parental authority, but had ended up by declaring its support for those very institutions—by portraying the family as an Arcadia. . . .

[Alcott thus] became a traitor to her destructive cause, and was in the end responsible for an act of construction, the creation of the Arcadian family novel. In England, meanwhile, construction had not yet been achieved. Kingsley, Carroll, and MacDonald had shaken the foundations of faith and had exposed the hollowness of the old ideas

upon which children's literature had been built; but they had scarcely managed to put anything in their place. They left that to a new generation of writers.

Ruth K. MacDonald

SOURCE: "Louisa May Alcott's *Little Women:* Who is Still Reading Miss Alcott and Why," in *Touchstones: Reflections on the Best in Children's Literature, Vol. 1,* Children's Literature Association, 1985, pp. 13-20.

Louisa May Alcott's books continue to occupy space on library shelves, and some of her novels can still be found in bookstores. At least part of the reason that children, especially girls, continue to read Alcott is that her books are highly recommended by adults who read them when they were children, and who find rereading them similar to visiting an old friend. For children today, however, the experience of Alcott cannot be so comfortable; her books are certainly not as exhilarating as much of the modern fiction available for children, and Alcott's style, with its frequent copious descriptions and occasional authorial intrusions, is somewhat archaic, perhaps even obsolete, quite different from the simplified vocabularies and syntax of many modern novels. Certainly the multi-cultural, quickly paced urban lives that many American children lead today would not predispose them to the leisurely, sentimental journey that Alcott offers. Yet that journey still has much to offer them.

There is another large group of readers who keeps Alcott's reputation alive. One need only note the many titles of critical and biographical works on Alcott in the past decade to realize that academic women find Alcott fascinating. Perhaps this interest exists because, as Janice Alberghene has pointed out, Alcott deals with many of the issues that modern women still face: how to combine marriage and a career, how to be a professional in a world which may judge women's efforts to be inferior, how to assert one's principles and rights without so offending the powers that be that the granting of those rights is jeopardized. In short, Alcott is a feminist, who struggles to combine both womanly duties and manly pursuits; the tension that results from this struggle keeps academic readers interested, and they in turn help to keep Alcott's reputation alive.

Little Women, Alcott's first and best novel for children, continues to receive the most attention. Once a reader is hooked on Jo March's conflict between societal expectations about "little women" and her own aspirations to be somebody, to do something worthy of praise, he (or more likely she, as I will call the reader from now on) is likely to continue through the whole Alcott canon. The other books are less satisfactory, but good enough so that the reader keeps on reading. If she is lucky, she will discover Alcott's gothic short stories, and perhaps ever her adult novels, though modern editions of these works are few, and unlikely to be found anywhere but in college libraries. If she does find these adult works, the vivid contrast between Miss Alcott, "the children's friend," and the sometimes anonymous or pseudonymous voice of the adult works, may force her to pause and reevaluate those works otherwise uncritically perceived as perfectly charming and appropriate for children.

Of course, Alcott's children's books seem to be quite safe to recommend, especially from the point of view of the modern censor; unlike a good deal of modern "problem literature" or "new realism" for children, Alcott no longer shocks the reader with her subject matter. There are no promiscuous, drug-dealing anorexics here, and ever since "Christopher Columbus," Jo March's favorite expletive, ceased to offend even the most delicate sensibility, no one has seen fit to criticize the language. Alcott and her family were all believers in and pursuers of social reform throughout their lives, but there is nothing in *Little Women* that reveals that authorial predisposition, and even in Alcott's time, most readers found little to take exception to. Even those readers, past or present, who know that the South won the War Between the States, find this Civil War novel set in New England worthy of their total approbation.

From the point of view of the child reader, furthermore, there is much real appeal in the warmth of the family relations. Marmee is hardly ever really angry; certainly she never raises her voice at her daughters, and she is always willing to explain why she says what she says and does what she does. She is never peremptory, never harried, and only occasionally does the reader see a crack in her maternal veneer. The sisters may have on-going squabbles, but even these, for the most part, seem under control. The girls are basically good and easy to sympathize with. And like good girls in fairy tales, they get the traditional reward at the end: parental approval for their hard work and achievements, and loving husbands and children. Though the sisters never get to be princesses, their husbands are attractive and attentive, and their lack of wealth is not so troubling, since there always seems to be enough to keep the families happy, without spoiling them on the one hand and depriving them on the other.

Americans have always celebrated the golden isolation of the home from the turbulence of the outside world. From Puritan times, colonists saw the family as the model upon which the commonwealth was based and believed in the sanctity of the family unit. Americans are inventors of the idea of home as more than just a dwelling, of the terms "hometown" and "homesick." So as a group, we like and enthusiastically recommend portrayals of such happy homes, in the faith that such portrayals can perpetuate a sense of the value of home in our young.

Little Women seems to offer that sort of portrayal and to be a safe, unthreatening book. But Alcott deserves the benefit of the doubt about her conventionality. We need to suspend our modern standards of judgment, and try to see the work through the eyes of Alcott's contemporaries.

In its own time, *Little Women* was unique in its restrained impulse to preach. By modern standards, Alcott intrudes

Louisa May Alcott, 1876.

herself into the novel entirely too often to be acceptable; but by the standards of her time she stood on her soapbox hardly at all. She did not preach to children about right behavior, but rather let characters and readers work out their own conclusions through the situations and actions in the novel. Marmee may be full of good advice, but she does not offer it unless asked, and only in amounts appropriate to the situation.

To the reader used to dealing with juvenile delinquents in realistic fiction, the girls may seem nearly perfect already; but before Alcott, no one else had even tried to create faulty characters worthy of improvement. Good characters were models; bad characters incorrigible and exemplars of the negative results of their actions. Alcott's abilities in fully-rounded characterization alone earn this novel a place in the canon.

Modern readers have lost their taste for the sentimental novel and may find Alcott somewhat treacly and lacrimose; but here too Alcott shows her restraint. By the standards of her time she was not manipulating the reader to tears to the extent that other sentimental writers did, and though she does have one deathbed scene, it is short by comparison to those of her contemporaries, and certainly short of melodramatic excess. She did not introduce the death simply to indulge the readers' demands for bathetic release, but because her readers had demanded a continuation of her original March family story. The original story was based on her own family; and since her own sister had died, she felt justified in presenting her death as part of the autobiographical reality of the narrative.

It is clear, then, that the March family story is not a simple sentimental formula without any dramatic tension or interest. And while children are hardly literature's best or most articulate critics, I think that at some level even they realize that Alcott has more on her mind and in her writing than just her loving, charming, fictional family happily living together in genteel poverty. For the young reader old enough to read and remember carefully, there will be a clear message about the value of being comfortable in clothing rather than being stylish, about the intrigue of a personality that is not restrained in saying what it wants and in laughing out loud, however boisterously, at jokes. As modern as parents are now be trying to be in raising their daughters, there are still a number of rules about being a "lady" which every little girl at some time comes to resent. Jo March articulates clearly her resentment at the restraints that the "little woman" role imposed upon her. She may be admonished by her sisters and mother for her frankness in responding, but she articulates for the reader socialized enough to know that one does not always say what one thinks that such strictures are unfair and uncomfortable. Jo receives little rebuke; the reader receives none. So there is vicarious criticism of the prevailing social order on behalf of the reader, and yet she need not worry about the consequences.

For Alcott, the only way to do manly things in a man's world while still being a woman was to be competent at the housewifely arts, such as cooking, cleaning, and sewing, while at the same time pursuing other interests outside the home. The compromise she posits here is a workable answer to the modern girl's and woman's dilemma about combining male and female. In fact, it is one which will probably guarantee success in both sexes' domains. In her last book, *Jo's Boys,* Alcott complained more stridently about the burdens which such a dual role places on a woman, and encouraged the co-eds at Laurence College to consider spinsterhood and career as an acceptable alternative to combining marriage and family; but she did not dare to take such an outspoken stand earlier in her career. And even in *Jo's Boys,* homemaking is still a worthy choice of career for a woman to dedicate her life to. At the same time, Alcott did not discourage women from pursuing careers outside the home. And she suggests quite clearly that work is ennobling and rewarding; having one's own money, however small the sum, gives one status in the world and a feeling, if not the actual achievement, of independence and autonomy. Work is also a healthy solution to depression about the unfairness of life, and to the langor of inactivity. Though her solution may have encouraged several generations of readers to try it for themselves—after all, if Marmee and Jo March could do it, why shouldn't they?—it has also led contemporary women to question the stress that such a burden places on such "Super Women." But for many readers, Alcott solves a problem to which there seemed to be no solution.

Even though the surface of the novel suggests that everything is placid and graceful in the relations of the family members, the careful reader realizes that there is a great deal of sibling rivalry going on in *Little Women.* The tension, subtly presented so that Alcott's less perceptive readers could not object to the novel's surface, does much to enhance the novel's appeal. When Amy burns Jo's notebook, Jo's anger surfaces, and the reader feels that Jo would be more than justified in killing Amy. After all, Amy's provocation is simply childish pique; Jo will not let her come along to a theater outing with Laurie and herself, certainly not a substantial enough provocation to justify Amy's heinous destruction of Jo's hard and irrecoverable work. When Jo goes skating with Laurie later in the same chapter, Amy once again traipses after them, invading their comaraderie the same way she wanted to in the first place. Once again, Amy provokes, and Marmee, as idealized as she is, does not intrude to prevent Amy from being a brat. When Amy nearly drowns by falling through the ice, Jo feels remorse, and all is forgiven between the sisters—but not for long. Throughout the novel, Jo and Amy continue to irritate each other. Amy criticizes Jo's mannish manners; Jo criticizes Amy's social pretentions. Though the rivalry is never again as clearly demonstrated as in this chapter, it is always present as a continuous source of interest and realism.

Marmee's status as the ideal American mother was not nearly as clear in Alcott's original version of the novel. For example, when Marmee first enters the door in chapter one, in the version that most girls read today, a revision that Alcott substituted after the first two editions, Alcott describes her as "a tall, motherly lady, with a 'can-I-help-you' look about her which was truly delightful. She was not elegantly dressed, but a noble-looking woman . . ." The first edition gives a much more revealing description, one perhaps much closer to Alcott's estimation of her own mother: "a stout, motherly lady, with a 'can-I-help-you' look about her which was truly delightful. She wasn't a particularly handsome person, but mothers are always lovely to their children . . ." Alcott edited out her frankness about her mother's physical appearance here and elsewhere, and eliminated many of the mother's quick retorts and willingness to comment on others faults; yet the traits still persist, revealed primarily in Marmee's pursed lips, which Marmee tells Jo and the reader is her way of containing her temper. When irascible Aunt March ungraciously consents to lend Marmee the money she needs to rush to the side of her stricken husband, Marmee reads the letter containing Aunt March's reply with the telltale configuration of lips.

When Marmee lets the girls follow their own self-indulgent inclinations to do no work for the summer in order to pursue idleness, she again reveals her humanity as she forces the experiment to a disastrous ending. During the first week of the experiment, she and the household servant try to fill in the gaps that the girls' idleness have left in the household labor force; but by the end of the week she gives the servant a day off to rest and deliberately absents herself, so that the girls will have to shift for themselves, and will appreciate more sincerely the efforts made on their behalf during the earlier part of the week. Marmee does not really allow events to follow their own course to calamity; she forces the issue, giving play to her own anger about having been unacknowledged and unappreciated in the early part of the week. As sister Meg reports,

> Mother isn't sick, only very tired, and she says she is going to stay quietly in her room all day, and let us do the best we can. It's a very queer thing for her to do, she don't act a bit like herself; but she says it has been a hard week for her, so we mustn't grumble, but take care of ourselves.

As the reader soons finds, there is much more anger beneath Marmee's surface than implied by the charming, loving, maternal bosom presented to the world.

As Nina Auerbach has pointed out, there is a lot to be said for the seductive power of that maternal bosom. As much as Marmee's maternal instincts are otherwise innocuous, her love is so all-accepting and her desire to be a mother to all comers so all-consuming, that she manages to convince her daughters, and even the boy next door, that life as her child is a permanent status. Auerbach notes that although the novel purports to be about growing up, its equally salient message is that, in the fictional world of this novel, one need never grow up. One can remain Marmee's chosen and cherished darling forever if one so desires. The sisters seldom chafe at the maternal apron strings. Even when they marry, they barely move away from home, being able to stand a separation of only a few houses down the street. This offer of eternal childhood explains much of the book's charm. Not only is Marmee the perfect mother, she is also eternally available, both to the reader in the stasis in which she exists in the book, and to her daughters. As Marmee herself says when a troubled Jo comes to her for advice about Meg's impending marriage, "It is natural and right you should all go to homes of your own, in time; but I do want to keep my girls as long as I can."

The book also continues to be read, I think, because of its appeal to the pleasures of consumerism—an apparent contradiction to the spiritual values it proclaims. John Bunyan's spiritual guide *The Pilgrim's Progress* is a specifically posited model for the March sisters to follow, for as early as chapter one they all decide to shoulder their burdens and go forward in their earthly progresses to their eventual heavenly perfection. But as spiritual and highminded as the sisters are supposed to be, the reader tends to agree with Jo March's famous opening line in the novel, "Christmas won't be Christmas without any presents." Though the line shows Jo and her sisters to be utterly misguided spiritually, it also shows them thoroughly and sympathetically possessed by the pleasures of consumption inevitably associated with the Yuletide season. Though the girls complain of their poverty, they do not seem so poor to the modern reader, who has lost the conception of genteel poverty as socially embarrassing. And for all their protestations about their material sacrifices since the family's financial reverses, they don't miss out on much: they still go to the fancy balls and have special dress-up clothes and hair styles to match. They may not have fancy foods, but certainly there is always enough at the table, and their simple gustatory pleasures are so convincingly described that it hardly seems as though they are missing anything. Even something as simple as a cup of coffee, a rare treat for the sisters, is offered to them in the novel at a time when both they and the readers particularly appreciate its aroma, flavor, and caffeine-derived stimulation. Just after their mother rushes off to be with their stricken father at his Civil War post, the household servant and long-time friend realizes that the sisters need something both to distract them from the parental absences and to lift their spirits. The coffee, not only because it is a rarity but also because it is a physical stimulus at a point in the book where spiritual and emotional descriptions have predominated, cheers both fictional character and reader. As important as prayer and self-examination are supposed to be in the novel, sometimes nothing works as well as a new dress or a snack.

Though *Little Women* is not the educational novel that *Little Men* or *Eight Cousins* is, still Alcott's concern for educational reform according to the precepts of her father's rather unconventional ideas does much to attract the modern young reader. Bronson Alcott did not believe in corporal punishment, but rather, in correction by moral suasion and learning from the consequences of one's actions. He did not believe in rote memorization, but rather in learning from experience. Most of all, he did not believe that most education went on in the classroom. His educational ideas were rooted in his conception of the child as innately good, someone who was willing to learn and to be good if only learning and goodness were put in his way. These ideas do not seem so radical now, but in his daughter's time, they were nearly scandalous—especially when one considers that they were combined with his ideas about co-education of the sexes and racially integrated classrooms. Perhaps the attraction for the modern young reader is that these educational ideas are centered on what children are and not on what they are supposed to be; and as theoretical and irrelevant as Bronson's ideas might seem to today's reader, she will no doubt find appealing the fact that none of his characters ever seem to spend much time in a dreary classroom.

Little Women established for Louisa May Alcott a popular and critical success, which her writing for adults had failed to do for her. Perhaps because *Little Women* was so lucrative, and because her family had long been destitute, she continued to use some of the formulae from *Little Women* in her later novels. The reader who continues on through the Alcott canon finds much that is familiar, if not as vigorous as in the original presentation. There are more comments about women's rights and about education; there are more good characters who appear in the novels in order to be made better. There is even a recreation of Jo march, in a niece of Jo's, also named Josie, who appears in *Jo's Boys*. There are other dying children, other girls trying to find careers for themselves and proper mates. Alcott did not tamper with a good thing once she found it, but repeated it as long as her public would continue to buy and read. But she never achieved again what she had in *Little Women,* and it is on this one book that her reputation continues to be based.

Zena Sutherland and May Hill Arbuthnot

SOURCE: "Modern Books Begin: *Little Women,*" in *Children and Books,* seventh edition, Scott, Foresman and Company, 1986, pp. 74-5.

During the Victorian period there was an increasing awareness of, and response to, children's needs. In England the awareness was most evident in the work of Charlotte Yonge (1823-1901), who wrote family stories based on her own happy childhood, and some school stories, sentimental in tone, moral in intent, and realistic in approach. Her prolific output (well over a hundred books) was read avidly by children of the period.

The epoch-making book in the United States was a modest story of family life. *Little Women,* like Charlotte Yonge's books, was based on the author's own family experiences. The author, Louisa May Alcott (1832-1888), submitted the manuscript hesitatingly, and her publisher told her as gently as possible how unacceptable it was. Fortunately, he felt some qualms about his judgment and allowed the children of his family to read the manuscript. They convinced him that he was wrong. Those astute little girls loved the book, and it has remained popular with children since its publication in 1868. The story is as genuine a bit of realism as we have ever had. Family life is there—from the kitchen to the sanctuary of the attic, from reading to giving amateur dramatics in which the homemade scenery collapses. But right as all the details are, the reason adults remember the book is the masterly characterizations of the four girls. No longer are people typed to represent Ignorance or Virtue; here are flesh-and-blood girls, as different from each other as they could well be, full of human folly and human courage, never self-righteous, sometimes irritable but never failing in warm affection for each other. This ability to make her characters vividly alive was Louisa May Alcott's gift to modern realism for children.

John Rowe Townsend

SOURCE: "Domestic Dramas: *Little Women,*" in *Written for Children: An Outline of English-Language Children's Literature,* third revised edition, J. B. Lippincott, 1987, pp. 61-2.

The life and work of Louisa May Alcott (1832-88) have been written about endlessly, and undue brevity here will no doubt be forgiven. She was the daughter of the unworldly if brilliant philosopher and educationist Bronson Alcott and of his necessarily practical wife Abba May. The March sisters and 'Marmee' were portraits of her own family, and *Little Women* (1868) was based largely on incidents in their own lives. It was a gifted editor, Thomas Niles of the Boston firm of Roberts Brothers,

who persuaded Louisa May to write a girls' story when she would rather have produced 'a fairy book'. She noted in her journal: 'I plod away, though I don't enjoy this sort of thing. Never liked girls or knew many, except my sisters; but our queer plays and experiences may prove interesting, though I doubt it.'

When it was finished, she and her editor both thought it rather dull, but *Little Women* was an immediate success and was followed by *Little Women, Part 2* (better known in England as *Good Wives*) in 1869, and by half a dozen books that dealt with the March family of later years, as well as some about other characters. The last of the *Little Women* series, *Jo's Boys,* appeared in 1886. I have not read all the later books, and what I have read failed to hold me; it is, however, on the two parts of *Little Women* that Louisa May Alcott's reputation rests. The qualities that account for its success are obvious: truth, warmth, simplicity, intimacy. The Marches are a real family you might have known. Jo March, based on the author herself, is the obvious inspiration of many a later heroine, and the very name of Jo still seems to bear her imprint.

There is some sermonizing in *Little Women*; but there is also human reaction against sermonizing. (When Jo has been indulging in it, her friend Laurie asks, 'Are you going to deliver lectures all the way home?' Jo says, 'Of course not; why?' Laurie says, 'Because if you are, I'll take a bus.') Laurie, I fear, has never seemed quite like masculine flesh and blood to me. I suspect that he is the nice girl's dream-boy-next-door: handsome, attentive, and unlikely to attempt anything more dangerous than holding hands. Yet the dismay still felt by readers when they realize that Miss Alcott will not let Jo marry him suggests that I am in the minority, and that most readers see them both as real people. There is no point in adding speculation on Miss Alcott's motives for keeping Jo and Laurie apart; but does Jo cop out by accepting the staid Professor Bhaer? It could be argued that she cops out sooner than that, for at the end of *Little Women* she is improved to the extent that she 'neither whistles, talks slang, nor lies on the rug as she used to do.' Already that is not the real Jo; the Jo we remember is the one who does these unladylike things.

Little Women marks not only an increased truth-to-life in domestic stories, with children seen as people rather than examples of good and bad; it also marks a relaxation of the stiff and authoritarian stereotype of family life persisting from the still recent times when the Fifth Commandment came first and the earthly father was seen quite literally as the representative of the heavenly one. ('Henry,' said Mr Fairchild to his son, 'I stand in place of God to you, whilst you are a child.' [Mary Martha Sherwood, *The Fairchild Family,* (1818)].) This mellowing was necessary before the family story, of which *Little Women* is the first great example, could come into its own. A relationship between rulers and subjects had to be replaced by one of mutual affection. The family story could not work in an atmosphere of repression or of chilly grandeur. The key characteristic is always warmth.

Beverly Lyon Clark

SOURCE: "A Portrait of the Artist as a Little Woman," in *Children's Literature: Annual of the Modern Language Association Seminar on Children's Literature and the Children's Literature Association,* Vol. 17, 1989, pp. 81-97.

Alcott as submissive, Alcott as subversive, Alcott as ambivalent—these are dominant themes in recent reflections on Louisa May Alcott. The same themes appear in Alcott's own writing about writing, when she writes about Jo March. Though Alcott gives some play to subversive ideas of self-expression, her overt message is that girls should subordinate themselves and their language to others. A little woman should channel her creativity into shaping the domestic space or shaping her soul. She can enact *Pilgrim's Progress* and learn to live as a Christian—to live by God's Word, or by John Bunyan's word, not by her own.

Nineteenth-century male authors send a very different message to their readers. Jan B. Gordon notes that in works as diverse as the Alice books, Mill's *Autobiography,* and *David Copperfield,* the child "must reverse or otherwise overturn a prescriptive text that had kept him in a figurative prison." The opposite is true for the girls in *Little Women.* Laurie may complain that "a fellow can't live on books," rebelling against prescribed texts as other males do, but Jo must learn to stifle her rebelliousness and to forgive Amy for burning the only manuscript of her book, Jo's attempt to find her own voice.

In her other works Alcott shows a similar reluctance to rebel. Her adult novel *Work* may in effect rebel against its predecessor *Jane Eyre,* but only in the service of a higher submission. The heroine, Christie, objects to Charlotte Brontë's portrayal of Rochester: "I like Jane, but never can forgive her marrying that man, as I haven't much faith in the saints such sinners make." Then Christie enacts her objection to *Jane Eyre* by marrying not the Rochester-like Mr. Fletcher but David Sterling, a type of St. John Rivers, with whom she undertakes missionary work at home; and a symbolic bedroom fire is caused not by the madwoman in the attic but by Christie's dangerous penchant for books. Alcott rebels against the romance of *Jane Eyre* not so much to find her own voice as to submit herself to the divine and masculine allegory of *Pilgrim's Progress.* Christie's very name recalls those of Christian and Christiana, and in her progress through temptations she eventually achieves a state of grace, with the help of a character compared to Mr. Greatheart. Thus Alcott's rebellion against a predecessor text is not so rebellious after all: it is a reworking of the secular *Jane Eyre* in order to submit to the higher truths of *Pilgrim's Progress,* a reworking that underscores the searing dangers of books to women. She rebels not to find her own voice but to modulate it in the heavenly chorus.

In *Work* Alcott stifles her predilection for the lurid and sensational, much as she has suppressed her blood-and-thunder tales (first by publishing them anonymously or under a pseudonym and then by turning instead to juve-

niles). In a telling entry in her diary, at age eighteen, she notes, "Reading Miss Bremer and Hawthorne. The 'Scarlet Letter' is my favorite. Mother likes Miss B. better, as more wholesome. I fancy 'lurid' things, if true and strong also." Eighteen years later, in her own writing, Alcott has submitted to the preferences of her mother, the arch-representative of the family, giving up the gothic for domestic realism, banishing the "skeleton in the closet." Or hiding "behind a mask," as so many of Alcott's strong gothic heroines do, concealing her passions and longings behind the passionless and virtuous facade of her "marble women." Alcott's reworking of *Jane Eyre* (one of fifteen items in an 1852 list of books she liked) is more a self-chastisement for her sneaking fondness for things gothic, more an act of penitent submission to Christian godliness than a rebellion against a predecessor text.

In *Little Women,* too, Alcott stifles the sensational—or at least hides it. In the first volume it still lurks just below the surface. Thomas H. Pauly points to the contrast between the romantic literature that the girls read and their plain lives, a contrast that signals both Alcott's innovation, the way she calls "attention to the drama and impact that could attend the commonplace," and also the "notable deficiencies that Alcott perceived in the very environment she strove to recommend." Or perhaps in *Little Women* the two tendencies are in creative tension, the sensational not yet as fully repressed as it will later be: Ann Douglas suggests that "Alcott hoped to let sensational and domestic fiction educate each other."

Still, the surface message in *Little Women* is that the March sisters should aspire to domesticity and moral goodness. *Little Women* may not enforce submissiveness as much as some of Alcott's other books for girls do—Jo is remarkably rebellious for a nineteenth-century girl. And some of her eventual taming may result from Alcott's sense that fiction for girls ought to teach feminine virtues—Alcott may simply have been acceding to the constraints of the form. Yet she chooses to submit to these constraints (and also to the constraint of writing popular books that will earn money for her family). Jo, too, eventually submits to the constraints of what her culture considered seemly feminine behavior.

According to this cultural definition of the feminine, art and fiction are suspect, self-control preferable to self-expression. Such self-control requires control of language; and, significantly, the two girls with artistic aspirations, Amy and Jo, are also the two who need to learn greater control of their language. Janice Marie Alberghene has suggested that each tries "to forge a personal style," Amy having too great a weakness for the ornamental, Jo for the sensational. Certainly Jo is fond of slang and strong language, of saying "pegging away" for "studying," and of using phrases like "desperate wretches," making Meg chide her for using such "dreadful expressions." Later, in volume two, Jo is largely cured of her weakness, perhaps in part because she has acted out its extreme manifestation by becoming Mrs. Malaprop at a masquerade party (much as she seems to be cured of writing partly from having sampled the extremes of thrillers and virtual sermons).

Amy, too, is guilty of excess in both art and language in volume one but overcomes both excesses by the end of volume two. Early on, she tries to use impressive words but commits malapropisms, using "label" for "libel," "samphire" for "vampire," "fastidious" for "fascinating." Likewise, she is fond of drawing ludicrous caricatures, which "came fluttering out of all her books at unlucky moments." By the end of the first volume, though, she has learned to control her language and to channel her creativity into religion, to model her life after *Pilgrim's Progress,* to meditate in front of a picture of the Madonna instead of drawing one herself. What creativity she does allow herself is a tribute to domestic bliss: she sketches the engaged Meg and Mr. Brooke. By the end of the second volume she recognizes her own lack of genius and happily submerges personal in domestic achievement, tastefully arranging curtains rather than an artist's draperies. She may be allowed the indulgence of molding a model of her baby, but only in case this second Beth dies, "so that, whatever happens, I may at least keep the image of my little angel."

Much as art should not be Amy's supreme goal, writing should not be Jo's. Jo should outgrow it, like her strong language and her tomboy exuberance. Alcott undermines the value of writing, yet she cannot dismiss it altogether, for she herself is Jo, she herself is writing. Initially, Alcott endorses writing; especially in the first volume, fiction allows Jo to enact her masculine fantasies of power. She can assume male roles in the plays that she writes and in meetings of the Pickwick Club, where, as Augustus Snodgrass, she gives her word as a gentleman. Writing fiction gives her an arena where she can express herself, express her anger, instead of just tightening her lips to suppress it as her mother teaches her.

The other girls, too, though less strikingly, find in the stories they invent an outlet for self-expression—and also self-revelation—before they submerge themselves in domesticity. For *The Pickwick Portfolio,* the family newspaper, Meg writes a romantic story of the Lady Viola's wedding to an apparently impoverished suitor, unconsciously anticipating her own marriage to John Brooke. House-wifely Beth writes a homely tale of the life of a squash, grown by a farmer, baked by a little girl, and eaten by the Marches. Irresponsible Amy writes a note of apology for not writing anything.

Stories similarly allow self-expression and self-revelation when a group of young people plays Rigmarole, a game in which players take turns telling a story, one picking up the thread where another leaves off. Although the game affords Alcott a chance to display stylistic virtuosity—the segments are variously romantic, gothic, adventurous, humorous, or Polonius-like combinations thereof—it also sheds light on the characters. It reveals the tellers' literary tastes and hints at matters important to them. Mr. Brooke, for instance, tells of a poor knight who tames a colt and longs for a captive princess, much as he has been taming Laurie and longing for Meg. Shy Beth characteristically prefers not to participate—as if she knows the dangers of fiction and chooses not to indulge.

The game also celebrates creativity and self-expression, as becomes clearer if we compare it to a similar game in Charlotte Yonge's popular family story, *The Daisy Chain* (1856). Quite possibly Alcott wrote her episode in response to the British one, for Alcott's game is introduced by a British visitor, and the whole chapter plays Britain against America: the American friends, as if inspired by "the spirit of '76," defeat the British family at croquet, even though one of the British boys has cheated; nor is the British young lady's tendency to condescend to young women who earn money, as Meg does, endorsed. On some level, it seems, Alcott wants to show how the American family story can outdo the British, and how accepting money for one's writing (instead of channeling it to religious and other charitable causes, as Yonge did) is worthy. In any case, while all the players of Alcott's Rigmarole have been influenced by their favorite reading, the segment told by the boy who cheated at croquet is even more derivative, jumbling together phrases and facts from a single book—from *The Sea-Lion,* as Laurie recognizes. And it's clear that such plagiarism is not praiseworthy.

In *The Daisy Chain,* however, a kind of plagiarism is endorsed. The story game is, to begin with, rather different: various people tell someone stories incorporating an agreed-upon word until the person can guess what the word is. The story segments are related semantically rather than syntactically, metaphorically rather than metonymically. The game thus invites allegorical stories, focused

Alcott, 1887.

on the key word, rather than the wide-ranging inventiveness fostered by Rigmarole. The young girl Flora tells of a girl who becomes the first woman to achieve the glory of ascending Mont Blanc; the story is a thinly veiled allegory of Flora's own ambitions, particularly her later political ambitions for her dullard husband. Her father tells of a hummingbird who considers itself "vain and profitless" but whose master tells it that by valuing its own bliss and praising its master it "conduces to no vain-glory of thine own, in beauty, or in graceful flight, but . . . art a creature serving as best thou canst to his glory." As for the heroine, Ethel, an engaging and lively girl like Jo, she too tells a story distinguishing between worldly and heavenly glory, about princes competing to serve the ladies Vana Gloria and Gloria: the one prince, trying to conquer worlds, finally discovers Vana Gloria to be vain and ugly; the other, staying at home and being good to his subjects, finds his Gloria, still lovely, as he dies. Here is an allegory particularly apt for Ethel, who learns to seek her glory—to glory in her duties—close to home.

Significantly, Ethel does not invent her story; she has modified a tale from an old French book. Yet such plagiarism does not call forth censure here, implicit or otherwise, as it does in **Little Women.** Far from it. Ethel has enacted what the story preaches—by not seeking earthly glory through her own originality but, in a devout and womanly fashion, assimilating the moral in another's work.

As for the secret word in Yonge's story game, it is, of course, "glory." And much as we have learned its true meaning in these transparent allegories, so do we learn it in the book as a whole. The young people are not to pine after earthly glory, we are later told, but to discover that "charity is the true glory" and that letting God's will be done can release an exulting "cry of Glory."

Thus is the reader invited to read *The Daisy Chain,* more chained by religious allegory than **Little Women,** just as its language game is more constrained. For, compared to Ethel, Jo is granted considerable freedom; Ethel is more willing than Jo to accept her constraints, more willing to give up her writing. The differing imports of their nicknames are emblematic. Josephine lays claim to male prerogatives when she becomes Jo. Ethel, on the other hand, is short for Etheldred. As a younger child she had been nicknamed King Etheldred the Unready—King for short—the overt significance being her childhood tendency to be a little slapdash with household duties. Yet the nickname is also male, appropriate for someone who chafes more than her sisters do against traditional expectations for women. She finally settles, however, for the feminine Ethel, thus reversing Jo's progress, outgrowing the male and becoming female. Or rather, Jo's progress is a little more complex, for when in later volumes Jo becomes Aunt Jo or Mrs. Jo, both gender oxymorons, she highlights the tensions between the two tendencies toward domestic and literary creativity that she continues to embody.

Not all the stories in **Little Women** are as self-expressive as the Rigmarole ones are; some are constrained by alle-gorical shaping. In the chapter called "Burdens" each girl tells a story, or rather a vignette, of her experiences that day. These stories are not so much outlets for self-expression as reflections on each pilgrim's progress. The girls are morally shaping their lives, allegorizing them, rather than creatively expressing their feelings. Jo tells of interesting Aunt March in *The Vicar of Wakefield* in lieu of Belsham's Essays; Meg tells of a disgrace in the society family where she works as a governess; Amy tells of the embarrassing punishment meted out to a fellow pupil; Beth tells of seeing Mr. Laurence's act of kindness to a poor woman. True, the stories are expressive insofar as the girls reveal aspects of themselves. It is fitting that Jo tell a story about the attractions of fiction, that Meg tell a story about the attractions of society, that Beth tell a story of selfless generosity, that Amy tell a story of the horrors of embarrassment (anticipating her own experience later at school). Yet the girls are learning, in their monitory stories, to channel their feelings in socially acceptable ways: they are learning both how to behave (like Mr. Laurence, not like the fellow pupil) and how to channel storytelling.

The culmination they should aim for is the selflessness of Marmee—a selflessness and devotion she then enacts by glossing their stories. For Marmee tells a transparent allegory about four girls who learn to become happy by counting their blessings: "One discovered that money couldn't keep shame and sorrow out of rich people's houses; another that, though she was poor, she was a great deal happier, with her youth, health, and good spirits, than a certain fretful, feeble old lady, who couldn't enjoy her comforts; a third that, disagreeable as it was to help get dinner, it was harder still to have to go begging for it; and the fourth, that even carnelian rings were not so valuable as good behavior." Just as the girls tell stories here to shape their lives more than to express their feelings, Marmee provides a final shaping, one that unifies the stories, much as she unifies the family. Furthermore, she subtly revises the moral of Jo's potentially subversive story—from the pleasures of fictional escape to the advantages of Jo's own lot—much as she subtly revises, redirects, Jo herself.

Writing is thus double-edged, enabling expression or repression, or both. Some of Jo's other fictions likewise aim not so much at self-expression as at accommodation: they allow her, as she grows older, to come to terms with domesticity. She works through her adjustment to domesticity, in part, by writing of it in "A Song from the Suds." The poem joins the virtues of domesticity and moral goodness. She can physically "wash and rinse and wring" and wants further to "wash from our hearts and souls / The stains of the week away." Her writing here has been tamed to laud domestic and moral virtues—as has Alcott's own in **Little Women.** And again Jo follows a male model, Bunyan, for she creates an allegory out of the ordinary. Yet for all its surface compliance the poem is subtly subversive. There's humor in the mere idea of "A Song from the Suds" as moral literature. And instead of simply living *Pilgrim's Progress,* as Marmee has enjoined, Jo is rewriting it, much as Alcott herself has done.

Thus Alcott remains ambivalent—about writing, about self-expression, and about gender roles. A key emblem of her ambivalence is Jo's cutting of her hair, ambiguously masculine and feminine. The daring action itself may be "masculine," as may the shorn hair, but the sacrifice of a prized possession for the benefit of others—so that Marmee can travel to her ailing husband—is "feminine." Further complicating the gender valence is the echo of Samson and Delilah. For Delilah was active, not passive, and Samson's shorn hair became a sign of masculine weakness. The traditional gender boundaries were blurred, decisive action associated with the female, long hair associated with physical strength. Moreover, Jo plays Delilah to her own Samson—she is ambiguously, perhaps ambivalently, both artist and art object, both Samson and Delilah.

By the end of the first volume, though, Jo becomes more object than artist, more conforming, less wildly imaginative: her father is proud of her for becoming "a young lady who pins her collar straight, laces her boots neatly, and neither whistles, talks slang, nor lies on the rug as she used to." Jo learns to restrain her exuberance, in both writing and action, and to submit to her proper role—and to God: to submit both to the Word and to the words of Bunyan's text. She must learn to curb her "abominable tongue"; she must channel her creativity into living, "replac[ing] her pen with a broom"; she must forgive Amy for burning a precious manuscript. Thus Jo's writing recedes into the background, eventually stopping. At the end of the first volume she is presumably still writing, but we see less of it and its fruits. It could be that she no longer needs to act out her melodramas and instead channels her earlier public exuberance into writing done behind the scenes. More likely, though, Alcott simply had to submerge this self-expressive writing since, according to the ethic she wanted to espouse, submerging the self and caring for others are more suitable to a little woman than self-dramatization and self-expression.

Jo's submersion in domesticity can be gauged, in part, by the submersion of her fictions, including her dramatic fictions. On the first Christmas the melodramatic adventures of Don Roderigo and Zara are so compelling that both stage scenery and "dress circle" collapse. Even here, though, Alcott feels the need to justify staging Jo's play: "It was excellent drill for their memories, a harmless amusement, and employed many hours which otherwise would have been idle, lonely, or spent in less profitable society." She is not altogether comfortable about giving free reign to creativity. Certainly such exuberant self-expression is not appropriate for the grown women the little women want to become. As Karen Halttunen suggests, the play "permits Jo's theatrical violation of true womanhood only within a larger ritual of family harmony," enabling Jo to act out "the moral struggle raging within her" and thereby "to control the destructive potential of her inner demon." The following year the drama is muted and more fully absorbed into the life of the family—the girls seem to follow Marmee's early advice and recognize that *Pilgrim's Progress* "is a play we are playing all the time in one way or another . . . not in play, but

in earnest." The melodramatic romance of Don Roderigo and Zara has become the more prosaic one of John Brooke and Meg. The play is absorbed not only into the plot but also into metaphor: the volume has become "the first act of the domestic drama called 'LITTLE WOMEN.'" Much as Jo learns to suppress anger, all the girls—and the narrator—learn to suppress melodramatic fictions.

And much as drama gives way to drama metaphor, fiction gives way to fiction metaphor: the stories of the Pickwick Club and the game of Rigmarole dwindle, by the end of the first volume, to story metaphors. Meg no longer needs romantic fictions because she lives her own novel: she "felt like the girls in books"; John might act "like the rejected lovers in books"; he then "looked decidedly more like the novel heroes whom [Meg] admired." As the narrator tells us, "Now and then, in this work-a-day world, things do happen in the delightful story-book fashion." The volume concludes when "Father and Mother sat together, quietly re-living the first chapter of the romance which for them began some twenty years ago."

This taming of exuberance, this attempt to control it through metaphor, reverses the movement of the contemporary *Alice's Adventures in Wonderland* (1865). Lewis Carroll did not attempt to justify his excursion into fiction by making it moral. He simply sought to entertain Alice Liddell and to find a means of self-expression. Thus the book literalizes metaphor: "mad as a hatter" engenders a Mad Hatter; "mock turtle soup," a Mock Turtle. The book is profoundly liberating, granting the imagination creative freedom—even if Carroll does try to recant at the end, making the adventure just a dream. *Little Women,* on the other hand, metaphorizes the literal. It grounds Jo's early imaginative flights, and it similarly grounds the dangerously fictive, constraining it in metaphor. Like the budding poet in Alcott's "Mountain Laurel and Maidenhair," Jo "put her poetry into her life, and made of it 'a grand sweet song' in which beauty and duty rhymed so well that the . . . girl became a more useful, beloved, and honored woman than if she had tried to sing for fame which never satisfies." Still, the mere existence of the fiction metaphors may remind us of the earlier fictional flights, of the potential for imaginative, not just imaginary, freedom.

The effects of this shift in *Little Women,* this absorption of fictions into the plot, are several. One is to show the domestication and maturing of the little women: they have outgrown their childish reliance on stories and now live them, as they try to live *Pilgrim's Progress.* Another is to lift the book itself into the never-never land of story: the book loses some of its reality, becoming more of a romance, receding from our everyday world in part because of its saccharine sweetness but also because of its metamorphosis into the fiction it has previously enclosed. The fiction metaphors may remind us that we are, after all, reading a fiction—and thereby give us enough distance to call the pronouncements it seems to endorse into question. In any case, because of the shift from fiction making to living, Jo is no longer primary author and mover; she can no longer direct Meg in a play or in life. And her loss of authority may account for some of her indignation that Meg wants to marry and leave her sisters.

The devaluation of writing continues in the second volume. For here writing is a means, not an end. It is, first of all, a means of earning money, to send Beth and Marmee to the seashore. Writing is more womanly if its goal is self-sacrifice and kindness to others, if self-expression is subordinate to self-abnegation. Alcott's ambivalence is nowhere so clear as in the kind of writing that she allows herself and Jo to pursue—"popular" writing to earn money for others, not "serious" writing for the selfish purposes of art.

Elsewhere in the second volume writing is similarly a means, though not always unambiguously so. When Jo is feeling despondent, Marmee urges her to write to make herself happy—a therapy that largely works. Some degree of self-expression is permissible, it seems, as medicine, though the line dividing therapy and creativity is not entirely clear. But the two samples of Jo's writing that we see in the second volume, both poems, are less ambiguous: both achieve crucial nonartistic ends, their artistry subordinated to utility. Compared to the lively pieces in the first volume, these two are plodding and pedestrian. The first, Jo's poem about Beth's dying, allows Jo to express some of her grief and to tell Beth that she has not lived in vain, that others have benefited by her example. The second, a meditation on four trunks in the garret, revealing some of Jo's loneliness and longing for love, appears in a publication that Professor Bhaer reads—and it brings him courting. Jo acknowledges that it is "very bad poetry," but the Professor points out that "it has done its duty," beauty once again subordinated to—made to rhyme with—duty.

Even more striking is how dangerous art has become. At first, in volume two, the effects are relatively benign. Jo's overdeveloped imagination leads her to believe Beth in love with Laurie, "and common sense, being rather weakened by a long course of romance writing, did not come to the rescue." The consequences here are trifling. Later, as Jo is lured to write thrillers for the sake of money, a worse danger looms: "She thought she was prospering finely; but, unconsciously, she was beginning to desecrate some of the womanliest attributes of a woman's character. She was living in bad society; and, imaginary though it was, its influence affected her, for she was feeding heart and fancy on dangerous and unsubstantial food, and was fast brushing the innocent bloom from her nature by a premature acquaintance with the darker side of life, which comes soon enough to all of us." Beyond such possible excesses, though, writing is simply not what a little woman should aim for. Jo's beloved Beth urges her to follow the claims of love and duty: "you'll be happier in doing that than writing splendid books or seeing all the world; for love is the only thing that we can carry with us when we go, and it makes the end so easy."

Jo essentially does stop writing when she marries, and she channels her creativity into telling stories to her household of boys and composing a song for a festive occasion.

True, bookishness has brought Jo and her Professor together: they read Hans Christian Andersen; he gives her a volume of Shakespeare; they attend a literary dinner. Yet the Andersen is simply sugarcoating for Jo's German lessons, the dinner a disappointment. Books are insufficient in themselves, but they may serve a useful end. And that end is marriage and domesticity. Early on, Jo is bookish, with a metaphoric family: her stories are "dutiful children whom good fortune overtakes"; she herself, a "literary spinster, with a pen for a spouse, a family of stories for children." She ends, though, with a true family, and bookishness is metaphoric; when the Professor becomes intimate with Jo he will read "all the brown book in which she keeps her little secrets." The metaphoric family becomes actual, the actual bookishness metaphoric. At the end of volume two as at the end of volume one, fiction is channeled into metaphor. Jo does state, "I haven't given up the hope that I may write a good book yet, but I can wait, and I'm sure it will be all the better for such experiences and illustrations as these." Such a teasing reminder of Jo's earlier bookishness may subvert some of Alcott's surface message—and may also remind us that we are reading a book, only a book, and can thus question its pronouncements. But the surface message remains clear: as long as she is happy and busy and dutiful—as a proper woman, a wife and mother—Jo should feel no great call to write.

In the first continuation of *Little Women,* in fact, she feels none. The only writing she does in *Little Men* is in her Conscience Book, where each week she records the virtues and follies of the boys at Plumfield. Again, the writing is instrumental, here (as in Alcott's own works) an instrument of moral growth. Not until *Jo's Boys,* published nearly twenty years after *Little Women,* does Alcott allow Jo the writing she allowed herself. And then it is only because Jo has been fretting for something to do while sick, has hoped to lighten her family's financial burdens, and has wanted to buy Marmee some peace and comfort at the end of a hard life. Furthermore, it's not dangerous gothic tales that Jo indulges in but domestic realism. Still, Alcott calls this return to writing "Jo's last scrape"—and not just because Jo's popularity makes her the prey of autograph hounds. Despite all the rationalizations, writing remains morally dubious. Later, Jo and Laurie collaborate on a Christmas production, one far different from the melodrama of Don Roderigo and Zara in *Little Women.* For this one is a tribute to motherhood: "I'm tired of love-sick girls and runaway wives. We'll prove that there's romance in old women also." The play thus provides closure to the family saga that began with a Christmas play so long ago. But the tenor of the final play exalts the everyday rather than the exotic, the dutiful rather than the beautiful, echoing the shift in Alcott's own writing from the gothic to the domestic.

Fortunately, even if she was dubious about its justification, Alcott herself continued to write. She could justify her writing by doing it out of a sense of duty: she earned money to feed her family, and her fiction was an instrument of good, teaching girls how to become proper women. Alcott may have espoused women's rights, including suffrage, but in her books as in her life the greatest good was not individual rights and self-fulfillment but loyalty and service to the family; she was a "domestic feminist," seeing the family as the key to reforming society. Though she sometimes needed to escape her family in order to write and rented a room in Boston, the family almost always took precedence over her liberal causes, over herself, over her writing.

Alcott couldn't write just for the sake of writing, for the joy of creating. She may have continued beyond the point of financial necessity partly because she liked indulging in writing, but her avowed goal was always security for the family. Perhaps the only way she could permit herself to write was to pretend, even after her family was secure, that she was writing only for the sake of the family. Or, to put it another way, the act of writing itself may have been liberating, but Alcott paid for such self-indulgence by making the writing instrumental, by sacrificing herself and her writing to duty. The liberating pen was also its homonym: confinement could give birth to creativity but could also abort it.

Caryn James

SOURCE: "Amy Had Golden Curls; Jo Had a Rat. Who Would You Rather Be?" in *The New York Times Book Review,* December 25, 1994, pp. 3, 17.

Was there ever a more passive-aggressive trio than those whiny little March sisters, Meg, Jo and Beth? Meg, the dutiful oldest, sighing as she tosses off her frequent complaint that it is dreadful to be poor, but she can bear it; Jo such a martyr she lops off her hair to sell for quick cash, when she could easily have borrowed the money from her aunt; Beth wasting away and not once snarling about it. Only Amy, the spoiled baby of the family, refuses to beg for attention. She simply accepts it as her due. The pretty one who marries the handsome boy next door. Amy is the pampered princess of *Little Women.* That's what I liked about her.

Among female readers and especially writers, there is no more sacred a cow in all of literature than *Little Women.* We are supposed to have worshiped Jo, identified with her, found in her a role model for our writing lives. Louisa May Alcott clearly adored Jo, her idealized self, and generations of readers have fallen in line behind her.

In 1968, 100 years after the book first appeared, Elizabeth Janeway praised the independent Jo in *The New York Times Book Review,* calling her "the tomboy dream come true" and a "New Woman." In 1977, Carolyn Heilbrun wrote, "Jo was a miracle," a role model for "girls dreaming beyond the confines of a constricted family destiny." And more recently both Perri Klass and Anna Quindlen have cited Jo as a model who inspired them as professional writers.

You can't argue with other people's childhood memories. But *my* girlhood memory is that books were usually about fantasies, not career plans, and I wanted to be Amy. The idea of New Womanhood hadn't trickled down to me yet. Amy had golden curls; Jo had a pet rat. Who would you rather be?

For years this was my guilty secret. Then the new film version of *Little Women* approached promising Winona Ryder as a Jo for the 1990's. The March sisters became a topic of conversation and I discovered a group of secret-sharers who had always found Jo to be actively annoying. She was loud, imperious, altogether obnoxious. The cult of Jo has conspired to make her a proto-feminist saint and *Little Women* a tract, but a great deal of that comes from cultural hindsight. The novel admits many more ambiguous readings and imaginative possibilities.

As a girl, I read *Little Women* the way I read fairy tales. I wanted to be the princess in "Cinderella," too, but I didn't think I'd grow up to be royal (at least not until I heard about Grace Kelly and Wallis Simpson). It never occurred to me that Amy was a pathetic weakling or that "Cinderella" should have come with a warning label. "This story contains a woman who depends on a man. It may be dangerous to your economic self-sufficiency later on."

Part of the enduring charm of *Little Women* is that each March sister still has her followers, and the anti-Jo's haven't turned out any the worse for it. Some of my best friends say they wanted to be Beth: these are women who, as Alcott might have put it, now earn their livings by their pens. Being Beth was a sure-fire way to get attention, but dying seemed a little extreme to me. I identified with the responsible Meg, but the character you long to be is never the one you most resemble. Amy went to Europe, traipsed through the Palais-Royal and fell in love with the dashing Laurie; then she married him. Jo moved to a boarding house in New York, where the bearish Professor Bhaer scolded her for writing sensational stories; then she married him anyway. Choosing Amy as a heroine was, as Alcott would not have put it, a no-brainer.

I wasn't the only one who wanted to be Amy. Louisa May Alcott envied her, too.

In a journal entry written a few years before *Little Women,* Alcott notes that her youngest sister, May, the real-life model for Amy, was being sent to art school by a magnanimous neighbor. With the pity-me tone that would soon creep into the Marches, Alcott wrote about her sister. "She is a fortunate girl, & always finds someone to help her as she wants to be helped. Wish I could do the same, but suppose as I never do that it is best for me to work & wait & do all for myself."

A common theme in biographies of Alcott is her complicated relationship with May. Part lavish love and part reined-in resentment, it is copiously documented in Louisa Alcott's journals. Louisa paid for her sister to go to Europe to study art, but she was always keenly aware of her self-sacrifice. In 1873, she described a day: "Cold and dull; but the thought of May free and happy was my comfort as I messed about."

It's not much of a jump from there to *Little Women,* especially when Jo learns that Aunt March will be taking Amy to Europe in her place: "'Amy has all the fun and I have all the work. It isn't fair, oh, it isn't fair!' cried Jo passionately." Then Jo turns on Amy and says, "You hate hard work, and you'll marry some rich man, and come home to sit in the lap of luxury all your days." Jo means those words as a curse, not a compliment, but a little girl reading them could certainly reach a different conclusion.

And when college boys come to visit the March sisters, whose side should we be on when Alcott writes: "They all liked Jo immensely, but never fell in love with her, though very few escaped without paying the tribute of a sentimental sigh or two at Amy's shrine"? In many ways Amy was the sister Louisa longed to be, though not the one she most resembled.

There were many trade-offs and seesaw changes in the sisters' lifelong competition. Amy was a mediocre artist in *Little Women* (as an adult, I hardly remembered that she painted at all), a judgment that turned out to be prophetic. May illustrated the first edition of *Little Women,* and critics faulted her lifeless drawings when they noticed them at all.

With Louisa a public success, it seemed only fair that May should have the upper hand in private life. When she was 37 and spending more time in Europe than in Concord, May married a man 15 years younger than she was. This left her spinster sister looking to the afterlife for comfort. "How different our lives are just now!" Louisa wrote in her journal. "I so lonely, sad and sick; she so happy, well and blest. She always had the cream of things, and deserved it. My time is yet to come somewhere else, when I am ready for it."

They both arrived somewhere else far sooner than they expected. Within two years of her marriage, May gave birth to a child and died weeks later. "Of all the trials in my life I never felt any so keenly as this," Louisa wrote of May's death. Yet even then there were compensations. May left her daughter, named Louisa May, in the care of her sister Louisa, who raised the child until she herself died eight years later, only 55.

In the 1990's, grown-up readers of *Little Women* tend to see both Alcott and Jo as flawlessly strong, shining heroines, forgetting how much Alcott improved her life in her fiction. Jo sold her hair as a heroic gesture because she was too proud to beg Aunt March for money. In real life, Alcott lost her precious three and a half feet of brown hair helplessly. She caught typhoid pneumonia while nursing solders during the Civil War, and while she was delirious doctors ordered her hair cut off. *Little Women* transforms Louisa the victim into Jo the willful.

If some people can't tell Jo from Louisa, even more believe that Jo is Katharine Hepburn. The Jo cultists may not like to admit it, but they get a lot of mileage from Ms. Hepburn's performance in the 1933 movie. From then on, Jo's image mingled with that of the typical Hepburn heroine. She is smart, spirited, confident—though in a heavily made-up, movie-star way. She even looks glamorous when her hair is cropped. Ms. Hepburn's Jo is a vast improvement over Alcott's, and the George Cukor film more quaintly enjoyable than the 1949 remake.

Yet June Allyson, in the 1949 version, seems truer to my sense of Alcott's Jo. She is loud and abrasive, a stumble-bum foolishly grinning at her own clumsiness. Amy, on the other hand, is Elizabeth Taylor, preserved forever in her stunningly beautiful youth. (Joan Bennett was never very convincing as the baby Amy in 1933, possibly because Ms. Bennett was expecting a baby of her own. By the end of filming, Amy was conspicuously pregnant, Cukor was reportedly shooting her from the waist up, and the costume designers were grateful for 19th-century pinafores.)

The novel and the old movies of *Little Women* haven't held up as well as you might think. It's surprising to look back and realize that the book is crammed with preachy, do-good lessons from Marmee. The earlier films pared down the sermons, yet kept a cloying, saccharine tone.

The latest movie version, in keeping with the image of Jo as saint, runs wild with Alcott's moralism. A humorless Marmee (Susan Sarandon) preaches about the evils of corsets and the value of women's education. In New York, Jo takes part in a conversation decrying sexism and racism. All these concerns were important in the abolitionist, suffragist, temperance-minded Alcott family, but dragging them into the movie clumsily and without historical context simply reveals how the film strains to make this 19th-century novel relevant today.

Ms. Ryder's character lives through the same events as the previous Jo's. But her tomboy ways (not a pair of clean white gloves to her name!) no longer matter. Stereotypes of girls and boys have broken down so much in the past few decades that Jo seems no more or less than an ordinary girl. She does grow up to be an unfortunately pedantic one, though. "Do you know the word 'Transcendentalist?'" she asks Professor Bhaer.

In the midst of this misguided *Little Women,* it is Professor Bhaer who carries on a tradition, though it is a Hollywood tradition. With each film version, the professor gets better looking. Alcott made it clear that Jo, that sexless martyr, married an older, unattractive man because she found in him a soul mate and intellectual equal. Faithfully, Ms. Hepburn's Jo married the grizzly Paul Lukas. But June Allyson's Jo got the romantic (if distinctly non-Germanic) Rossano Brazzi. And the latest Jo is luckiest of all. Her Professor Bhaer is Gabriel Byrne, who hasn't looked so handsome or romantic since he played Byron in Ken Russell's "Gothic." He apologizes for being harsh in his criticism of Jo's writing: he takes her to the opera, where they sit in the wings and he kisses her. This sentimental courtship is an extreme perversion of the novel, of course. But the fairy tale romance is the most appealing part of a movie that labors to make Alcott seem more modern than she really is.

Louisa May Alcott, in her heavenly "somewhere else," may be tearing out her hair in grief as this latest version of her story. Or maybe not. Perhaps this is her revenge. Finally, Jo is pretty and marries the handsome man in the room next door. He even knows the word "Transcendentalist." Finally, Jo is more like Amy.

Meanwhile, the latest movie Amy (played as a girl by Kirsten Dunst and as a woman by Samantha Mathis) is a pallid blonde who carries on a pallid romance with Laurie. Some people have always seen her this way, but I say: Jo has all the fun and Amy gets second-best. It isn't fair, oh, it isn't fair!

Little Women was never my favorite Louisa May Alcott novel, anyway. The one I loved was *Eight Cousins* (tossed off in 1875, when Alcott was a literary star, much in demand). It's the story of a 13-year-old orphan named Rose, who lives in a big house with her kind maiden aunts, Peace and Plenty. Her rich guardian, Uncle Alec, is a seafaring doctor who brings her rainbow-colored scarves and beautiful embroidered jackets from Asia. The family has a maid about Rose's age who becomes her best friend—which means her best friend has to clean up after her! Best of all, she has seven male cousins, all of whom live nearby, all of whom adore her, in the days when you could marry your cousin. Now that was a fantasy worth having. That book was worthy of the Amy I know.

Additional coverage of Alcott's life and career is contained in the following sources published by Gale Research: *Concise Dictionary of American Literary Biography, 1865-1917; Dictionary of Literary Biography,* Vols. 1, 42, 79; *Major Authors and Illustrators for Children and Young Adults; World Literature Criticism;* and *Yesterday's Authors of Books for Children,* Vol. 1.

Alois Carigiet
1902-1985

Swiss author and illustrator of picture books.

Major works include *A Bell for Ursli* (written by Selina Chönz, 1950), *Florina and the Wild Bird* (written by Chönz, 1953), *The Snowstorm* (written by Chönz, 1958), *Anton the Goatherd* (1966), *The Pear Tree, the Birch Tree, and the Barberry Bush* (1967).

INTRODUCTION

The first illustrator to receive the Hans Christian Andersen International Children's Book Medal, Carigiet is regarded as a gifted artist whose works, distinguished by his sumptuous watercolors, are considered marvelous introductions to Switzerland. He made his debut into the world of children's literature with the publication of *A Bell for Ursli,* the first of three books for primary graders that he illustrated for Swiss poet Selina Chönz. Set in the Swiss Alps, a setting Carigiet knew and loved, this story depicts the adventures of Ursli, a little shepherd boy, with colorful full-page spreads of splendid Swiss scenery, simple local customs, and warm family interaction. Working closely with Chönz—sometimes preceding, sometimes following her text, which is written in the Romansh dialect—Carigiet captured the essence of the irrepressible Alpine lad who, like Heidi of an earlier time, became an immediate and universal favorite of young readers. Although Carigiet later created several picture books of his own, a few of which have been translated into English, none were as successful as the ones he illustrated for Chönz. Critics have praised him for his vibrant, stylized technique, which features childlike bold lines to contrast the intriguing detail of his memorable settings. Many other authors asked Carigiet to illustrate their works, but he declined any subject outside his own personal experience.

Biographical Information

The seventh of ten children, Carigiet was born the son of a peasant farmer in the village of Truns in the canton of Graubünden, East Switzerland. He grew up in the Grison Alps, among the upland meadows, valleys, and villages he recreated so vividly in his picture books. After ten years of schooling in Chur, capital of the canton, Carigiet served an apprenticeship as a decorator. Moving to Zürich, he worked as a commercial artist and stage designer, teaching himself painting, drawing, and lithography. He began to paint in earnest during a six-year period in the village of Platenga near his birthplace, where he endeavored to become recognized as one of Switzerland's finest artists. In 1945 the teacher and poet Selina Chönz asked him to illustrate a book, later published in English as *A Bell for Ursli,* that she wrote in verse for her pupils. "This excel-

lent book," recalled Carigiet, "threw a sharp light on my own childhood memories." Chönz lived in Guarda, considered one of the loveliest villages of the Engadine, and Carigiet was given a studio in her old house which served as the model for Ursli's home. The house itself was surrounded by snowcapped mountains on three sides, home of the flora and fauna that the artist often depicted in his pictures. Appearing soon after World War II, when other countries were still struggling to survive, the trio of books resulting from the Chönz-Carigiet collaboration owed no small part of its success to the brilliant printing capacity of the Zürich publishers Schweizer Spiegel Verlag. Marriage and the responsibility of educating his children took Carigiet back to Zürich, where he became noted for his wall murals. He continued to do graphic design and book illustration, including those for elementary school textbooks for the canton of Zürich. He died after a long illness in 1985.

Major Works

A Bell for Ursli introduces in simple rhyme and big bright pictures the little Swiss shepherd who, determined to join the spring procession of bell ringers, runs away from home, spends a lonely night under the stars, and climbs incredible heights to bring back the largest cowbell of them all. Children worldwide were attracted to this ambitious lad, his life in the high Alps, and the final family supper table scene with the huge bell on the empty guest chair; the book sold more than one and a half million copies. Carigiet's second effort with Chönz, *Florina and the Wild Bird* (1966), focuses on Ursli's sister Florina and a bird she rescues and ultimately frees at edelweiss heights. Written in verse and illustrated with Carigiet's unique angular perspective and large colorful landscapes, the result was described by the *Christian Science Monitor* as "utterly delightful." The third and last of Carigiet's trilogy with Chönz, *The Snowstorm,* tells of Florina's narrow escape from an avalanche, thanks to brother Ursli, and their winning of the prize for best decorated sled. Ellen Lewis Buell stated: "The pictures are just as handsome as we've come to expect of Alois Carigiet, an evocation of Swiss life and landscape that is both sensitive and vigorous." Carigiet himself wrote several books for children, including three which have been translated into English. The first of these, *Anton the Goatherd,* describes a summer day in the life of a boy who sets out to find three of his missing goats in the Alps. Although critics felt the text weak in comparison to those by Chönz, they noted that Carigiet again captures the beauty of mountain and valley from his own childhood memories. *The Pear Tree, the Birch Tree, and the Barberry Bush,* cited as a model of various textural surfaces in *The Child's First Books* by Donnarae MacCann and Olga Richard, is a birdwatching story set in the Alps, while *Anton and Anne* (1969) describes how two cousins are rescued by helicopter after an alpine landfall.

Awards

Florina and the Wild Bird was listed among the *New York Times* Choice of Best Illustrated Children's Books of the Year in 1953. *Anton the Goatherd* won the Swiss Juvenile Book Prize in 1966. *The Pear Tree, the Birch Tree, and the Barberry Bush* appeared on the honor list of the German Juvenile Book Prize in 1968. Carigiet was awarded the Hans Christian Andersen International Children's Book Medal for his body of work in 1966.

AUTHOR'S COMMENTARY

Alois Carigiet

SOURCE: "Winners of the Hans Christian Anderson Award 1966," in *Bookbird*, No. 4, 1966, pp. 3-9.

A very good spirit—probably the one entrusted with the care of children in this unkind world—is solely responsible for me coming from the narrow mountain valleys of my home, standing here before this world-wide and illus-

trious assembly and receiving this great honour for my work as a painter of children's books.

Whenever something so unexpected happens to a simple mortal, people in my country say: "That was not sung to him in his cradle." To verify this precept in my case I would have to be able to ask my dear mother, who has long been dead, the modest but wise farmer's wife. She would probably be quite indignant and say, "What on earth are you talking about, child, of course I never sang to you about Ljubljana."

No, dear mother, of course it must be true that you never dreamed of honours and medals, and yet somehow the melody of those years, when I, one of ten, tried to catch hold of a corner of your apron, is the deepest cause and reason why I am here.

Those years, the years of my happy mountain childhood, linger in my memory like an unforgotten tune. They prepared me for my work with books for children, they supplied the decisive stimulus when I was faced with that task.

My first confrontation with it happened a good twenty years ago in Zurich, the city that was later to become the cradle of the International Board on Books for Young People, in the course of my first meeting with Selina Chönz, the authoress from the Canton of Graubünden. On that occasion she gave me the first version of a children's book, then called "Uorsin" and which later became *A Bell for Ursli* (English version Oxford University Press, London, American: Henry Z. Walck, New York). This excellent book was in Engadin Romance, an idiom similar to my own mother tongue, and even if the action was set in the Engadin, the story of the little farm boy threw a sharp light on my own childhood memories.

At that time I had just given up my profession of commercial artist, in which I had been reasonably successful, and lived mainly in my native mountains, following my own vocation as a free-lance painter.

At intervals I spent a few brief weeks as a guest at the Chönz's house in Guarda, one of the most beautiful Engadin mountain villages. In the pine-panelled attic room of that hospitable house I painted most of the pictures for *A Bell for Ursli, Flurina and the Wild Bird* and *The Snowstorm.* The poetess Selina Chönz and I always discussed the layout of the story, and when these talks had shown the way, sometimes even during our conversations, I sketched and painted. The authoress then wrote the final text—in particular that of *Flurina* and *The Snowstorm*— after the pictures had been completed. That may be the reason why I am inclined to reject the term "illustration" for my work on children's picture books. I believe that my books are perhaps not illustrated stories for children but rather picture-books with accompanying texts. (I should like to acknowledge gratefully the painstaking care of the Swiss Spiegel Verlag, Zurich, and the art printers Orell-Füssli in the publication and printing of my books.) Far be it from me to assert the primacy of one or the other of these stylistic forms of children's books. Certainly the only essential point is that each achieves its own perfection and gets across to the child. While travelling along this road, I made a wonderful and surprising discovery.

I painted my pictures for children, as I like to put it, in a desire for the lost paradise of childhood, and I desired no end other than to transmit something of the light that brightened my own childhood to all children near and far, and in particular to city children.

Would the children of the world hear my voice and understand the language of my pictures?—I cherished no very great illusions on that score.

What happened then was like a small miracle for me.

The child answered!

He answered with his agreement, his belief, his enthusiasm, his joy.—

Letters written in many childish hands piled up in my

study, together with many drawings of Ursli's bell, Flurina's wild bird and the three goats Zottel, Zick and Zwerg (They might become Bushy, Billy and Baby in translation). They all bear eloquent witness to the echo raised by my efforts in the hearts of so many children.

These tokens of acceptance were a great gift to me. They were both a satisfaction and a reassurance.

I patiently listened to the many requests from competent and incompetent authors and publishers at home and abroad who wanted me to provide pictures for fairy-tales and children's stories. Much as I would have liked to comply with all the requests, my answer had to be a simple "No."

On the one hand my work for picture books was and is only a sideline, as it were, and my much more extensive tasks at the easel, on walls or the lithographic stone leave me little time for book illustrations. Moreover, I lack the living relationship and depth of experience to illustrate other people's texts. Therein, I believe, lies the secret of the success of the children's books that I have painted. I

From A Bell for Ursli, *written by Selina Chonz. Illustrated by Alois Carigiet.*

have experienced Ursli's and Flurina's world with wide-awake senses and I have wandered all over the rocks and heights where Maurus, the goatherd, searched for his three goats.

In conclusion may I be permitted to say that the same friendly spirit of childhood who, as I said at the beginning, led me here today, guided me on those steep paths and lonely walks in the mountains of Graubüden.

My gratitude today primarily goes to this spirit, whether it looks at us with the eyes of children or dwells in the hearts of men. But I also want to thank the International Board on Books for Young People, and in particular its founder Mrs. Jella Lepman, for their faith in me and my work.

The honour and distinction conferred on me today is really due to that friendly spirit working in children and, through us, *for* children.

I sincerely hope and desire that all nations may realize and appreciate more fully the immense cultural importance of the International Board's fight for juvenile literature, against the flood of mediocre and plain bad publications threatening the child. I have dedicated my work as a painter for children to this cause.

GENERAL COMMENTARY

The Christian Science Monitor

SOURCE: "In a Swiss Mountain Village," in *The Christian Science Monitor,* May 4, 1967, p. B2.

From time to time over the past several years, Switzerland has sent the American children a new book about a Swiss mountain village. With every other page filled with what looks like a glorious, original watercolor, these books are marvelous mediums for bringing the mountains, farms, and flowers of Switzerland across the Atlantic. So good are the illustrations by Alois Carigiet that the rather mediocre stories (perhaps the fault of the translator) are easily forgiven and forgotten. For *Anton the Goatherd,* Alois Carigiet won the 1966 Hans Christian Andersen medal. In this book Alois Carigiet also provided the story of a goatherd who saved three lost goats despite a minor injury. Now Mr. Carigiet's New York publishers—Walck—have reissued three of the earlier books which he illustrated: *A Bell For Ursli, The Snowstorm, Florina and the Wild Bird.* The stories are all by Selina Chönz. In the first, the illustrations are not quite as lavish, constant disaster lends a pall to the second, while the third, in which a little girl befriends a wild bird, is utterly delightful.

Bettina Hürlimann

SOURCE: "Alois Carigiet," in *Bookbird,* Vol. IX, No. 4, December, 1971, pp. 74-9.

Alois Carigiet is a child of the mountains. He has remained so, and all of his works are testimony of it.

Born in 1902 in Truns in the Grisons, where he still lives today, he grew up in a peasant family of eleven children. At the age of 17, he moved to Chur, the canton's capital, to finish his training as a painter and decorator.

However, this sort of work could hardly satisfy the intelligent and talented young man; he educated himself further on his own and became a graphic artist in Zurich, where he found great stimulus. He began with applied graphics, posters for travel offices, textile advertisements, magazines and book jackets. For ten years he also designed the settings for Zurich's famous political cabaret "Cornichon", in which many well-known authors and actors of the day took part.

Nevertheless, he had enough from advertising and applied graphics and moved with his family back to his mountains, to the village of Platenga, where, in the solitude of nature, he devoted himself to a new discipline of seeing and creating and dedicated himself completely to free-lance painting and drawing. From this time on both became the media of expression of his own feelings and thoughts alone.

The spontaneity of his message, his technical skill, so well-trained through his work in the applied arts, his colour and power of expression quickly brought him a good name among the painters of his generation. Especially in Chur and Zurich, but in other places as well, one can find murals by him, and his name appears more and more often as the illustrator of works from his region. The long bibliography of his works is evidence of this.

Carigiet already belonged among the leading artists in Switzerland as the poet and teacher Selina Chönz asked him in 1945 to illustrate a story in poetry which she had written for her pupils. Selina Chönz wrote in the Romanic languages and German and lived in one of Switzerland's prettiest villages, in Guarda in the Engadine.

In Guarda, as in many other villages in the canton, it was customary to ring in the spring with cow bells. The children walked through the streets ringing their bells, and naturally each child wanted to have the biggest and loudest bell.

The first and today still the most impressive picture book by Alois Carigiet was done on this motif. The wild beauty of nature, the adventure of a little runaway, the loneliness of a starry night in the mountains, the anxiety of his parents, his return to the wonderful security of a warm home—all these simple and timeless themes are dealt with here with a matchless freshness. It stands to reason that 25 years ago this expressive vitality was something quite new and astonishing.

The only European who was capable at that time, in the midst of war and post-war misery, of creating similarly bold and vital works for children was the Czech Jiri Trn-

From Florina and the Wild Bird, *written by Selina Chonz. Illustrated by Alois Carigiet.*

ka with his unparalleled illustrations of the first book of verse by Hrubin.

With Carigiet's work a vanishing world was held fast in word and picture as well. Reality a few years ago, it is gradually retreating to the far-away fairytale land. The later volumes, **Florina and the Wild Bird** and **The Snowstorm,** with verses by the same author, varied the theme with other adventures and added other characters to that of Ursli.

With **Anton the Goatherd** Carigiet began a new series of picture books, now grown to include three volumes deriving from his own childhood memories with the text by the illustrator. These books, too, were bound to be successful, and if the wild colours and spontaneity of the first volumes are missing, they are documents of Carigiet's childhood, reason enough for publication.

In the fifties, the readers of the canton of Zurich appeared, illustrated with thumb-nail masterpieces for children by Carigiet and Hans Fischer. It is no surprise that, besides in these most important and widely-read works, Carigiet's name appears in innumerable popular and bibliophilic works. He has also illustrated the fairy tales of the Grisons.

A crowning point of his career was reached as he received the Hans Christian Andersen Medal of the International Board on Books for Young People in Ljubljana five years ago. In a handsome smock frock, the rough figure of the painter stood up and thanked not only the jury for their decision but also his origin, above all his mother, for the gift which has made it possible for him to delight us anew with such works of art.

Carigiet's picture books, especially **A Bell for Ursli,** have been published in many countries, and the love for the little boy with the big bell and his bold adventures unites their children, as did, many years ago, Heidi and the other child characters of the Swiss mountain world.

Patricia Cianciolo

SOURCE: "The Artist's Media and Techniques," in *Illustrations in Children's Books,* second edition, Wm. C. Brown Company Publishers, 1976, pp. 58-93.

Alois Carigiet uses vivid and brilliant watercolors in his book Illustrations. A recipient of the Hans Christian Andersen Award in 1966, Carigiet is expressionistic in his style. His illustrations for *A Bell for Ursli* and *The Snowstorm* highlight the gaiety of the Swiss festival for which the children in the stories are preparing. Many of his illustrations in *A Bell for Ursli* and *The Snowstorm,* as well as in *Florina and the Wild Bird,* all written by Selina Chonz, are sumptuous full-color spreads. Each is suggestive of a huge mural. Carigiet's scenes of the Swiss villages and mountains portray Switzerland as a "paradise" that one must be certain to visit as soon as possible.

TITLE COMMENTARY

📖 *A BELL FOR URSLI* (written by Selina Chönz, 1950)

New York Herald Tribune Book Review

SOURCE: A review of *A Bell for Ursli,* in *New York Herald Tribune Book Review,* November 12, 1950, p. 8.

> High in the mountains, far
>   and blue,
> There lives a small boy just like
>   you.
> See the wee village, small but neat?
> His is the last house in the street.

So Ursli's story in verse begins, and we enter again that high, cold beautiful world of the Engadine in Switzerland. Here is a hard-working small boy who wants to lead the Procession of Bells, but can only borrow a tiny bell for the festival, "to ring the winter out." So Ursli climbs through the snow to his father's summer hut high in the mountains, and brings back the biggest bell of all. What a bell! What a journey! What joy when Ursli leads the procession!

The big, gay, modern, funny pictures are enchanting. The verses will appeal widely to the very young. for they have a clever way of pointing to what is in the pictures. It all is as clear as the mountain air, for small Americans who never yet have seen the Alps, nor heard of a life like Ursli's. Here is that Swiss educational intelligence quietly bearing fruit.

As for the printing done in Zurich, it is absolutely superb—the text in gray, these brilliant colors against the snow, and the really black backgrounds for some scenes indoors. Where in America is printing done like this? Hurrah for the Swiss craftsmen, thanks to the lovely city of Zurich, welcome to Ursli!

Ellen Lewis Buell

SOURCE: A review of *A Bell for Ursli,* in *The New York Times Book Review,* November 12, 1950, p. 35.

One of the freshest picture books of the year, **Ursli's Bell** comes from Switzerland. The story-poem is based on the annual Procession of the Bells, during which the village boys ring out the winter and ring in the spring with cowbells. Ursli is determined to have a big bell, "one 'large and loud,' and help the big boys lead the crowd." He wasn't one to be put off with a tiny tinkle bell, not he. So in search of a proper bell he climbs the hazardous mountain and spends the night alone in a mountain hut. The verses are light and gay. The pictures, of the cockeyed Bemelmans school, are at once sophisticated and childlike, resplendent with color and beautifully printed.

Virginia Kirkus' Bookshop Service

SOURCE: A review of *A Bell for Ursli,* in *Virginia Kirkus' Bookshop Service,* Vol. XVIII, No. 22, November 15, 1950, p. 675.

A rambling, winding rhymed tale about a boy and a bell in Switzerland with enchanting full page, full-color illustrations by Alois Carigiet. Ursli lives in a tiny village in the mountains with his father and mother ("Who toils all day for Ursli's sake.") When the Spring Festival comes around, when all the boys march with bells to celebrate the end of winter, Ursli is much cast down when he is given only a small tinkling bell. Then Ursli decides to do something about it, and after a night's adventure comes home with the biggest bell of all. Although the spoofing epic stumbles elegantly into inverted predicates now and then, the gaiety of the rhyme with the pictures of the sharp-nosed villagers and snow, sky, mountains and animals, glitters on every page.

Marc Simont

SOURCE: "Notes about Artists and By Artists about Their Work: *A Bell for Ursli,* in *The Illustrator's Notebook,* edited by Lee Kingman, The Horn Book, Incorporated, 1978, pp. 61-2.

The final judgment upon looking at a picture book—as in looking at a painting, piece of sculpture, reading a book, etc.—rests on the amount of enjoyment we derive from it. When methods and techniques become so important they can't be overlooked, the intensity of enjoyment value is cut.

When I was asked to mention a recent picture book that I liked, *A Bell for Ursli* came to my mind, but, in order to give specific reasons for my choice, I had to go back and take another look.

The illustrations by Alois Carigiet have three important points in their favor—first, they are in harmony with the text; second, they are beautiful pictures; third, they hold together as a unit.

As illustrations they complement the story perfectly. Color is used for what it can do to a picture, not just as a means to define objects. When an object can be used to advantage, however, as in the case of the great, big beautiful bell, the opportunity is not overlooked. Aside from working well with the story, the illustrations hold their own as individual pictures, and this is done without disturbing the cohesiveness of the book.

It is a well-planned, beautifully executed piece of work done in excellent taste.

📖 FLORINA AND THE WILD BIRD (written by Selina Chönz, 1953)

Virginia Kirkus' Bookshop Service

SOURCE: A review of *Florina and the Wild Bird,* in *Virginia Kirkus' Bookshop Service,* Vol. XXI, No. 16, August 15, 1953, p. 531.

Selina Chonz' delightful book, *A Bell for Ursli,* won wide acclaim in 1950. Here is another one about the same Swiss family and its heroine is Florina, Ursli's sister who rescues a wild ptarmigan from a marauding fox. At the mountain hut where they have come to pasture the goats for the summer long-legged, active Florina raises the bird. There's sadness when it must be set free, but when Florina goes in search of it, she finds a lovely crystal high in the crags, sees her bird safe, and goes home happily. Moving rhyme and again the large narrative pictures by Alois Carigiet tell a story as gleaming as the mountains themselves.

Ellen Lewis Buell

SOURCE: A review of *Florina and the Wild Bird,* in *The New York Times Book Review,* November 8, 1953, p. 40.

A Companion volume to the lovely Swiss picture book, *A Bell for Ursli,* this introduces Ursli's sister, Florina. (She must have been away on a visit when the first book was written.) Now it is summer and Ursli and Florina help their parents drive their three goats up through the flow-

From Anton the Goatherd, *written and illustrated by Alois Carigiet.*

ery Alpine meadows to their mountain hut. There Florina rescues a fledgling from a fox, rears it tenderly and, inevitably, is torn between her love for her pet and the bird's need of freedom. A daughter of the free mountain country, Florina makes the right decision—with an unexpected consolation at the end.

Ursli's story was, in miniature, a comedy-adventure; Florina's is more poignant, which is good, since companion volumes need not be twins. Like the earlier story, this is told in verse and in notable pictures, dramatic in color and design.

Claire Huchet Bishop

SOURCE: A review of *Florina and the Wild Bird,* in *The Saturday Review,* New York, Vol. XXXVI, No. 46, November 14, 1953, p. 66.

Those who liked *A Bell for Ursuli* will enjoy this book which comes to us from Switzerland. It tells how Florina found a wild bird and cared for it, and how finally she never was so happy as when she let it go free.

This very sweet story is in free verse easy enough for young readers. If you happen to see the world in a sort of angular way you will like the fresh and gay-colored pictures. A book with a Christmasy touch.

Polly Goodwin

SOURCE: A review of *Florina and the Wild Bird,* in *Chicago Sunday Tribune,* November 15, 1953, p. 7.

High in the Swiss Engadine mountains Florina spends golden, carefree summers with her parents and her brother, Ursli. One day she finds a motherless baby bird, which she shelters and loves until it grows and longs to be free. Ursli persuades her to let it go and, reluctantly, they see it rocket into the sky. Not until the harvest is over and Florina comes down the mountain, does her wild bird reappear and flutter a loving farewell. A companion to *A Bell for Ursli,* this exceptionally lovely Swiss picture book will bring equal joy to small children. They will love the rhyming verses, full of imagination and gayety, and the large, richly colored pictures showing Florina against the wild beauty of the mountains.

Margaret Ford Kieran

SOURCE: A review of *Florina and the Wild Bird,* in *The Atlantic Monthly,* Vol. 192, No. 6, December, 1953, p. 96.

[I'll] give a loud "Huzza!" to *Florina and the Wild Bird* by Selina Chonz. Perhaps you remember *A Bell for Ursli* by the same author. If you do, it will not be necessary for me to whip up your enthusiasm for the story or for the beautifully fluid illustrations of Alois G. Carigiet. The

setting here, as in the earlier book, is the Swiss Alps, and the lilting verses recount an adventure that has all the suspense of the poem known familiarly as "The Night Before Christmas."

Virginia Haviland

SOURCE: A review of *Florina and the Wild Bird,* in *The Horn Book Magazine,* Vol. XXIX, No. 6, December, 1953, p. 452.

A welcome companion to that earlier distinctive Alpine picture book, *A Bell for Ursli.* Again, full-page modern water-color mountain scenes have been printed in Zurich with the sharp vividness of original paintings. They tell as clearly and as gaily as the facing pages of verse the simple, childlike story of how, when the family goes to their summer hut, Ursli's sister Florina rescues a baby ptarmigan and rears it as a pet until it is ready for freedom.

THE SNOWSTORM (written by Selina Chönz, 1958)

Virginia Kirkus' Service

SOURCE: A review of *The Snowstorm,* in *Virginia Kirkus' Service,* Vol. XXVII, No. 15, August 15, 1958, p. 658.

It is lamentable that the author-illustrator team of Selina Chonz and Alois Carigiet, whose *A Bell For Ursli* and *Florina and the Wild Bird,* received such warm acclaim, should suffer so disastrously at the hands of an inadequate translation. This story of Florina and Ursli's ordeal in a snowstorm and of their love for an old weather tree is beautifully illustrated,—one is transported to the exhilarating atmosphere of the Swiss countryside—and doubtless, there is a story here. But the awkward and monotonous quality of the rhymed couplets through which the story is told, all but makes one dizzy. A straight prose version of the text might have resulted in a uniquely charming book, but *The Snowstorm* as it now reads, is a distorted reflection of an enticing promise.

Ellen Lewis Buell

SOURCE: A review of *The Snowstorm,* in *The New York Times Book Review,* September 7, 1958, p. 40.

This is the third picture book about Ursli and Florina, Swiss brother and sister, to appear in America, and even as the earlier two differed in mood, so does this. *A Bell for Ursli* was a lighthearted comedy; *Florina and the Wild Bird* was a poignant tale of a sensitive girl's dilemma. This is primarily adventure, but its telling is not nearly so dramatic as the situation promises. Ursli sends Florina to the spinning woman for tassels to decorate their sled; on the way home Florina is burled by an avalanche but is rescued by her brother in time for an ending full of gaiety and *gemütlichkeit.* Unfortunately, the excitement is over almost before the reader has a chance to savor the shock of danger. And the English translation, in rhyme, is so bumpy that one feels as if he'd been riding over an old road. But if the story is shaky, the pictures are just as handsome as we've come to expect of Alois Carigiet, an evocation of Swiss life and landscape that is both sensitive and vigorous.

Margaret Sherwood Libby

SOURCE: A review of *The Snowstorm,* in *New York Herald Tribune Book Review,* October 26, 1958, p. 15.

As a pictures book **The Snowstorm** vies with the other beautiful books by this author and artist about the Swiss children Florina and Urali, Alois Carigiet's illustrations shiver with the cold or glow with the happy warmth of barn and home. Young children can follow almost all the action without the words. They can see the children planning to trim their sled for the carnival, Florina's dash to the village for extra tassels, the accident in the avalanche on the way home, her rescue—thanks to the old "weather tree" and Ursli—and the clever and triumphant decoration of their sled. It is an appealing plot weakened in the telling by halting and forced rhymes where simple dramatic prose would have been so much more effective.

Margaret Warren Brown

SOURCE: A review of *The Snowstorm,* in *The Horn Book Magazine,* Vol. XXXIV, No. 6, December, 1958, p. 463.

Although Carigiet's art is far from traditional, this lovely book somehow has the old-fashioned flavor of the classic picture book. It is the large pictures, in full color, which count. The story has been translated from the original German into rhymes which seem awkward and halting. But words are almost unnecessary—the pictures, with all their fascinating detail, tell the story of Florina, caught by an avalanche in the Swiss Alps and rescued by Ursli in time to win the prize for the best decorated sled in the children's sledding party.

Kurt Werth

SOURCE: A review of *The Snowstorm,* in *The Horn Book Magazine,* Vol. XXXVI, No. 1, February, 1960, pp. 26-7.

The Snowstorm by Selina Chönz, illustrated by Alois Carigiet, is one of my favorite books of 1958. The text in the English translation is a simplified version of the original German story and easy to read even for young children. The pictures are beautifully reproduced and the book as a whole has atmosphere, charm and lightness. Alois Carigiet has departed from the heavy outlines of his first book, *A Bell for Ursli.* His drawings now are softer in line and color and children will feel a relationship with their own art work.

Snow is always a fascinating experience for the young. I remember my first drawings as a child were often inspired by the merry happenings of a winter day. Snowball fights and ice skating on a frozen pond, trudging home dead tired and hungry as wolves after hour-long activities on the ice, thick snowflakes coming down—this was winter. These scenes I tried to put down again and again on the loose pages of my sketchbook.

I find this spirit again in Carigiet's pictures—they are felt and done with the heart of a child. All the details which are so important, epic and humorous, the accuracy of the scene, the nearness of nature expressed very realistically, are designed in a great style.

One of my favorite illustrations, the scene in the barn where Ursli is feeding a calf, with the horse, the cows, goats, and sheep at their mangers, is an example of powerful drawing and harmonious colors. The grain of the boards, horizontal and vertical, the texture, the movement of the lines, and the naïve, refined forms are a great achievement. I like especially how the warmth of a stable is depicted, with the oil lamp shedding its light on the scene, contrasted by the wintry cold outside shown by a few snowflakes in the open door. The vivid colors in the drawing of the children's party at the end of the book, with music, dancing and eating, should arouse the delight of every child. It is the gayest picture and at the same time the effective finale of the story.

ANTON THE GOATHERD (1966)

Virginia Kirkus' Service

SOURCE: A review of *Anton the Goatherd,* in *Virginia Kirkus' Service,* Vol. XXXIV, No. 21, October 15, 1966, p. 1097.

Klingelingeling. . . . That is the sound of the little bell around the neck of Zock, the smallest goat in the flock. Each morning Anton the goatherd takes Zock, Zick and Zack and all the other goats of the Swiss village up to the meadows to spend the day. Stina, the old mistress of Zack, Zick and Zock warns Anton— "take care . . . you know what they are like!"—but Anton listens with only half an ear. That very day, the three disappear. After searching a long time, Anton hears the soft tinkle of a little bell. To reach the goats, Anton must jump a swift stream. He hurts his ankle but he finds Zick, Zack and Zock safe, and they all return to a warm welcome in the village. That night, Anton dreams about his adventures. In his sleep, he hears the tinkle of the little bell. "(It) grows quieter and quieter until it finally disappears. The only sound . . . is the gentle breathing of the little goatherd." The illustrations are gay and fresh the story is short and to the point—it's the nicest way to go off to sleep.

Marian H. Scott

SOURCE: A review of *Anton the Goatherd,* in *School*

From The Pear Tree, the Birch Tree, and the Barberry Bush, *written and illustrated by Alois Carigiet.*

Library Journal, Vol. 91, No. 22, December 15, 1966, p. 45.

"Zack, Zick and Zock are three nanny goats who live in a small village high up in the mountains. . . . Anton is a goatherd; he herds all the village goats and takes them up to the meadows each morning." So begins a charming tale of a brave young goatherd who goes through a storm to rescue the three wandering goats. The well-known illustrator here tells his own tale, based on memories of his childhood in the Swiss Alps. Distinctive and colorful water-color paintings on every page, of the goatherd and his horn, the Swiss mountainside, and picturesque village scenes are similar to those this artist did for the stories by Chönz.

Ruth Hill Viguers

SOURCE: A review of *Anton the Goatherd,* in *The Horn Book Magazine,* Vol. XLIII, No. 1, February, 1967, pp. 56-7.

The story tells of a summer day in the mountains with a little goatherd, who at the end of the day must search far and long for three wayward goats who do not come with the others when he calls. The simple story is told in the present tense, making it seem no real story at all. Slightness of text is a weakness of all the Carigiet picture books, but those written by Selina Chönz are more interesting than this one. Since the artist has just won the Hans Christian Andersen Award, it is a pity that the new book is not better. The story must have been contrived merely to hold together the pictures, which have lovely colors and interesting detail but are lacking in depth and are little more than repetitions of illustrations in the earlier books.

Bookbird

SOURCE: "Swiss Juvenile Book Prize 1966," in *Bookbird,* Vol. V, No. 2, 1967, p. 42.

Zottel, Zick und Zwerg is the fourth picture book by the Bundner artist. His earlier works, *Schellenursli, Flurina und das Wildvöglein* and *Der grosse Schnee,* have long enchanted children and parents throughout the world. They are all based on stories by Selina Chönz and have been translated into many languages.

The new work, where Carigiet is both author and illustrator, is the story of a goatherd in the canton of Graubünden. Three of this goats, whom he was supposed to watch especially, disappear from the herd. He goes searching for them in a thunderstorm and hurts himself on the way, but manages to bring all his charges safely back home. In a dream the animals whom he met during the day appear to him and thank him for his loving care.

There are many appealing facets to this simple story:

> the painter's quiet home-sickness for the country of his boyhood; the simple life in the mountains of Graubünden, remote from tourism and phony folklore; the biblical story of the good shepherd.

The pictures have become more delicate, more transparent, more fragrant. The sheen of the memory of a happy mountain childhood lies over them.

THE PEAR TREE, THE BIRCH TREE, AND THE BARBERRY BUSH (1967)

Kirkus Service

SOURCE: A review of *The Pear Tree, the Birch Tree and the Barberry Bush,* in *Kirkus Service,* Vol. XXXV, No. 11, June 1, 1967, p. 640.

A barberry bush is better protection for a bird's nest than a tall pear tree is, observes the Tubak family from their quaint house up in the Swiss Alps: magpies steal glittering things, and crows rob chaffinch nests. It's a bird-watcher story of small appeal further limited by a stilted and sometimes overly sentimental text, but the illustrations are superb—full page pencil and watercolor, they are fresh, bright and unaffectedly delicate, communicating the Swiss setting and tenderness of the story far better than the narrative. No one will forget the pictures (or remember the plot).

Zena Sutherland

SOURCE: A review of *The Pear Tree, the Birch Tree and the Barberry Bush,* in *Bulletin of the Center for Children's Books,* Vol. 21, No. 2, October, 1967, p. 23.

An oversize picture book from the Swiss winner of the 1966 Hans Christian Andersen award. The illustrations have a breezy vitality, bright color, and a rather engaging, blithe treatment of the human frame. The story is not strong: A family's home is sheltered by a large pear tree and a birch tree; in one live some crows who rob a chaffinches' nest, in the other a pair of magpies who steal a favorite possession. In the barberry bush lives a hedge sparrow, protected by the thorns of the barberry from

would-be predators; her fledglings grow up safely and fly away for the winter.

Mary Belle Long

SOURCE: A review of *The Pear Tree, the Birch Tree and the Barberry Bush,* in *School Library Journal,* Vol. 14, No. 4, December, 1967, p. 45.

Dominec Tubak, his wife and two children live in a little house high in the Swiss Alps. Their life is quiet, their pleasures simple. Near the house are a pear tree, a birch, and a barberry bush. Bird neighbors include chaffinches, crows, magpies, and hedge sparrows. The only conflict in the story revolves around the quarrelsome crows and the thieving magpies. The translation is smooth and rhythmic. Large illustrations in soft color in Carigiet's usual style are beautiful, as they show the changing seasons and the children, but not enough happens to interest children. Recommended to large picture book collections as an example of the work of an outstanding artist.

ANTON AND ANNE (1969)

Kirkus Reviews

SOURCE: A review of *Anton and Anne,* in *Kirkus Reviews,* Vol. XXXVII, No. 17, September 1, 1969, p. 924.

At a price as steep as Anton's mountains, a book that doesn't make the grade in any circumstances. Carigiet's pictures, which have sometimes compensated for a slight story, are here all too often as unaccented as an abstract expressionist canvas—jagged strokes rend them, multitudinous forms crowd them. Only in a few instances, as when Anton is crossing the glacier's expanse on his way to visit Uncle Tim and Cousin Anne in the city, and again when the three are returning through the snow to Anton's village, do the elements of the composition stand forth clearly and tellingly. What passes for a plot concerns the children's yearning to ride in a helicopter (seen at the airport) and its fulfillment when one gives them a lift after part of the path home has fallen away. Nothing is made of the city cousin-country cousin aspect, and one locale is an quaintly sugared as the other. Not a likely spot for a helicopter to fetch up.

The Christian Science Monitor

SOURCE: "A Glance at the Winners," in *The Christian Science Monitor,* November 6, 1969, p. B1.

Until Alois Carigiet won it for his illustrations to **Anton the Goatherd,** Europe's Hans Christian Andersen Medal was always awarded to a writer. His paint is bright, fresh with that just-applied look, and the printer faithfully records even hairline penciling. His children are full of movement.

In his *Anton and Anne* Anton visits his cousin, a journey-length away, across high mountains. The children nearly get lost in a snowfield, but those who are reading the book in English will find most of its fascination lies in the alien, beautifully recorded landscape and in children caught up in an unfamiliar routine.

Sidney D. Long

SOURCE: A review of *Anton and Anne,* in *The Horn Book Magazine,* Vol. XLV, No. 6, December, 1969, p. 664.

Pictures of stunning beauty and a text that is too cumbersome and wordy to be effective characterize the Hans Christian Andersen Medal-winner's latest book. The classic situation of a country cousin—Anton—visiting his relatives—Anne and Uncle Tim—in the city enables the author-artist to depict scenes of Alpine splendor as well as lovely views of a European city's fountains, flower stalls, bridges, zoo, and airport. When they are at the airport, Anton and Anne develop a great longing to ride in a helicopter; and their wish is granted at the end of the story when a helicopter rescues them from a mountain predicament, and whirls them safely to Anton's home "high up in the Grison Mountains."

Josette A. Boissé

SOURCE: A review of *Anton and Anne,* in *School Library Journal,* Vol. 16, No. 4, December, 1969, p. 40.

Suffering slightly from a literal translation: e.g., "Even the pilot is smiling all over his face," Carigiet's story is redeemed by colorful, airy watercolors with a myriad of detail that crisply portray life in the Grison Mountains of Switzerland. Anton goes to the city to visit his Uncle Tim and Cousin Anne, and there delights in the zoo, the arriving and departing planes at the airport, etc. Accompanied on his mountain-hiking trip home by Uncle Tim and Anne, Anton's adventure is capped by a rescue-ride in a helicopter when a crumbled mountain path bars the threesome's terrestrial progress. Children who can't yet read can follow the story through the full-page illustrations; the oversized book (9 5/8" X 12 5/8") offers a visual appreciation of another country's culture. However, the price is steep for a slight story and sometimes stilted text.

Zena Sutherland

SOURCE: A review of *Anton and Anne,* in *Bulletin of the Center for Children's Books,* Vol. 23, No. 7, March, 1970, p. 108.

An oversize book affords the author-illustrator a splendid opportunity to paint large-scale, effective pictures of mountain scenery and a few particularly delectable ones of a Swiss town. The story, originally published in Switzerland under the title *Maurus und Madleina,* has a modest plot: Anton goes from his rural home to visit his cousin Anne in the town, where they go sightseeing; on the trip back, Anne and Uncle Tim accompany Anton, and they are rescued, when trapped by a landfall, by a helicopter. Not very substantial and sedately written, but the action does have a focus and the illustrations are lovely.

Joseph H. Schwarcz

SOURCE: "The Roles of Natural Landscape," in *Ways of the Illustrator: Visual Communication in Children's Literature,* American Library Association, 1982, pp. 55-64.

Fascinating in their own special way are illustrations where nature, its shapes and forces, represent aspects of the protagonist's state of mind; where, in other words, emotions are projected onto the landscape, and expressed visually.

In Carigiet's *Maurus and Madleina,* [*Anton and Anne*], Maurus the village boy sets out to visit his girl cousin in the city, has to cross white rocks and a very steep mountain slope, where he has to proceed on a narrow, partly decayed path, keeping close to the rocks. While the illustration includes realistic elements, its force lies in the strongly marked, scraggy, nervous lines of the almost perpendicular threatening slope, reinforced by a few broken trees, the only horizontal line being the thread-like meandering path on which the boy wearily advances. Thus expression is given to the anxiety and dynamic tension gripping him. Yet the triangle formed by his body and by the stick he supports himself with, introduces an element of balance, of decision.

Additional coverage of Carigiet's life and career is contained in the following sources published by Gale Research: *Contemporary Authors,* Vols. 73-76, 119; and *Something about the Author,* Vols. 24, 47.

Eloise Greenfield

1929-

African-American author of fiction, nonfiction, picture books, and poetry.

Major works include *Honey, I Love and Other Love Poems* (1978), *Childtimes: A Three-Generation Memoir* (1979), *Nathaniel Talking* (1989), *Night on Neighborhood Street* (1991).

For information on Greenfield's career prior to 1980, see *CLR,* Vol. 4.

INTRODUCTION

A writer of both prose and poetry for young people, Greenfield has received praise for her positive and hopeful stories, poems, and biographies about contemporary African Americans. Designed to inspire confidence and self-esteem in children, her books offer realistic portraits of loving family relationships and are often lauded for their sensitive portrayal of childhood joys and fears. Although many of the themes in Greenfield's works—such as friendship and coping with change—are universal, she acknowledges a political agenda as well, noting the need for sound role models for black youth. Without sugarcoating the everyday problems of modern life, she addresses such difficult realities as death, divorce, poverty, insecurity, and loneliness. Greenfield creates proud, strong-willed characters who know and like themselves and are comfortable expressing their feelings. These protagonists draw strength from the support of stable families, providing a positive picture of what it means to grow up African American.

Biographical Information

Greenfield was born in Parmele, North Carolina and raised in Washington, D.C. during the decade of the Great Depression. Washington was racially segregated at that time; Greenfield writes: "There were a lot of things we couldn't do and places we couldn't go. Washington was a city for white people. But inside that city, there was another city. It didn't have a name and it wasn't all in one area, but it was where black people lived." When Greenfield was nine years old, her family moved to Langston Terrace, a new housing project where they found a supportive community of African Americans. Greenfield spent much of her free time as an adolescent reading at the Langston branch of the public library, where she later worked part-time while attending college. She began writing in her early twenties, soon after her marriage to Robert J. Greenfield in 1950. Working as a clerk-typist in a government office, Greenfield initially wrote rhymes and songs as a creative diversion. She later completed several short sto-

ries for adults, some of which were published in *Negro Digest* (later *Black World*) between 1965 and 1974. Her first book for children, *Bubbles,* was published in 1972.

Major Works

Childtimes: A Three Generation Memoir is an autobiography written by Greenfield with her mother and grandmother. In this work, Greenfield uses the experiences of her own family to represent the obstacles facing all black people, emphasizing that these challenges can be surmounted with the support of strong family bonds. Many of Greenfield's stories and collections of poetry focus on similar themes, highlighting warm and positive images of life in urban African-American communities. *Grandmama's Joy* (1980) is a sensitive portrait of the relationship between child-protagonist Rhondy and Grandmama, who are forced from their home by rising costs. Rhondy helps her distraught grandmother have the strength to face their dilemma when she reminds her of the accident that killed Rhondy's parents and left the young girl in Grandmama's care. At that tragic time, Grandmama looked at the orphaned infant in the hospital and thought, "That's Grandmama's joy. Long as I got my joy, I'll be all right." Greenfield explores a child's emotional growth in *Grandpa's Face* (1988), another story of love between generations. In this work, Tamika is frightened and confused when she opens the door to her grandfather's room and sees him rehearsing lines for a play, expressing a harsh, angry face to which she is unaccustomed. This unsettling experience causes Tamika to become sullen and misbehave, angering her parents. Grandpa takes her to the park, where Tamika reveals her concern and is reassured of her Grandpa's unfailing love. The poetry in *Nathaniel Talking* demonstrates the power of confidence and positive thinking for children in eighteen first-person poems that offer nine-year-old narrator Nathaniel B. Free's "philosophy" and his description of the world around him. Several of the poems imitate musical rhythms from various eras, surveying a variety of African-American musical forms from twelve-bar blues to rap, each honoring a member of Nathaniel's family born in that time period. *Night on Neighborhood Street* is likewise a poetic tribute to black American society. In this book, Greenfield once again celebrates the power of love in a modern, urban community, exploring the everyday worries and delights of the younger residents of a city block. Of this collection, which includes five poems that can be read with a rap beat, Gale W. Sherman writes: "The nighttime urban Black world Greenfield depicts is one of nurturing friends and families alongside the stark realities of a present-day world with unemployed fathers, drug dealers, and scary boarded-up houses. While portraying the real world with the good and the bad, *Night on Neighborhood Street* gives readers a sense of security and hope for the future." Greenfield has also written three well-received biographies for young readers: *Rosa Parks, Paul Robeson,* and *Mary McLeod Bethune.*

Awards

Greenfield received the first Carter G. Woodson Award in 1974 for *Rosa Parks*, the Irma Simonton Black Award that same year for *She Come Bringing Me That Little Baby Girl*, and the Jane Addams Children's Book Award in 1976 for *Paul Robeson*. She was given the Boston Globe-Horn Book Award for nonfiction in 1980 for *Childtimes: A Three-Generation Memoir* and the George C. Stone Award for *Honey, I Love and Other Poems* in 1990. She won the Coretta Scott King Award three times, in 1978, 1990, and 1991, for *Africa Dream, Nathaniel Talking,* and *Night on Neighborhood Street*, respectively. Greenfield was honored with a citation for her body of work from the Council on Interracial Books for Children in 1975.

AUTHOR'S COMMENTARY

Eloise Greenfield

SOURCE: "Writing for Children—A Joy and a Responsi-

bility," in *Interracial Books for Children Bulletin,* Vol. 10, No. 3, 1979, pp. 3-4.

It is a joy to write for children. In addition to the satisfactions that derive from creative activity, there is a sense of sharing the world with someone who hasn't been in it very long. It's a joy.

And yet, there are times when I wonder why anyone would want to write, to suffer the pain and frustration of trying to trigger a flow of words that won't come, and be racked by the fear that a door has slammed and locked the words inside forever. At those times I have to say to myself, "This has happened before, I've had this terror before, the words will come, they'll come." I try to remember that although words do sometimes flow unbidden from their source, it is often just this suffering, this tension, that awakens my African muse.

Almost every writer has experienced this terror and the rush of relief and gratitude that accompanies, finally, the rush of words. It is not easy, therefore, to admit that the Muse is not infallible, that she must be continually challenged as to the validity of her offerings, but we must have the courage to face that fact. Our audience is too vulnerable, too impressionable, for us to entrust our art entirely to this force that lies somewhere in the subconscious mind, that repository of accumulated knowledge, attitudes and emotions. Both the rational and the irrational, the healthful and the harmful reside there as the result of a lifetime of conditioning.

In this society, our conditioning has been, to a great extent, irrational and harmful. This country was built on a foundation of racism, a foundation which is only slightly less firm after centuries of Black struggle. Attitudes toward women, toward men, attitudes regarding age, height, beauty, mental and physical disabilities have been largely of the kind that constrain rather than encourage human development. To perpetuate these attitudes through the use of the written word constitutes a gross and arrogant misuse of talent and skill.

Librarians, no less than writers, have a responsibility to challenge their own conscious and subconscious beliefs, as well as the validity of the books they select. Standing as they do between authors and children, they are the conduit through which book messages flow. The importance of their role as selector cannot be overemphasized. Nor can the importance of the question they must ask: What is the author saying?

There is a viewpoint which denies the relevance of this question, that holds art to be sacrosanct, subject to scrutiny only as to its esthetic value. This viewpoint is in keeping with the popular myth that genuine art is not political. It is true that politics is not art, but art is political. Whether in its interpretation of the political realities, or in its attempts to ignore these realities, or in its distortions, or in its advocacy of a different reality, or in its support of the status quo, all art is political and every book carries its author's message.

In the area of Black-oriented literature, much of what is communicated is venomous. Considerable attention has been devoted by sociologists to the study of the targets of racial abuse and oppression. The trauma, the damage to the spirit, the stifling of creativity, the threat to mere physical survival, have all been well-documented. Not enough attention, however, has been given to the study of those who, because of their conditioning, manifest delusions of grandeur, delusions that the whiteness of their skin makes them somehow special. The necessity to keep these delusions well-nourished, to fortify them against any invasion of reality, makes these people menaces to society. Some of them are writers. They wield word-weapons, sometimes overtly, sometimes insidiously, yet they disclaim all responsibility for what they say, being merely objective observers of the human scene, or secretaries transcribing the dialogue of characters over whom they have no control. Is it the writer's fault that the characters just happen to be racist?

Children need protection from these word-weapons. They need protection in the form of organizations such as the Council on Interracial Books for Children and Black literature journals such as *Black Books Bulletin,* and they need librarians who care. The library can and should become the center for regular and systematic education of children in the dynamics of racism as it occurs in literature. Even the youngest school-age child can be told: "There are some people in the world who are very sick. Some of them are so sick that they don't want you to know what a wonderful being you are."

Until children are knowledgeable enough to defend themselves, racist books must be kept out of their reach, as any other deadly weapon would be. To say this is not to demean the intelligence of children, but to recognize the power of communication to influence the thought, emotions and behavior not only of children, but also of adults. The tens of billions of advertising dollars effectively spent each year attest to this fact. And consider this—there must have been a time in our recent history when there was only one Farrah Fawcett-Majors, and now there are at least three in every square mile of the North American continent.

The books that reach children should: authentically depict and interpret their lives and their history; build self-respect and encourage the development of positive values; make children aware of their strength and leave them with a sense of hope and direction; teach them the skills necessary for the maintenance of health and for economic survival; broaden their knowledge of the world, past and present, and offer some insight into the future. These books will not be pap—the total range of human problems, struggles and accomplishments can be told in this context with no sacrifice of literary merit. We are all disappointed when we read a book that has no power, a story that arouses no emotion, passages that lack the excitement that language can inspire. But the skills that are used to produce a well-written racist book can be used as well for one that is anti-racist. The crucial factor is that literary merit cannot be the sole criterion. A book that has been chosen as worthy of a child's emotional investment must have been judged on the basis of what it is—not a collection of words arranged in some unintelligible but artistic design, but a statement powerfully made and communicated through the artistic and skillful use of language.

We are living now in a period of rapid growth comparable to that one year in the life of adolescents when they have trouble keeping up with the changes occurring in their bodies. We are struggling to keep up with our new understanding as we unlearn myths that have existed for hundreds—in some cases thousands—of years, and as we challenge the concepts that have defined us and our goals.

Webster's New World Dictionary, for example, defines the word success as: "the gaining of wealth, fame, rank, etc." I am incensed each time I read it. To take beings who have the potential for infinite growing, infinite giving of their ideas and talents, of their caring, and to commend for their greatest efforts aspirations that glorify two of the basest of human attributes—greed and egotism—and not be ashamed to set it down in print, is a harsh self-indictment by the society in which we live. And this from a society that boasts of being civilized.

But we are learning. Though few of us here today will live to see it, there will come a time when positive attitudes will be so ingrained in the fabric of our society, so pervasive, that constant examination of our artistic expressions will no longer be necessary. Our art will reflect us, and we will be in a state of health. For now, though, we have work to do. We will make mistakes sometimes. We will have periods of conflict and confusion. But we owe it to children, we owe it to posterity, and we owe it to ourselves to persevere. Our place in history demands it.

GENERAL COMMENTARY

Rosalie Black Kiah

SOURCE: "Profile: Eloise Greenfield," in *Language Arts,* Vol. 57, No. 6, September, 1980, pp. 653-59.

Since her first children's book, ***Bubbles,*** (now titled ***Good News***) was published in the early 1970s, Eloise Greenfield has found writing for children a joy. This is evidenced in the thirteen books, including one book of poetry, that she has written for the delight of children. She cares about children and how words can make them feel. Commenting on the wonder of words she states:

> I want children to think, but I also want them to feel something. If I don't touch their emotions, then I have failed to that extent.

Mrs. Greenfield was in her early twenties when she began writing. Before that time she had given little thought to it. She cannot recall the moment when she decided to write except that working as a GS-3 clerk typist in a government office became very boring and provided the incentive for writing. Her first effort consisted of rhymes which she shared only with family members. "I didn't submit these early rhymes for publication, rather it was just something I wanted to do." Soon she was caught up in the excitement of moving words around on paper.

From rhymes she went to writing music and lyrics for songs, accumulating some ten taped songs which she still has. She describes them as "corny." Once she submitted one of her songs to a local television show that invited the audience to send in original songs which would eventually be published and played on the air. A few weeks later, she received a letter from the program director stating that the show was going off the air. Laughingly she recalls that she didn't know whether her song had anything to do with the cancellation of the show.

Writing adult short stories was her next venture and she decided at this point to give herself a test. The test would consist of writing three stories and submitting the manuscripts for publication. If all three stories were rejected, she would have failed her test. They were and she was convinced that she had no writing talent. Several years passed and she learned that even with talent, there are certain writing techniques that must be mastered.

Getting a manuscript published was not easy for her. As is the case with most writers, Mrs. Greenfield received many rejections. This did not discourage her, rather she continued to study the techniques of writing and to submit her manuscripts. The rejection slips continued to arrive for five years. But she wanted to write even if she did not get published. "I was more disappointed than discouraged," she stated. Using the *Writer's Market,* she eventually got a poem published in the *Hartford (Conn.) Times* on the editorial page. This was her first break. Two years later she discovered *Negro Digest* (later *Black World*) in the neighborhood drugstore and began sending her short stories to the magazine. They liked her work and published several of her stories between 1965 and 1974.

Mrs. Greenfield's first book for children, *Bubbles,* was written in 1966. It was rejected about ten times and finally published in 1972. In 1977 it was newly illustrated and reissued under the title *Good News.*

Good News is the story of James Edward and his elation over the discovery that he could read. Wanting to share the good news with his mother first, James Edward is disappointed when Mother is too busy to share his excitement. Bursting with his good news and eager to share it with someone, he settles for telling his baby sister who is too young to understand. James Edward's excitement comes over well in this story, which also conveys a compassionate picture of affection between a brother and a sister.

In 1971, Mrs. Greenfield joined the staff of the District of Columbia Black Writers Workshop. This organization, founded by Annie Crittenden, a playwright, had as its purpose to bring together writers, both published and unpublished, to share their common interest. New writers would read their manuscripts to the group and have them critiqued. The workshop, which disbanded in 1975, was divided into several different groups: fiction, non-fiction, poetry, playwriting, and children's literature. It was here that she met award-winning author Sharon Bell Mathis, who at that time was the head of the Children's Literature Division. Mrs. Greenfield later succeeded Mrs. Mathis as the head of this division.

Rosa Parks (1973) a Crowell Biography, was a direct result of Mrs. Greenfield's association with the D. C. Black Writers Workshop. (At the time she joined, Sharon Bell Mathis and Ophelia Settle Egypt were writing books in this series—*Ray Charles* and *James Weldon Johnson,* respectively.) The book received the first Carter G. Woodson Award, given by the National Council for the Social Studies. This easy-to-read biography is about the Montgomery, Alabama woman whose courage started the bus boycott led by Martin L. King, Jr.

Sister (1974), Mrs. Greenfield's first novel for young people, embraces many aspects of the human experience—life, death, love, laughter, sadness. All are carefully documented by Doretha (or "Sister," as she is known to the family) in a book she calls her "Doretha Book," which observes her older sister withdraw from the family following the death of the father. About Doretha, Mrs. Greenfield observes, "I could write about a child who was shy because I know that experience very well."

Mrs. Greenfield's fourth book for children, *She Came Bringing Me That Little Baby Girl* (1974), was the recipient of the 1974 Irma Simonton Black Award, a selection made by children, under the sponsorship of the Bank Street College of Education. This is the story of Kevin and his disappointment when instead of bringing home a little brother from the hospital, mother brings a little sister. Not only is Kevin disappointed but also a bit jealous. The author shows in this work that, "Every child has a place in the family. Parents have enough love for all of their children."

Aside from her most recent book *Childtimes,* Mrs. Greenfield does not consider her books autobiographical. Rather, she draws from those things she has experienced, observed, heard about, and read about. Then she combines them, changes them and finally develops them into her stories. Such was the case with the character of Grandpa Jack in *Sister.*

> When my grandfather was almost ninety years old, he told me about his father who had been a slave as a child, and his grandfather, Grandpappy Jack, who was a slave from Guinea, West Africa. Grandpappy Jack became a shoemaker in Edgecombe County, North Carolina, and he had a reputation for being extremely protective of his children. I put all of this together to create the composite character of Grandpa Jack.

A line from Lucille Clifton's poem, "Good Times," was used as an epigraph to capture the mood of the story:

". . . oh children think about the good times." Commenting on this, Mrs. Greenfield maintains, "We have pain, but we can look to the good things in our lives to help us get past the painful periods. We can lean on those things and on the people who love us."

Children will delight in the experiences of Janell and her imaginary playmate Neesie, in the warm and humorous picture book entitled, *Me and Neesie,* a 1975 ALA Notable Children's Book. This is a simple story of a little girl's imagination and how it almost causes trouble when her aunt comes to visit.

Paul Robeson (1975) and *Mary McLeod Bethune* (1977) are the second and third in the Crowell Biography series written by Eloise Greenfield. *Paul Robeson* was the recipient of the 1976 Jane Addams Children's Book Award and the 1976 Runner-up for the Coretta Scott King Award. This is a brief biography for young readers about the life and times of a black man who was a famous singer, actor and fighter for equal rights. Written in language that children can understand, the author presents highlights of Robeson's life from childhood through adulthood.

The biography of Mary McLeod Bethune depicts the life of this black pioneer educator. The author provides the young reader with a story that is as beautiful as it is informative. In writing the biographies of black Americans, Mrs. Greenfield is carrying out what for her is a mission "to make children aware of the people who have contributed to the struggle for black liberation."

"There must be a story there" is one of her favorite lines, hence the flicker of a picture book entitled, *First Pink Light* (1976). Mrs. Greenfield tells it this way:

> One Christmas, when my nephew, Darren, was five or six years old, he received a camera as a gift, but no flash attachment. He'd gotten up at 3:00 a.m., as so many children do on Christmas, and he wanted to use his camera immediately. My sister explained that he needed daylight and suggested that he go back to bed and sleep until morning. But he said, "No," that he'd sit up and wait for daylight, and that's what he did. Then he went outdoors and took pictures of the trees. As soon as my sister told me about it, I said, "There must be a story there."

With this basic theme of a child waiting and of the dawn, she began working on the story. She described how she got up early one morning to see what dawn looked like, although she had seen it before. But this time she wanted to really look. That she did, seeing the sky turn pink in streaks, just before the sun comes up. From this came a story of the innocence and beauty of a child's world.

In the story, Tyree, a typical four year old, is determined to stay up and greet his daddy after a month's absence. He gets angry with his mother and feels she doesn't understand when she tells him he has to go to bed. A compromise is reached when Tyree is permitted to sit in the big chair with his pajamas on and wait. He is also told that he will know when daddy is coming when he sees the

Greenfield's high school graduation photo, 1946.

"first pink light" in the sky. Of course Tyree falls asleep before dawn, but settles in with the feeling that he had won. This is a cozy story of family love and a theme that dominates all of the stories by the author.

In 1978, the Coretta Scott King Award, which is given annually to the author of a book published during the preceding year which exemplifies the life and philosophy of Martin Luther King, Jr., went to Eloise Greenfield and illustrator Carole Byard for *Africa Dream* (1977). The rich life and culture of the African continent are captured in this beautifully illustrated picture book. It tells of a child's dream of crossing the ocean and landing in "Africa, Long-ago Africa." The author weaves in an abundance of information about the culture as well as the heritage of Africa as the text and the illustrations flow in a melodic mood.

I Can Do It By Myself (1978) marked the beginning of the writing team of Lessie Jones Little and Eloise Greenfield (mother and daughter). Mrs. Greenfield's mother began her writing career at the age of sixty-seven in 1974. This is the first of two children's books resulting from their collaboration. The story relates the experiences of young Donny as he attempts to establish his own independence. It is mother's birthday and he has plans to go by himself to purchase a plant to give her as a gift. A few obstacles stand in his way but this does not prevent him from completing his mission. There is warmth, humor, and family love portrayed in this story.

Cited as a 1978 ALA Notable Book, *Honey, I Love and Other Love Poems* (1978) is Eloise Greenfield's first collection of children's poems. There are sixteen poems in all that encompass the everyday experiences of a young black girl. These are poems about warm loving relationships with family, friends, and schoolmates. The theme is captured in the last two poems in the book that speak of the child's ability to love and above all else, love herself:

Love don't mean all that kissing
Like on television
Love means Daddy
Saying keep your mama company
　till I get back
And me doing it

I love
I love a lot of things
A whole lot of things
And honey,
I love ME, too.

Mrs. Greenfield also wrote the poem that was featured on 1979 bookmark for Children's Book Week.

Eloise Greenfield discusses the theme of *Talk About a Family* (1978):

Families come in various shapes. There is no one shape that carries with it more legitimacy than any other. All of them are legitimate. In the case of divorce and separation—the problems that parents have—the children can go on and build their own lives regardless of the problems of the parents. Children *have* to go on and build their own lives.

This serious theme is handled perceptively and sensibly as young Genny learns to cope with and accept the new "shape" the family is taking. Her mother and father are planning to separate and she makes every effort to prevent this. It is through the help of an elderly widower friend that Genny beings to realize that some things can never remain the same.

Mrs. Greenfield comments on books for children that present problems, social or otherwise:

When I write about problems, I like to leave children with hope. I don't think it's constructive just to give them a rundown of the problems they already know they have. I feel that I must leave them with some kind of hope or some direction they can take toward solutions.

The theme of family life runs throughout all of her books. "I look back on my childhood with pleasure. It wasn't perfect, but overall it was a very joyful part of my life."

We share her childhood and that of her mother and grandmother in her most recent book entitled *Childtimes: A Three-Generation Memoir* (1979). This second book written with her mother, Lessie Jones Little, is the story of the childhood days of the three women. They reconstruct the times they used to have as children. Each experience, though set in a different time, is rich in human feeling and strong family love.

Concerning the title, *Childtimes: A Three-Generation Memoir,* Eloise Greenfield explains:

We wanted to take just one family and show what black people have given to their children. Even though they had to face the utmost in opposition and harsh conditions, and with almost nothing in the way of material things, they somehow provided their children with real childhoods. So we could take our experiences and they could represent the experiences of other black people.

When asked if her daughter would write the next chapter to this book, she replied:

I hope that someday, maybe ten years from now, my daughter will put her experiences on paper. Not necessarily for publication, but for the family, just to keep the story moving forward.

Recently, the proprietors of a children's bookstore expressed to Mrs. Greenfield their hope that children who read *Childtimes* will write down the childhood experiences of their parents and grandparents. Mrs. Greenfield hopes that children will, at least, add their own experiences to this book. "Compare their lives," she says, "with what our lives were like in each of the three sections. Theirs will be the fourth section."

Eloise Greenfield was born in Parmele, North Carolina. She grew up in Washington, D.C., where she and her husband now live. Mrs. Greenfield is the mother of a son and a daughter, both adults now. How much help does she get from her husband and family? "They often read my manuscripts before they are submitted and I value their opinions. Usually at least one of them will read the manuscript before I send it out. They are very supportive, but honest. They will tell me if they think something doesn't work; and I ask their opinions if I run into problems or if I'm not sure about something. I call them my in-house editors."

Since most of her books are aimed at the young reader, it is important that there be complete unity between the text and the illustrations. Mrs. Greenfield's books have not suffered from a lack of quality art work. Her books have been illustrated by Carole Byard, Moneta Barnett, George Ford, Leo and Diane Dillon, Jerry Pinkney, and John Steptoe.

Why did she decide to write exclusively for children rather than remaining with her short stories for adults?

When I joined the D.C. Black Writers Workshop, I

met Sharon (Bell Mathis) and she was so deeply involved in children's literature and talked so passionately about the need for good black books that it was contagious. Once I realized the full extent of the problems, it became urgent for me to try, along with others, to build a large collection of books for children. It has been inspiring to me to be a part of this struggle.

Finally, she says, "I would like to have time to write an occasional short story, and some other things, but I don't feel any urgency about them. It seems that I am always being pushed from inside to do children's books, those are more important."

Gale W. Sherman

SOURCE: "Hip-Hop Culture Raps into Children's Books," in *Bookbird,* Vol. 33, No. 1, Spring, 1995, pp. 21-5.

The emergence of hip-hop and rap music "can be traced back to the tribes of Africa, back to James Brown sliding across the stage at the Apollo, [and] back to the chatter of men-folk inside the barber shop." But the actual birth moment of this "new urban blues" occurred when DJ Hollywood and Lovebug Starski hooked up their speakers, turntables, mixer, and microphones on the streets of Harlem during the summer of 1977. The subculture which emerged that summer, as an underground music movement, has grown into a major force influencing many aspects of American life, including speech, fashion designs, and television programs.

In his linguistic explanation of the words "hip-hop" and "rap," language critic and historian William Safire noted that the use of the word "rap" to describe speech can be traced to the fourteenth century. However, it was not generally used in this sense until the 1960s and did not make its entry into the dictionary until 1970. "Within a decade," Safire observed, "the noun was used attributively in *rap music,* labeling the rhythmic rhyming lines set to an insistent beat." *The Dictionary of Contemporary Slang* tells us that *rap,* meaning "to talk, converse, or discuss," was first used in Black American speech and subsequently adopted by white hipsters, beatniks, and finally hippies. Although the exact origin of this use of the word is unclear, possible etymologies include a shortening of *rapid* (speech), *rapport,* or *repartee.* The term might come simply from the similarity between talking and tapping ("rapping") on a drum or other surface; this might fit an origin among jazz musicians (rap session). Alternatively, in archaic slang a *rapper* was someone who talked to the authorities, and this notion may have become generalized in Black argot into "talk." All of these explanations have in common the association of rap not with music, but with speech and its own cadences. It is in its essence spoken poetry.

Eloise Greenfield's **"Nathaniel's Rap"** was one of the first published rap poems for children. Greenfield has written over 20 children's books, accurate portrayals of African-American children, their lives, and their history.

With the importance music has played in her life since childhood, it was natural for her to pioneer the use of the rap rhyme scheme and verse form in children's literature.

"Nathaniel's Rap" launched an 18 poem collection entitled *Nathaniel Talking* (1988). Using the rap rhythms Black children are familiar with, nine-year-old Nathaniel thinks about his world and his place in it—his family life, his day-to-day experiences, and his future. The poem begins:

> It's Nathaniel talking
> and Nathaniel's me
> I'm talking about
> My philosophy
> About the things I do
> And the people I see
> All told in the words
> Of Nathaniel B. Free
> That's me
> And I can rap
> I can rap
> I can rap, rap, rap
> Till your earflaps flap . . .

As with rap generally, readers are easily caught up in the strong rhythm of this poem and might find not only their earflaps flapping but also their feet tap-tapping!

Though **"Nathaniel's Rap"** is the only rap poem in this collection, all 18 poems resonate with Greenfield's carefully chosen words and rhythms. She evocatively portrays Nathaniel as a spirited Black child in touch with his being and the beat of his environment. As the first writer in the field of children's literature to include rap, Greenfield set a high standard.

Three years later, *Night on Neighborhood Street* was published. This celebration of African-American neighborhood life has 17 original poems, including five which can be read with a rap beat: **"Little Boy Blues," "Fambly Time," "When Tonya's Friends Come to Spend the Night," "Buddy's Dream,"** and **"Lawanda's Walk."** The nighttime urban Black world Greenfield depicts is one of nurturing friends and families alongside the stark realities of a present-day world with unemployed fathers, drug dealers, and scary boarded-up houses. While portraying the real world with the good and the bad, *Night on Neighborhood Street* gives readers a sense of security and hope for the future.

TITLE COMMENTARY

📖   *FIRST PINK LIGHT* **(1976; revised edition, 1991)**

Publishers Weekly

SOURCE: A review of *First Pink Light,* in *Publishers Weekly,* Vol. 238, No. 50, November 15, 1991, p. 72.

The creators of *Nathaniel Talking* and *Night on Neighborhood Street* again pool their considerable talents for a sympathetic and accessible tale. Like a one-act play, the story's scope is small: a boy talks his mother into letting him wait up for his father's return. The focus here is not on just the events, however, but also on the emotions involved—Tyree's elation with the cardboard fort he hides in while his mother does her homework, his sweetly transparent manipulations to get his way and, finally, as the "first pink light" of dawn appears, his welcome surrender to sleep. Accordingly, [Jan Spivey] Gilchrist's illustrations focus on those windows of emotion, the faces. Her portraits are suffused with ardor and affection, and help create fully realized characters. Kudos also to this duo for their loving depiction of an African American family with a strong father figure. This tender book is a valuable addition—but needn't be limited—to the multicultural bookshelf.

Kathleen T. Horning

SOURCE: A review of *First Pink Light*, in *Booklist*, Vol. 88, No. 8, December 15, 1991, p. 773.

A newly illustrated edition of a story first published in 1976 once again combines the talents of the author and illustrator of *Nathaniel Talking*. Preschooler Tyree anxiously awaits the return of his father, who has been away from home for a month taking care of Tyree's grandmother. Even though his mother tells him his daddy won't be home until daybreak, Tyree is adamant about staying up so he can hide in a cardboard box underneath the dining-room table to surprise his daddy. After some marvelously realistic negotiating, mother agrees to let Tyree sit in a rocking chair at the living-room window, watching for the "first pink light" of dawn. As the evening wears on for the tiny sentry, his wise mother suggests that a pillow and blanket might make his post more comfortable. She is right, of course, and soon Tyree is fast asleep. Greenfield's humorous yet poignant story unfolds entirely through Tyree's believable actions and interactions, achieving a depth of character and drama rarely seen in realistic stories of and for preschoolers. . . . As a read-aloud selection either one-on-one or for groups of preschoolers, this will delight the grown-ups as well as the children.

Karen James

SOURCE: A review of *First Pink Light*, in *School Library Journal*, Vol. 38, No. 1, January, 1992, p. 90.

Tyree is determined to stay awake until his father, who's been away from home for a month, returns in the morning. He wants to hear " . . . daddy's hard shoes on the steps, and hear his daddy's key clicking in the door." Mother finally tucks him in a chair to wait. Tyree does fall asleep, but it doesn't matter in the pleasure of his father's homecoming. Without sentimentality, and in flowing natural language, Greenfield shows the loving inter-

action of a young black child and his parents. Gentle watercolor illustrations enhance the feeling of a close family relationship. Tyree's emotions, from his stubborn refusal to go to bed to his fight to keep awake, are shown in his posture and on his face. The father is a handsome, smiling man set against a background of the warm "first pink light" of morning. First published in 1976 and illustrated by Moneta Barnett, the story has been given an updated look with full-color illustrations and a larger format. There is more emphasis on closeups of Tyree, and the faces of all three characters are more individualized and realistically expressive. This is a loving family story that will have strong appeal for a new generation of children.

📖 *TALK ABOUT A FAMILY* (1978; revised edition, 1980)

Beryle Banfield

SOURCE: A review of *Talk About a Family*, in *Interracial Books for Children Bulletin*, Vol. 11, No. 8, 1980, pp. 16-17.

I hereby declare Eloise Greenfield a national treasure! This extremely gifted and sensitive writer consistently produces exquisitely wrought works which illuminate key aspects of the Black experience in a way that underlines both its uniqueness and universality. Small triumphs, special relationships and crises of survival are portrayed in a manner that strikes a responsive chord in all readers. You have to care about the people Eloise Greenfield writes about. You have to feel about them. . . .

Talk About a Family explores the effects of parents' constant conflict and eventual separation on their children who love them both very much. Genny, the hero of the story, is confident that her brother Larry, who is due home from the army, will heal the rift between her parents. When even Larry fails, Genny is upset and angry. Mr. Parker, a friend and neighbor, helps her to realize that although her family situation has changed, there is still a great deal to cherish and hold onto. Genny then considers the different shapes of different families. Concerning the new shape of her own family, she muses "me and Kim and Mac and Larry and Mama, me and Kim and Mac and Larry and Daddy. Two circles. Two circles linked together. That was their shape for now. She would have to get used to it."

📖 *GRANDMAMA'S JOY* (1980)

Judith Goldberger

SOURCE: A review of *Grandmama's Joy*, in *Booklist*, Vol. 77, No. 1, September 1, 1980, p. 44.

Rhondy knows all the ways to make her Grandmama smile; she dresses up, sings like a TV star, and looks for pretty things in the yard to give her. But today, Grandmama won't smile. "We have to leave our yard," she explains. The house they have lived in is too expensive now. As sometimes happens, the child is more resourceful than the adult. Rhondy begs Grandmama to retell the story of their coming together; how, after the accident that killed Rhondy's parents, the older woman came to get Rhondy in the hospital. Rhondy reminds Grandmama of her words then: "Long as I got my joy, I'll be all right," and a sad morning ends with a long, warm hug. The substance of the incident is expressed in perceptions and words of emotion. Likewise the illustrations [by Carole Byard], done in soft, deep charcoal, focus on facial and body expression. This is the portrait of a relationship, revealed less as story than as the unfolding of love.

Zena Sutherland

SOURCE: A review of *Grandmama's Joy,* in *Bulletin of the Center for Children's Books,* Vol. 34, No. 2, October, 1980, p. 32.

Hazy charcoal drawings, deftly composed but a bit repetitive, illustrate a brief story nicely told but not quite substantial enough to hold most primary grades readers. Rhondy tries to cheer her grandmother on a day when Grandmama seems depressed and preoccupied. Finally she reminds her of the accident that killed her parents, and how Grandmama looked at her in the hospital and thought ". . . that's Grandmama's joy. Long as I got my joy, I'll be all right." Rhondy asks if she is still Grandmama's joy; Grandmama is upset because poverty is forcing them to move, but for the first time she smiles. Rhondy is still her joy, and will be wherever they live. A gentle story is tenderly told, but it has a static, fragmentary quality.

Betty Valdes

SOURCE: A review of *Grandmama's Joy,* in *School Library Journal,* Vol. 27, No. 2, October, 1980, p. 135.

A sensitive story that shows the loving relationship between Grandmama and Rhondy, whom she has raised since Rhondy was a baby and her parents died in a car accident. Rhondy's several attempts to cheer the sad woman fail, and Rhondy learns why: they must move to a cheaper home. But the girl is persistent and cheers her by reminding her of the love they share. Beautiful charcoal illustrations contribute to the mood that permeates the story.

Nieda Spinger

SOURCE: "Honest Pictures of Black Life," in *Freedomways,* Vol. 21, No. 1, first quarter, 1981, pp. 67-8.

Rhondy and her grandmama don't have much in the way of possessions, but they have each other. Ever since Rhondy was a baby, her grandmama has always said, "Long as I got my joy [meaning Rhondy], I'll be all right." But one day Grandmama isn't all right. Grandmama looks

sad, and Rhondy wants to make her smile. How about singing a popular song, and dancing like they do on television? No, that doesn't work. Rhondy knows her grandma likes pretty things from the garden, so she brings her a shiny rock. But the older woman cries. Rhondy figures that something very serious is wrong, but she also figures that their mutual love will see them through.

Author Eloise Greenfield and illustrator Carole Byard combine their talents in presenting a tender story that is also socially significant because it deals honestly with the housing dilemma burdening many older people who live on fixed incomes.

Grandmama cries when Rhondy gives her the stone because it sparks memories of the good times she has had in a home she can no longer afford. "We have to leave our yard, Rhondy," Grandmama said, crumpling the napkin in her lap. "We have to move. The rent here is too much for me now. I had to find us another place to live."

For an instant, Rhondy and her grandmother share the same despair at the prospect of having to leave their familiar surroundings. But for Rhondy, their love is the bottom line no matter how big the problem. Embracing her grandmother Rhondy asks to hear her favorite story—the one about the day she came to live in Grandmama's house that ends with the line, "Long as I got my joy, I'll be all right." When Grandmama fails to smile as has been customary when she speaks the last line, a worried Rhondy asks, "Grandmama? Am I still your joy?" Grandmama is then reminded that even though they must face change, they still have what is most important—each other.

ALESIA (1981)

Zena Sutherland

SOURCE: A review of *Alesia,* in *Bulletin of the Center for Children's Books,* Vol. 35, No. 5, January, 1982, p. 85.

Although the jacket flap says of eighteen-year-old Alesia Revis' reminiscences that they are "in her own words," there is no clarification of Eloise Greenfield's role as principal author. The comments are dated, like journal entries, over a half of the year 1980 although a preface indicates that it was in 1972, when Alesia was nine, that she was hit by a car while cycling. While the persistent and successful efforts to improve as much as she could and to accept what she couldn't change are admirable, the book has a documentary quality; perhaps it is because Alesia's valor is seen in retrospect that it seems robbed of impact.

Denise M. Wilms

SOURCE: A review of *Alesia,* in *Booklist,* Vol. 78, No. 11, February 1, 1982, p. 706.

When Alesia Revis was nine years old, she was struck by

a car while riding her bicycle and was pronounced dead on arrival at the hospital. But Alesia lived, fought back, and at 17 "can walk some now, if I hold on to a wall or a piece of furniture or somebody's arm, or if I push my wheelchair." She writes of her life today as a high school student who's interested in boys, music, and friends and who isn't sure what she'll do upon graduation. The narrative isn't always smooth, and the diary approach makes for some disjointedness. But Alesia's buoyant nature is apparent, and the inherent message that disabilities don't make one a nonperson won't be lost on readers. That she is black will have further meaning to minority youngsters who are disabled and in need of a role model. Accompanying charcoal drawings [by George Ford] are often stiff; a center packet of photographs [by Sandra Turner Bond] is much more effective at capturing Alesia and her surroundings.

Karen Harris

SOURCE: A review of *Alesia,* in *School Library Journal,* Vol. 28, No. 7, March, 1982, pp. 157-58.

Alesia's journal covers the seven months that span the end of her junior year in high school and the first months of her senior year. In it she recounts her partial recovery from a disabling accident and her progress from immobility to being able to walk with braces and a cane, as well

Greenfield's children, Monica and Steve.

as her school, social and work experiences. Many of the entries report the everyday concerns of an adolescent; others focus on the problems of adjusting to an impairment, particularly to the insensitive reactions of some people and the unwavering support of others. . . . Both drawings [by George Ford] and photographs [by Sandra Turner Bond] are used to illustrate this slim title, but the former fail to capture the vitality and charm of Alesia—qualities evident in the latter.

Catholic Library World

SOURCE: A review of *Alesia,* in *Catholic Library World,* Vol. 53, No. 9, April, 1982, p. 401.

While riding her bicycle through a Washington, D.C. alley, nine-year-old Alesia Revis was hit by an automobile. She was pronounced dead at the hospital. Alesia, however, did not die and eight years later she is still amazing people with her courage and optimism. Alesia's condition has progressed from immobility, to use of a wheelchair, to the assistance of a cane. This diary of Alesia's last year in high school relates her active life with a loving family and friends. Self-pity has no place in this young lady's life. Alesia speaks in a candid fashion about herself. The conversational tone makes very pleasant, interesting reading. She is friendly, full of fun and has a great sense of humor.

Jonetta Rose Barras

SOURCE: "Essence of Poetry," in *Freedomways,* Vol. 22, No. 2, second quarter, 1982, pp. 117-19.

Alesia is the result of a first-time collaborative effort between an award-winning author of children's literature, Eloise Greenfield, and a young girl from her neighborhood, Alesia Revis. It is the story of Alesia's near fatal accident and her life thereafter, told in the form of journal entries in language that is straightforward and intense.

Writing about the accident in the prologue, Greenfield sets the tone:

> Alesia was having a good time. She and her friend Percy were racing on their bikes flying down the alley to see which one could go faster . . . a car was coming that day . . . headed straight toward Alesia. She never saw it. When they got her to Providence Hospital she was pronounced DOA—Dead On Arrival.
>
> But Alesia didn't die. . . .

Alesia is a poignant story that offers insight into the life of a disabled girl. The authors convey her hopes and dreams as she progresses from a five-week coma to her high school graduation. The entries pinpoint the problems that are common to persons with disabilities and the insensitivity sometimes displayed by able-bodied individuals:

> When mama used to take me grocery shopping in my

wheelchair, little children would come up to me and they'd stare and ask a whole lot of questions.

I used to get tickled. But it's not funny when grown people start staring. . . . Some people move way away from me when they see me in the wheelchair like they're afraid they might catch my disability. . . .

Greenfield and Revis teach us not to take for granted the common everyday experiences of using an elevator, walking up a flight of stairs, dancing and other activities. For most people, the breakdown of an elevator at a subway station would only force them to take the stairs. But for Revis and her mother it could become a major dilemma:

One time Mama took me downtown on the subway, and when we got off, the elevator wasn't working, and there was this long, steep flight of steps we had to go up. A man and a woman came over and helped Mama carry me in the chair all the way up those steps. I don't know what we would have done if they hadn't offered to help.

Even the thought of walking can expand into a poetic fantasy:

Walking, real walking is gliding.

And you don't need any assistance—not a wheelchair or a crutch or anything or anybody. You just glide.

The book also dispels the notion that disabled persons don't have experiences similar to those of their able-bodied counterparts. Alesia writes about parties, sleeping late, boys and a range of activities in which girls her age often engage:

I went to a high school basketball game tonight and I met a nice guy. He came over at half time and said hello and things like that. . . . Mama came to get me all early and messed up everything, but he did ask me for those seven little digits—my phone number. . . .

Journal entries spanning the months of March to October 1980 note such experiences as rained-out picnics and such thoughts as Alesia's plan to walk without assistance across the stage at graduation to receive her diploma—"Nobody around me, waiting to catch me. Just me myself, Alesia."

Regrettably, this beautifully told story is not well served by George Ford's illustrations and Sandra Turner Bond's photographs. The drawings are tight in contrast to the fluid quality of Greenfield and Revis' language. The photographs, while sharp and revealing, add a textbook feeling and a sterile, impersonal flavor to an extremely personal account.

This book will provide able-bodied children with the opportunity to come in contact with the real and tangible experiences of a disabled person and to learn that the disabled are people too. In addition, their sensitivity to those disabled people around them will be sharpened. For a disabled reader, Alesia's story may prove inspiring and helpful. All readers may expect to be affected by this journey through eight months of a particular young life, the rendering of which is marked by, not the form, but the essence of poetry.

Caryl-Robin Dresher

SOURCE: A review of *Alesia,* in *Interracial Books for Children Bulletin,* Vol. 13, Nos. 4 & 5, 1982, p. 7.

It is rare to find truly positive literature about an individual who is disabled—and even rarer to find such works about a person of color who is disabled. *Alesia* is such a rare find.

Alesia tells of her childhood, the accident that caused her disability, her recovery period and her experiences at a school where "all the children . . . are disabled." All this is told in a straightforward, matter-of-fact way; Alesia is not consumed with self-pity. Another plus: Alesia's family includes her in all aspects of family life—sometimes that is not easily achieved.

Alesia is also a typical teenager; she loves Fridays because she gets to sleep late the next day and "talking to her girlfriends in the recreation room." She goes to many parties and loves to dance ("I can do it pretty well if I lean against something for support"). Her insights are real without being overly dramatic or simplistic. With honesty, she confides that "Sometimes I get lonely when everybody else is busy and I'm the only one sitting around." Alesia is very real and any teenager could identify with her.

The illustrations and photographs realistically depict different facets of Alesia's life. *Alesia* teaches us about growing up and gives us a view of a girl *who just happens to be disabled.* The book is highly recommended.

UNDER THE SUNDAY TREE (1988)

Kirkus Reviews

SOURCE: A review of *Under the Sunday Tree,* in *Kirkus Reviews,* Vol. LVI, No. 1, September 1, 1988, p. 1322.

Selecting 20 paintings by a Bahamian artist who paints in a vibrant, primitive style, Greenfield provides complementary verse celebrating island life. With their bold colors, masterful designs, and rhythmic reiteration of forms, [Amos] Ferguson's paintings (dated from as early as 1969 to the present) capture the people and scenes they portray so well that no additional text is really necessary. However, some of Greenfield's poems are lovely in their own right—e.g., **"This Place,"** which echoes the subtle pattern of a somber line of trees: "this place is quiet / no shouts may enter / no rolling laughter / but only silent tears / to carry the feelings / forward in waves / that wash the children / whole." Although some of the poems are simply explanatory, she wisely doesn't force interpretations but uses the art to give her own creativity wing. A fine, unusual book.

Kathleen Whalin

SOURCE: A review of *Under the Sunday Tree*, in *School Library Journal*, Vol. 35, No. 2, October, 1988, p. 153.

Under the Sunday Tree is too special for just once-a-week reading. Greenfield's 20 exuberant poems are matched by the bright colors of [Amos] Ferguson's life-filled paintings. Ferguson's native Caribbean glows as vividly in the words as in the full-page primitive pictures—"It takes more than a wish / to catch a fish / you take the hook / you add the bait / you concentrate / and then you wait" (from **"To Catch a Fish"**) or "The sun shone too hot / the veil wouldn't stay / the pianist never / came to play / but love is what made it / a perfect day" (**"Wedding Day"**). Savor the perfect collaboration between two master image-makers, for this book offers readers a chance to "fill their lives with warmth and sun / enough to carry home for winter / when their trip is done."

Steven Ratiner

SOURCE: "Poetry Report Card: Grades from A to C," in *The Christian Science Monitor*, November 4, 1988, p. B7.

Under the Sunday Tree . . . [pairs] the naif paintings of Bahamian artist Amos Ferguson with the childlike verses of Eloise Greenfield. The life of the island's black community is the subject of the book, and both writing and artwork take an approach that is direct, personal, and intriguing. The familiar figures and everyday events take on the special grandeur peculiar to a child's perspective.

Despite a few stilted rhyming passages, the poems are playful and full of feeling. With Ferguson's dazzling color combinations and flattened perspectives, the result is a world of innocence that children will relate to, and one that will make them take a closer look at "home."

Lois Fields Anderson

SOURCE: A review of *Under the Sunday Tree*, in *The Horn Book Magazine*, Vol. LXIV, No. 6, November/December, 1988, p. 796.

There is a special contagious quality in Eloise Greenfield's poetry. Rhythmic vitality permeates the verses, and their musical texture gives a sense of place. That place, the Bahamas, is effectively portrayed in the primitive paintings of Amos Ferguson. His brightly colored illustrations reflect an island life not often seen by the tourist. Like the patches of a quilt, the poems and paintings together reflect the spirit of the native islanders. We read their thoughts and take a glimpse into their daily lives. The book contains twenty poems and paintings celebrat-

ing a variety of subjects, including nature, family, occupations, special places, and dreams. The first poem, **"That Kind of Day"**—accompanied by Ferguson's rural landscape, blue skies, brown cottages with sun-framed doorways, and trees rich with fruit—is a joyful invitation to the reader. "It's that kind of day / and that kind of season / when the breeze is sweet / and the cool air calls / 'Come out!'" With a vocabulary well within the reach of seven- and eight-year-olds, the spirited collection can also be read aloud to a general audience.

Roger Sutton

SOURCE: A review of *Under the Sunday Tree*, in *Bulletin of the Center for Children's Books*, Vol. 42, No. 4, December, 1988, p. 97.

A more symbiotic collaboration than most picture poetry books, this makes it hard to tell where poem leaves off and picture begins. Greenfield gives voice to portraits: "pineapples, pumpkins, chickens, we / carry more than the things you see / we also carry history." Through cool planes of green and blue, [Amos] Ferguson creates a peaceful ocean shore that makes visible Greenfield's "place I know / where children go to find / their deepest feelings." Sometimes contemplative, often funny ("It takes more than a wish / to catch a fish") the poems glide and bounce with rhythmic effects echoed in the bold paintings, which are naively drawn and iconographic, and formally patterned with two-dimensional perspectives. For **"The Brave Ones"** ("We hear the bell clanging / we come in a hurry / we come with our ladders and hoses / our hoses") Ferguson paints a stylized house afire, its straight lines surrounded by bomb-like blobs of smoke and a wreath of flame around the chimney, all capturing the danger and excitement of the poem. **"The Sailboat Race"** sounds and looks ready to rush off the page. The last poem is a marvelously festive toast from both poet and illustrator: "let's lift our punch / to the bunch / (that's us) . . . this toast we'll repeat / each time we meet / and now, my friends— / let's eat". Crisply designed, with poem and painting on facing pages, the collection is supposed to be "an affectionate portrait of life in the Bahamas," but given the breadth of vision contained herein, the book extends far beyond the Caribbean.

GRANDPA'S FACE (1988)

Publishers Weekly

SOURCE: A review of *Grandpa's Face*, in *Publishers Weekly*, Vol. 234, No. 18, October 28, 1988, p. 78.

To Tamika, her grandfather's face tells her everything about him, changing from "glad to worried to funny to sad." But one day, when Tamika watches her grandfather practicing lines for a play, she sees his face change into a face she had never seen before—a mean, cold, angry face that scares her; she is afraid that he will look at *her* like that. Naughty as can be, Tamika tests the limits of her grandfather's patience, but still that face does not appear. When he finds out why Tamika has misbehaved, her grandfather explains that the face she saw was just a pretend face. With eloquence and a penetrating glimpse of the fears of children, Greenfield has written a moving story about the reliability of love.

Gratia Banta

SOURCE: A review of *Grandpa's Face,* in *School Library Journal,* Vol. 35, No. 3, November, 1988, p. 88.

Muted realistic paintings [by Floyd Cooper] complement this story of Tamika, a young girl who grows emotionally through love. Tamika loves her Grandpa, and at the theater she watches him turn "into another person." While he is practicing in a mirror, however, she sees a part of his personality that she does not understand, and it frightens her. "It was a hard face. . . . It was a face that could never love her or anyone." These are powerful words that evoke an unforgettable and horrible visual image, and Tamika acts out her inner turmoil at a catastrophic family dinner scene. Striking, in text and illustration, is the moment when Grandpa catches up with Tamika, and gently all is resolved. Greenfield's other books, *Grandmama's Joy* (1980) and *Honey, I Love and Other Love Poems* (1978), like the works of Ezra Jack Keats, Sharon Bell Mathis, Jeannette Caines, and Charlotte Zolotow, are strong statements about love. The black characters in *Grandpa's Face* do not serve any didactic purpose; they simply love and grow. The carefully chosen combination of visual details and large abstract areas support the notion that love is not always clearly definable. It is a rich life for Tamika and for those who experience and grow, and these are rich visual images to support that belief.

Kirkus Reviews

SOURCE: A review of *Grandpa's Face,* in *Kirkus Reviews,* Vol. LVI, No. 21, November 1, 1988, p. 1604.

"Grandpa's face told everything about him . . . even when he was mad with Tamika, his face was a good face, and the look of his mouth and eyes told her that he loved her." But Grandpa is an actor, and one day Tamika sees him privately practicing a face with "a tight mouth and cold, cold eyes . . . that could never love her or anyone." Dismayed, she acts out her fear at the dinner table, slopping food about and distressing her parents; it's Grandpa who realizes that her uncharacteristic behavior comes from some hidden trouble, who draws her out and then helps her to understand that the fearsome face was just pretend and could never be aimed at her.

Poet Greenfield tells this warm family story with tenderness and grace; and [illustrator Floyd] Cooper makes an outstanding debut. The realistic, full-color double spreads are rich in earth tones and vibrant colors; the faces—especially the crucial expressions on Grandpa's mobile visage—are well characterized and convey emotion with subtlety and precision (also, Tamika's body-language after her trauma is especially poignant). The well-composed backgrounds develop a strong sense of place—a city street of well-kept brownstones, a lovely park touched by the setting sun.

Denise M. Wilms

SOURCE: A review of *Grandpa's Face,* in *Booklist,* Vol. 85, No. 6, November 15, 1988, p. 576.

Tamika loves her grandfather's face. Its expressiveness intrigues her, and even when she's done something wrong, she's reassured by the deep caring she sees in his eyes. One day, when Grandpa is privately rehearsing a role he has in a play, Tamika is shocked at the hard, cold, face he displays. Could her treasured Grandpa turn that face on her one day? The prospect upsets Tamika so much she misbehaves at the dinner table and then fearfully watches her grandfather's reaction. But love is still apparent in his face, and when the two talk afterwards (Tamika confesses her fear), Grandpa reassures her that he could never regard her with anything but love. [Floyd] Cooper's illustrations underscore the story's emotional warmth. Though his faces are of uneven quality (some secondary characters appear stiff), the scenes are full of the closeness that exists between Tamika and her grandfather. The close-knit family here is black, the young-old connection so vibrantly portrayed universal.

Mary Harris Veeder

SOURCE: A review of *Grandpa's Face,* in *Chicago Tribune—Books,* January 1, 1989, p. 4.

Tamika loves her grandfather's face, mobile and expressive, "and the look of his mouth and eyes told her that he loved her." One day when she watches him practice with his script and assume the expressions his character must play on stage, she becomes frightened and confused about which is the true grandfather. While many children do not have actor grandfathers, all of them need a simple loving story about the way a grown-up can put on different faces for adult situations without losing love for the child.

Hanna B. Zeiger

SOURCE: A review of *Grandpa's Face,* in *The Horn Book Magazine,* Vol. LXV, No. 2, March/April, 1989, p. 197.

Tamika and her grandpa have a very loving relationship; she spends a great deal of time with him, listening to his stories and going for "talk-walks" to the park or around the neighborhood. Tamika has learned to watch his face for changing feelings, knowing that even when he is angry, his eyes still say he loves her, and she can kiss "the sturdy brown of his face." Grandpa is an actor with a theater group, and often Tamika goes to see him perform.

One day, opening the door to his room to ask for a story, Tamika sees him reading his lines in front of a mirror. As she watches, his face changes and becomes hard, cold, and hating. Frightened that her beloved grandpa might look at her that way, she is unable to tell anyone about her fear. At the dinner table she mopes and plays with her food, making her parents angry and, finally, upsetting a glass of water onto Grandpa's shirt. Wisely, Grandpa takes Tamika off to the park for one of their walks and is able to comfort her and assure her of his love.

NATHANIEL TALKING (1989)

Publishers Weekly

SOURCE: A review of *Nathaniel Talking,* in *Publishers Weekly,* Vol. 235, No. 20, May 19, 1989, p. 82.

The rhythm of Greenfield's text is infectious from a very early line: "It's Nathaniel talking / and Nathaniel's me / I'm talking about / My philosophy / About the things I do / And the people I see / All told in the words / Of Nathaniel B. Free / That's me." Her sentiments are equally affecting, but in a more sobering way; Nathaniel wonders when he'll ever be old enough not to have to answer a question "I don't know," and he remembers his mother, who has died: "Mama was funny / was full of jokes / was pretty / dark brown-skinned / laughter." His experiences are warmly universal, as are [Jan Spivey] Gilchrist's depictions of his joyful and sorrowful moments, and both poetry, picture and mood come together in one wistful moment when Nathaniel says, "I know life ain't no piece of pie . . . I know I got to try."

Kirkus Reviews

SOURCE: A review of *Nathaniel Talking,* in *Kirkus Reviews,* Vol. LVII, No. 12, June 15, 1989, p. 916.

The thoughts and opinions of Nathaniel B. Free, who—like Clifton's Everett Anderson—is a child of deep, genuine feelings and a penetrating eye.

Nathaniel's ruminations, like Everett's, are delivered in

Greenfield with her mother in the playground at Langston Terrace, her childhood home, in 1973.

poetic vignettes (several have appeared previously in magazines); whether written in the cadences of rap, with the structure of a blues song (an essay on which is appended), or in some freer rhythm, all lend themselves to reading aloud and to easy comprehension. Nathaniel remembers making faces, and friends, with a girl in kindergarten; watching Grandma play "the bones"; and his feelings of loss at Mama's death a year ago. He's also wise beyond his years, thinking about how stupid he is to get into a fight and how, even when he's old and gray, he still won't know everything.

Kathleen T. Horning

SOURCE: A review of *Nathaniel Talking,* in *School Library Journal,* Vol. 35, No. 12, August, 1989, p. 146.

"It's Nathaniel talking / and Nathaniel's me / I'm talking about / My philosophy" begins a stellar collection of 18 first-person poems. Like Greenfield's *Honey, I Love* (1978), the collection as a whole characterizes an individual black child through the child's lyric impressions of self and the surrounding world. Here, the child is a little older, his world a little wider. Nathaniel is a confident nine-year-old, making observations about his life, sifting through bittersweet memories of his past, and dreaming of his future. . . .

While all the poems remain true to a nine-year-old's perspective, the mature poet's playfulness with words and rhythms gives resonance, depth, and unity to the collection as a whole. For example, each generation of Nathaniel's extended family is distinguished by a poetic tribute to a musical form associated with their era, from **"Nathaniel's Rap"** ("I can rap / I can rap / I can rap rap rap / Till your earflaps flap"), to **"My Daddy,"** a poem written according to the lyric and rhythmic formula of the 12-bar blues, to **"Grandma's Bones"** in which words and rhythms imitate the sound of a folk instrument which has its origins in Africa. Overall, *Nathaniel Talking* will strike a chord of recognition in children everywhere, and is sure to set feet tapping and earflaps flapping.

Denise Wilms

SOURCE: A review of *Nathaniel Talking,* in *Booklist,* Vol. 86, No. 8, December 15, 1989, p. 830.

This collection of simple poems presents reflections of childhood from a black American boy's point of view. Greenfield's at her best with the winning bouyancy of **"Nathaniel's Rap"** ("It's Nathaniel talking / and Nathaniel's me / I'm talking about / My philosophy / About the things I do / And the people I see / All told in the words / Of Nathaniel B. Free / That's me"). Also effective are a couple of selections that follow a twelve-bar blues structure; the implied melody gives the verses extra punch. The poems touch on many subjects and express some healthy, down-to-earth views, with a distinct emphasis on pride and positive thinking. A few of the poems

are flat, with neither fresh images nor salient points to make them come alive. Nevertheless, this will prove a highly welcome item where books on the African American experience are needed.

Mary M. Burns

SOURCE: A review of *Nathaniel Talking,* in *The Horn Book Magazine,* Vol. LXVI, No. 5, September/October, 1990, p. 613.

It is not often that a book of poetry can successfully contain a variety of verse forms while simultaneously maintaining the sense of a single voice. Eloise Greenfield meets the challenge brilliantly, eliciting from the reader an immediate emotional response to the ideas, the rhythms, and the imagery. The voice belongs to nine-year-old Nathaniel B. Free, an appropriate name for a child who can rap about his philosophy of life in the introductory poem and then provide specifics in the succeeding pages, as in the concluding lines of **"My Daddy"**: "yeah my daddy sings the blues / and he plays it on that old guitar / he ain't never been on TV / but to me he's a great big star." Some lines recall other poets—the poignant tone of Gwendolyn Brooks or the heart-scalding similes of Langston Hughes, for example—but they are never derivative or imitative. Similarities lie rather in the recollection of common experiences and shared emotions. What is particularly unique is the poet's use of varied musical forms, from "bones" to blues to rap, slipping easily from one to another just as a child might replicate the sounds and voices of his environment. The book concludes with directions for composing a twelve-bar blues poem. Jan Spivey Gilchrist's illustrations—sculptured, expressive, black-and-white representations—match the vitality and dynamism of the text. It is this bonding of the verbal and the visual that gives so strong a sense of unity to the whole. A marvelous book in subject, execution, and design—one not to be missed.

NIGHT ON NEIGHBORHOOD STREET (1991)

Kirkus Reviews

SOURCE: A review of *Night on Neighborhood Street,* in *Kirkus Reviews,* Vol. LIX, No. 14, July 15, 1991, p. 931.

As "dusk spins from daylight" on Neighborhood Street, some children sing and play on the sidewalk, others trot sleepily to bed or lie wakeful. Juma gets a good-night hug from his Daddy; the Robinsons have "fambly time"; Tonya's mother entertains her daughter's friends at a sleepover and—later that night—"blows lullaby sounds" with her horn out over the silent street. Except for **"The Seller"** ("when the seller comes around / . . . all the children go inside / . . . they know his breath is cold") and **"The Meeting,"** about an ever-angry neighbor, Greenfield's poems have a peaceful tone that is perfectly matched in [Jan Spivey] Gilchrist's gentle, dreamy paintings, where brown skins glow with a warm light against soft-focus backgrounds of shadowed walls and deep, starry sky. A winning combination.

Denia Hester

SOURCE: A review of *Night on Neighborhood Street,* in *Booklist,* Vol. 87, No. 22, August, 1991, p. 2156.

Neighborhood Street will very likely strike a familiar chord in the young and the old. It's a timeless place of everyday sights, sounds, and smells woven together in a tapestry of homespun, lyrical verse. Children chant jumprope rhymes, the church congregation sings "Hallelujah," and the smell of hot, buttered bread lingers in the air. [Jan Spivey] Gilchrist's soft paintings do not depict the city streets as much as the expressive faces of the families and friends that make up a neighborhood—not a Mr. Rogers-type neighborhood, but a real community where the drug dealer plies his trade and an abandoned house inspires tales of ghosts dancing in the moonlight. The magical and the everyday reside comfortably together on Neighborhood Street and make it well worth the visit.

Eve Larkin

SOURCE: A review of *Night on Neighborhood Street,* in *School Library Journal,* Vol. 37, No. 9, September, 1991, pp. 245-46.

Warm shades of blues, greens, and lavenders as well as the characters' gently, glowing shades of browns perfectly capture *Night on Neighborhood Street.* Each of Greenfield's poems deals with everyday concerns and delights of African-American city children: a lonely boy gazes at the moon, waiting for his "best, best friend" to come home; a newborn baby swaddled in pink cries because she's "too tiny a girl / for this big new world." Nerissa tries to cheer her unemployed father and ill mother "by telling them the best old / bedtime jokes." The most powerful poem is **"The Seller,"** who "comes around / carrying in his many pockets / packages of death." The final poem depicts a young mother playing a trumpet on a porch late at night. She "blows lullaby sounds / into the silence / the children hear and smile / their sleep deepens / and they are at peace / with the night." A warm, triumphant book that will be wonderful to share with a group or in a more cozy situation.

Roger Sutton

SOURCE: A review of *Night on Neighborhood Street,* in *Bulletin of the Center for Children's Books,* Vol. 45, No. 2, October, 1991, pp. 37-8.

Greenfield's collection of seventeen poems acutely captures the sounds and sights of an evening in an urban black community. Some verses softly lilt ("rocking the baby / rocking the baby / swish, swish / swish"); some bounce along ("When Tonya's friends come to spend the night / Her mama's more than just polite"); some are soothing nocturnes ("only light and shadow / play on the sidewalk now / it is the time when / darkness and stillness meet / and most are asleep / on Neighborhood Street"). Both big-city realities, such as scary boarded-up houses and drug pushers, and any child's home truths, such as being afraid of the dark, are here, but a loving array of parents, children, and friends gives the book as a whole a cozy sense of security.

Mary M. Burns

SOURCE: A review of *Night on Neighborhood Street,* in *The Horn Book Magazine,* Vol. LXVII, No. 6, November/December, 1991, p. 750.

Through a series of poems accompanied by [Jan Spivey Gilchrist's] sensitive, handsome paintings, executed in gouache with pastel highlighting, readers are brought into a community which is at once unique and universal. Remarkable for unselfconscious use of varied rhyme schemes and verse forms, the text reads aloud beautifully. Appropriately, poetic diction is controlled by subject and personae so that the conversational tone enhances the sense of intimacy conveyed by the illustrations. The arrangement is equally notable: the first poem, **"Neighborhood Street,"** evokes a particular time and place as "dusk spins from daylight" and children play singing games; the concluding selection reflects a later hour "when darkness and stillness meet / and most are asleep / on Neighborhood Street." In between, the focus shifts from individuals, as in **"Little Boy Blues,"** which poignantly captures a child's longing for his best friend's return, to groups such as that portrayed in **"The Meeting."** There are moments of stark realism, as in **"The Seller,"** in which the children turn their backs on a drug dealer "carrying in his many pockets / packages of death," or **"Nerissa,"** in which the small heroine tries to help her ailing mother and out-of-work father "by telling them the best old / bedtime jokes." And there are moments of pure joy and playfulness as in **"Goodnight, Juma"**—a dialogue between a loving parent and a child trying to postpone bedtime—or **"Fambly Time,"** a contemporary, and livelier, version of Longfellow's "The Children's Hour." A lovingly produced book, beautifully designed and illustrated, which presents a balanced portrait of life as it is—celebrating ordinary joys, commenting on problems and sadness, but most of all conveying hope in family solidarity and the power of love.

Mary Harris Veeder

SOURCE: A review of *Night on Neighborhood Street,* in *Chicago Tribune—Books,* February 9, 1992, p. 7.

Seventeen poems look at what's happening in a city neighborhood on one night, as children might see it. The mixture of lives and moments is realistic. Some children approach the night with family games, others with a terror of the dark. Some children are walking away from the offers of a drug pusher; some are in a noisily happy church service. [Jan Spivey] Gilchrist's illustrations catch the burdens and the joys of these children.

Phyllis G. Sidorsky

SOURCE: A review of *Night on Neighborhood Street,* in *Childhood Education,* Vol. 68, No. 3, Spring, 1992, p. 178.

These poems are about evening doings in an African-American neighborhood—babies being tucked in bed, girl friends sharing a sleepover, children experiencing both bedtime fears and happy dreams. Even the ugly intrusion of drug pushers is included. The theme, however, is warmth and solid reaffirmation of family values.

Lee Galda, Donna Diehl and Lane Ware

SOURCE: A review of *Night on Neighborhood Street,* in *The Reading Teacher,* Vol. 46, No. 5, February, 1993, pp. 412-13.

Eloise Greenfield's commitment to telling the "true story of the African American people" is evident in the eloquent poems in *Night on Neighborhood Street.* This is a wonderful book, a collection of poems celebrating the love that can exist in families and neighborhoods and exploring the feelings of children, both happy and sad. The emotions Greenfield conveys are beautifully captured by Jan Spivey Gilchrist's full-color paintings. You will want to frequently read this book aloud to children of all ages.

BIG FRIEND, LITTLE FRIEND; DADDY AND I . . . ; I MAKE MUSIC; and MY DOLL, KESHIA (1991)

Publishers Weekly

SOURCE: A review of *My Doll, Keshia; I Make Music; Daddy and I . . . ; Big Friend, Little Friend,* in *Publishers Weekly,* Vol. 238, No. 45, October 11, 1991, p. 62.

The creators of *Nathaniel Talking* and *Night on Neighborhood Street* here introduce a series of board books featuring black children that describe everyday activities familiar to all kids. The, first three books [*My Doll Keshia, I Make Music,* and *Daddy and I . . .*] are written in simple, if occasionally strained, rhyming verse and concern a boy and girl who play with a doll; a girl and her parents who make music together; and a boy and his dad doing household chores. The fourth—and strongest—story [*Big Friend, Little Friend*], told by a boy who enjoys playing with two friends is written in pithy sentences that beginning readers will easily master. The volumes' themes of the rewards of working and playing together are reinforced by [Jan Spivey] Gilchrist's cheerful if repetitious illustrations, which focus on each tale's characters but contain little background detail.

Kirkus Reviews

SOURCE: A review of *Daddy and I . . . ,* in *Kirkus Reviews,* Vol. LIX, No. 20, October 15, 1991, p. 1353.

[*Daddy and I* is the] best of four board books by a Coretta Scott King Award team. The small boy who narrates describes a happy day helping Daddy—laundry, cleaning, etc.—varied with a ball game, a book, and an affectionate hug. Poet Greenfield's language is straightforward but graceful; [Jan Spivey] Gilchrist's illustrations are a little clumsy here, but do convey the pair's warmth and sense of purpose. Of the other titles, *I Make Music* has the strongest text; *Big Friend, Little Friend* is an adequate concept book; and *My Doll, Keshia* suggests a parenting role model. None of these is ideal—all are slight and undemanding; still, they meet a real need for simple books about African-Americans.

Liza Bliss

SOURCE: A review of *Big Friend, Little Friend; Daddy and I . . . ; I Make Music; My Doll, Keshia,* in *School Library Journal,* Vol. 37, No. 12, December, 1991, p. 92.

Four board books that feature African-American characters and cover several areas of a young child's experience (playing with pals of various ages, enjoying a parent's company, experimenting with musical instruments, and having a favorite doll, respectively). . . .

This foursome is a functional unit, offering en masse a variety of approaches to life situations (*Daddy and I* seems to feature a single parent, for example, while a two-parent household shows up in *I Make Music*) and avoiding stereotypes (e.g., a boy with a doll in *My Doll*). Greenfield's sweet and simple texts are in verse in all but *Big Friend.* Although all of these titles stand alone, their combined success is greater; they represent a range of topics, moods, and emotions seldom seen in this format.

Kathleen T. Horning

SOURCE: A review of *Big Friend, Little Friend; Daddy and I . . . ; I Make Music; My Doll, Keshia,* in *Booklist,* Vol. 88, No. 8, December 15, 1991, pp. 772-73.

Four board books feature day-to-day activities of young African American children, described in brief, first-person narratives. *Big Friend* compares and contrasts the ways in which a small boy interacts with and plays with a friend who is older than he is and a friend who is younger. *Daddy* recounts the many things a young boy and his daddy do together: "We go to the store, I carry the bread. / I turn the page when the book is read." In *I Make Music,* a little girl lyrically describes a variety of ways she makes music, from playing a toy xylophone to tapping her thigh. Another little girl talks about playing with her doll in *My Doll.* Although the children pictured in each volume appear to be older than the typical board-book audience, the simple, patterned texts, child-centered concerns, and clear, boldly colored illustrations will make the books appealing to toddlers.

Maeve Visser Knoth

SOURCE: A review of *Big Friend, Little Friend; Daddy and I . . . ; I Make Music; My Doll, Keshia,* in *The Horn Book Magazine,* Vol. LXVIII, No. 1, January/February, 1992, p. 59.

Confident, happy African-American children leap off the pages of these board books. All four feature Greenfield's characteristic poetic language in their descriptions of everyday situations and early relationships. *Big Friend, Little Friend* tells the story of a child who learns from an older friend and is able to share his knowledge and skills with a younger friend. *I Make Music* and *My Doll, Keshia* are simple stories about young girls who, in their play, take pride in themselves. In *Daddy and I* a young boy and his father enjoy playing basketball and doing laundry together. Eloise Greenfield's skillful use of language and rhythm elevates the four books from the mundane to the delightful, and [Jan Spivey] Gilchrist's watercolor-and-ink illustrations are warm and lively. The books are published in board-book format, but the concepts and stories are appropriate for preschoolers past the board-book stage. Four positive, immediate portraits of young children and their daily lives and important relationships.

Geeta Pattanaik

SOURCE: A review of *Big Friend, Little Friend; Daddy and I . . . ; I Make Music; My Doll, Keshia,* in *The School Librarian,* Vol. 40, No. 1, February, 1992, p. 15.

These four board books show the different relationships a little girl has with those around her: her doll, her mother, her father, and her friends. The characters are all black, but the emotions are universal. I like this set. The books introduce various concepts and achieve this in simple rhyme. There is not too much to read, so they are ideal picture books for beginners. The positive images of race and gender are very strong. Some of the pen and wash drawings are better than others, though the covers are all very well drawn. The books could be used effectively with lower infant classes. They are sturdy and will withstand considerable wear and tear.

KOYA DELANEY AND THE GOOD GIRL BLUES (1992)

Publishers Weekly

SOURCE: A review of *Koya DeLaney and the Good Girl Blues,* in *Publishers Weekly,* Vol. 238, No. 56, December 20, 1991, p. 82.

Sisters Koya and Loritha get along very well, though they don't always see eye to eye. Koya never loses her temper and does her best to keep everyone happy. Her sister's propensity for being accomodating doesn't sit well with Loritha when she is double-crossed by Koya's best friend, Dawn. Instead of sticking up for Loritha, Koya continues to be buddies with Dawn so that *her* feelings won't be hurt. In a rather dramatic, epiphanic moment, Koya realizes that it's okay to be angry sometimes, and finally gives Dawn a piece of her mind. All is forgiven, and the three girls are friends again. Meanwhile, such events as a double-dutch contest and a visit from the DeLaney sisters' cousin, a famous pop singer, keep Greenfield's plot rolling along at a sprightly clip. Youngsters will warm up immediately to the feisty Koya, a '90s Pollyanna with a witty edge.

Kirkus Reviews

SOURCE: A review of *Koya DeLaney and the Good Girl Blues,* in *Kirkus Reviews,* Vol. LX, No. 2, January 15, 1992, p. 114.

As neatly summed up in Jan Spivey Gilchrist's attractive jacket art, there are several themes in this warm school-and-family story, set near Washington, D.C. Koya is distressed by a falling-out between her sister Loritha and her best friend Dawn, the result of a spiteful trick Dawn plays on Loritha just before a "double-dutch" contest. The jacket's swirling jump-ropes with the two girls suggest a treble clef—even more important than the team competition is a visit from cousin Del, a popular singer. Del's fans' adulation leads to Koya getting in touch with her own emotions: though her inability to express her justifiable anger at Dawn has delayed resolving the bad feelings among the three girls, when the fans drown out Del's music with their enthusiasm her indignation erupts; and once she's felt it, Koya creatively learns to combine righteous anger with her habitual tactic when she's upset—telling jokes, for which she has a special gift.

The resolution here is a tad simplistic, and the adults—though admirable role models—seem a little too good to be true. (Still, it's grand to read about a pop idol who turns down his sound to protect young ears and picks up the litter his admirers have left by his host's door.) The girls are credible and more subtly drawn, their troubles and triumphs engaging. Meanwhile, Greenfield (a much-honored author and poet) narrates with grace and clarity, weaving her several themes into a carefully structured, thought-provoking story that should be a long-lived favorite.

Denia Hester

SOURCE: A review of *Koya DeLaney and the Good Girl Blues,* in *Booklist,* Vol. 88, No. 12, February 15, 1992, p. 1104.

Sixth-grader Koya DeLaney's special talent is the gift of laughter. She loves finding the funny side of things and

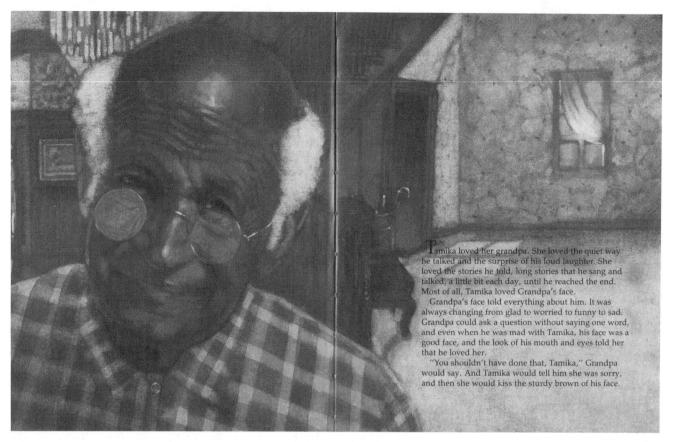

Tamika loved her grandpa. She loved the quiet way he talked and the surprise of his loud laughter. She loved the stories he told, long stories that he sang and talked, a little bit each day, until he reached the end. Most of all, Tamika loved Grandpa's face.

Grandpa's face told everything about him. It was always changing from glad to worried to funny to sad. Grandpa could ask a question without saying one word, and even when he was mad with Tamika, his face was a good face, and the look of his mouth and eyes told her that he loved her.

"You shouldn't have done that, Tamika," Grandpa would say. And Tamika would tell him she was sorry, and then she would kiss the sturdy brown of his face.

From Grandpa's Face, *written by Eloise Greenfield. Illustrated by Floyd Cooper.*

making other people laugh, especially when things get sticky. And things get very sticky indeed when Koya's older sister is betrayed by Koya's best friend. Further complicating matters is the much-awaited visit of cousin Del, a famous pop musician. The rift with her sister and the somewhat disappointing reunion with her cousin force Koya to do a little growing up and to get in touch with her true feelings. Koya is afflicted with the good-girl blues; the same could be said of this novel. It wants very hard to please, perhaps at the expense of real dramatic tension. But Koya is likable, and this portrait of a close-knit African American family is welcome.

Roger Sutton

SOURCE: A review of *Koya DeLaney and the Good Girl Blues,* in *Bulletin of the Center for Children's Books,* Vol. 45, No. 7, March, 1992, pp. 179-80.

Koya's sister Loritha, and Dawn, friend to both sisters, have quarreled, and Koya's caught in the middle. This tale of sixth-grade feuding is enlivened by a frisky protagonist: Koya mugs and makes jokes and is constantly exasperating her friends and families with her desire to keep everyone happy, even at the expense of her true feelings. Loritha says, "You make me sick. You always have to be so . . . so *good.* Miss Good Girl." The fight

between the sisters is complicated not only by the double-dutch jump-rope tournament that started the whole thing, but also by the fact that the girls' cousin Del, a pop star, is coming to visit. Although the theme of Koya's denial of anger seems imposed upon the story rather than growing out of it, the book is a good mix of exciting and ordinary events, and the happy—if rushed—conclusion will appeal to genre fans. Along with Emily Moore's *Whose Side Are You On?,* this is one of too few school-and-family stories to feature a black cast and community.

Helen E. Williams

SOURCE: A review of *Koya DeLaney and the Good Girl Blues,* in *School Library Journal,* Vol. 38, No. 3, March, 1992, p. 237.

Koya is a bright, giggly African-American sixth grader who lives with her parents and older sister, Loritha. Loritha and her best friend are members of the double-dutch jump-rope team and are practicing for the championship competition. When a rift develops between the two friends, and during subsequent events, Koya tries to be the peacemaker and "good girl" until the role gives her the blues. When she finally screams her displeasure, she realizes that anger is an appropriate and healthy emotion to be expressed rather than subdued. Her relationships with family and friends improve almost immediately. This has a somewhat laborious beginning, but the plot eventually unfolds into an enjoyable story with credible characters and conflicts.

Joyce Graham and Susan Murphy

SOURCE: "Growing Up Black: Fiction about Black Adolescents' Experiences," in *Journal of Reading,* Vol. 36, No. 7, April, 1993, pp. 590-92.

Koya has always tried to be a "good girl," but when her older, famous cousin comes to town to do a benefit concert and to visit her school, the furor is difficult for Koya to handle. She learns a great deal—how to manage her desire to share in her cousin's glory, how to protect her cousin's privacy, how to express her anger toward her best friend's jealousy, and how to help her sister see that Koya loves her. Koya has understanding parents who guide and support her through the experience. What she discovers about herself convinces her that she needs to be true to herself and cannot always please everyone.

WILLIAM AND THE GOOD OLD DAYS (1993)

Publishers Weekly

SOURCE: A review of *William and the Good Old Days,* in *Publishers Weekly,* Vol. 240, No. 31, August 2, 1993, p. 79.

Once again Greenfield displays commendable sensitivity in this story about an African American boy who must cope with a beloved grandmother's illness. William reminisces about the "good old days" before Grandma got sick and lost her sight. He longs for the times at Grandma's restaurant—a nurturing world full of loving family and friends—"where all those happy *people*-sounds would make my food taste extra, extra good." Eventually William begins to focus on the "good *new* days," planning how Grandma can help him plant flowers despite her blindness. Greenfield captures not only the language of a child but also a credible reaction to the decline of a grandparent: anger, sadness, compassion and, ideally, the courage to accept and move forward.

Kirkus Reviews

SOURCE: A review of *William and the Good Old Days,* in *Kirkus Reviews,* Vol. LXI, No. 17, September 1, 1993, p. 1144.

Young William thinks about his ailing grandmother, just home from the hospital, remembering the good times in her small diner and hoping for more of them when she's feeling better. His changing moods are wonderfully evoked in [Jan Spivey] Gilchrist's paintings; sadder memories, rendered in sepia tones, brighten into warm browns and yellows as William plans a happier future. Aside from one unrealistically artful line—about Grandma "back in the good old days, last year when I was little"—the boy's voice and the progression of his thoughts are natural and childlike. Uncontrived comfort for young readers disturbed by a family member's illness.

Quraysh Ali

SOURCE: A review of *William and the Good Old Days,* in *Booklist,* Vol. 90, No. 2, September 15, 1993, pp. 156-57.

Everyone called her Mama, and that's why Grandma named her restaurant Mama's Kitchen. The folks in the neighborhood loved her and her cooking so much that sometimes they'd help her wash the collard greens. It was William's favorite place to be, but now everything has changed. Grandma is ill, and "her eyes don't see anymore." Someone else owns the diner, and little William misses the good old days of last year. He must find peace and come to terms with the pain he feels. Feeling sad and angry, William blames a fly for all the trouble. Quite simply, it makes him feel better. He gradually learns to accept and adapt to the situation. Greenfield writes in a voice that's warm, and William's reflections are filled with a truly touching emotional sensitivity and innocent disregard for time. [Jan Spivey] Gilchrist's watercolor and chalk artwork appears to be ripped from a piece of memory. Through the juxtaposition of flashback and simultaneous moment, she captures the triumphant testament to the perseverance of hope.

Anna DeWind

SOURCE: A review of *William and the Good Old Days,* in *School Library Journal,* Vol. 39, No. 11, November, 1993, p. 79.

William likes to think about the way his Grandma used to be—before she got sick and lost her eyesight. He likes to remember her hugging people, cooking at her restaurant, and letting him pick out any kind of juice he wanted to drink. But that was in the good old days, last year when he was little. Now, after a long hospitalization, Grandma is back home, but she is still ill. William's memories develop into anticipation of the good days ahead, when he can sit with her in the garden and plant flowers just the way she tells him to. This poignant exploration of a child's feelings of loss, sorrow, and hope features a closely knit African-American family and community, lovingly depicted in paintings that combine realistic renderings of people against impressionistic, swirling backgrounds of color and line. A wonderful sense of neighborhood permeates the pages of this touching book.

Enola G. Aird

SOURCE: A review of *William and the Good Old Days,*

in *The New York Times Book Review,* November 14, 1993, p. 55.

Ms. Greenfield's *William and the Good Old Days* is a rich, beautifully woven and inspiring tale about how illness changes a woman, a little boy, a family and a neighborhood.

William tells how all of a sudden, "about a week or a day" after swatting a fly, his Grandma got sick and had to be hospitalized for a long time. She returns home. But "her eyes can't see anymore" and she will never be the same. Pained and struggling to explain the inexplicable, William reminisces about a time, "last year when I was little," when Grandma was well.

The little boy remembers a strong woman whom everybody called "Mama," who commanded respect and made people happy. She was the driving force behind Mama's Kitchen, which was not just a restaurant but a center of neighborhood life. He remembers the place, which is no longer a part of his family, where "every day the same people used to come . . . to eat their dinner," and where customers helped out because they wanted to.

It was a place where William learned the value of being part of a community. He'd visit with friends at Mama's Kitchen on Saturdays, when people gathered to watch, talk, laugh and eat together, and when "all those happy *people*-sounds would make my food taste extra, extra good." Those days are no more.

But William doesn't live in the past. He is a friend to his grandmother now—calling every day to cheer her. He visits often and, unafraid to love and care for his not-well Grandma, he hugs and kisses her and makes his peace with the "good *new* days" to come.

📖 *SWEET BABY COMING* (1994)

Publishers Weekly

SOURCE: A review of *Sweet Baby Coming,* in *Publishers Weekly,* Vol. 241, No. 1, January 3, 1994, p. 80.

Though aimed primarily at youngsters anticipating the arrival of a new sibling, [this cheerful board book is] likely to appeal to any toddler who likes looking at drawings of babies. The narrator of *Sweet Baby Coming* uses rhyming verse to convey both her excitement and her anxiety about her brother- or sister-to-be: "Is the baby

going to like me? / Will the baby want to stay? / Mommy says our baby loves me more and more each day." [Jan Spivey] Gilchrist's delicate but realistic watercolors show an African American youngster touching her mother's stomach, getting a reassuring cuddle, listening for the baby's heartbeat and, finally, greeting her new little brother.

📖 *ON MY HORSE* (1995)

Kathie Krieger Cerra

SOURCE: A review of *On My Horse,* in *The Five Owls,* Vol. IX, No. 3, January/February, 1995, p. 58.

In this poem for young children, a child describes the joy, real and imaginary, of riding on a horse at the horse park. The first section, in rhythmic rhymed couplets, tells of the child's tame ride accompanied by Mr. Morse, who protects him from falling off the tall horse. The middle section, prefaced by the words, "I wish that I could ride alone, my horse and I out on our own," is written in free verse with occasional internal rhyme. This section creates the child's imaginary ride, wild and free, racing through open grass, walking through woods, and jumping a stream. The last section returns to the rhymed couplet form and the end of the child's real and imaginary ride "Pretending is over and we are three, Mr. Morse, my horse, and me."

This pleasing balance of form and expression is joined by full-color pictures [by Jan Spivey Gilchrist] that are spread over both pages, supporting the text by lying beneath the print on the page and by reflecting each event in the child's experience and imagination. The sixteen pages of the book are printed on thick stock that is clearly meant to survive frequent examination by little hands. *On My Horse* is part of a series of Let's Read Aloud books by HarperFestival, a series designed to encourage parents to read aloud to their preschool children. Indeed, *On My Horse* is a perfect book for a child to savor while riding on a parent's lap.

Additional coverage of Greenfield's life and career is contained in the following sources published by Gale Research: *Contemporary Authors New Revision Series,* Vol. 43; *Major Authors and Illustrators for Children and Young Adults*; *Something about the Author,* Vols. 19, 61; and *Something about the Author Autobiography Series,* Vol. 16.

David C(arpenter) Knight

1925-1984

American author of nonfiction.

Major works include *Science ABC* (1962), *Copernicus: Titan of Modern Astronomy* (1965), *The First Book of Berlin: Tale of a Divided City* (1967), *The Tiny Planets: Asteroids of Our Solar System* (1973), *UFOs: A Pictorial History from Antiquity to the Present* (1979), *The Moving Coffins: Ghosts and Hauntings Around the World* (1983), *Robotics: Past, Present, and Future* (1983).

INTRODUCTION

A prolific and respected author of nonfiction for young people, Knight is best known for his introductory works on various aspects of science. His writings, frequently commended for their straightforward and highly readable style, offer a broad range and historical view of human scientific endeavor from the efforts of such figures as Isaac Newton and Nicolaus Copernicus to more modern achievements such as robotics and space colonization. Knight also explores pseudo-scientific issues of frequent interest to young readers, among them the existence of UFOs (Unidentified Flying Objects), ESP (Extra-Sensory Perception), and ghosts. While typically seen as well organized and carefully crafted, Knight's works are sometimes criticized as unimaginative. Some reviewers have noted errors and inaccuracies in his science books, and others have remarked that his works fail to adequately address important social, economic, and political aspects of the scientific issues they examine. Nevertheless, Knight is credited with introducing science to a wide audience, accomodating young readers of all ages with topics and treatments that are relevant and of interest. Many commentators have commended Knight's objective approach to his subject matter, and his works, usually well-illustrated with photos and other graphics, have generally been well received.

Biographical Information

Knight was born in Glens Falls, New York, the son of magazine editor H. Ralph Knight and painter Dorothy (Weed) Knight. He received a bachelor of arts degree from Union College in 1950, and briefly attended the Sorbonne in Paris the following year. Knight began his career as an editor in 1954 with the *Pacific Coast Review*; he moved to Prentice-Hall the following year and remained there until 1959, when he accepted a position with Franklin Watts, Inc. Watts published Knight's *The First Book of Sound: A Basic Guide to the Science of Acoustics* in 1960, and many of his works thereafter. Knight also spent several years in the late 'sixties as a journalist in the U.S. Naval Reserve, a vocation that took him to Berlin and

culminated in his *The First Book of Berlin: Tale of a Divided City*. Over the course of the next two decades, Knight continued to write prolifically, completing several works for his "Let's Find Out" series for primary graders and dozens of educational books for older students. He died in 1984.

Major Works

The majority of Knight's works are science-related. *Science ABC,* a typical alphabet book in which each letter represents some aspect of science or technology (A is for Air, B is for Bridge), stands out as one of his few books for very young readers. More complex works include *Comets* (1968) and *The Tiny Planets: Asteroids of Our Solar System,* each of which examines its subject in terms of physical characteristics, behavior, history, and significance. This approach is also used in Knight's works dealing with medicine, physics, geology, meteorology, oceanography, zoology, and technology. In his biographies, including those of Isaac Newton, Nicolaus Copernicus, and Robert Koch, Knight highlights the struggles and sacrifices that have been made by such men in their hopes to further human knowledge. Among his titles of a more popular nature, *UFOs: A Pictorial History from Antiquity to the Present* and *The Moving Coffins: Ghosts and Hauntings Around the World* reflect another of Knight's favorite topics, the supernatural. In these titles and his numerous other books documenting unexplained phenomena, Knight maintains that appearances of ghosts, UFOs, and the like have been recorded throughout history and therefore should be studied from a scientific perspective. Leading readers through a series of haunting accounts, Knight encourages them to keep an open mind to the existence of inscrutable forces and beings.

TITLE COMMENTARY

📖   *THE FIRST BOOK OF SOUND: A BASIC GUIDE TO THE SCIENCE OF ACOUSTICS* (1960; revised edition, 1965)

Virginia Kirkus' Service

SOURCE: A review of *The First Book of Sound,* in *Virginia Kirkus' Service,* Vol. XXVIII, No. 19, October 1, 1960, p. 869.

The study of acoustics has many implications, both of a practical and theoretical nature. In this text the author defines sound, the mechanisms of sound production, the voice, the ear, sound and energy, the effect of environment on sound, the sound barrier, sound in relation to the atom, and many other pertinent and timely aspects of acoustical concepts. A list of experiments and a glossary of facts further support this elaborately illustrated book which is recommended to school libraries.

The Booklist and Subscription Books Bulletin

SOURCE: A review of *The First Book of Sound,* in *The Booklist and Subscription Books Bulletin,* Vol. 57, No. 13, March 1, 1961, p. 428.

The cause, characteristics, and behavior of sound are lucidly explained in this well-organized introduction to the science of acoustics. A number of experiments with sound and a condensed summary titled "A checklist of sound facts" are appended. Illustrated with many drawings, diagrams, and photographs.

Eric Linfield

SOURCE: A review of *The First Book of Sound,* in *The School Librarian and School Library Review,* Vol. 14, No. 1, March, 1966, p. 117.

Luckily this book is sub-titled 'A basic guide to the sci-

ence of acoustics'. Otherwise potential buyers and borrowers might be misled into thinking that it might be a simple introduction to sound for young juniors. However, this is an excellent information book for the intermediate years from nine to thirteen. One must commend the illustrations especially for here is a very apposite fusion of text and diagram, text and photograph and photograph with diagram.

Sound is an appealing topic. It provides plenty of opportunity for simple experiments which illuminate complex ideas. David Knight has been most successful in the experiments which he has introduced in the text and he has added a useful appendix of further sound experiments. His explanations are both concise and meaningful and the publishers are to be complimented on producing a popular science book for children which enables understanding to develop whilst factual information and experimental discovery are presented with equal emphasis.

📖   *ISAAC NEWTON: MASTERMIND OF MODERN SCIENCE* (1961)

Virginia Kirkus' Service

SOURCE: A review of *Isaac Newton: Mastermind of Modern Science,* in *Virginia Kirkus' Service,* Vol. XXIV, No. 1, January 1, 1961, p. 15.

Smaller print and material geared more appropriately for 13 to 15 here but biographical facts and scientific discoveries are integrated. Many young readers will be surprised to learn that Newton did poorly at his schoolwork. Not until he decided to defeat the class bully, both physically and intellectually, were any indications of genius exhibited. A description of the world of science before Newton enhances appreciation for his achievements. His discoveries of the laws of motion and those of gravitation and optics won him fame within his own lifetime.

📖   *ROBERT KOCH: FATHER OF BACTERIOLOGY* (1961)

Zena Sutherland

SOURCE: A review of *Robert Koch: Father of Bacteriology,* in *Bulletin of the Center for Children's Books,* Vol. XVI, No. 4, December, 1962, p. 61.

A good biography of the great German bacteriologist whose contributions were made both in identification and isolation of specific diseases, and in inventing and perfecting techniques of bacteriological research. A most useful book, although the writing style is quite mediocre. Scientific descriptions are accurate, the book has a good balance between personal and professional life, and the explanations of Koch's work are clear. A glossary of medical terms and an index are appended.

The Junior Bookshelf

SOURCE: A review of *Robert Koch: Father of Bacteriology,* in *The Junior Bookshelf,* Vol. 27, No. 5, November, 1963, p. 285.

A fascinating scientific detective story with bacteria as the killers. This life story of Koch brings out his early genius, that genius being dependent on his painstaking attention to details, and a certain amount of luck common to most vital discoveries. Though a scientist, Koch is shown as a man like other men, but ready to sacrifice himself in the battle against disease in many forms—tuberculosis, anthrax, malaria, etc. There is a very useful glossary. Well recommended.

SCIENCE ABC (1962)

Alice Dalgliesh

SOURCE: "Travel Here and There," in *The Saturday Review,* New York, Vol. XLV, No. 17, April 28, 1962, p. 31.

This tiny ABC slipped down in the package of books from Watts and almost got lost—which would have been too bad, because small boys especially are going to like it. A is Air and Z is Zero—praise be, not Zebra. Capital, small, and script letters given, but the script seems a bit elaborate for beginning writers. Printed in blue throughout, the pictures are pedestrian though workmanlike.

Zena Sutherland

SOURCE: A review of *Science ABC,* in *Bulletin of the Center for Children's Books,* Vol. XV, No. 9, May, 1962, p. 144.

A very small book that combines the letters of the alphabet with a rather random selection of some science material and some informational material that is not scientific. The read-aloud factual material is on one page, a pedestrian illustration on the facing page; each page of text gives the letter and capitalizes that letter whenever it occurs at the beginning of a word on the page. For example, "B is a Bridge / Engineers Build Bridges Big and strong. Bridges lead over rivers and Bays." It is confusing when the text capitalizes other letters, as it does for N: "N is Newspapers / People read Newspapers / To find out what's New. Newspapers are Printed On Printing Presses."

Emily Maxwell

SOURCE: A review of *Science ABC,* in *The New Yorker,* Vol. XXXVIII, No. 40, November 24, 1962, p. 222.

For those small children whose minds are teeming with unanswered questions of a scientific nature, there is a tiny alphabet book called "Science ABC," by David Knight, with pictures by Gustav Schrotter. "C is Clouds. When dark Clouds Cover the sky, It means rain is Coming. Clean white puffy Clouds Mean Clear weather. . . . W is Water. We say Water is Wet. But sometimes it is hard and cold. Then it is ice. And sometimes Water is hot and misty. Then it is steam. . . . S is a Star. At night the Sky is full Of Shining Stars. Each Star is really a Sun. Our own Sun is a Star. . . . O is the Ocean. Ships sail Out Over the Ocean. Oysters, fish, and lobsters Live in the Ocean. How many Oceans are there? Only One—the Ocean has no end." This is a completely unpretentious book, printed in blue on white paper with plain, primerlike pictures that make no effort to be charming. The alphabet is shown in capitals, small letters, and script.

JOHANNES KEPLER AND PLANETARY MOTION (1962)

Virginia Kirkus' Service

SOURCE: A review of *Johannes Kepler and Planetary Motion,* in *Virginia Kirkus' Service,* Vol. XXX, No. 17, September 1, 1962, pp. 837-38.

First a mathematician and then an astronomer, Johannes Kepler (1571-1630) overcame tremendous odds: lifelong illness, personal disasters, religious and political oppression, and financial difficulties, to become the founder of theoretical astronomy. In this thoroughly researched biography we are immersed in the difficult life and times of the Counter-Reformation. With painstaking care the author describes Kepler's poor childhood, his clerical training, teaching jobs, his arrival in the world of the great as imperial mathematician to Rudolf II at Prague, his methods of deduction and calculation resulting in his theories concerning the speed of planets and the shape of their orbits. His new laws exploded the accepted Ptolemaic explanation of the universe, but not without considerable opposition from the scientists of his day and the Catholic Church. Heavily weighted with technical detail, this book has great value but only for the young adult with a mania for mathematics and/or astronomy, their history and evolution.

Best Sellers

SOURCE: A review of *Johannes Kepler and Planetary Motion,* in *Best Sellers,* Vol. 22, No. 22, February 15, 1963, pp. 437-38.

An offering of the *Immortals of Science* series, this biography presents a warm and informal portrait of the famous astronomer. The author has done a fine job in combining the picture of Kepler's friendly personality with a simple explanation of his great discoveries of the Planetary Laws which he formulated. Certainly, Kepler could have become bitter and disappointed with the many obstacles that he had to face in his career of research and teaching. Persecuted by many, even Catholics, for his religion, caught in the midst of the Thirty Years' War, often separated from his family and constantly fighting the spectre of poverty, Kepler managed to maintain equanimity in the face of all. Although often distracted from his tasks of research, he worked when he was able and finally succeeded in working out the problem of how the planets move through the sky. For a period he worked with Tyco Brahe, and after Brahe's death he used the latter's observations to prove his own theories. This book is recommended for scientifically-inclined young people.

Dorothy Schumacher

SOURCE: A review of *Johannes Kepler and Planetary Motion,* in *School Library Journal,* Vol. 9, No. 7, March, 1963, p. 171.

A biography of the German scientist whose laws of planetary motion laid the foundation for Newton's discoveries. His personal life, scientific achievements, and historical background are well covered. In a comparison of this book with Arthur Koestler's biography of Kepler, *The Watershed,* the vivid and artistic style of Koestler makes Knight seem pedestrian, and a little dull. Knight's scientific explanations, however, are simpler and less technical and, therefore, the book can be used with younger readers and is recommended for that purpose.

K. L. Franklin

SOURCE: A review of *Johannes Kepler and Planetary Motion,* in *Natural History,* Vol. 72, No. 10, December, 1963, p. 9.

Johannes Kepler, a contemporary of Galileo, lived during troubled times in a turbulent country. All scientists know that Kepler's contributions to astronomy were the basis for much of Newton's work, but few know about his life. This gap can be remedied by turning to *Johannes Kepler and Planetary Motion,* by David C. Knight. Without resorting to imaginary conversations and guessed-at thoughts, the author succeeds in making Kepler come alive; a person who was often ill, often frustrated, and sometimes elated. In matters of astronomy, however, the author is quite weak. Kepler's important "Rudolphine Tables" are never described, although allusions are made to their significance. A knowledgeable reader will understand the section dealing with relative distances to planets, but others may be greatly confused. And Kepler's greatest law, which relates the distances and periods of the planets, is never shown to be the powerful tool it became (after modification by Newton) for deriving the masses of celestial bodies in orbits. It is surprising that so little astronomy figures in this book, but Mr. Knight's account is a highly readable biography of Johannes Kepler.

THE FIRST BOOK OF DESERTS: AN INTRODUCTION TO THE EARTH'S ARID LANDS (1964)

John Imbrie

SOURCE: A review of *The First Book of Deserts: An Introduction to the Earth's Arid Lands,* in *Natural History,* Vol. 73, No. 9, November, 1964, p. 11.

The arid lands of the earth, including the great deserts, have a perennial allure for those of us who live in wetter areas. *The First Book of Deserts,* by David C. Knight, examines these regions from a scientific point of view (although the author is not a scientist), and the reader is rewarded with a book that is accurate, informative, and well written. The illustrations are striking and are integrated with the text. Many aspects of deserts are covered, including their origin, the life that dwells there, the formation and migration of dunes, and mirages.

Margery Fisher

SOURCE: A review of *The First Book of Deserts: An Introduction to the Earth's Arid Lands,* in *Growing Point,* Vol. 5, No. 3, September, 1966, p. 761.

A sound and authoritative survey, without undue simplification, for twelve and upwards mainly. The author starts by defining the climatic and geological conditions behind the fact of arid lands, discusses the types of desert and dune, describes ways of finding and conserving water, and ties everything to desert inhabitants and their necessary way of life. The illustrations are varied, the aerial photographs especially good.

Eileen Bowker

SOURCE: A review of *The First Book of Deserts,* in *The School Librarian and School Library Review,* Vol. 14, No. 3, December, 1966, p. 369.

Do not be misled by the title, for this is no watered-down simple introduction to deserts written for the young child.

Reinforced by many superb black-and-white photographs and some sketches, the book deals mainly with arid desert wastes. In geographical terms, Mr. Knight explains their *raison d'être* and the basic types found, as well as considering the natural forces that shape and determine the topography and ecology of such hostile environments. The sections dealing with desert plants, creatures and human habitation are particularly interesting.

Although the text is more suitable for the secondary child, an able top junior will learn much if he is selective. The good index will help him. I consider this book excellent value.

THE SCIENCE BOOK OF METEOROLOGY (1965)

Best Sellers

SOURCE: A review of *The Science Book of Meteorology,* in *Best Sellers,* Vol. 24, No. 20, January 15, 1965, p. 411.

The author writes clearly and succinctly on the many

aspects of the science of meteorology. However, young readers will not pick up this book and read cover-to-cover. Rather, the volume is of more use as a reference tool and source of information on questions that might arise in the study of weather. An excellent index, a glossary of terms and the wealth of illustrations make the volume an attractive reference tool. The volume does not deal simply with the elements that go into weather forecasting, but attempts to "examine the characteristics of the basic stuff with which meteorology is directly concerned—the air of our atmosphere, . . ." The book deserves a place in every high school library.

Elizabeth F. Grave

SOURCE: A review of *The Science Book of Meteorology*, in *School Library Journal*, Vol. 11, No. 6, February, 1965, p. 58.

A comprehensive guide to an understanding of the fundamentals of modern meteorology. Includes a thorough study of the many aspects of our atmosphere and much recent material on such topics as the Van Allen radiation belts, air pollution and control, and use of meteorological satellites. Excellent illustrative material on almost every page: diagrams showing the movement of air currents, charts used by the Weather Bureau, weather instruments, weather maps, etc.

Isaac Asimov

SOURCE: "Views on Science Books," in *The Horn Book Magazine*, Vol. XLI, No. 2, April, 1965, pp. 187-88.

[I] am pleased to report on . . . [a book] which I consider to be the best children's book yet in its field. [In *The Science Book of Meteorology*, David C. Knight] discusses all aspects of the weather, from the invention of the barometer to the causes of smog, from the action of the sun to that of the weather satellites. My only reservation is that occasionally the text is interrupted rather distractingly by solid pages of photographs and diagrams.

Science Books: A Quarterly Review

SOURCE: A review of *The Science Book of Meteorology*, in *Science Books: A Quarterly Review*, Vol. 1, No. 1, April, 1965, p. 22.

One of the better elementary descriptive introductions to the field of meteorology. Most of the basic elements of the subject such as the structure of the atmosphere, clouds and precipitation, weather systems and forecasting, as well as some recent information about satellite meteorology and instrumentation are included in this book. It also contains many helpful diagrams and pictures. The numerical data contained in the text are accurate, except that on page 32, the heat balance diagram is incorrect in certain particulars; on page 102, the vertical circulation picture is

incorrect; and on page 105, the jet stream speeds of 400 mph are questionable. While the explanations of processes and systems manage to convey a useful idea of what is going on, they sometimes lack rigor. This readable book will serve the interested layman who desires a realistic statement on the field of meteorology as it exists today.

COPERNICUS: TITAN OF MODERN ASTRONOMY (1965)

Elizabeth F. Grave

SOURCE: A review of *Copernicus: Titan of Modern Astronomy*, in *School Library Journal*, Vol. 12, No. 4, December, 1965, p. 89.

A thoughtful work on the life and times of Nicolaus Copernicus. The author describes the early years of Copernicus in the household of his uncle, the powerful Bishop of Ermland, and his student days at Bologna and Padua. Copernicus was an original thinker concerned with a new theory of the universe. His belief in an earth in motion in a heliocentric system was contrary to the accepted Ptolemaic idea. This volume with its abundant source material and superior illustrations gives evidence of careful research.

The Booklist and Subscription Books Bulletin

SOURCE: A review of *Copernicus: Titan of Modern Astronomy*, in *The Booklist and Subscription Books Bulletin*, Vol. 62, No. 9, January 1, 1966, pp. 444-45.

The author elucidates what little is actually known about the life of Copernicus against a graphic background of the world in which he lived. A very general description of his great manuscript, *De revolutionibus*, is given along with brief explanations of the Ptolemaic and heliocentric systems and an account of the gradual acceptance of the Copernican theory. Appendixes include Osiander's preface and Copernicus' dedication to Pope Paul III. Photographs, diagrams, and line drawings complement the well-written text which will be useful for those studying or interested in astronomy.

Isaac Asimov

SOURCE: "Views on Science Books," in *The Horn Book Magazine*, Vol. XLII, No. 1, February, 1966, pp. 78-9.

A series called Immortals of Science consists of biographies of famous scientists intended, usually, for the junior high-school level. Those I have seen are uniformly good, but now I have come across *Copernicus, Titan of Modern Astronomy* by David C. Knight, which is the best so far. (I would suspect that this one is more suitable for senior high school.) Copernicus' exciting life as a scientific revolutionary, churchman, government functionary, diplomat, and participant in some unusual intrigue on the frontiers of Europe is extraordinarily well told, with a straightforward clarity that makes for more drama than any amount of silly, fictional conversation.

More than that, Knight has taken his biography seriously as a background against which to teach the history of science. The last half of the book includes a brief history of astronomy prior to Copernicus and an *excellent* consideration of Copernicus' theory. The original dedication and preface of *De Revolutionibus Orbium Coelestium* by Copernicus are given (the passages are often referred to but rarely seen in other books), and most curious of all, every known portrait of Copernicus is presented at the end. No teenager who is seriously interested in astronomy should miss this book.

 ### THE FIRST BOOK OF MARS: AN INTRO-DUCTION TO THE RED PLANET (1966; revised edition, 1973)

Milton B. Wenger

SOURCE: A review of *The First Book of Mars: An Introduction to the Red Planet,* in *School Library Journal,* Vol. 12, No. 8, April, 1966, p. 104.

Before Mariner IV relayed the 22 close-up photographs of Mars in July 1965, it was believed this planet was most like our earth in composition and history. The photographs showed, however, that it is more like the moon. The significance of this research is that Mariner IV failed to discover earthlike features in its scan of one percent of the Martian surface. Mr. Knight in his interesting book describes the flight itself and the meaning of the photographs.

The Booklist and Subscription Books Bulletin

SOURCE: A review of *The First Book of Mars: An Introduction to the Red Planet,* in *The Booklist and Subscription Books Bulletin,* Vol. 62, No. 16, April 15, 1966, pp. 832-33.

A well-written, scientific text, supplemented by excellent photographs, charts, and drawings, presents known facts and various astronomical theories past and present about Mars, including the latest discoveries revealed by Mariner IV's "fly-by" in 1965. It also discusses the intriguing folklore and fiction which has been inspired by the Red Planet and the possible future exploration and use of Mars by man.

Science Books: A Quarterly Review

SOURCE: A review of *The First Book of Mars,* in *Science Books: A Quarterly Review,* Vol. 2, No. 1, May, 1966, p. 16.

Mr. Knight has presented an up-to-date summary of the

story of Mars in a concise but readable text that is illustrated with well chosen diagrams and photographs. He has described our present understanding of Mars and the observations leading to this knowledge. The story begins with a description of the Mariner IV flight. A comprehensible account is presented of the launching, control, experiments, and results. Having thus gained the reader's attention, Mr. Knight then gives an account of the folklore of Mars with emphasis on Orson Welles' 1938 radio drama. A conventional account of facts concerning Mars and the history of these discoveries completes the story.

The Christian Science Monitor

SOURCE: A review of *The First Book of Mars,* in *The Christian Science Monitor,* May 5, 1966, p. B7.

This is one of the best books on the Red Planet yet brought out for readers of 12 up. It includes a simple but informative review of the Mariner 4 close-up pictures of that planet. These pictures are reproduced. Together with some of the better telescopic views of Mars, they show the reader as much as now can be shown him of what the planet looks like. The book is well written. It neither talks down nor beyond its readers.

Isaac Asimov

SOURCE: "Views on Science Books," in *The Horn Book Magazine,* Vol. XLII, No. 5, October, 1966, pp. 584-85.

The first third of this book (written for the junior high-school student) is devoted to the story of Mariner IV, which took close photographs of Mars in 1965. The space probe is described, and every one of the twenty-one pictures it took is reproduced and identified. There is even the reproduction of an IBM card of "ones" and "zeros," which gives an idea of the manner in which the information is received on Earth before it is converted into a picture. Once the attention of the young reader is effectively captured, Mr. Knight returns to the beginning with a systematic description of the astronomy of Mars. Until something better than Mariner IV happens (such as a soft landing on Mars) this book is safe.

K. L. Franklin

SOURCE: A review of *The First Book of Mars,* in *Natural History,* Vol. 75, No. 9, November, 1966, p. 25.

This is a well-written, factual account of the Mariner IV mission to Mars, with enough background information about the red planet to show the import of the new observations. The author has restricted himself to telling just what is required to establish man's interest in Mars, from the Babylonians to Orson Welles, and the spectacular result of that interest in the space age. His discussion of the achievements of the Mariner IV fly-by is not so complete as to be tiring, but it is enough to indicate what was new and surprising, and even tantalizing. Again, here is a book that may stimulate a certain kind of youngster to plan a career in what may be termed space engineering.

Philip Morrison and Phylis Morrison

SOURCE: A review of *The First Book of Mars,* in *Scientific American,* Vol. 215, No. 6, December, 1966, p. 141.

Knight's book—brief, handsome, with a ground-based color photograph of the planet—is meant for readers from 12 up. . . . [It shows] all 21 of the Mariner IV photographs. He tells the stories well: the Orson Welles radio program, the misnamed "canals," the strange little moons, the polar caps (with a long sequence of photographs). The book fulfills its title splendidly.

Ovide V. Fortier

SOURCE: A review of *The First Book of Mars: An Introduction to the Red Planet,* in *School Library Journal,* Vol. 20, No. 1, September, 1973, p. 84.

This revision of the 1966 edition covers the treatment of Mars in folklore and fiction, the findings of earthbound astronomers, and the results of the recent Mariner spacecraft flights. Since 1966, when only one space craft (Mariner 4) had made it to Mars, three other craft which carried much better instrumentation (Mariners 6, 7, and 9) have also collected and sent back to earth data about Mars. The inclusion of these newer findings makes this a useful replacement for the earlier book.

Science Books: A Quarterly Review

SOURCE: A review of *The First Book of Mars: An Introduction to the Red Planet,* in *Science Books: A Quarterly Review,* Vol. IX, No. 3, December, 1973, pp. 254-55.

Mr. Knight's style is designed for elementary grades, but the reader must understand erosion, spacecraft orbits, biology of plants and animals, gravitational capture, solar heating, etc. The style is unacceptable for college students, although the facts and descriptions are often at college level. The book starts with fairly complete descriptions of the NASA Mariner flights to Mars and the well-selected photos obtained on them. Distances traveled, times, experiments performed, and data obtained are accurate and fairly complete. The author is less complete in his description of Mars as a planet in the Solar System. However, his summary of the history of Mars investigations is excellent, with accurate accounts of the "canals," H. G. Wells and Orson Welles science fiction, and speculation about the moons, Deimos and Phobus. (Some of the theories he describes are not accepted by scientists, and he omits Carl Sagan's explanation of color changes as due to dust.) The *First Book of Mars* is more up-to-date than most other published books on the subject, but it is less accurate scientifically, and it is inconsistent in format and content.

LET'S FIND OUT ABOUT MARS (1966)

Marguerite M. Murray

SOURCE: A review of *Let's Find Out About Mars,* in *School Library Journal,* Vol. 13, No. 1, September, 1966, p. 162.

Attractively illustrated, this book fills a need in the primary grades for readable material about space. It is directed to [the second and third grade level, and] . . . includes the discoveries shown in the pictures taken by Mariner 4 of Mars. Though the writing is rather choppy, the author has handled reasonably well the fact and fancy surrounding Mars, and, with the help of the pictures, has provided a stimulating atmosphere of excitement in discovery.

Science Books: A Quarterly Review

SOURCE: A review of *Let's Find Out About Mars,* in *Science Books: A Quarterly Review,* Vol. 2, No. 3, December, 1966, p. 184.

The reader will learn something about Mars from this book, but to do so he must plod along with a pedestrian text and illustrations that exhibit little imagination. Some statements are misleading, indicating that the text should have been checked by a specialist in astronomy prior to publication. The makings of a good book are in evidence, but there were slip-ups along the way. The book will be satisfactory for the child who is willing to work for his learning—it will not attract the casual reader.

LET'S FIND OUT ABOUT MAGNETS (1967)

Virginia Kirkus' Service

SOURCE: A review of *Let's Find Out About Magnets,* in *Virginia Kirkus' Service,* Vol. XXXIV, No. 24, December 15, 1966, pp. 1286-87.

The child who is looking for answers to his questions will find none of them here. He'll find out that "Nobody makes lodestones. They just come that way in nature"; he'll find out that "Magnets can be made in all different shapes . . . But (they) always attract iron and steel things best." The disregard of experimental method, the lack of logical ordering of information, make this far inferior to several other simple books on the subject.

Alphoretta Fish

SOURCE: A review of *Let's Find Out About Magnets,* in *School Library Journal,* Vol. 13, No. 6, February, 1967, p. 60.

In this simple, well-written text the reader is given the usual information about magnets contained in most first-

and second-grade textbooks and in many other general trade books, e.g. that like poles attract and unlike ones repel, that magnets are useful and are found in many places in the home, that the greatest force of a magnet is at the North and South Poles, that the force of a magnet will act through water, etc. Unfortunately, the questions of how magnets attract and repel and how we know these and other facts are not explained.

Science Books: A Quarterly Review

SOURCE: A review of *Let's Find Out About Magnets,* in *Science Books: A Quarterly Review,* Vol. 2, No. 4, March, 1967, p. 267.

Although there are many children's books about magnets, because of their interest in the subject there is always room for another good one. Mr. Knight begins with the story of the early Greeks and their "lodestones," explains the principles of magnets, their shapes and sizes, and some of the many uses of magnets in familiar things about the school and home. The do-it-yourself activities teach useful principles and skills that are related to the methods and content of modern science teaching in elementary schools.

Zena Sutherland

SOURCE: A review of *Let's Find Out About Magnets,* in *Bulletin of the Center for Children's Books,* Vol. 20, No. 8, April, 1967, p. 125.

A good first science book for the primary grades reader. The text is continuous; the illustrations show white and Negro children doing simple experiments and demonstrations. The pictures are large and clear; the print is large and clear; the explanations of basic magnetic phenomena are lucid. The book begins with a brief description of the Grecian knowledge of lodestones; it concludes with some examples of the use of magnets in such familiar objects as a refrigerator door or an automatic can-opener.

📖 LET'S FIND OUT ABOUT TELEPHONES (1967)

Zena Sutherland

SOURCE: A review of *Let's Find Out About Telephones,* in *Bulletin of the Center for Children's Books,* Vol. 20, No. 10, June, 1967, p. 155.

Intended as an introduction to the topic of telephones and how they work, this book gives only a smattering of information, some of which seems extraneous. The illustrations are in some cases susceptible to misunderstanding; the text is written with some disparity, since the child who can understand "The telegraph could send messages between cities by electricity over a wire" is probably well aware that when "You see people talking over telephones

every day. What they are doing is telephoning, called *phoning.*" This slightly patronizing note is again evident in the comment that Bell's first telephone "was a funny looking thing."

📖 LET'S FIND OUT ABOUT WEATHER (1967)

Kirkus Service

SOURCE: A review of *Let's Find Out About Weather,* in *Kirkus Service,* Vol. XXXV, No. 13, July 1, 1967, p. 743.

One more assemblage of small words and large pictures that organizes the child's observations and supplies a few explanations, here regarding the role of the air in "making weather." The explanations are likely to satisfy only a very young or torpid child; for others they will raise as many questions as they answer: Lightning. "How does it get there? Lightning is really giant sparks of electricity. Electricity shoots through a storm cloud. . . ." *How does it get there?* In the long sequence of weather books, this is a whistle stop, worth noticing only if you need another pause between evocation and elucidation.

Science Books: A Quarterly Review

SOURCE: A review of *Let's Find Out About Weather,* in *Science Books: A Quarterly Review,* Vol. 3, No. 2, September, 1967, p. 123.

The basic facts of weather phenomena are explained for the very young reader with accompanying illustrations that enable him to relate the text to his own visual experience. The concluding section on weather forecasting, introduced by an illustration of a weather map on a television screen, will capture the interest of many youngsters who will want more information and hence "older" books on the subject. There are two minor technical errors. It is misleading to speak of the blanket of air around the earth as being "hundreds of miles thick"; the blanket of air involved in weather phenomena is comparatively thin—about 20 miles. There is also the usual nonscientific confusion of "heat" content and "temperature"; admittedly difficult to explain to novices. The illustrations of a thermometer should have indicated the Fahrenheit scale.

Elizabeth Hone

SOURCE: A review of *Let's Find Out About Weather,* in *School Library Journal,* Vol. 14, No. 2, October, 1967, p. 165.

A primary-grade teacher might find this book useful for its simple developmental ideas and analogies. The illustrations are quite acceptable. However, like many other children's books about weather, this volume does not clarify the two major concepts involved in understanding weather, namely, matter and energy changes, (the evaporation cycle) and convection currents.

THE FIRST BOOK OF BERLIN: TALE OF A DIVIDED CITY (1967)

Kirkus Service

SOURCE: A review of *The First Book of Berlin,* in *Kirkus Service,* Vol. XXXV, No. 19, October 1, 1967, pp. 1223-24.

This study of Berlin begins in the middle—with the Wall and attempts to cross it. In an obvious appeal to the emotions, Mr. Knight tells about (and shows) East Berliners sloshing through sewers, strapped under cars and digging tunnels to escape; an eighteen-year-old boy, killed in the attempt, lies bleeding to death beneath the barbed wire. Thus Berlin is not so much a city as a situation and much of the subsequent information is directed at explaining that situation. There's still room for a good deal of history before partition, blockade and Wall; still room to display the characteristic wit of Berliners; still room to visit the various quarters and the cultural attractions—but very little room for East Berlin, which the author seems not to know first-hand. The result is an informed, affectionate portrait of West Berlin today, of the whole city in calmer days, between the propaganda at front and back. If you don't object to the tone, it could be useful—it is the first with the most *about* Berlin. Good photos and maps, too.

The Christian Science Monitor

SOURCE: "Some Tickets to Faraway Places," in *The Christian Science Monitor,* November 2, 1967, p. B8.

The tragedy of a divided city is graphically portrayed in **The First Book of Berlin,** by David C. Knight. The book draws its young readers in by beginning with a series of accounts of dramatic escapes by East Berliners over the Wall. The author then goes back to the city's beginnings as a village in the 1200's and in crisp style gives its history through the Electors, Frederick the Great, Hitler, and finally to its present divided state. Especially interesting are the photographs which show much of Berlin before its destruction in World War II. Maps and an index complete this fine book.

Dallas Y. Shaffer

SOURCE: A review of *The First Book of Berlin: Tale of a Divided City,* in *School Library Journal,* Vol. 14, No. 4, December, 1967, p. 82.

This book is filled with information on Berlin's history and culture. The writing style is clear, concise, and straightforward except for a few instances of strongly disparaging adjectives: the East Berlin police dogs are "half starved" and the Russian troops are "sullen." The author does an excellent job of presenting the material, including information not found in most other books, e.g. the background of the June 17, 1953, uprising in East Berlin. The

photographs are dramatic, including many before and after pictures of war damaged areas. There are several maps, some of them historical. An attractive and useful book.

The Booklist and Subscription Books Bulletin

SOURCE: A review of *The First Book of Berlin: Tale of a Divided City,* in *The Booklist and Subscription Books Bulletin,* Vol. 64, No. 12, February 15, 1968, pp. 700-01.

Surveying the history and present status of Berlin, the author focuses most clearly on the division of the city and the Wall which separates the free Western and the totalitarian Eastern sectors. The portrait of present-day West Berlin conveys the spirit of its people as well as its physical appearance and cultural attractions. Maps and many well-chosen photographs highlight the discussion.

LET'S FIND OUT ABOUT INSECTS (1967)

Paul Walker

SOURCE: A review of *Let's Find Out About Insects,* in *The New York Times Book Review,* November 5, 1967, p. 56.

As a science primer, [this book] skips about over too much ground and its random facts are not always clarified by the illustrations. Drawings are labeled with terms not explained in the text ("carboniferous," "triassic"); insects are inexplicably drawn out of proportion (a mosquito on a girl's hand is the size of a hummingbird); and in the sequence on the metamorphosis of a butterfly, the larva shown belongs to one species, the chrysalis and imago to another.

Science Books: A Quarterly Review

SOURCE: A review of *Let's Find Out About Insects,* in *Science Books: A Quarterly Review,* Vol. 3, No. 3, December, 1967, pp. 240-41.

An attractive little book for preschool and beginning readers that will acquaint them with some of the diversity of the insect world, provide a few interesting details on morphology and habits, and serve to sharpen their visual acuity as they observe insects in nature. The book was tried out on a few children at a summer camp, and they and their counselors liked it. It provides a good foundation for more detailed and sophisticated books for children such as *The Insect World,* by Norman M. Lobsenz (1962).

LET'S FIND OUT ABOUT EARTH (1967; revised edition, 1975)

Kirkus Service

SOURCE: A review of *Let's Find Out About Earth,* in

Kirkus Service, Vol. XXXVI, No. 1, January 1, 1968, p. 11.

This is a rather poorly conceived introductory level book about the earth in space which covers the gamut from historical conceptions of the flat earth to earth as an orbiting planet. Along the way it too briefly skims across definitions of terms like *planet, gravity, atmosphere* and *continents,* equally slighted are concepts like the tilt of the earth's axis and its relation to seasonal variation, and the decrease of gravity with distance. In an incorrect statement regarding the weightlessness of astronauts, Mr. Knight perpetuates the fallacy which pervades the popular press but which is unacceptable in a science book. (The astronautic flight is usually an orbital flight which by its very nature cannot be "weightless" in any valid sense of the word; otherwise the space ship would not retain orbit.) The confusion of the sensation of weightlessness with the actual state thereof may not be a topic to be explored at this age level (an observation which applies to other concepts in this book), but difficult notions should not be replaced with skewed information.

Science Books: A Quarterly Review

SOURCE: A review of *Let's Find Out About Earth,* in *Science Books: A Quarterly Review,* Vol. 3, No. 4, March, 1968, p. 294.

This reading book offers factual information on the solar system in general and on the earth and moon in particular. The earth's lithosphere, hydrosphere, and atmosphere are sketched in the simplest terms. Illustrations make up about half the book; in artistic quality these are uniformly good, and most of them elucidate the text. The guidance of an understanding teacher will, however, be needed to explain the alternations of day and night and the march of the seasons.

Jacqueline Carr

SOURCE: A review of *Let's Find Out About Earth,* in *Appraisal: Children's Science Books,* Vol. 9, No. 1, Winter, 1976, pp. 23-4.

The simple, accurate text of this book covers the physical geography of planet Earth: its roundness, night and day, the passage of a year, the reflected light of the moons, the atmosphere, the seasons, continents and oceans, gravity, and the possibility of new knowledge through space exploration. The text is poorly supported by illustrations, which are brightly colored but dull in their stylized oversimplifications. This is a good book for primary readers.

Harry C. Stubbs

SOURCE: A review of *Let's Find Out About Earth,* in *Appraisal: Children's Science Books,* Vol. 9, No. 1, Winter, 1976, p. 24.

This is supposed to be a revised edition, but the revision seems to have consisted largely of adding distances in kilometers, without regard to significant digits, to the distances already given in miles. Walking around the earth would indeed be a journey of "almost 25,000 miles," but if the figure is to be rounded off that much there is no excuse for adding in parenthesis "40,234 kilometers." It would have been less misleading, if so many digits were to be used, to call the circumference 24,903 miles (40,077 km). I cannot fault the omission of Jupiter's fourteenth moon, which was not discovered until after the book was published; but the thirteenth was reported in the summer of 1974, and Saturn's tenth has been known for several years now. The discussion (explanation?) of seasons is not incorrect, but not very adequate in my opinion; it is a section where author and artist could have collaborated much more closely and effectively.

THE FIRST BOOK OF THE SUN (1968)

Kirkus Service

SOURCE: A review of *The First Book of the Sun,* in *Kirkus Service,* Vol. XXXVI, No. 1, January 1, 1968, p. 15.

An extremely competent introduction to the phenomena connected with the sun. One of problems of the series is that the title can be misleading, and this is far more than a simple beginning for the immature mind. It ranges through historical and mythical conceptions of the sun and the solar system; narrows in on the star to explore its surface granulation and feculae and the prominences, flares and corona of its atmosphere; and concludes with hypotheses concerning the nature of the sun's energy, and ideas about its past and future. The many photos are well-chosen and very informative; the text is lucid and interesting to the point of excitement.

Milton B. Wenger

SOURCE: A review of *The First Book of the Sun,* in *School Library Journal,* Vol. 14, No. 8, April, 1968, p. 140.

How big is the sun? What physical properties does it have? David Knight answers these and other basic questions about our sun and explains clearly many theories about it, in his smooth and factual text. The illustrations range from pictures showing ancient beliefs about the sun to striking recent photographs and drawings of the solar system. The author explores new theories about our galaxy, the sun's surface and atmosphere, the interior of the sun, and solar energy. The book includes historical background on the sun and some speculations on its future. This is an authoritative introduction to a study of this body and to basic astronomy.

Science Books: A Quarterly Review

SOURCE: A review of *The First Book of the Sun,* in

Science Books: A Quarterly Review, Vol. 4, No. 3, December, 1968, p. 193.

Various descriptive aspects of the sun are covered in this short book, including brief discussions of its place in the universe, early beliefs concerning its nature, and its effects on terrestrial life. The writing style is clear for the level intended, and the coverage is adequate. The book however is cursory in many respects, there being very little discussion of the interrelation of solar phenomena and physical principles. Moreover, accounts of the basic physics of the sun and of theories and explanations of phenomena contain many inaccuracies. For example, the assertion that the solar wind is part of the solar corona is highly questionable. It is not true, either, that the sun is overhead at noontime, as the book implies. Centrifugal force is used to explain why planets stay in orbit, and this is erroneous.

Zena Sutherland

SOURCE: A review of *The First Book of the Sun,* in *Bulletin of the Center for Children's Books,* Vol. 23, No. 3, November, 1969, p. 48.

An excellent discussion of the composition of the sun, the thermonuclear reactions that produce solar energy, observable phenomena, and the theories scientists have about all of these. The material is well-organized, with a description of the universe and our galaxy, a section on sun-worship in past cultures, and discussion of earlier astronomical theories preceding the major portion of the text. The book is lucidly written and there is a separate section on techniques and instruments used by scientists in obtaining solar information. The continuous text is organized by topic headings; the photographs and diagrams are clearly captioned, and an index is appended.

📖 *COMETS* (1968)

Kirkus Service

SOURCE: A review of *Comets,* in *Kirkus Service,* Vol. XXXVI, No. 11, June 1, 1968, p. 608.

An anatomy of comets, including their parts, their composition, a little of their history as recorded by man, and even a short tabulation of some of the most famous. This clear account is useful because of the scarcity of competent books on the subject, in contrast to a few pages or a section. Included here is a section on cometary orbits, understandable if brief, which has wider value as a geometry of all orbiting objects. The photographs are quite good and useful for the illustration of some otherwise difficult terms. Some of the more famous astronomers (Newton, Halley) and their finds in the area of cometry are discussed in a semi-biographical form, which adds a personal dimension. Although the book is competent and worth purchasing, *the* book on comets for the young audience is still to come.

The Christian Science Monitor

SOURCE: A review of *Comets,* in *The Christian Science Monitor,* November 14, 1968, p. 14.

Comets, by David C. Knight, covers the story of comets from ancient myths to the latest scientific theories. It's interesting, informative and probably would please many youngsters in grades 5 and up. If only the author had put more color into his writing, this could be an outstanding book. He has brought together a lot of good material, including some fascinating old pictures of myths about comets, and sketches of actual comets. But his style lets him down with its matter-of-fact dryness. He could have had fun with his material and still kept it authoritative. Yet this may be only a quibble, for it is generally quite a good book.

Philip Morrison and Phylis Morrison

SOURCE: A review of *Comets,* in *Scientific American,* Vol. 219, No. 6, December, 1968, p. 126.

The schoolish appearance of this book makes it look as though it were meant for fifth-graders, who indeed can grasp it, but the richness of its text, photographs and diagrams extends its readability and interest upward many years. Much is owed to the paintings of famous comets from the American Museum of Natural History, reproduced here in black and white, and the excellent astronomical photographs from the big telescopes. The six-tailed comet of 1744 was a wonder; Halley's comet is treated in an excellent chapter. Only sun-grazers are somewhat slighted. The great Siberian explosion of 1908 is very sensibly ascribed to a comet head falling to earth.

Harry C. Stubbs

SOURCE: A review of *Comets,* in *The Horn Book Magazine,* Vol. XLV, No. 2, April, 1969, pp. 190-92.

Mr. Knight provides a very good mixture of history, observational fact, and theory in an account aimed at the upper-primary student. Much of it is funny—comet cartoons and even tales of a comet pill. Ancient drawings and modern photographs, portraits of astronomers and diagrams of orbits combine very well to build up the currently held ideas about comets—and the uncertainty of those ideas. Mr. Knight seems to favor the cloud-of-shot picture of the comet, rather than the stones-in-ice theory of Dr. Whipple. I do not share his opinion, but must grant that he has presented both views fairly.

In many of the photographs, the background stars show as lines because the camera was tracking the comet. I failed to see this explained anywhere in the book. It is a very minor point, but it did strike me that the author was overlooking a good chance to illustrate the point he makes on page eight—that the direction of a comet's tail is not much of a guide to its space motion. Contrasting Comet

Brooks and Comet Morehouse would have been meaningful, I should think, even to fifth-graders.

THE WHISKY REBELLION, 1794: REVOLT IN WESTERN PENNSYLVANIA THREATENS AMERICAN UNITY (1968)

Phillip Haag

SOURCE: A review of *The Whiskey Rebellion, 1794: Revolt in Pennsylvania Threatens American Unity,* in *School Library Journal,* Vol. 15, No. 6, February, 1969, p. 90.

Clearly and concisely, Mr. Knight discusses the financial plight of the emerging American nation and Alexander Hamilton's excise tax on whiskey that was designed to relieve the monetary crisis. Without casting aspersions on Hamilton's ability, the author shows why the tax was an unfair one and how it created more problems than it solved. The infuriated farmers in western Pennsylvania, the people primarily affected by the tax, revolted. Federal troops were sent in, resulting in bloody conflict and a severe rupture in national unity. The principal federal and insurgent leaders involved are carefully covered in this well illustrated and thoroughly indexed book, which will be useful supplementary reading in American history units.

The Booklist and Subscription Books Bulletin

SOURCE: A review of *The Whisky Rebellion, 1794: Revolt in Pennsylvania Threatens American Unity,* in *The Booklist and Subscription Books Bulletin,* Vol. 65, No. 14, March 15, 1969, p. 836.

An almost itemized account of a local historical incident which the author explains is of national significance as an example of the newly created U.S. government's power to enforce obedience to its laws. He describes the circumstances which gave rise to the insurrection and the peaceful and violent protests of the rebels which were quickly suppressed by Federal force.

METEORS AND METEORITES: AN INTRODUCTION TO METEORITICS (1969)

Kirkus Reviews

SOURCE: A review of *Meteors and Meteorites: An Introduction to Meteoritics,* in *Kirkus Reviews,* Vol. XXXVII, No. 3, February 1, 1969, p. 113.

This is properly conceived of as a companion to Knight's recent *First Book of Comets.* The text is very similar in style—perhaps a little more encyclopedic. A wealth of information on known meteorites, their locations, craters and history is presented in relevant sections. Some of the photos are effective but they don't compare in excitement with those available in newspapers and magazines. More-

over, there is little indication of the intrinsic importance of the topics covered. It is a fuller source of information than LaPay's *Space Nomads* (which dates back to 1961) though not a better book and certainly not more interesting reading.

Franklyn M. Branley

SOURCE: A review of *Meteors and Meteorites: An Introduction to Meteoritics,* in *School Library Journal,* Vol. 15, No. 8, April, 1969, p. 129.

A dully written though mostly accurate introduction to the subject of meteorites aimed at school libraries. Mr. Knight discusses types of meteorites, possible sources of meteoroids, meteor showers, etc. The book is, at times, omissive and confusing, and includes some questionable statements. For example, references to the origin of meteors are contradictory; tektites are said to be found on or near one of the three great circles of the earth but there is no follow-up explanation of which circles are meant; questionable references are made to an unknown species of bacteria reportedly found on a meteorite. There is no bibliography—a decided lack in a book of this sort—but there are some 40 photographs, prints, and engravings from the files of the American Museum of Natural History and photographs from other institutions, as well as helpful, captioned charts and diagrams. Unfortunately the visual support can't make a dull or confusing text better.

Science Books: A Quarterly Review

SOURCE: A review of *Meteors and Meteorites: An Introduction to Meteoritics,* in *Science Books: A Quarterly Review,* Vol. 5, No. 1, May, 1969, pp. 24-5.

The various types of meteoric material are described and profusely illustrated with photographs from many sources to provide an introduction for advanced elementary and junior high students. The style is generally suitable for students in those groups, but a few technical terms from geometry and chemistry (ordinarily obtained in senior high courses) may require the use of reference works. The book is factually correct, but the text omits recent developments (space-probe detection of meteoroids, the Prarie Network of meteor cameras, meteoric dust on the moon) and fails to mention several of the illustrations. The lists of meteor showers, meteor craters, and meteor falls are useful, but the many descriptions of individual meteorites become boring to the reader. The most serious defect is the omission of Harvard College Observatory's major work during the 1930's and the comparatively recent (1963) detection of organic material in the Orguille meteorite. The work may be useful as a reference in some junior high science courses.

Ben W. Bova

SOURCE: A review of *Meteors and Meteorites: An In-*

troduction to Meteoritics, in *Appraisal: Children's Science Books,* Vol. 2, No. 3, Fall, 1969, p. 14.

The author obviously knows his subject well, but presents it in a dust-dry manner. Several technical concepts that are difficult for children to grasp are tossed in with little or no explanation. Much of the most exciting aspects of meteorics is glossed over in favor of long recitations of where various meteor craters are, and how meteorites have been brought to museums. Greatly missed are discussions of astroblemes, the role of meteorics in understanding the origin of the solar system, and a fuller discussion of the biological traces found in certain types of meteorites. Missed most of all is excitement.

Allison Hamlin

SOURCE: A review of *Meteors and Meteorites: An Introduction of Meteoritics,* in *Appraisal: Children's Science Books,* Vol. 2, No. 3, Fall, 1969, p. 13.

The most appealing feature of this rather cut-and-dried introduction to meteorics is its illustrations, engravings, photographs and charts from the American Museum of Natural History and other first rate sources. In accurate but somewhat textbookish style, the author distinguishes between meteoroid, meteor and meteorite and attempts to give the history and pertinent scientific facts about each. Explanations are not always detailed enough for the student who lacks background. There is room for a lucid and vividly written trade book more up to date than La Paz's *Space Nomads* or Zim's *Shooting Stars* for younger readers. This title will be useful, but will not fire the interest of the unenthusiastic student.

📖 *LET'S FIND OUT ABOUT ROCKS AND MINERALS* (1969)

Science Books: A Quarterly Review

SOURCE: A review of *Let's Find Out About Rocks and Minerals,* in *Science Books: A Quarterly Review,* Vol. 5, No. 3, December, 1969, p. 237.

This discussion of rocks and minerals is superficial, even for the intended reader. Defining a mineral as "something in nature that isn't a plant or an animal" gives the child a false impression of what a mineral is. Color would add greatly to the comprehension of the illustrations, and photographs should be substituted for the drawings of minerals in the identification chart. The description of rocks, their formation and uses is interestingly developed. Other features of the book include a list of field trip equipment, a list of museums and exhibits of rocks and minerals in the U.S. and Canada, and a list of books for elementary level rockhounds.

Ann E. Matthews

SOURCE: A review of *Let's Find Out About Rocks and*

Minerals, in *Appraisal: Children's Science Books,* Vol. 3, No. 1, Winter, 1970, p. 22.

This text has a standard approach to the popular subject of rocks and minerals. It will appeal to students who are pebble pups. Many times the statements made are stated as truth such as: "Our earth is a great ball of rock." Therefore it fails to convey the tentative nature of geologic investigation. Young children should be exposed to this. However, it does encourage student investigation of sensory perceptions of common rocks.

Marion H. Perkins

SOURCE: A review of *Let's Find Out About Rocks and Minerals,* in *Appraisal: Children's Science Books,* Vol. 3, No. 1, Winter, 1970, p. 22.

The text is too simple for the subject matter it attempts to cover. A hodgepodge of bits of information about rocks and minerals. Poorly organized, the author skips from one kind of rock to another and doesn't tell enough about any one kind to make the book interesting or very clear to the reader. In 63 pages he gives a few characteristics of rocks in general (4 in particular); says rocks are made of minerals of which he names 5 varieties; mentions fossils in rocks; tells of the effects water and wind have on rocks; the uses of rocks and minerals; methods of mining, etc. In closing he lists basic items for a field trip and some common rocks and minerals you can expect to find. One redeeming feature is a listing of larger museums in the United States and Canada where rocks and minerals can be found.

📖 *LET'S FIND OUT ABOUT THE OCEAN* (1970)

Pat Barnes

SOURCE: A review of *Let's Find Out About the Ocean,* in *School Library Journal,* Vol. 17, No. 4, December, 1970, p. 82.

A clearly written, concise introduction to basic oceanography, this includes simple facts on tides, marine life, currents, etc. A question-and-answer approach is sometimes used, with concepts presented in logical, developmental sequence and the causes and effects of phenomena delineated. The black and aqua illustrations are both decorative and detailed; the book as a whole could best be used on a second-grade level. Comparable in content to Barlowe's *Oceans* (1969), this has a simpler vocabulary and will be better for primary readers.

Science Books: A Quarterly Review

SOURCE: A review of *Let's Find Out About the Ocean,* in *Science Books: A Quarterly Review,* Vol. 6, No. 4, March, 1971, p. 304.

David Knight provides the reader with a compact book which attempts to present a very broad view of oceans and oceanography. As seems to be typical of books of this sort, questionable statements abound. What will be the perceptions of the youngster who reads this statement: "The hot sun beating down on the surface of the ocean makes water rise like mist into the air." Will he believe that there is no evaporation unless it is hot? Unless the sun is "beating down?" Will he believe that under the circumstances which are described, water defies gravity and "rises?" Scientists and science educators alike deplore the current state of the typical citizen's scientific literacy. Books such as this one would appear to do little to improve matters.

Wayne Hanley

SOURCE: A review of *Let's Find Out About the Ocean,* in *Appraisal: Children's Science Books,* Vol. 4, No. 2, Spring, 1971, pp. 21-2.

This volume may be a little heady for small children since it tells considerably more about oceans, marine biology, and oceanography than the average adult knows. Nevertheless, it accomplishes the task through about 90 per cent illustration and 10 per cent text, and both illustrations and text are easily grasped by even beginning readers. It answers such questions as the difference between oceans and seas, why whales are not fish, tides and waves, etc.

📖 *AMERICAN ASTRONAUTS AND SPACE-CRAFT: A PICTORIAL HISTORY FROM PROJECT MERCURY THROUGH APOLLO 13* (1970; revised edition as *American Astronauts and Spacecraft: A Pictorial History from Project Mercury through the Skylab Manned Missions,* 1975)

Julian Scheer

SOURCE: A review of *American Astronauts and Spacecraft,* in *The New York Times Book Review,* January 17, 1971, p. 14.

American Astronauts And Spacecraft, edited by David C. Knight, contains biographical sketches of the astronauts and a glossary of space terms. But the real meat is the 200 official photographs. They carry the reader from Project Mercury through Apollo 13 (the most recent, and almost ill-starred, lunar attempt). It's hard to find anything the editor left out of this pictorial history for young teenagers: John Glenn running on the beach; the blackened spacecraft at Canaveral in which three astronauts died; color photographs of the earth from space; the lunar surface; spacecraft in orbit; and close-ups of the astronauts.

Zena Sutherland

SOURCE: A review of *American Astronauts and Space-*

craft: A Pictorial History from Project Mercury through Apollo 13, in *Bulletin of the Center for Children's Books,* Vol. 24, No. 9, May, 1971, p. 139.

An oversize book in photograph-and-caption format, the pictures taken from official NASA files and the text, based on material in NASA archives, giving highlights of each of the three United States space programs: Projects Mercury, Gemini, and Apollo. Although a few diagrams give some details of space capsules, there is little information about spacecraft; the book focuses on the training, liftoff and splashdown, and facts about flight details and statistics. A brief review of the flights in each of the three programs preceded the pictorial material; the text ends with the Apollo 13 mission. Biographical notes on the astronauts, a glossary of terms, and an index are appended.

Science Books: A Quarterly Review

SOURCE: A review of *American Astronauts and Spacecraft: A Pictorial History from Project Mercury through Apollo 13,* in *Science Books: A Quarterly Review,* Vol. 7, No. 1, May, 1971, p. 80.

Photographs, caption material, biographies of the astronauts, a glossary, and an index all related to the United States program in manned spaceflight make up this volume. Projects Mercury and Gemini are described and the Apollo moon-landing program is covered up through Apollo 13. The 24 colored photographs are beautifully reproduced and include the now famous picture of the earth seen from distant space. There are many more black-and-white photographs. Many of the captions could be improved by including more detail. They appear similar to press releases. This volume is a useful addition to the record of manned space flight. However, the book is marred by numerous minor errors.

Science Books: A Quarterly Review

SOURCE: A review of *American Astronauts and Spacecraft: A Pictorial History from Project Mercury through Apollo 13,* in *Science Books: A Quarterly Review,* Vol. 8, No. 2, September, 1972, p. 174.

The manned space program is famous for the number of outstanding photographs it has produced. A collection of these photographs which emphasizes the human aspects of the Mercury, Gemini, and Apollo programs together with brief biographies of the United States Astronauts is here assembled into book form. It is an enjoyable and easy way to learn something about the manned space program, and the pictures are great!

Ovide V. Fortier

SOURCE: A review of *American Astronauts and Spacecraft: A Pictorial History from Project Mercury Through* the Skylab Manned Missions, in School Library Journal, Vol. 22, No. 5, January, 1976, p. 47.

A reprint of the 1970 edition with a 48 page supplement describing the four subsequent Apollo and three Spacelab missions. The new material presented here is a series of photographs with lengthy captions covering participants preparations, lift-off, space activities, landing, and homecoming for each mission. The original 14 pages of biographies, the glossary, and the index have not been brought up to date, thus seriously decreasing the book's value as a reference.

David G. Hoag

SOURCE: A review of American Astronauts and Spacecraft: A Pictorial History from Project Mercury Through the Skylab Manned Missions, in Appraisal: Children's Science Books, Vol. 9, No. 2, Spring, 1976, pp. 26-7.

For the youngster still fascinated by America's manned space exploits, this would be a great book. Almost two hundred pages have one or more photos from the Mercury, Gemini, Apollo, and Skylab programs. There are twenty-eight more pages of biographies of the Astronauts, a glossary, and an index. A few pages describe each program, and the paragraphs describing each photo are disappointing. In these sterile words, don't expect to find any little known facts, any unusual stories of interest, or anything much beyond a listing of names, locations, and numbers describing the orbits and times of the missions. However, the excellent selection of photos makes up for it all.

POLTERGEISTS: HAUNTINGS AND THE HAUNTED (1972)

Kirkus Reviews

SOURCE: A review of Poltergeists: Hauntings and the Haunted, in Kirkus Reviews, Vol. XL, No. 20, October 15, 1972, pp. 1207-08.

The assertion that "Poltergeist phenomena happen. That much science admits. Like it or not these strange occurrences are a part of our world . . ." sets the tone for one of the least defensible forays into parapsychology of the current season. The twelve reported cases of RSPK (recurrent spontaneous psychokinesis)—spanning the centuries from the Drummer of Tedworth in 1661 to the bottle-popping "Seaford Disturbances" which shook Long Island (and rated a review in Reader's Digest) in 1958—are full of appropriately creepy bangings, knockings and flying objects. And the inclusion of lengthy visits with the Borley Rectory's ghostly nun and the talking mongoose "Gef" on the Isle of Man suggest that Knight is not averse to a good story even when it goes beyond the boundaries of classic poltergeist activity. But unfortunately Knight's researches don't proceed with the critical acuity of Georgess McHargue's investigation of Facts, Frauds and

Phantasms. His speculation on causes runs to theories about the existence of electromagnetic forces "as yet unknown to science," "ectoplasmic pseudopods" and the notion that an "astral" body splits off from the "focus" person ("no one to date has disproved it"), and his proofs are based largely on assurances that witnesses to the remarkable events were "cultured and intelligent" people. Finally, there are directions on what to do should your home become afflicted with poltergeist activity—"Panic and hysteria should be avoided at all costs" and "an atmosphere of tact, understanding and openmindedness . . . should be maintained." It all depends, of course, in what spirit you read this kind of thing, but Daniel Cohen's travels In Search of Ghosts were conducted in a less credulous manner without spoiling the fun. The poltergeist remains a fascinating, elusive beast, but we pity the gullible youngster who has this particular manifestation dropped in his lap.

Karla Kuskin

SOURCE: A review of Poltergeists: Hauntings and the Haunted, in The Saturday Review, New York, Vol. LV, No. 46, November 11, 1972, pp. 76, 78-9.

[This book] is an intriguing collection for anyone who likes ghost stories. But a poltergeist is not your ordinary ghost. The word is German for "racketing" or "noisy spirit," and such creatures haunt specific people (young people), not places. There was, for example, the poltergeist in Amherst, Nova Scotia, who spent 1878 taunting and terrifying a nineteen-year-old named Esther. Bedclothes flew from her bed, lighted matches dropped from her ceiling, and that was only the beginning. Or the poltergeist who showed up in Seaford, Long Island, in the late Fifties at the James Herrmanns' to focus its bottle-top-popping attentions on the Herrmanns' twelve-year-old son. It also threw china and furniture around. Not to mention "Gef," who spent ten years with a family on the Isle of Man. He claimed to be an eighty-year-old Indian mongoose, was extremely talkative, and killed rabbits by strangling them with his tiny, yellow, three-fingered hands. Mr. Knight ends with some theories and advice in case you are confronted by a poltergeist of your own.

The Booklist

SOURCE: A review of Poltergeists: Hauntings and the Haunted, in The Booklist, Vol. 69, No. 13, March 1, 1973, p. 649.

Drawing on both original and secondary sources a lay Fellow of the American Society for Psychical Research explores 11 poltergeist cases of the last few centuries. The sprightly individual stories are preceded by description of poltergeist activity in general and followed by theories concerning the phenomena and guidelines for persons encountering it. A short list of books for further reading is appended. Intriguing fare for readers of ghost tales.

R. Baines

SOURCE: A review of *Poltergeists: Hauntings and the Haunted,* in *The Junior Bookshelf,* Vol. 42, No. 2, April, 1978, pp. 104-05.

Poltergeists, says David Knight, are noisy ghosts which haunt people, rather than places. Themselves usually invisible, they have their own line in physical manifestations, and progress from comparatively minor tricks like stripping beds and pulling hair to hurling and smashing crockery, lighting fires and making photographs run with human blood.

This book contains accounts of eleven such hauntings, which take place in a variety of places and countries. The house of a seventeenth century Tedworth magistrate echoed with ghostly drumming; a particularly malevolent poltergeist in Tennessee caused blockages and swellings in the mouth of the master of the house to such an extent that he starved to death; at Stratford, Connecticut, a spirit manufactured stuffed effigies from clothing found about the house.

Unfortunately, eleven consecutive accounts of similar hauntings have a tendency to monotony which the pedestrian style of this book does little to dispel.

THE TINY PLANETS: ASTEROIDS OF OUR SOLAR SYSTEM (1973)

Kirkus Reviews

SOURCE: A review of *The Tiny Planets: Asteroids of Our Solar System,* in *Kirkus Reviews,* Vol. XLI, No. 7, April 1, 1973, p. 391.

A clear and systematic if less than sparkling report on the asteroids, the thousands of miniplanets (some only a few miles or less in diameter) which occupy the vast interplanetary space between Mars and Jupiter. Knight begins with a chronological review of the earliest discoveries and most notable asteroids, briefly noting their separate peculiarities as they appear, then describes their "physical nature" (actually their distribution, variously elliptical orbits, groupings, rotations, etc.) and considers different theories about their origin, finally surveying their present and possible use to science as guides to further knowledge of the solar system. Like the asteroids the book is relatively slight but it fills a gap on the juvenile astronomy shelves.

Harry C. Stubbs

SOURCE: A review of *The Tiny Planets,* in *The Horn Book Magazine,* Vol. XLIX, No. 3, June, 1973, pp. 293-95.

David C. Knight's *The Tiny Planets* lies in the realm of pure astronomy. This is a good, workmanlike summary of the history, nature, and—believe it or not—usefulness of the asteroids (which are only apparently starlike, in spite of the name). The chapters on physical nature and theories of origin are particularly good; the few slips I caught would be serious only to the purist. The description of Hermes' orbit as being "nearly circular" fits poorly with its actual eccentricity correctly given in the table at the end. The statement . . . that the asteroids "must have surface temperatures very near absolute zero" will startle the average physics teacher (who will, I trust, promptly ask his students to explain what is wrong with it). Still, I am happy to add the book to my school-use library.

Science Books: A Quarterly Review

SOURCE: A review of *The Tiny Planets: Asteroids of Our Solar System,* in *Science Books: A Quarterly Review,* Vol. IX, No. 3, December, 1973, pp. 254-55.

In an interesting discussion of the discovery, composition, origin, and possible uses of the asteroids, the author captures the spirit of adventure that was an important factor motivating 19th century astronomers in their search for the elusive objects that populate the region between Mars and Jupiter. The chapter entitled "Physical Nature" is particularly good; density, mass, weight, orbital configuration and distribution of asteroids are discussed. The author deals briefly with "Kirkwood's gaps" (empty regions of unknown origin in the asteroid zone) and Lagrangian points (which explain the existence of the "Greek" and the "Trojan" clusters of asteroids which travel along the orbit of Jupiter). The book has a crisp appearance with clear, highly readable type. Illustrations are for the most part the standard ones that have been seen before; however, they do augment the text and are not merely decorations to break up the text.

Alden C. Belcher

SOURCE: A review of *The Tiny Planets: Asteroids of Our Solar System,* in *Appraisal: Children's Science Books,* Vol. 7, No. 1, Winter, 1974, p. 22.

A comprehensive introduction to the asteroids, *The Tiny Planets* is wonderful! The subject is introduced in a stimulating manner and developed logically. Mr. Knight adheres totally to facts and is painstakingly careful to explain new terms or concepts. His information is scientifically accurate. He has produced a work which will inform some members of his intended audience. Others it will surely stimulate to further study and will linger as a reference. In all, it is very good reading, well in keeping with the "painless" learning concepts of today.

Nancy Bell

SOURCE: A review of *The Tiny Planets: Asteroids of Our Solar System,* in *Appraisal: Children's Science Books,* Vol. 7, No. 1, Winter, 1974, p. 22.

A thorough study of asteroids, both historic and scientif-

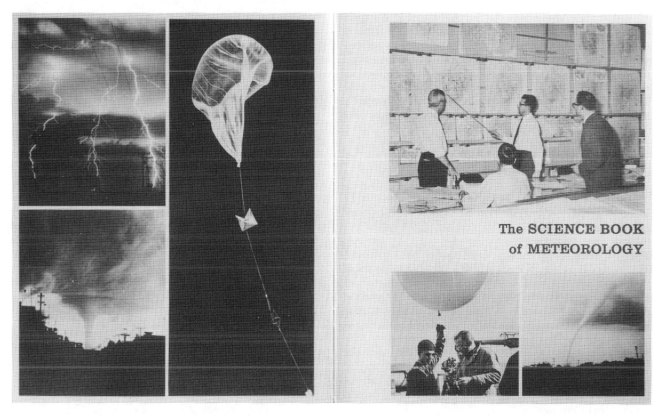

Title page from one of Knight's many introductory science books.

ic, this volume will prove fascinating reading for the more sophisticated science student who has already made some study of the solar system. The topic of asteroids is rarely covered with much detail in more general volumes on the solar system. *The Tiny Planets* is a most enjoyable answer to this need. The chapter on history and discovery is quite readable, as much a good story as scientific fact. The chapters which present more technical information on asteroids, their orbits, natural characteristics, etc. are well organized and simply stated. Occasionally one might wish for more and clearer diagrams and drawings. However, with a bit of concentration, the student can almost always decipher the illustrations. The final chapter, which deals with the use of asteroids, presents just enough information to pique the imagination. Most certainly this is not a book for beginners. The information is quite sophisticated while the absence of many pictures and the presence of long chapters assume mature reading skills. However, this should prove a most successful book for amateur astronomers and solar system enthusiasts.

THIRTY-TWO MOONS: THE NATURAL SATELLITES OF OUR SOLAR SYSTEM
(1974; revised edition as *The Moons of Our Solar System*, 1980)

Kirkus Reviews

SOURCE: A review of *Thirty-two Moons: Natural Satel-*

lites of Our Solar System, in *Kirkus Reviews,* Vol. XLII, No. 5, March 1, 1974, pp. 249-50.

Though, other than Earth, most of the planets in our Solar System have environments too hostile for man to consider landing upon them, the four giant planets and Mars each possess a system of natural satellites—or "moons"—from which it is at least conceivable that man could observe their more forbidding planets. Knight considers each of these 32 moons (including the one orbiting the Earth), in relation to its mother planet, relating stories of its discovery, hypotheses of its origins, and new information gleaned from space probes. We even learn that conditions which may be favorable to the emergence of life are known to exist on Titan, one of Saturn's moons. The lucid text, further clarified by the inclusion of photographs, drawings, diagrams, and a relevant glossary, is a worthy successor to *The Tiny Planets.*

The Booklist

SOURCE: A review of *Thirty-two Moons: The Natural Satellites of Our Solar System,* in *The Booklist,* Vol. 70, No. 20, June 15, 1974, p. 1154.

This survey of our solar system's moons describes historical and contemporary research findings on both the satellites and their primaries, or planets around which they revolve. The well-designed volume provides clearly labeled diagrams along with descriptive material on each moon's discovery, physical nature, and spatial relationships to neighboring satellites. In addition, many controversial theories on the origin, composition, and interaction of certain bodies in our solar system are explored in context. This should be considered a companion work to less specialized volumes, particularly since it assumes a degree of familiarity with some basic concepts on the part of the reader. Includes a glossary.

Science Books: A Quarterly Review

SOURCE: A review of *Thirty-two Moons: The Natural Satellites of Our Solar System,* in *Science Books: A Quarterly Review,* Vol. X, No. 3, December, 1974, p. 252.

A well-written, definitive but brief survey of the natural satellites of the solar system. There is considerable speculation on the origin of this system. We know there had to be an origin, but Mr. Knight indicates that the precise mechanism is unknown to us now and that many astronomers believe it may remain so for a long time. In introducing each family of moons, the author provides some background on the planet and thoughtfully includes the most current findings on their physical characteristics. The description of the earth's moon is excellent, and the author echoes what has become a self-evident truth: despite the Apollo moon landings our knowledge of the physical characteristics of the moon is still hazy and fragmentary. The sizes, motions and other characteristics of the satellites are developed together with scale drawings showing the orbits. While today these are isolated, tiny worlds, perhaps at some time in the distant future they will assume a key role in the continuing development of space flight. One unfortunate error does crop up in the book. Knight writes: ". . . a person on Mars would see Phobos rise in the east and set in the west three times every Martian day. . . ." Actually, because the period of Phobos is 7 hours 39 minutes it would rise in the west and set in the east. Aside from this obvious error this is a competently written reference work and is thus recommended.

Harry C. Stubbs

SOURCE: A review of *Thirty-two Moons,* in *The Horn Book Magazine,* Vol. LI, No. 1, February, 1975, pp. 74-5.

Thirty-two Moons is rather disappointing, especially after the author's earlier book on comets and meteors. I am not blaming Mr. Knight because a thirty-third moon (another one for Jupiter) was tentatively reported a few months after his book came out. But I am bothered by the impression of hasty research recorded without clear understanding or careful thought. The most bothersome error, repeated by the author several times, consists of stating that a satellite's diameter is uncertain and then giving a value for the body's density to two or more significant figures. This is silly, not just unscientific; density varies inversely with the cube of the diameter for any given mass. "Estimates of . . . [Miranda's] diameter vary from about 100

to 200 miles. Its density is 5 times that of water". If the mass is known (which it isn't, with any real accuracy), the body would be eight times denser with the smaller diameter than with the larger.

Also designed to make an astronomer blink is the statement, "Mars, with its small mass, could not hold a body with a size comparable to that of our moon." And judging by the illustration on page 35, the author, illustrator, and editor are all unfamiliar with *Gulliver's Travels:* The discoverers of Mars' moons in that book were the Laputans, not the Lilliputians. The distance from Saturn to Rhea is wrong both in the text and in the diagram; it is 327,000 miles, not 237,000. The diagram, at least, should have caught someone's eye, and the correctly given periods should have provided a warning. The orbits of Rhea and Dione could not be a mere 2,000 miles apart without involving gross mutual perturbations—and without having periods very much closer together in time. One gets the impression that no one familiar with astronomy was involved with editing the book.

Selina Woods

SOURCE: A review of *Thirty-two Moons: Natural Satellites of Our Solar System,* in *Appraisal: Children's Science Books,* Vol. 8, No. 2, Spring, 1975, pp. 26-7.

A simply organized, concisely written text which includes a brief and somewhat difficult introduction to theories concerning the origin of the solar system and a short discussion about the importance of studying a planet's natural satellites. The book then discusses known facts about each planet's moon in our solar system. Although much of the material relating to the moons could be handled by younger students, the introductory material is rather heavy reading. Some potential questions that might have been answered in the text and weren't included: How do scientists estimate the density of a moon that is far away and about which very little is known? If a planet is made up of hydrogen, what is solid hydrogen? etc. This may seem a bit picky—in general the book is a very good one for junior high up. Clear and well-labeled line drawings, a glossary, and an index accompany the text.

Margaret L. Chatham

SOURCE: A review of *The Moons of Our Solar System,* in *School Library Journal,* Vol. 26, No. 10, August, 1980, p. 65.

Thirty-two Moons (Morrow, 1974) has been retitled and extensively revised to include results from analysis of moon rocks and Apollo data plus photos and data sent back from Mars by the Viking mission, from Jupiter and its moons by the Voyager probes, and from Saturn by Pioneer 11 as well as some Earth-based discoveries. A few outdated statements remain, and Uranus' rings are not mentioned. This is still unusual in its focus on moons, though its coverage of all planets (except Pluto) that have moons makes it more generally useful than the title implies. Asimov's *Saturn and Beyond* (1979) contains no photos but supplements Knight's presentation with many diagrams and observations about moons' orbits and what could be seen from moons of various planets.

Jonathan C. Gradie

SOURCE: A review of *The Moons of Our Solar System,* in *Science Books & Films,* Vol. 16, No. 2, November/ December, 1980, pp. 71-2.

The Moons of Our Solar System, an introduction to the natural satellites of the planets, was previously published as *Thirty-two Moons.* This revision incorporates fascinating photographs from the recent flybys of Jupiter and Saturn. The author starts with the earth's moon, then goes on to Mars, Jupiter, Saturn and finally Uranus and Neptune. Each satellite is described both historically and scientifically. Unfortunately, the descriptions are disorganized enough to confuse readers of any age. There are occasional sensationalistic tidbits (the Kepler and Swift pre-discovery articles about two Martian moons is purely coincidental) and physical misconceptions (a satellite can be as massive as the primary; thorium, tantalum and uranium are elements, not minerals). The author has failed to mention such important observations as the remarkable grooves of Phobos and the rings around Uranus discovered in 1977. The pictures and historical accounts are worthwhile, but the scientific errors and physical misconceptions more than negate their usefulness.

Daphne Ann Hamilton

SOURCE: A review of *The Moons of Our Solar System,* in *Appraisal: Science Books for Young People,* Vol. 14, No. 1, Winter, 1981, p. 41.

So much has been discovered about the natural satellites in our solar system since the publication of *Thirty-two Moons* in 1974 that this revised edition should be welcome as it is fascinating. I have not been able to compare it with its predecessor, but the changes—which must be substantial—appear to have been smoothly incorporated into the text; it reads extremely well. Knight moves outward from Earth's moon—the "first" satellite and so far the only one actually visited by humans—to that of Pluto—discovered in 1978 and about which almost nothing except its existence is known. I was engrossed throughout and was constantly being surprised by unexpected facts— a situation not limited to the results of the recent Jupiter and Saturn fly-bys. There are a few minor flaws: "day" is always used for rotational times as meaning an earth day, though this is never explained, and considering that each planet and satellite has its own "day" length, some acknowledgement of this fact should be given; a photograph of Neptune and its two satellites does not in fact show Nereid at its indicated position, although the caption says it was found by photographs! Also, in the "wind-up" section, the author postulates that future astronauts

may choose Io as a base from which to study Jupiter, when Voyager data indicates that the radiation level that close to Jupiter would be lethal (not to mention its highly volcanic surface). Still, these are relative quibbles about a book which I would recommend for any juvenile astronomy collection exceeding a half dozen books. There is a glossary and an index.

FROM LOG ROLLER TO LUNAR ROVER: THE STORY OF WHEELS (1974)

Science Books: A Quarterly Review

SOURCE: A review of *From Log Roller to Lunar Rover: The Story of Wheels,* in *Science Books: A Quarterly Review,* Vol. X, No. 2, September, 1974, pp. 160-61.

The story starts in 3500 B.C., ends with the lunar rover and touches many bases in between, not all of them germane to the author's thesis. If his intention is simply to draw attention to the ways in which the wheel is used in everyday life, then he has succeeded. Unfortunately the treatment seldom rises above the level of gee-whizzism, and in some instances the text may mislead the young reader. (Examples: "Other kinds of wheels help people, too. A driver couldn't steer his bus or car without a steering wheel. A ship's captain couldn't control an ocean liner's rudder without a wheel." The author frequently uses the term "wheel" alone when "wheel and axle" should have been used.) Perhaps these are only quibbles, since the book is primarily a history book. There are no serious historical errors, but more emphasis on the energy-conserving aspects of simple machines would have added much to the usefulness of the book in science classes.

Shirley A. Smith

SOURCE: A review of *From Log Roller to Lunar Rover: The Story of Wheels,* in *School Library Journal,* Vol. 21, No. 1, September, 1974, p. 87.

Competent and straightforward, this covers the development, types, and applications of the wheel. The greater part of the book explains the probable evolution of the wheel, its use in antiquity, and the correlation between its refinement and man's technological advance. Only two pages, however, are devoted to space-age applications of the wheel, and the black-and-pink illustrations are accurate but undistinguished. There is nothing here which cannot be found in other titles for middle graders such as Buehr's *The Story of the Wheel* (1960).

David G. Hoag

SOURCE: A review of *From Log Roller to Lunar Rover: The Story of Wheels,* in *Appraisal: Children's Science Books,* Vol. 7, No. 3, Fall, 1974, p. 28.

It is surprising to find described in this book so many

ways that wheels have been used on vehicles and by machines through the ages. And it is a pleasure to find these descriptions so interesting. The author has not penetrated the subject very deeply but what he presents is accurate and should be informative to the early reader.

Heddie Kent

SOURCE: A review of *From Log Roller to Lunar Rover: The Story of Wheels,* in *Appraisal: Children's Science Books,* Vol. 7, No. 3, Fall, 1974, p. 28.

The story of man's discovery, development, and use of the wheel is a long and interesting one. This very simple and straightforward telling of the wheel's history is for second-to-fourth graders both in vocabulary and content. The material in the book is presented in such a way that it could be used either in a science class or for a social studies report. Profusely illustrated (there is at least one picture on nearly every page) by drawings in shades of black and salmon pink, the book is attractive, inviting, and easy to assimilate. From the first log disc cut by a prehistoric inventor, all the way to the astronauts' Lunar Rover, the development of the wheel and man himself has gone hand in hand. . . .

YOUR BODY'S DEFENSES (1975)

The Booklist

SOURCE: A review of *Your Body's Defenses,* in *The Booklist,* Vol. 71, No. 13, March 1, 1975, p. 694.

A serviceable overview of the physiological processes that keep the body in a healthy state. Knight begins by noting the "early warning" functions served by such reactions as pain or fever and the "early defense" presented by the body's layer of skin. The disease-provoking role of various antigens, the production of protective antibodies, and a simplified view of immunology give an understandable picture of the body's capacity to cope with illness. A concluding chapter offers familiar suggestions for maintaining general health—proper diet, rest, exercise, and good hygiene. Some irritatingly stiff, amateurish drawings of people are offset by occasional photographs and helpful diagrams. A glossary is appended.

Leone R. Hemenway

SOURCE: A review of *Your Body's Defenses,* in *School Library Journal,* Vol. 21, No. 8, April, 1975, p. 54.

In clear, basic terms Knight describes the function of the senses, the skin, the blood, antigens and antibodies, immunization and other defense systems which protect the human body from disease. Interspersed throughout is information on historical discoveries and the limitations of present immunization practices. A useful glossary and index and a superfluous section on standard hygienic do's

and don't's conclude the coverage. A good supplement to other elementary physiology and hygiene books which include but do not focus on elements of immunology.

Gerald S. Golden

SOURCE: A review of *Your Body's Defenses,* in *Science Books & Films,* Vol. XI, No. 1, May, 1975, p. 38.

The basic mechanisms by which the body protects itself from accident and disease are discussed simply, clearly and accurately in this volume. The major emphasis is on defenses against infectious diseases. A logical sequence of presentation is followed. There is initial discussion of the concept of homeostasis, followed by chapters on protective reflexes and mechanical barriers to infection. The main theme is then picked up, and white cells, antigens, antibodies and immunizations are covered in some detail. A discussion of several problems of immunology and basic health guidelines follows. Broader implications of immune mechanisms such as problems of allergy, neoplasia and autoimmune diseases are also introduced. There is an accurate, complete glossary and an excellent index. The major shortcoming is a lack of depth in the discussion of most areas. This limits the usefulness of the book to a young age group, but it does serve very well as a lucid introduction to a complex field.

Zena Sutherland

SOURCE: A review of *Your Body's Defenses,* in *Bulletin of the Center for Children's Books,* Vol. 28, No. 9, May, 1975, pp. 149-50.

A comprehensive discussion of the intricate system of defenses in the human body, from the simple sensory reactions and the defensive functioning of the skin and the mucous membranes to the more complicated action of antigens and antibodies. Knight describes the immunity system and its aberrations, and concludes with a chapter on basic health care: cleanliness, diet, adequate sleep, etc. The text is accurate, the subject interesting, but the book is weakened by the solid passages of close print and by the inadequate labelling of illustrations. A glossary of terms and a relative index are appended.

EAVESDROPPING ON SPACE: THE QUEST OF RADIO ASTRONOMY (1975)

Kirkus Reviews

SOURCE: A review of *Eavesdropping on Space: The Quest of Radio Astronomy,* in *Kirkus Reviews,* Vol. 43, No. 9, May 1, 1975, p. 525.

An admirably clear, basic and straightforward introduction, beginning with a simple explanation of wave phenomena and proceeding to more than ordinarily personable summaries of the work of radio astronomy pioneers.

With this for background, the descriptions of different types of radio telescopes can be better understood and appreciated. Similarly readable and to the point is the survey of some of the discoveries of radio and radar, astronomy, such as the baffling quasars, compact pulsars and incredibly dense black holes (you might call them collapsestars)—and the interstellar molecules, including organic ones, which offer a spot of encouragement for Cyclops, that other radio astronomy project undertaken to investigate the possibilities of interstellar communication.

Harry C. Stubbs

SOURCE: A review of *Eavesdropping on Space: The Quest of Radio Astronomy,* in *The Horn Book Magazine,* Vol. LI, No. 4, August, 1975, pp. 398-99.

Mr. Knight's *Eavesdropping on Space* contains a history and a description of radio astronomy. The photographs are pertinent; the explanations clear and generally correct; and as a science-fiction enthusiast, I particularly liked the final chapter about interstellar contact between intelligences. There are a few slips. [One] might infer that all nonthermal radiation comes from synchrotron action; I understand that the colliding galaxies explanation of Cygnus A is a good many years out of date; and the explanation of the rotation rate change of pulsars does not require a liquid core. Simple conservation of angular momentum will do it. However, these errors fall into the category of those I sometimes like to see in a book—the kind that remind an alert student that the printed word is not infallible. They did not spoil my enjoyment of the book.

Ovide V. Fortier

SOURCE: A review of *Eavesdropping on Space: The Quest of Radio Astronomy,* in *School Library Journal,* Vol. 22, No. 4, December, 1975, p. 60.

Radio astronomy had its beginnings in the 1930's when radio waves emanating from celestial sources were first detected. Without going into much technical detail, Knight discusses the instruments, methods, and discoveries of radio astronomers as well as the various types of antennae used and the significance of the discoveries. This book is a worthwhile acquisition because it covers a subject not found in many other books and because it will not quickly become outdated.

Frances Doughty

SOURCE: A review of *Eavesdropping on Space: The Quest of Radio Astronomy,* in *Appraisal: Children's Science Books,* Vol. 9, No. 1, Winter, 1976, p. 23.

This clearly written exposition of radio astronomy begins with a definition of the radio universe and continues with detailed information on the history and present state of radio astronomy. All terms in the text are italicized and

briefly defined; there is a glossary and an index. The book is not easy to read because it contains a wealth of unfamiliar material. However, it will reward the persistent.

David E. Newton

SOURCE: A review of *Eavesdropping on Space: The Quest of Radio Astronomy,* in *Appraisal: Children's Science Books,* Vol. 9, No. 1, Winter, 1976, p. 23.

Just about anything that anyone could possibly want to know—and much more—about the specialized topic of radio astronomy is to be found in this impressive volume. The author provides a fascinating description of the historical development of radio astronomy, of the facilities now available, and of the work being done. My only objection is in the publisher's advertisement that this book is suitable for children of ages seven to nine years. Neither the subject matter nor the writing style is appropriate to students at less than the junior year in high school, in my judgment.

THOSE MYSTERIOUS UFOS: THE STORY OF UNIDENTIFIED FLYING OBJECTS (1975)

Judith Goldberger

SOURCE: A review of *Those Mysterious UFOs: The Story of Unidentified Flying Objects,* in *The Booklist,* Vol. 72, No. 8, December 15, 1975, p. 579.

A theme with popular appeal, explored in an unintimidating manner. A more or less chronological approach is taken, in which the story of the U.S. Air Force's Project Blue Book figures prominently along with accounts of UFO sightings. The author enticingly presents material but leaves questions of fact open to speculation. A fine array of black-and-white photographs enhances the accounts.

Ovide V. Fortier

SOURCE: A review of *Those Mysterious UFOs: The Story of Unidentified Flying Objects,* in *School Library Journal,* Vol. 22, No. 6, February, 1976, p. 46.

UFO's have been appearing off and on for many years. Some have been traced to unusual manifestations of ordinary things—cloud formations, balloons, planets, etc. Others have not been accounted for satisfactorily. It is these mysterious ones which provide the interesting material for Knight's book. He does a very good job of presenting the facts and claims without trying to interpret them. A well-done review for those interested in the subject.

Richard J. Merrill

SOURCE: A review of *Those Mysterious UFOs: The Sto-*

ry of Unidentified Flying Objects, in *Science Books & Films,* Vol. XII, No. 1, May, 1976, pp. 36-7.

The history of UFO sightings over the past 80 years is given. Many specific instances are described in detail, presumably based on written reports. Investigations and reports (e.g., the Condon Committee) are described. Speculations about visitors from space are identified as such. Excellent use is made of photographs and drawings, and an index is provided. The text is interesting and clearly written, and the book tends to convince the reader that many UFOs are real and have not been adequately explained.

David G. Hoag

SOURCE: A review of *Those Mysterious UFOs: The Story of Unidentified Flying Objects,* in *Appraisal: Children's Science Books,* Vol. 9, No. 3, Fall, 1976, p. 27.

There is general professional agreement that Unidentified Flying Objects, UFO's, have been observed numerous times. There is no agreement as to the cause of many of these sightings. The author of this book has attempted objectivity in this subject. The believers who are certain these UFO's are due to some extraterrestrial phenomena may also feel the author was far too objective. The skeptical observer, and this reviewer, can complain that the book lacks sufficient rigor in separating what was reported by the UFO witnesses from what is offered as theory about these strange manifestations. The book should be fun for the curious youngster, though. Many photographs purported to be those of UFO's fill this easy-to-read book. Some of the stranger unexplained cases are described along with those later to be proven fraudulently perpetrated.

LET'S FIND OUT ABOUT SOUND (1975)

Beryl B. Beatley

SOURCE: A review of *Let's Find Out About Sound,* in *Appraisal: Children's Science Books,* Vol. 9, No. 1, Winter, 1976, p. 24.

As is usual with this author, this is a very clear and well-presented introduction to sound, profusely illustrated with large, clear, colorful drawings which are very helpful in reinforcing the text. There is no index, but this is not a necessity. The author discusses various types of sounds, vibrations, how sound waves travel, why there is a delay in sounds reaching the ear, etc. Five-year-olds may find it a little difficult to grasp some of the concepts such as vibration, and air being made up of molecules; but with the help of a parent or teacher, there is much here to keep an inquisitive child interested and questioning and understanding. . . .

David G. Hoag

SOURCE: A review of *Let's Find Out About Sound,* in

Appraisal: Children's Science Books, Vol. 9, No. 1, Winter, 1976, p. 24.

David Knight has skillfully written a particularly good science book for the very young reader. The effort he has made in introducing scientific concepts is evident in the careful organization and exposition of the material. A surprising quantity of science is in the forty pages, and the clarity has not suffered. The illustrations are for the most part clear. Simple experiments are described which help. It is an excellent book in introducing a technical subject to the first or second grades.

HARNESSING THE SUN: THE STORY OF SOLAR ENERGY (1976)

Kirkus Reviews

SOURCE: A review of *Harnessing the Sun: The Story of Solar Energy,* in *Kirkus Reviews,* Vol. XLIV, No. 10, May 15, 1976, p. 605.

A nuts-and-bolts survey of solar energy research from the tinkerers and dreamers spanning hundreds of years to today's working solar cookers, furnaces, and water heaters. "Enough technology already exists to begin using sunshine to heat and cool homes and buildings," and though the economic obstacles to solar electricity are greater, solar cells are already used extensively in space and "there must be a better way" than the present wasteful process of growing artificial silicone crystals. Proposals for the future, many "obviously still in the visionary stage," include solar farms, satellite power stations, "ocean-thermal-difference" plants, windmills, bioconversion, and a solar hydrogen generator which would solve the central problem of storing transportable energy to use where and when the sun's not shining.

Denise M. Wilms

SOURCE: A review of *Harnessing the Sun: The Story of Solar Energy,* in *Booklist,* Vol. 72, No. 19, June 1, 1976, p. 1407.

A timely presentation in view of solar energy's growing attractiveness as a cheap and constant source of power. After an introductory look at some of the pioneers in solar technology, Knight explains several systems for collecting sunlight; this lays the base for a look at some of the current uses of solar energy in simple, inexpensive solar cookers used in India, in hot water heaters mass-produced in Japan, or in an increasing number of successful experimental homes. Solar electrical production is shown to be prohibitively expensive because of delicate and difficult manufacture of solar cells, though these do power U.S. satellites. Later chapters explore the possibilities of exploiting wind power or using the differences in ocean top and bottom temperatures to obtain power; some drawing board plans for solar farms and a national solar power facility are also included. The text is straightforward and, for the most part, easily understandable, though a few explanations of how solar cells transform sunlight into electricity may be too technical for some.

Ovide V. Fortier

SOURCE: A review of *Harnessing the Sun: The Story of Solar Energy*, in *School Library Journal*, Vol. 23, No. 1, September, 1976, p. 134.

Not nearly as well done as most of Knight's space and astronomy books, this focuses on devices to convert solar radiation directly to heat and also allots some space to sunlight-to-electricity converters. Although the book covers the important work in the field, it has some serious shortcomings: the economic aspects of using the free energy from the sun to reduce dependence on fossil fuels are not adequately treated; technical terms are frequently misused; and, definitions are often circular.

Donald E. Marlowe

SOURCE: A review of *Harnessing the Sun: The Story of Solar Energy*, in *Science Books & Films*, Vol. XII, No. 3, December, 1976, p. 133.

This is a good compilation of the state of the art in solar energy utilization—a topic of substantial importance to the citizenry. It is very nearly unbiased, although slightly optimistic, in contrast to many other writings on this topic. Very little is presumed regarding the reader's prior scientific understanding, and no mathematics is required to follow the discussion. Every effort is made to help the reader develop the necessary fundamental basis for the main topic. Knight's historic treatment is outstandingly thorough, particularly his discussion of solar heating. By contrast, the historic discussion of the solar generation of electricity is less thorough. Perhaps readers should be warned that books on a topic such as this one will lose value with time. Although current in 1975, it will be out-of-date in five or six years.

Christine McDonnell

SOURCE: A review of *Harnessing the Sun*, in *Appraisal: Children's Science Books*, Vol. 10, No. 1, Winter, 1977, p. 27.

The topic of solar energy is explained in depth and with remarkable clarity by this book. It is a nicely balanced blend of history, theory, current examples and future possibilities. Many anecdotes and inventions are included to demonstrate the effects and applications of solar energy, giving the book vitality. There are numerous photographs and drawings, as well as a glossary and index. This will appeal to ten-to-fourteen-year-olds, and should interest even those readers who are not science buffs. This is an attractive and useful addition on a timely topic.

David E. Newton

SOURCE: A review of *Harnessing the Sun*, in *Appraisal: Children's Science Books*, Vol. 10, No. 1, Winter, 1977, p. 27.

This is an excellent book for anyone who would like to accumulate a lot of information about the historical background, current conditions and future prospects of solar energy as a source of power for humankind. It scores high on categories such as accuracy, up-to-dateness, and thoroughness, but I doubt that it will have very much appeal to children. This is too much like a "textbook" in science, with large accumulations of facts on far too many pages. I counted, for example, twenty-seven discrete bits of factual information on the first five pages of the text. I also worry a bit about the author's tendency to treat the question of solar power as if it were entirely a scientific and technological problem. He asks, at the beginning of chapter three, "Why has it taken man (sic) so long to utilize the sun's light for energy purposes?" Throughout the long discussion that follows, he gives only cursory attention to the social, political, and economic dislocations that would be associated with the use of solar energy. Some might argue that those issues are too sophisticated for children to deal with. The level of scientific treatment in this book, however, does not permit this author that excuse.

📖 *BEES CAN'T FLY, BUT THEY DO: THINGS THAT ARE STILL A MYSTERY TO SCIENCE* (1976)

Kirkus Reviews

SOURCE: A review of *Bees Can't Fly, But They Do: Things That Are Still a Mystery to Science*, in *Kirkus Reviews*, Vol. XLIV, No. 14, July 15, 1976, p. 797.

Though scientists have discovered how bumble bees fly (it involves flapping their wings some 18,000 times a minute), they're still in the dark, according to Knight, as to why some people can walk on hot coals, all snowflakes are hexagonal, cats find their way home from miles away, Australian aborigines have ESP, lemmings self-destruct, and water witching works. It's as motley a lot of mysteries as ever were assembled in the name of science, and in fact science has little to do with Knight's treatment. His two or three pages per mystery barely mention possible explanations though much could be said, for example, about recent laboratory investigations of yogis' mind-over-matter control. Elsewhere he states flatly—take it or leave it—that all aborigines have the ability to know what's going on at a distance; and he tells us that water witching is endorsed by "no less than five Nobel Prize winners" (a most unscientific appeal to authority) and reports astounding claims as fact, without citing a source.

Publishers Weekly

SOURCE: A review of *Bees Can't Fly, But They Do:*

Things That Are Still a Mystery to Science, in *Publishers Weekly,* Vol. 210, No. 4, July 26, 1976, p. 79.

The intriguing title should invite the curious (including grownups) and perhaps spread a feeling of respect for nature and its mysterious ways. Aerodynamicists know that the small wings of a bee and the size of its body preclude flight. This contradiction led scientists to study the insect's "impossible" ability. They found that the bumble bee flaps its wings an amazing 18,000 times to fly for one minute. Other phenomena are discussed though not explained, for their causes are still secret: why do trees, unlike other living things, keep growing until they die, why is each snow crystal a hexagon, each flake unique, what's the mystery behind the razor-sharp proven extrasensory power of the Australian Aborigines? These and other puzzles are concisely explored here.

Marcy Kimlin

SOURCE: A review of *Bees Can't Fly, But They Do: Things That Are Still a Mystery to Science,* in *School Library Journal,* Vol. 23, No. 2, October, 1976, p. 108.

Although the title and introduction lead readers to believe that this book discusses scientific phenomena, the body of the account deals with dubious, unsubstantiated mysteries, e.g., firewalking by Fiji tribesmen in which inferences are made that all the Islanders can perform this feat without harm; the blanket assertion of Australian Aborigines' power of ESP when only one isolated event is recounted. Unreliable as a science book, and as for sensationalism, the Believe It or Not titles are more entertaining.

Ethanne Smith

SOURCE: A review of *Bees Can't Fly, But They Do: Things That Are Still a Mystery to Science,* in *Appraisal: Children's Science Books,* Vol. 10, No. 2, Spring, 1977, p. 32.

In six brief chapters Mr. Knight introduces children to six still unexplained wonders of the world: people who can walk on burning coals or logs without harm; cats who can return alone to a distant home; snowflakes, that are always hexagonal; Australian aborigines, who know things as they happen at a distance; the lemmings' suicidal rush to the sea; and the ability of dowsers to locate hidden water with forked sticks. Occasional interesting incidents enliven the presentation of facts. The author stresses that scientists have never been able to discover logical causes for these apparent miracles, which have been witnessed by many people for centuries. The introductory chapter presents other scientific puzzles as well. Why does a goldfish stay small in a bowl but grow to perhaps two feet in length if in larger bodies of water? And why do trees keep growing as long as they live? The title of the book refers to one mystery that *has* been solved. The bee is too heavy for its wings to be able to fly—according to

the logic of aerodynamics, that is. But it *does* fly, by beating its wings hundreds more times per second than other insects. The unexciting illustrations do not add life to the text, but the latter is readable and will serve to whet the child's appetite for more detailed information on these endlessly fascinating miracles of nature.

COLONIES IN ORBIT: THE COMING AGE OF HUMAN SETTLEMENTS IN SPACE (1977)

Kirkus Reviews

SOURCE: A review of *Colonies in Orbit: The Coming Age of Human Settlements in Space,* in *Kirkus Reviews,* Vol. XLV, No. 10, May 15, 1977, p. 542.

In a sort of brief for the far-out utopia proposed by Princeton physicist Gerard K. O'Neill, Knight envisions space communities which provide earth with all her energy needs, obtain their building materials from the moon, and carry on the usual functions—agriculture, recreation, learning—in a deliberately earthlike but pollution-free environment so superior to ours that the mother planet, relieved of population and other pressures, will become "a beautiful place to visit" on which "most people would not want to locate permanently." In his usual unpadded style Knight explains the Lagrangian points which are likely sites for future colonies, describes O'Neill's twin cylinder model for such habitats, and discusses their design, construction, and possibilities for technologically controlled better living. Like most such projections at this level, it's more advocacy than examination, but Knight avoids a gee-whiz tone, and his presentation is crisp and clear.

Harry C. Stubbs

SOURCE: A review of *Colonies in Orbit: The Coming Age of Human Settlements in Space,* in *The Horn Book Magazine,* Vol. LIII, No. 6, December 1977, pp. 691-92.

David Knight has included history in **Colonies in Orbit,** mostly to bring out the human changes and scientific developments which would make space settlements not merely desirable but perhaps inevitable—if our technological culture lasts long enough. He mentions the stories of Jules Verne and Edward Everett Hale, both of whom gave correct impressions of space conditions and orbit phenomena—though the former was not as correct about weightlessness as Knight implies. If Verne's moon travelers had survived the initial shot, they would have been floating free in the projectile for the entire voyage, not just at the gravity plateau between Earth and moon. The book largely deals with the O'Neill "L5" proposal, the colony at the Lagrangian point which follows the moon by sixty degrees on the latter's orbit. The author covers well the problems and advantages of the proposed colony, though he makes a few errors. The potential hollow of the L5 point is far from spherical in shape. The trouble with the giant planets as colony sites is not gravity—except for Jupiter and Neptune the gravities of these bodies are not much greater than Earth's—but other conditions, such as pressure, temperature, atmospheric composition, and the probable lack of a solid surface. I am mystified by the statement that the earth's soil, rich in atmospheric gases, can be compressed into containers and released in the station. Surely this is an editorial error; the author must know better. I also disagree with his statement that a tennis ball in low gravity conditions would travel slowly; this would happen only if it were hit very gently. If it were hit hard, it would go just as fast as it would on Earth or anywhere else. The book contains a glossary and an index.

Ovide V. Fortier

SOURCE: A review of *Colonies in Orbit: The Coming of Human Settlements in Space,* in *School Library Journal,* Vol. 24, No. 6, February, 1978, pp. 65-6.

After briefly reviewing early ideas about colonizing space, Knight describes in detail a proposal by Professor G. K. O'Neill of Princeton University to build and continually replicate "habitats" in orbit around the earth. These colonies would become so nearly self-sufficient and attractive that most human activity would cease on the earth, which would then become a beautiful park. The book is almost identical in content to Frederic Golden's *Colonies in Space: the Next Giant Step,* though it is not quite as well written. Still, either title would be useful in any up-to-date space collection.

Allan Moose

SOURCE: A review of *Colonies in Orbit: The Coming Age of Human Settlements in Space,* in *Science Books & Films,* Vol. XIV, No. 1, May, 1978, p. 41.

To the science fiction buff, the idea of human colonies in space is intriguing and appealing. In recent years a small number of physicists and NASA scientists have seriously studied the feasibility and design of earth-orbiting space colonies. This little book is a presentation of some of the results of these studies. As a popularization, the work is credible. The book is clearly written with good illustrations and a glossary. To be a realistic project, space colonies must offer potential benefits, tangible and intangible to humans. The benefits listed, which include solution of the population problem and the energy problem, are not entirely convincing. Such problems might be better solved by intelligent management of earth resources. Intangible psychological factors—rather than potential practical benefits—will probably have greater influence on the ultimate building of space colonies. I suggest this book for those who are interested in visionary applications of science and technology. As such it might be considered for collateral reading in general science studies. The book might also stimulate interested students to investigate the topic further.

 DINOSAUR DAYS (1977)

Publishers Weekly

SOURCE: A review of *Dinosaur Days,* in *Publishers Weekly,* Vol. 212, No. 16, October 17, 1977, p. 84.

In all the world, it's hard to find a child who isn't enchanted by the prehistoric beasts which vanished eons ago. Knight addresses himself to his potentially vast readership most effectively. His text is simple, easily assimilated and never condescending. He describes the many kinds of ancient reptiles, tells what they lived on and where and reports what scientists believe was the reason they died out. Tongue-twisting names like Elasmosaurus, Pteranodon, Corythosaurus and others are followed by their phonetic spellings, a thoughtful touch. And [Joel] Schick's drawings are marvels of accuracy and professionalism, set against landscapes as they must have been, millions of years ago, before the arrival of the first humans on earth.

Michele Woggon

SOURCE: A review of *Dinosaur Days,* in *School Library Journal,* Vol. 24, No. 5, January, 1978, pp. 78-9.

Essential introductory facts about dinosaurs are presented here. Following a one-page chronology of the age of reptiles is a useful guide to selected dinosaurs presenting pronunciation of names, physical descriptions, and information on habits and habitats. A conclusion advances theories on the extinction of prehistoric animals. The text, using a minimum of scientific-technical terminology, is accurate and, while condensed, is not oversimplified. . . .

Barbara Elleman

SOURCE: A review of *Dinosaur Days,* in *Booklist,* Vol. 74, No. 9, January 1, 1978, p. 748.

A brief introduction to the age of dinosaurs describes the physical world in which the creatures lived and explains how scientists, through the study of fossils, have come to their conclusions. Although one statement, "Dinosaur fossils are mostly bones, teeth and eggs," is misleading (fossils are the mineral remains of bones), researchers will find this a worthwhile source. Especially helpful is the breakdown of 18 different kinds (with pronunciations), such as brontosaurus, diplodocus, stegosaurus, and pteranodon, which gives specific details concerning size, eating habits, movement, and method of attacking enemies.

THE HAUNTED SOUVENIR WAREHOUSE: ELEVEN TALES OF UNUSUAL HAUNTINGS (1977)

Kirkus Reviews

SOURCE: A review of *The Haunted Souvenir Warehouse:*

Eleven Tales of Unusual Hauntings, in *Kirkus Reviews,* Vol. XLVI, No. 3, February 1, 1978, p. 108.

There's comic potential in the behavior of souvenir items at the Tropication Arts Miami warehouse: beer mugs, combs, rubber daggers, zombie highball glasses—all made in the Far East and stamped with Florida symbols—suddenly begin falling off the shelves, floating through air, and bouncing across the floor. Knight, however, plays it straight ("It is thought that these young persons [poltergeists' foci] are suffering from deep inner emotional conflicts, perhaps sexually oriented, and that somehow this releases forces"), and he follows the story with further tales of hauntings . . . on a British golf course, a Scottish beach, a Barbados churchyard, and so on up to the famous (in ghost story circles) gardens of Versailles. Which makes this just another round of visitations, some of them re-appearances, strictly for those who can never get enough of the little man—or woman in white—who wasn't there.

THE SPY WHO NEVER WAS AND OTHER TRUE SPY STORIES (1978)

Saul J. Amdursky

SOURCE: A review of *The Spy Who Never Was and Other True Spy Stories,* in *School Library Journal,* Vol. 25, No. 4, December, 1978, p. 54.

The stories of ten different spies representing five countries are recounted in this book. Americans include Nathan Hale, Lydia Darragh, Emma Edmonds, Peter Ortiz, and Francis Gary Powers. Alexander Scotland and Major William Martin worked for the British; Mata Hara sold her allegiance to the Germans; and Rudolf Abel spied for the Russians. Knight avoids nationalism fairly well but his stories lack creativity and imagination. Most of the people he discusses are fairly well known and he adds no new information.

Booklist

SOURCE: A review of *The Spy Who Never Was, and Other True Spy Stories,* in *Booklist,* Vol. 75, No. 8, December 15, 1978, p. 681.

Ten true accounts of men and women known for their spying activities—including Emma Evelyn Edmonds, so adept at disguises that she served as a regular in the Union army, later becoming a spy; "Major William Martin," the fictitious British officer of World War II's Operation Mincemeat; Soviet spy Rudolf I. Abel; and U-2 pilot Francis Gary Powers, the man for whom Abel was exchanged in 1961. Subject matter is high interest, and sketches are straightforward and largely noninterpretive. Each runs approximately 10 to 15 pages in length with chapterlike headings providing artificial pause breaks in the story.

Juanita Moore

SOURCE: A review of *The Spy Who Never Was and Other*

True Spy Stories, in *High/Low Report,* Vol. 2, No. 4, December, 1980, p. 2.

The Spy Who Never Was relates the espionage efforts of ten notables, including Nathan Hale, Mata Hari and Francis Gary Powers. If only the stories were as exciting as the description on the book's jacket! In fact, the jacket summarizes the adventures so well that reading the story is almost anticlimatic. Considerable sequential description in a short, choppy sentence structure prevents minimal, if any, identification with the characters or suspense. The more "exciting" stories are placed in the middle of the book and I doubt a reluctant reader would bother reading long enough to encounter these.

Designed as high low material for junior and senior high students, *The Spy Who Never Was* will present some difficulties for these readers. While the print size is favorable, the book appears dull—lacking photos or illustrations which would have been helpful. Also it is not a consistent 4th grade reading level and the vocabulary can be quite technical. Probably most crucial is that the author assumes both geographical and historical background which many reluctant readers will not possess.

This book does have potential use for reluctant readers in a social studies content class if specific individual stories were used to supplement lessons. Also it might be of interest to older adults in an adult literacy program for they would be more likely to possess the geographic and historic knowledge to enjoy the stories. Generally, however, it is a book that is neither exciting nor motivating and I could not recommend it as an addition to a high low library. It's one of those that have the potential of gathering dust.

GALAXIES: ISLANDS IN SPACE (1979)

Denise M. Wilms

SOURCE: A review of *Galaxies: Islands in Space,* in *Booklist,* Vol. 75, No. 13, March 1, 1979, p. 1092.

Readers who got a first introduction to galaxies in Berger's *Planets, Stars and Galaxies* would find this a convenient next step in their learning process. Besides providing a basic definition of these "chief bodies in the universe," Knight recounts what astronomers now know or theorize about galaxies' functioning: their birth and presumed life cycle, their interaction, star-making, and their unimaginable sizes and speeds. Explanations are nontechnical; only occasionally are they simplified in a way that falls short of concreteness.

Kirkus Reviews

SOURCE: A review of *Galaxies: Islands in Space,* in *Kirkus Reviews,* Vol. 47, No. 12, June 15, 1979, p. 688.

Knight begins with our galaxy, playing up the "mysterious" ring around the center which is both moving and expanding outward (potentially dangerous to earth? astronomers aren't sure). He then ranges outward to other galaxies, which were first verified in 1925 by Edwin Hubble who also established the classification system described here, and to the groups and clusters and superclusters into which they fall. Finally, Knight skims over current theories of galactic evolution, recent findings and ideas about the "violent processes" taking place in their centers, and speculation about the future of the universe—all of which has been more fully investigated elsewhere, though without the galaxy orientation. A neat summary overall, without Asimov's patient detail or Branley's sense of shared inquiry.

Carolyn Caywood

SOURCE: A review of *Galaxies: Islands in Space,* in *School Library Journal,* Vol. 26, No. 1, September, 1979, p. 158.

In this book galaxies are used as steppingstones through a history of modern astronomical discoveries to current theories about the origin and future of the universe. A great deal of new information is presented, especially the reasoning behind popularized theories of quasars and black holes (the author makes clear how much is still speculation). Various new means of observation such as spectroscopes and radio telescopes are discussed. The explanation of star catalogs will clarify why Andromeda, for example, is also called M31 and NGC 224. Knight's book will not only update the collection, but will broaden readers' understanding of astronomy.

Allan Moose

SOURCE: A review of *Galaxies: Islands in Space,* in *Science Books & Films,* Vol. XV, No. 4, March, 1980, p. 203.

This little book appears to be written for junior high school students. However, I found the level of the vocabulary much higher than that of the general writing style, so it is difficult to say whether it would be more appropriate for high school students. Furthermore, it is difficult to determine exactly what purpose it serves. One might regard it as a supplement to an introductory astronomy text. Certainly it covers some standard topics: the Milky Way, types of galaxies, clusters of galaxies, the evolution of galaxies. However, the author chose to include chapters on the expanding universe, quasars and black holes. These latter two chapters should have been left out and the discussion of the standard topics lengthened. As it is, the treatment is, in my opinion, too cursory with insufficient attention given to an orderly development of concepts.

📖 *UFOs: A PICTORIAL HISTORY FROM ANTIQUITY TO THE PRESENT* (1979)

Publishers Weekly

SOURCE: A review of *UFOs: A Pictorial History from Antiquity to the Present,* in *Publishers Weekly,* Vol. 216, No. 19, November 5, 1979, p. 67.

Was the fiery chariot witnessed by Ezekiel in 600 B.C. an alien spaceship? Were the angels descending Jacob's ladder really extraterrestrial visitors? Are theories about even earlier space flights valid? Knight's exploration of the phenomena that incite such controversy consists of pages chockful of drawings, articles, photos and newly unclassified data from the Air Force's Project Blue Book. The author's learned commentary accompanies this gratifyingly complete roundup of data on UFO sightings in all parts of the world through the centuries. He pays particular attention to "percipients" (people who claim close encounters of various kinds), including astronauts. The text gives equal time to believers and disbelievers in UFOs as vehicles from other planets and the book should interest both camps.

Daphne Ann Hamilton

SOURCE: A review of *UFOs: A Pictorial History from Antiquity to the Present,* in *Appraisal: Children's Science Books,* Vol. 13, No. 3, Fall, 1980, pp. 37-8.

This iconography of the UFO phenomenon contains drawings, photographs, and clippings from the middle ages through the present day. Items are arranged in broad chronological groupings, each of which is introduced by a page-and-a-half of text, but most of the information is in the extensive captions to the pictures. Although this results in somewhat incomplete and disjointed individual accounts, the problem can be at least partially resolved by further reading, and a bibliography is provided for that purpose. The author is successful in providing an unusually broad overview, and that in a style totally different from other books on the subject (which is why I have made no comparisons here). This is sure to be popular, and is, I think, interesting from either a pro or con viewpoint because it provides the nearest approach to "hard" evidence in the UFO controversy. Knight does not dodge the possibility of faking, and a few such photographs are included as examples, though the focus is, of course, on genuine "unidentifieds." My only objections were that newspaper clippings tended to be both fuzzy and incomplete, and that the Air Force's Project Blue Book is so thoroughly discounted as to make me wonder why the author bothered to quote their opinions on many of the photographs. A glossary and an index are also included.

Norman F. Smith

SOURCE: A review of *UFOs: A Pictorial History from Antiquity to the Present,* in *Appraisal: Children's Science Books,* Vol. 13, No. 3, Fall, 1980, p. 38.

As a scientist and a writer of science books, I readily acknowledge my limitations as a reviewer for this book and will defer rating to give only a description and comment. The book starts by tracing possible accounts of mysterious flying objects in ancient literature, art, and folklore. It then moves quickly up to "the modern UFO age," with page after page of newspaper clippings, stories, and grainy, out-of-focus photographs of lights and hub-cap-like objects in the sky. There are also many photographs of people who claim to have seen UFOs, photographs and maps of places where sightings were claimed to have taken place, and even photographs of people in the process of watching what they claimed to have seen—none of which would seem to prove anything. The story thins a bit when many photographs are explained as hoaxes or lens reflections, and when stories are doubted or debunked. But the claims of the "UFOlogists" and the investigative work of the Air Force on unrefuted sightings are also reported in detail. While there is no doubt of the author's interest in his subject, he does an acceptable job of maintaining an objective and neutral position in reporting his "history" of this controversial topic. But if this history is all (or even a typical sample of) the evidence the UFO craze has produced, the book hardly seems necessary. I concur with the comment of one expert quoted in the book: UFOs, he says, are a "frightening diversion in a jittery world."

📖 *SILENT SOUND: THE WORLD OF ULTRA-SONICS* (1980)

Denise M. Wilms

SOURCE: A review of *Silent Sound: The World of Ultrasonics,* in *Booklist,* Vol. 77, No. 7, December 1, 1980, p. 514.

The military, industrial, and biomedical applications of high-frequency sound are reviewed by Knight in terse, straightforward prose. The explanation of ultrasound goes into the physics of sound; waves, frequencies, compressions, and cycles are some of the elements explored. Technical language is occasionally empty—a pitfall when reducing complex ideas to simple explanations—but important terms are usually explained in context, and concepts do come across. There is no glossary, a real deficit where quick reference to terminology might be needed, but overall this will function sufficiently in introducing a modern development to browsers as well as research students.

Richard B. Zipin

SOURCE: A review of *Silent Sound: The World of Ultrasonics,* in *Science Books & Films,* Vol. 16, No. 4, March/April, 1981, p. 197.

This charming little book is just the right size and depth of content to satisfy the youngster who is becoming aware of and wanting explanations for the physical phenomena which occur. The author begins with a general introduction to the subject of ultrasonics including a brief survey of the physics involved, the generation of ultrasonic energy and the occurrence of ultrasound in nature. He then

discusses the most important applications of ultrasonics that relate to the oceans, as well as those which are found in science and industry and in biology and medicine. The final chapter attempts to look ahead to new, useful applications of ultrasonic energy. The treatment of the subject is clear and easy-to-read throughout; there are no major problems with the accuracy. The book is well illustrated—a requirement for books written at this level.

Harry C. Stubbs

SOURCE: A review of *Silent Sound: The World of Ultrasonics,* in *The Horn Book Magazine,* Vol. LVII, No. 2, April, 1981, pp. 213-14.

I was glad that the author opened the book by clarifying the distinction between *ultrasonics* and *supersonics.* For some years the terms have been used correctly but in an ambiguous and confusing fashion. Beyond that, this is as good a summary as I have seen of the practical uses to which we have been putting high-frequency pressure waves. Mr. Knight covers the underlying physical facts briefly and with no more mathematics than what is needed to explain the concept of frequency; the rest of the book is devoted to practical applications and apparatus. Some of these things—such as cleaning equipment and depth-measuring devices—have been around quite a long time; but much of the biological and medical material is quite new, at least to me.

I have only a general understanding of why these waves can be used both to destroy tissue—cancers and bacterial cells, for example—and also to scan safely the structural details of a living heart or an unborn baby. I realize that differences in frequency and energy are involved, although these factors are not connected as they are in electromagnetic radiation; but I wish the author had provided more detail at this point. Without it, I'm afraid some of the antiscientific people will start complaining about the dangers of such equipment and even try to get laws passed against it. Mere informed assurance that a particular device is safe is no longer likely to be accepted uncritically. I realize that many of these people will not be affected by detailed information, either; but it should at least provide the average citizen with some defense against the antiscientists.

Clarence C. Truesdell

SOURCE: A review of *Silent Sound: The World of Ultrasonics,* in *Appraisal: Science Books for Young People,* Vol. 14, No. 2, Spring, 1981, pp. 23-4.

Here is a technical topic explained in a clear, direct style. This book delivers exactly what the title and chapter headings imply. Complex vocabulary is held to a reasonable level, with most specialized terms neatly defined in context; however, some students in the intended audience (ages 10-14) may benefit from a technical dictionary or other vocabulary assistance. The five chapter headings accurately represent the range of content: *What Is Ultrasonics?*; *In The Sea*; *In Science and Industry*; *In Biology and Medicine*; *The Future*. Some of the more complex topics are accompanied by instructive diagrams or photographs, which make the book both interesting and attractive. Beginning with such deceptively simple things as grasshoppers and dog whistles, the author soon has us deeply involved with bats, sonar, fathometers, nondestructive testing, cleaning surgery, and the many other present and future applications of ultrasonics. A sound introduction, if you will, to an important, developing technology.

Margaret L. Chatham

SOURCE: A review of *Silent Sound: The World of Ultrasonics*, in *School Library Journal*, Vol. 28, No. 3, November, 1981, p. 106.

An overview of the diverse uses of ultrasonics: sonar, detection of flaws in castings or weldings, thickness gauges, cleaning of intricate constructions, joining or drilling, smokestack scrubbing, acoustic microscopy and substituting for or supplementing medical X-rays, with scanty background on history and how things work. The text is full of nonexplanations hiding in opaque technical language; the illustrations include a few useful diagrams among too many dull photos of black boxes. The book requires readers to have background on such odd subjects as the problems of cold-soldered joints and a fair acquaintance with basic medical terminology. This may be of some interest as an update on applications after students read a good, basic text such as Robert Irving's *Sound and Ultrasonics* (1959), but it is full of inaccuracies and omissions.

📖 *VIRUSES: LIFE'S SMALLEST ENEMIES* (1981)

Kirkus Reviews

SOURCE: A review of *Viruses: Life's Smallest Enemies*, in *Kirkus Reviews*, Vol. XLIX, No. 21, November 1, 1981, p. 1347.

A reasonably informative overview dealing with the discovery of "nonfilterable viruses"; their makeup; how they invade cells, and how cells fight back; the different viruses that infect bacteria, plants, animals, and humans, and the different families of each; and what we know of viruses' role in cancer and other diseases. In process of discussing viruses at work, Knight must explain the structure and components of nucleic acid, and this could be clearer. So, at times, could Knight's sentence structure and his parenthetical disposal of unfamiliar terms. However, he does well enough with this difficult material to carry later discussions of virus and cell behavior. His survey of current approaches to fighting viral disease is enlivened by reference to several suggestive studies, and the diagrams and electron-microscope photos add dimension.

Denise M. Wilms

SOURCE: A review of *Viruses: Life's Smallest Enemies*, in *Booklist*, Vol. 78, No. 11, February 1, 1982, p. 707.

Knight's explanation of nucleotides, DNA, and RNA, vital to understanding how viruses work, is both technical and overly presumptive of background knowledge. It will require a studious reader who won't mind referring to the glossary now and again truly to comprehend what's going on. Coverage in other areas—pioneering discoveries in viral research, the classification of viruses, current scientific knowledge or theories about viruses and tumors, and the hope interferon holds as an antiviral agent—is much easier going. Numerous electron-microscope photographs provide effective illustration. Despite the aforementioned difficulty, this remains a useful introduction for the gifted or scientifically inclined.

Zena Sutherland

SOURCE: A review of *Viruses: Life's Smallest Enemies*, in *Bulletin of the Center for Children's Books*, Vol. 35, No. 7, March, 1982, p. 133.

In a well-organized and crisply written text, Knight describes what is known about viruses and what research resulted in that knowledge. He discusses the several kinds of viruses, explaining clearly how they infect their hosts and by what mechanisms they spread, reproduce, and destroy the tissues of the living plants, animals, or bacteria they infest; he cites some of the viral diseases, pointing out that there is increasing evidence of the link between viruses and cancer. A final chapter discusses current research in the field, including vaccines and interferon as well as studies that contribute to scientists' knowledge of immunology. A list of important events in the development of a body of knowledge in the field, a glossary, and an index are appended.

Nancy J. Horner

SOURCE: A review of *Viruses: Life's Smallest Enemies*, in *School Library Journal*, Vol. 28, No. 10, August, 1982, p. 118.

The nature, structure and intracellular behavior of viruses are methodically examined by a veteran science writer. Good photographs and diagrams support clear, highly detailed explanations. Bacteriophages and plant and animal viruses are differentiated and classified. Early research, covered by Rosenberg in *Vaccines and Viruses* (1971) and Loebl in *Fighting the Unseen: the Story of Viruses* (1967) is reiterated, lending drama and perspective to the long scientific search, but the primary emphasis is on current findings. This first book on the topic since the appearance of Nourse's *Viruses* in 1976 documents recent confirmation of viral involvement in disease, including children's diabetes, arteriosclerosis, schizophrenia, multiple sclerosis, allergies, mononucleosis and cancer. New understanding of the immune system, the implications of slow-virus research and the potentials of recombinant DNA are explored in this solid, well-written introduction to a complex and important subject.

Althea L. Phillips

SOURCE: A review of *Viruses: Life's Smallest Enemies,* in *Appraisal: Science Books for Young People,* Vol. 15, No. 3, Fall, 1982, p. 28.

The term "virus" is derived from the Latin word for poison. Although for many years it referred to any poison causing a disease, it now specifically refers to those infectious agents which are filterable or microorganisms too small to be seen by an ordinary optical microscope. A discussion of the three types of viruses, animal, plant and bacterial is presented by the author. An historical survey introduces the reader to some of the earlier virologists and their research: Dmitri Ivanovski (Russian bacteriologist), Martinus Beijerenck (Dutch botanist), Walter Reed (conquerer of yellow fever). An explanation of the nucleic acids DNA and RNA is necessary to the understanding of viruses and several pages are devoted to this subject. Viral makeup and classification of types are explained and interesting photographs and diagrams showing the various shapes and structures are an excellent addition to the text. Electron micrographs of certain viruses to certain cancers, the developments in the fight against viruses with vaccines and drugs and the protein interferon are dealt with. This book is a fine combination of fairly comprehensive text, diagrams and photographs arranged in an appealing format. A timely book on an important subject.

Edward Medzon

SOURCE: A review of *Viruses: Life's Smallest Enemies,* in *Science Books & Films,* Vol. 18, No. 2, November/ December, 1982, p. 81.

This author makes a valiant attempt to explain the nature of viruses and their effect on humans, animals, and plants. Much of the information is interesting and useful, although somewhat outdated. The history of virology is covered very well, but the recent events in the molecular biology of viruses are not mentioned. The chapter on virus structure is nicely presented and includes some electron micrographs and models. The life cycle of a virus is traditionally exemplified by bacteriophage, but little is said about the concepts of lysogeny or latency. The last chapter, on interferon, gives the reader some feeling for the excitement of science. Other developments, however, especially the work on the genetic analysis of virus replication and the use of DNA sequencing and cloning techniques, are not mentioned. A glossary and a list of historical events round out the book. Unfortunately, poor proofreading has left several errors that can mislead the naive reader. I cannot recommend this book until it has been revised.

THE BATTLE OF THE DINOSAURS (1982)

Publishers Weekly

SOURCE: A review of *The Battle of the Dinosaurs,* in *Publishers Weekly,* Vol. 223, No. 3, January 21, 1983, p. 84.

According to Knight, the ancient reptiles fought the longest, hardest battle of all to stay alive and remained on earth longer than any other creatures, over 150-million years. Named "terrible lizard" by the British scientist Sir Richard Owen, the dinosaur had to fight for food, to kill or be killed and to endure the uncertain climate in the prehistoric era. In concise terms, the author gives facts about dinosaurs large and small, information that stresses his convictions that survival for the species meant unremitting use of teeth and claws by the giants and other weapons by the little lizards. [Lee J.] Ames's drawings are mightily impressive and add considerably to a book that many young readers will want to own, since they are noted for their abiding interest in the extinct creatures.

Julia Rholes

SOURCE: A review of *The Battle of the Dinosaurs,* in *School Library Journal,* Vol. 29, No. 7, March, 1983, p. 179.

This new addition to the growing body of literature on dinosaurs emphasizes the more predatory species of dinosaurs. In addition to information concerning the size and diet of 29 dinosaur species, Knight also provides details about dinosaurs' behavior or physical features that would have been useful in battle. Several pages are also devoted to "Dino-Facts," assorted details about dinosaur life. Numerous black-and-white-drawings usually depicting battle scenes are included as well as an index and listing of museums where dinosaur bones can be viewed. Although the book does provide information about such lesser known dinosaurs as the Hypsilophodon and the Coelophysis, most of the material in *The Battle of the Dinosaurs* is familiar. This book should appeal to those readers primarily interested in the fighting aspects of dinosaurs. . . .

ROBOTICS: PAST, PRESENT, AND FUTURE (1983)

Kirkus Reviews

SOURCE: A review of *Robotics: Past, Present, and Future,* in *Kirkus Reviews,* Vol. LI, No. 1, June 1, 1983, p. 621.

A workmanlike entry in the robot lists, this defines the term—a robot performs useful human work automatically—to include such familiar household devices as thermostats and timed microwave ovens. The emphasis, though, which calls forth a historical survey of both ingenious automatons from ancient and medieval times and feedback devices from Jacquard and Babbage on, is on devices that combine computer brains with mechanical parts that parallel human limbs. The limb element, often consisting of a tube-within-a-tube arm with swivel wrist motion, gets a detailed, diagram-illustrated examination as one "playback" robot is taken through the different "points" in a particular welding operation. Readers are introduced also to sequence robots, transfer robots, and Mobots, who perform in danger zones by remote control. Knight sweeps readers through a number of fields where robots have proved useful, and treats them to a rosy picture of future robot servants in homes and elsewhere. Both more nuts-and-bolts oriented and more promotional in tone than Milton's *Here Come the Robots* (1981), this is for readers with a mechanical rather than a social interest.

Harry C. Stubbs

SOURCE: A review of *Robotics: Past, Present, and Future,* in *The Horn Book Magazine,* Vol. LIX, No. 4, August, 1983, p. 482.

The author begins with the regular clarification of the differences between an automaton and a robot, although the distinction is not always firmly maintained throughout the book (as it is not in everyday English!). Both, as he points out, have existed longer than most people realize, and they have been part of the reserve of authors for even longer. Most of the book deals with what the machines can and do perform in industry, around the home, and in the specialized situations of research.

Social questions about the balance between the loss of human jobs to machines and the gain in productivity which no human workers could provide are discussed; as usual, no final answer is reached. The book is a good, current survey, in reasonable depth, of the status of robots and automatons in human society.

Zena Sutherland

SOURCE: A review of *Robotics: Past, Present, and Future,* in *Bulletin of the Center for Children's Books,* Vol. 37, No. 1, September, 1983, p. 11.

Knight defines his terms, gives the history of robots, distinguishes between robots and automatons, and discusses, in separate chapters, robots in industry, medicine, and the home. He describes the differences between playback robots and sequence robots, and between open and closed loop control. The text concludes with a chapter on robotics in the future, predicting increasingly sophisticated sensory devices, unmanned assembly lines, and an increasing use of robots in the home, in medical and space research, and possibly (in all fields) to replace human labor at tedious jobs. The text is logically arranged and clearly written; an index gives access to the contents of a book on a subject that is alluring to many readers.

Ilene Cooper

SOURCE: A review of *Robotics: Past, Present, and Future,* in *Booklist,* Vol. 80, No. 1, September 1, 1983, p. 87.

There have been several good robot books in recent years that basically cover the same material. While Knight's book is neither as effective as D'Ignazio's *Working Robots* or as spirited as Milton's *Here Come the Robots,* this is competently written and can adequately serve as an extra book on a popular topic. Knight's thrust is both historical and futuristic. He mentions some of the earliest robots, including simple Egyptian robot figures, and discusses the use of robots in science, medicine, and space, explaining what the advent of computer brains has meant in these fields. One plus for the book is its clean format featuring good-sized, readable print.

Anne Raymer

SOURCE: A review of *Robotics: Past, Present, and Future,* in *Voice of Youth Advocates,* Vol. 6, No. 5, December, 1983, pp. 287-88.

Knight's unique survey traces the science of robotics as it evolved from ancient classical conceptions of mechanical men. Black and white photographs and sketches depict the toys, dolls and automatons of previous centuries that are the precursors of today's robots. Robots are shown to come in many shapes and sizes depending on the nature of the job they are needed to perform. As a result, they are often shown to be less trouble and more efficient than people which helps build a strong case as to why the robotics revolution is here to stay. This is not a book for the hobbyist wanting directions in how to build robots although it does cover well how particular types of robots work. It is less technical than Fred D'Ignazio's *Working Robots* which may make it more appealing to the casual reader. It also has a more practical slant than Barbara Krasnoff's *Robots: Reel to Real,* which is popular for its broader coverage of robots in movies and science fiction. As a reliable history by a respected science writer, this book can be recommended to young teens beginning to investigate the field.

Alfred B. Bortz

SOURCE: A review of *Robotics: Past, Present, and Future,* in *Appraisal: Science Books for Young People,* Vol. 17, No. 1, Winter, 1984, pp. 31-2.

The record of recent children's books on robotics is a sorry one. With the notable exception of Hilary Henson's *Robots* (1982), children's books on robotics are riddled with technical flaws. Unfortunately, David C. Knight's **Robotics** continues the trend. The book uses language well and has an interesting collection of photographs, drawings, and facts. I suspect that the librarian who reviews it will like it very much. Despite its strengths, however, I, as specialist, must rate it unsatisfactory.

Knight's most serious problem arises from his definition of robotics. He starts off well by stating, "A robot differs from an ordinary machine in that it is an automatic device that performs functions usually thought of as human." He also draws a good distinction between a robot and an automaton. But he then broadens his definition of robotics so far as to include thermostats, washing machines, dishwashers, clock radios, refrigerators, record players, water heaters, and toasters.

None of those devices should be considered robotic. By any serious standard, a robot includes considerable flexibility, adaptability, or programmability. Furthermore, most definitions of "robot" include a manipulative function. If the author includes thermostats and toasters, he should also include their mechanical analogs, float valves and flush toilets.

Later in the book, he adds teleoperated devices . . . to his collection of robots. These devices are undeniably fascinating and useful for manipulating hazardous materials and for extending a person's reach into previously inaccessible spaces, nevertheless they are not robots. The intelligence is not in the device, but rather in the human operator at the controls.

Knight also errs in his explanation of the difference between open-loop and closed-loop control. Closing the loop is *not* restarting the machine, although Knight explicitly, and by analogy to a toaster, says that it is. Closing the loop means making the machine continuously self-adjusting by using measurements to determine how close the machine is to achieving the desired effect.

In the chapter on home and office robots, the author describes "the information storage and retrieval robot," which is clearly what most people would call an elaborate data processing system. He compounds that error in the next chapter by stating that computers which write music, plan travel itineraries, and provide programmed instruction are also robots.

Knight also makes an error of a less fundamental, but still serious nature. He characterizes a microprocessor chip as "silicone" rather than "silicon." That indicates either poor editing or a lack of fundamental understanding in the computer field.

Finally, in the chapter on the future of robotics, he uncritically cites some projections that future robots may do such tasks as cooking, sweeping, lawn mowing, and baby sitting. Those projections should be qualified by noting the fact that robots do best in highly structured environments, while those tasks are, by their very nature, highly variable.

George Derderian

SOURCE: A review of *Robotics: Past, Present, and Future,* in *Science Books & Films,* Vol. 19, No. 3, January/ February, 1984, p. 150.

The title accurately describes the contents of this short book of six chapters. The second chapter, entitled "Origins and History," is particularly interesting and covers simple robot figures dating from about 2000 B.C. to the "Electro" introduced by Westinghouse at the 1939 World's Fair in New York. One of the famous automatons that the author describes in detail is the rooster perched on top of the great cathedral in Strasbourg, France; since 1350, it has flapped its wings, thrust out its tongue, and crowed at noon each day. Chapter four, "Robots in Home and Office," covers a number of interesting and more modern uses of robots. The banking robot ERMA (Electronic Recording Method of Accounting), which was introduced in the 1960s, can sort, post, record, and update twice as many bank accounts in one minute as a bank clerk can handle in one hour. More current advances in such equipment, however, are not adequately covered. The last chapter, "Robots and the Future," is also somewhat disappointing because the challenging problems of vision and intelligence are not fully discussed. Overall, the text and supporting illustrations are quite clear, and I recommend this book for junior-high school and high-school libraries.

THE MOVING COFFINS: GHOSTS AND HAUNTINGS AROUND THE WORLD (1983)

Sally Estes

SOURCE: A review of *The Moving Coffins: Ghosts and Hauntings Around the World,* in *Booklist,* Vol. 80, No. 9, January 1, 1984, p. 675.

Obviously a believer himself and hoping to convince others that "there are forces operating in dimensions beyond the cognizance of our five senses," Knight recounts in a straightforward but compelling fashion 21 documented cases of poltergeists, apparitions, and similar paranormal manifestations from 20 countries around the world. In Algeria in 1912, the ghosts of two dead Legionnaires, who had been good friends, apparently searched for each other within sight of the men of their garrison. In 1967 an attorney's office in Germany was besieged by poltergeist disturbances that included abnormal telephone activity; and in the U.S., a quiet Long Island home was the scene in 1958 of poltergeist phenomena that lasted more than a month, during which time parapsychologists documented 67 separate events. Soft, appropriately atmospheric black-and-white illustrations enhance a fascinating collection of "true" ghost stories that have no natural or physical explanations.

Candy Bertelson

SOURCE: A review of *The Moving Coffins: Ghosts and Hauntings Around the World,* in *School Library Journal,* Vol. 30, No. 7, March, 1984, p. 172.

In his collection of 21 "ghost stories that actually happened to real people in real situations," Knight has chosen well-documented cases of poltergeists and ghosts and relates them with a minimum of fictionalizing and no sensationalism. The foreword is helpful in putting the stories into the context of psychical research. Knight presents accounts of supernatural phenomena from all over the world, spanning almost two centuries, from the early 1800s to 1967. Included are ghosts of French Legionnaires seen in Algeria in 1912 and a tape recorder in Sweden in 1960 that recorded voices of the dead, notably Hitler's and Napoleon's. There are no photographs, but the black-and-white drawings enhance the eerie mood of the book. Only five of these stories are easily found in other books on this subject for young readers. Larry Kettelkamp, in *Mischievous Ghosts* (1980), includes one of these cases, and he does provide photographs. Three-quarters of the stories in *The Moving Coffins,* however, will be new to most young readers. This book is unique in its international range; Daniel Cohen's *The World's Most Famous Ghosts* (1978), for instance, contains mainly stories from the United States and England. Young readers clamoring for spooky ghost stories will not be disappointed with this one, and it will also be of use to those exploring the possibilities of parapsychology.

BEST TRUE GHOST STORIES OF THE 20TH CENTURY (1984)

Sally Estes

SOURCE: A review of *Best True Ghost Stories of the 20th Century,* in *Booklist,* Vol. 80, No. 20, June 15, 1984, p. 1469.

Comparable in format and treatment to *The Moving Coffins: Ghosts and Hauntings around the World,* this companion volume focuses on twentieth-century cases drawn from the literature of psychic research. Knight retells 20 unexplained incidents involving real people in real situations—among them, the ghosts of Versailles seen by two English school principals in 1901, the haunting of an ill-fated U-boat during World War I, and a number of poltergeist disturbances, including one in an army-navy surplus war goods shop that also qualified as a tactile case because someone felt a ghostly hand on his shoulder. As in the earlier book, Knight hopes to open readers' minds to the possibility of forces operating in dimensions beyond the knowledge of the five senses. A treat for both believers and nonbelievers.

Mary M. Burns

SOURCE: A review of *Best True Ghost Stories of the 20th Century,* in *The Horn Book Magazine,* Vol. LX, No. 4, August, 1984, pp. 486-87.

A former lay fellow of the American Society for Psychical Research, the author expresses his hope in the foreword that the twenty tales selected for retelling will "make readers aware that there are forces operating in dimensions beyond the knowledge of our five senses, and these can sometimes interact with our physical world in strange

ways." According to the dust jacket, the collection is designed as a companion volume to *The Moving Coffins: Ghosts and Hauntings Around the World* and considers representative cases of ghostly phenomena occurring or continuing to occur in the twentieth century. The tone is forthright, the style crisp and unadorned, and the subject matter fascinating; the combination of these elements is convincing. The experiences recorded are as varied as their locales: A bone stolen from an Egyptian tomb wreaks havoc on a British family; two English school principals on vacation in France in 1901 encounter the doomed Marie Antoinette in the gardens of Versailles as she would have appeared in 1789; a British artillery officer with little faith in supernatural manifestations plays a game of billiards with a ghostly opponent at an English manor house. Appropriate documentation is incorporated into the accounts of these and the other seventeen incidents; many of the stories also include descriptions of techniques used in psychical research.

Claire R. Gallam

SOURCE: A review of *Best True Ghost Stories of the 20th Century,* in *School Library Journal,* Vol. 31, No. 1, September, 1984, p. 130.

Knight's *Best True Ghost Stories of the 20th Century* will catch the eye of eerie story enthusiasts eager to discover further evidence that psychical events are real occurrences. In Knight's narration of 20 accounts featuring poltergeists, apparitions and unexplained voices, readers will find detailed case histories that have been reported to and studied by the Society of Psychical Research. These bizarre events take place around the world and involve historical figures such as Marie Antoinette as well as the more recent tragic heroes of World War II. Unfortunately, Knight's style is slow-paced and bland and [Neil] Waldman's illustrations do little to create an eerie atmosphere. All in all, a disappointment, since the nature of the material guarantees an automatic and eager readership.

Cosette Kies

SOURCE: A review of *Best True Ghost Stories of the 20th Century,* in *Voice of Youth Advocates,* Vol. 7, No. 4, October, 1984, p. 195.

A companion volume to the author's earlier *The Moving Coffins: Ghosts and Hauntings Around the World,* these nicely written stories include a variety of real ghost stories (apparitions) and some poltergeist tales. The most effective, to my way of thinking, are those cast in a traditional mode including the famous hauntings at Borley Rectory in England. Younger people, however, may be more delighted with more contemporary American settings, reminiscent of movies they have seen. The activities of various psychical societies in connection with some investigations is also included, giving a scientific flavor. Investigations following sightings, such as the ones recounted in the ghosts of Versailles, make some tales almost like detective stories. The mysterious element is well captured in the majority of the stories.

The illustrations [by Neil Waldman] are rather dreamy in nature, which complement the text well. These would be good to use in booktalk for a wide variety of ages, including adults and senior citizens. Everyone likes a good chilling ghost story on occasion, and this title provides a number of good ones.

📖 *"DINOSAURS" THAT SWAM AND FLEW* (1985)

Linda Callaghan

SOURCE: A review of *"Dinosaurs" that Swam and Flew,* in *Booklist,* Vol. 81, No. 19, June 1, 1985, p. 1402.

Various lesser known giant reptiles of prehistory are discussed in this slim volume suitable for reluctant readers and dinosaur fans. Knight traces the development of various giant reptiles through common ancestors, discusses adaptability, and examines current theories on the causes of the end of the dinosaur age. While sometimes choppy, the text is clearly written and features generous spacing, italicized terms, and pronunciations provided in parentheses. . . . A list of museums with reptile remains is appended.

Michael D. Jury and Floyd Jury

SOURCE: A review of *"Dinosaurs" that Swam and Flew,* in *Science Books & Films,* Vol. 22, No. 2, November/ December, 1986, p. 111.

This interesting book shows young children some of the less famous ancient reptiles. Along with the excellent black-and-white drawings, it should provide interesting and educational reading for young school-age children. The author does a good job of explaining the origin and characteristics of various air- and water-dwelling reptiles from the age of dinosaurs. Pronunciation guides aid the reader, and the dinosaur names are explained. The information is detailed and accurate except in one instance. The author lists *Pteranodon* as the largest flying reptile instead of *Quetzalcoatlus,* the Texas pterosaur, which is now considered to be the largest by many experts. Overall, the book serves its purpose well—to educate young readers about some of the "dinosaurs" that swam and flew.

Additional coverage of Knight's life and career is contained in the following sources published by Gale Research: *Contemporary Authors,* Vols. 73-76; and *Something about the Author,* Vol. 14.

Geraldine McCaughrean

1951-

(Also writes as Geraldine Jones) English author of fiction, retellings, and picture books.

Major works include *One Thousand and One Arabian Nights* (1982), *A Little Lower Than the Angels* (1987), *A Pack of Lies: Twelve Stories in One* (1988), *El Cid* (1989), *Gold Dust* (1993).

INTRODUCTION

McCaughrean is a highly regarded author of fiction and retellings for readers from elementary grades through high school. She has adapted a variety of classic tales: Greek myths and *The Odyssey,* works by Shakespeare and Chaucer, Scheherazade's yarns from the *Arabian Nights*, the legends of El Cid and St. George. In these retellings, McCaughrean has been lauded for her ability to capture the feel of remote and diverse settings through vivid, detailed descriptions of character, incident, and mood. Marcus Crouch writes that McCaughrean "saturates herself in the original until she has become part of it. Then she writes her own entirely independent book." Many commentators have cited the power of McCaughrean's imagery and her rich, eloquent prose, noting with favor her frequent use of simile and metaphor. Of this latter technique, McCaughrean has remarked, "[Likening] things to other things gives a kind of spurious unity to the world. . . . It adds a network of connections, that don't actually exist but give a sense of structure." McCaughrean also frequently explores the art of storytelling in her books. For example, *A Pack of Lies,* one of her original works, offers a wealth of stories-within-a-story, echoing the similar intricacy of her popular adaptation *One Thousand and One Arabian Nights.* Of this latter work, Ralph Lavender writes: "In some cases, a story lies within the story lying within a story, like images in a hall of mirrors; such mechanisms help to charge the fantasy with ever more intricate layers of meaning, so that it becomes the kind of fiction we can all live."

Biographical Information

McCaughrean was born in London and graduated with honors from Christ Church, Oxford. She has worked as both an editor and a staff writer for a British publishing firm, has written novels for adults, and translated a German picture book written in rhyme. She contends, however, that her "true talent lies in writing for children."

Major Works

McCaughrean's first novel for young people, *A Little Lower Than the Angels,* is set in fourteenth-century En-

gland, when religious Mystery Plays were dramatized by touring companies journeying throughout the country. In this story, eleven-year-old Gabriel joins such a troupe to escape his apprenticeship to an abusive stonemason. Garvey, master of the company, assigns Gabriel the part of the archangel in the group's play, then bribes members of the audience to help deceive him into believing that he has the power to heal. Eventually accosted by a piteous, despairing crowd who had hoped that they would be cured of the plague, Gabriel perceives the consequences of Garvey's chicanery and of his own vanity. Extolled for its evocation of medieval England, this tale of maturation concerns not only Gabriel's awakening but also the often illusory nature of reality and the lure of enticing fantasies. This theme is also evident in McCaughrean's second work of fiction, *A Pack of Lies.* In this book, protagonist Ailsa Povey is intrigued by the person of M. C. C. Berkshire, a stranger who convinces her to employ him at her mother's antique shop. Berkshire has a remarkable facility for concocting a tale for each item he tries to sell, every yarn tailored in style and pace to the type of book that he happens to be reading at the time and to the object being sold. Ostensibly, *A Pack of Lies* is an assembly of Berkshire's narratives, but, despite the subtitle "Twelve

Stories in One," there are eleven tales in the collection. As the story of Ailsa and Berkshire comprises the twelfth, McCaughrean leaves uncertainty as to whether Berkshire is a character of Ailsa's invention or vice versa. Hailed for its intriguing maze of narratives as an insightful look at the art of fiction, *A Pack of Lies* has also been compared to McCaughrean's retellings in its focus on the storyteller and the value of the tale. Similarly exploring human nature, reality, illusion and, according to Robert Dunbar, "the ties which link fiction and life," *Gold Dust* describes the effects of a gold rush on a small Brazilian town. McCaughrean's third original work of fiction for young people, the book has been acclaimed by Marcus Crouch as "an engrossing, funny, tragic blockbuster of a story."

Awards

McCaughrean won the Whitbread Award for Children's Literature in 1987 for *A Little Lower Than the Angels,* and received both the Carnegie Medal in 1988 and the Guardian Award in 1989 for *A Pack of Lies. Gold Dust* was shortlisted for the Smarties Book Prize, and received the Beefeater's Children's Book of the Year Award in 1994.

GENERAL COMMENTARY

Neil Philip

SOURCE: "Mining a Rich Seam," in *The Times Educational Supplement,* No. 4101, February 3, 1995, p. 14.

Geraldine McCaughrean's first commission as a professional writer was the famously difficult task of retelling *The Arabian Nights* for children. The resulting **One Thousand and One Arabian Nights** (1982) remains probably the best ever attempt. Its lush, exuberant language revels in the imaginative luxuriance of the stories.

Since then, McCaughrean has created something of a niche as a reteller of problematic texts, including **The Canterbury Tales** (1984) and now **Stories from Shakespeare** (1994). In addition, she has found time to publish three novels for adults, and three for children; *A Little Lower than the Angels* (1987) and *A Pack of Lies* (1988) both won awards and acclaim and her latest, **Gold Dust** (1993), was shortlisted for the Smarties Book Prize, and last week received the Beefeater's Children's Book of the Year Award.

Yet when I met Geraldine McCaughrean at her home in the Berkshire downs, she spoke of her work with real modesty: emphasising, for instance, her debt to the editors at her various publishing houses. It is the ingrained modesty of one who "was very unsuccessful at school" in the shadow of "brilliant" siblings. She left school with two A levels, and went to work as a secretary in the schools department of Thames Television. There her boss "sent me off to college", at Christ Church, Canterbury.

She realized almost immediately that she was not cut out to be a teacher, but "Fortunately Christ Church had this wonderful English department, really sensationally good. Suddenly people started asking my opinion on things, getting me to write essays. School largely consisted of cramming for exams; no one had ever asked me what I thought of a play. I couldn't believe it. I was mad keen on the theatre. So, suddenly, I came into my own".

Her feeling for the theatre permeates her Shakespeare retellings, which are dedicated to the Royal Shakespeare Company, though "I think it's really ironic that I was in the B group for English at school, considered unlikely to pass A level, and I end up adapting Shakespeare".

She wants her retellings "to catch the passion of the play; the thing that gives me pleasure when I go to see them, which is moments of extreme stress, crisis, tenderness. That's why the tragedies were infinitely easier to write than the comedies". She also wanted "to take the story and try to make it exciting for children. I think children have a strong sense of tragedy".

The shadow of Leon Garfield looms large, of course, over any modern retellings of Shakespeare. "I don't remember what I read of his when I was young, but I do remember wanting to be Leon Garfield when I grew up", she said. It is an absorbed influence, seen, for instance, in the lavish reliance on imagery that has been a feature of her work from the beginning. "I've always used simile and metaphor a lot. I think it's because likening things to other things gives a kind of spurious unity to the world. Everything is akin to everything else; it affiliates. It adds a network of connections, that don't actually exist but give a sense of structure".

There is something of Garfield, too, in the moments of spiritual crisis that sustain her narratives like the carved bosses in a cathedral roof. These have a sense of moral ambiguity, and of a suddenly revealed humanity that can be very moving. In *A Little Lower than the Angels,* for example, the cynical playmaster Garvey cavorts naked in church in celebration of his escape from the plague: "At the foot of the altar he stopped, his smooth, white plumpness daubed with bright colours by the sun through the stained glass. He stared down at his body, and large tears splashed on to the brilliant tattoos of light. He was filled with ecstasy at the miracle of his fat, sagging body". It is a moral rebirth.

Although *A Little Lower than the Angels* has a very convincing mediaeval setting, it was the result of imagination and intuition rather than painstaking research. "I'm not in the business of educating children. I'm in the business of entertaining them". A new novel started last year has been abandoned, at least for the time being, because "it died, under the sheer weight of research".

With **Gold Dust,** a ferocious farce with a tragic edge about a feverish gold rush in a Brazilian town, the writing became "fun" when she abandoned the research, thinking "Why am I doing this? I'm writing fiction, I can make it up! I don't have to find this out". The intense atmosphere of the book was conjured from the air: "Wantage library was as close as I got to Brazil". So McCaughrean's Brazil joins Masefield's Santa Barbara and Buchan's Olifa in English literature's oddly vivid shadow map of South America.

The exuberance of *Gold Dust*'s narrative momentum is anchored by the specificity of its images. Just as the story is about to leap away from reality it is pinned down with some precisely-observed detail. Geraldine McCaughrean compares this to a camera zooming in from middle distance on to a pair of hands, and observes, "My style is very affected by television. My brother and sister grew up virtually without television, because we didn't get a set until I was about 10, and they're older than I am. I can tell that our imaginations don't operate in quite the same way. My mind operates like a television camera. I think in terms of close-ups and pans and fades and cuts. Everything is visualized as if it's on a screen".

The filmic pace and construction of McCaughrean's tales, their inner momentum, is indeed striking. But the words themselves have equal weight with the visual strength. This camera is creating as well as recording.

All Geraldine McCaughrean's books—though most obviously her intricate weaving of fabulations in *A Pack of Lies*—echo the Chinese box stories-within-stories intricacy of *The Arabian Nights*. And as with the Nights, it is storytelling itself that is in the end both the point and the justification of the story. As the priest Father Ignatius says at the end of *Gold Dust,* "it was Fiction that saved the town".

TITLE COMMENTARY

📖 *ONE THOUSAND AND ONE ARABIAN NIGHTS* (1982)

Ralph Lavender

SOURCE: A review of *One Thousand and One Arabian Nights,* in *The School Librarian,* Vol. 30, No. 4, December, 1982, pp. 339-40.

It was E. M. Forster who drew our attention to the hold Shahrazad has over people's minds. We are all, like her, wanting to tell the rest of the story but making our listeners wait for it. And we are all, like the king, Shahryar, ruler of Sasan, wanting to know how it ends. But this sense of the ending is a more delicate matter than that: we all know that, inside the story, the characters must have lives after we have finished with them, living happily ever after; and we also know that, outside the story, there is a voice speaking directly to us. After all, the thousand and one Arabian nights and the stories told during them are literally a matter of life and death: without the stories

to keep the king in curious suspense, the queen's head will be cut off the next morning, because he believes all women to be fickle—'woman's love is as long as the hairs on a chicken's egg'—and there is no other way to prevent her ceasing to love him.

Geraldine McCaughrean's book is a splendid rendering of these stories. There are thirty-five of them here, some taking more than one episode, and although this is less than one story per night for one thousand and one nights, many are new to the children's versions commonly published. The favourites such as Sinbad, Ali Baba and Al-addin are here, but cleverly linked to others such as **"The two wazirs"** by means of a narrative logic which makes sense of the whole cycle, as well as of the lives of the king and queen. In some cases, a story lies within the story lying within a story, like images in a hall of mirrors; such mechanisms help to charge the fantasy with ever more intricate layers of meaning, so that it becomes the kind of fiction we can all live. This is made abundantly clear by the last four tales, which all carry their meanings closest to the king and the passions of his heart. And what these tales tell *us* is that sharing narrative imagination with another may be the highest proof of love there is.

The book's dust-jacket says that the style is 'clear, gripping and poetic', and for once this is a judgement that cannot be bettered. The imagery is brilliantly handled, illuminating each layer of meaning precisely when needed and with a diamond-sharp image. Perhaps the cycle falters once, when the ifrit of the lamp addresses Ala al-Din thus: 'And may I say how pleasant it is to be working for you again, master.' For this particular tale, this is the moment when a slipped coherence begins. And it might have been preferable to have had the book unillustrated. But these are minor cavils about an otherwise highly recommended book.

Anne Wilson

SOURCE: "A New Arabian Nights," in *Signal,* No. 40, January, 1983, pp. 26-9.

Long ago, in two desert kingdoms, the kings, who were brothers, were betrayed by their dearly loved wives. The wives and their lovers were executed, and immediately afterwards King Shahryar journeyed to see his brother. As he rode, the distant city walls trembled like a mirage, for his eyes were still full of tears, and, drawing near to King Shahzaman, he saw that his body too was like a tent smothered by a sandstorm as it bowed under the weight of his unhappiness. The brothers agreed that all women are worthless, and night fell in their hearts.

When King Shahryar returned to his own kingdom, unhappiness crept to the back door of his heart and unlocked it, letting in the enemies of Allah. He was afraid in his lonely bed when the black tent of night flapped around his heart, and he was also afraid of being betrayed again. So for three years the king of Sasan married a bride every day and beheaded her the next morning.

Eventually, there were a thousand spaces in the crowded streets of the bazaar and two thousand empty sandals, but the Wazir had two daughters. Shahrazad begged her father to marry her to the king so that one less daughter of Sasan would die.

> 'O Shahrazad,' he replied in vain, 'you are the oasis in the desert of my dry old soul. Do not empty yourself into the King's hands. He will only spill you.'

> The king was delighted with Shahrazad. 'Her face behind her veil is like the moon behind a cloud . . . Why did you not bring me this one before?'

> 'She is my daughter, noble king, my beloved daughter . . .'

We all know what happened, but has Shahrazad's story, together with her wonderful tales, ever been recounted in English so beautifully as in Geraldine McCaughrean's *One Thousand and One Arabian Nights?* My summary of the beginning of the story uses as much of her language and imagery as there is space for. The result may not be entirely happy but the original is spellbinding. The language in which the stories are told is a constant excitement throughout the book. There is never a tired phrase or image. Feelings and scenes are powerfully evoked, and Geraldine McCaughrean's arts show limitless versatility in the undertaking of a variety of narrative. Most strikingly, they conjure up, with all the force of a jinni, the Middle Eastern and Islamic world of the Nights.

Those repairing from this version to the seventeen almost unreadable volumes of Sir Richard Burton or the much more attractive translation of Mardrus and Mathers will not recognize very much, for Geraldine McCaughrean has given us a re-creation in miniature for Western children. She has greatly altered her sources in order to make a version which is nevertheless faithful and which takes us—adults and children alike—further into the heart of the Nights than any previous English version has done. We are given an account of only thirty-five nights and twenty-four stories, which include the famous Ali Baba, Sinbad (the first two voyages only) and Ala al-Din with his Wonderful Lamp. However, we are also given many stories that have never appeared in a collection for children before: romances and fairy tales which breathe of the palace, harem and desert journey, and folk tales, parables and narrative jokes which breathe of the street, bazaar, small farm and tent. The personal story of Shahrazad, which links her tales much as the sources do, can never have been told with so much warmth, suspense and appreciation of the ridiculousness of her situation. The book is illustrated by Stephen Lavis, in colour plates and Indian ink drawings, using a style which joins with the language in conjuring up the medieval Arab world.

Particularly distinctive in this re-creation are the narrative jokes. Perhaps the funniest is the story of the **'Everlasting Shoes'**, which have been so patched and overworked by their miserly owner over twenty years that they have become lethal. The extraordinary adventures of these in- animate, stinking objects, which lead their owner to accuse them of malice and conspiracy, are recounted with all the speed, economy and witty variation of repeated phrase essential to such a story. Abu Kassim's shoes, which made his feet look like 'two armadillos', were 'a byword' in Cairo. 'People would say, "This soup is as thick as Abu Kassim's left shoe" . . . or "That joke is as old as Abu Kassim's slippers."' But, one day, outside the Turkish bath, he put on someone else's elegant slippers and so begins his struggle with his unthrow-awayable, ever-recognizable shoes. Each fruitless attempt to dispose of the shoes brings disaster, and the enraged victims instantly identify 'Abu Kassim's famous footwear . . . "these legendary monstrosities" . . . the infamous slippers' at 'the scene of the crime'.

Another of the jokes is the better-known tale of the **'Wonderful Bag'**, described by its two competing claimants in court as containing increasingly glorious lists of objects, and eventually opened to discover old pieces of orange peel and three pips. Further stories about animals and humble human beings have novelty of content for Western readers and make shrewd fun of human antics, while also showing compassion and a concern with justice. Allah is an integral presence in the stories, without there being any moralizing.

The fairy stories are interesting to Western readers, especially the Muslim version of 'Cinderella', **'The Tale of the Anklet'**. Here the heroine flees from a harem, not a ballroom, and it is a dropped anklet, only three fingers wide, that is the clue to this girl fit to be a princess. Of course, the ugly sisters crush 'every caterpillar and beetle under their impressively monumental feet'. . . .

The stories of Ali Baba and Ala al-Din of the Wonderful Lamp are recent additions to the great collection, which contains stories from all over the Middle East and also India. Geraldine McCaughrean's chosen stories are not always to be found in both Burton and Mathers. Drawing on a number of sources, she offers her own variety of tales. We are given **'The Fisherman and the Bottle'**, where the fisherman outwits the dangerous jinni of the bottle; the tale of the scheming donkey in **'The Ox, the Donkey and the Farmer'**, and the story of the Land and Sea Abdullahs, where a merman brings amazing experiences to a fisherman. A story full of suspense is **'Pearl-Harvest'**, where the hero dares to enter the harem of the kalifa, pretending to be the kalifa himself, in order to find the girl he loves. Also included is the stirring, tragic romance of **'The Keys of Destiny'**, where a terrible desert journey leads to a secret city, betrayal and ill-fortune. **'The Lion's Revenge on Man-kin'** (in Burton, 'The Tale of the Birds, Beasts and the Carpenter') is a fine tale about the treachery and cruelty of humankind. In **'The Tale of the Little Beggar'** we see mankind in a different light. The beggar seems to be dead and to have been killed by a number of people, all of whom confess rather than see a fellow hanged. However, the fishbone that had been the initial cause of the trouble has been dislodged by the buffetings he has received, and he revives to tell the judge and court the next story Shahrazad has chosen.

Sinbad the Sailor, from One Thousand and One Arabian Nights, *adapted by Geraldine McCaughrean. Illustrated by Stephen Lavis.*

Shahrazad grows in her daring and her loving under the shadow of the sword. On the nine hundred and ninety-seventh night, she tells **'The Tale of the Leg of Mutton'**, about a woman who succeeds in marrying two men, thus doubling her income, without either of them knowing about the other. What is more, the husbands decide to continue the arrangement when they learn the truth. King Shahryar can hardly believe Shahrazad has dared to tell him such a story. "'Are you sick of life, Shahrazad, that you remind me of woman's deceitfulness? Do you think I haven't seen what trick you are playing to keep your head on your shoulders night after night?'" Shahrazad tells him the story of the Ebony Horse to show him a woman who loves a man as much as she, Shahrazad, (genuinely) loves King Shahryar.

It is now time I allowed readers to enjoy the book for themselves and to introduce it to children.

Neil Philip

SOURCE: "Authentic Voices," in *The Times Educational Supplemental,* No. 3472, January 14, 1983, p. 33.

The stories in *The Thousand Nights and One Night* are [not] amenable to nursery standards. Here it is not so much a question of abating or reducing the dominant mood, but of replacing it altogether. For the Arabian tales are a shamelessly erotic collection: the relations of the sexes are its overmastering concern. "Acceptable" stories dwelling on less earthy wonders can be extracted from the whole, but not without supplying a new context.

Geraldine McCaughrean's response to this problem [in her *One Thousand and One Arabian Nights*] has been to substitute loneliness, guilt and fear for King Shahryar's original erotic obsession, explaining that after he had executed his wife for infidelity, when others were asleep, "the black tent of night flapped around his heart. The creases of the empty pillow beside his head made faces at him, and the faces reminded him of his wife." This is a quite brilliant device, allowing the author to develop the relationship between Shahryar and the storytelling Shahrazad with subtlety and humour. In extended passages between the stories she builds up considerable tension as she shows the King fighting his own emotions: "Through the windows of his eyes, Shahrazad saw King Shahryar's heart turn away and dress itself in the hard armour of hate, and she was afraid for her life." No other children's version of the *1001 Nights* I know makes such convincing sense of this central question of the feeling between storyteller and listener. In addition, Geraldine McCaughrean provides in her prose an opulence of language, extravagance of image and vigour of expression to rival the voluptuous sensuality of the original. She chooses well-known stories—Aladdin, Sinbad—but also some overlooked ones, such as the Arabian Cinderella, **"The Tale of the Anklet"**, and a number of the very funny short tales: **"The Everlasting Shoes"**, **"The Price of Cucumbers"**, **"The Wonderful Bag"**.

M. Crouch

SOURCE: A review of *One Thousand and One Arabian Nights,* in *The Junior Bookshelf,* Vol. 47, No. 1, February, 1983, p. 44.

This replaces *Tales From The Arabian Nights* which was added to the Oxford Illustrated Classics in 1961. That earlier edition was notable for Brian Wildsmith's debut as an illustrator in colour. In other respects it was rather a dull volume, unenterprising in its choice of tales and relying on Edward Lane's rather stilted translation.

The new Arabian Nights is quite another matter. Geraldine McCaughrean has achieved a brilliant tour de force in what is not so much a translation as a thorough reworking of the tales. She gives us 33 stories, together with a prologue and an epilogue. The writer has been successfully daring in linking the tales with comment and dialogue between King Shahryar and Shahrazad, most of which is not even hinted at in the original, but which adds greatly to the relevance of individual stories and keeps the tension going right up to the thousandth night.

The Arabian Nights is a rich quarry from which the storyteller can hack out material, but it is full of pitfalls. For one thing, a majority of the tales are, if not pornographic, erotic in the extreme, just the stuff to keep a husband's mind off executions, but scarcely the thing for the kiddies. Many of them are also excessively wordy, their narrative line buried beneath a mass of convoluted sentences and much oriental poetry. Miss McCaughrean has been most skilful in selecting a range of stories, balancing romantic and humorous, tragic and heroic. The familiar tales are here: Sinbad, Ali Baba, Aladdin, the Ebony Horse, as well as many which will come as complete strangers, but as most welcome visitors, to most readers, child and adult. There are some nice fables, a delightful variant on Cinderella, comic anecdotes, and many more.

As to Miss McCaughrean's treatment, a single example must suffice. Here is the Powys Mathers translation of a passage in 'The Keys of Destiny': 'We rode beneath a burning sky for ten days, each as long to me as a night of evil dreams. . . . On the eleventh morning we came into a mighty plain which seemed to be made of grains of silver.' Miss McCaughrean renders this as: 'The rising and falling waves of desert sand-dunes washed away ten scorching days. The white hammer of the sun beat on my head until time itself was beaten out of shape. On the eleventh morning we reached the edge of a plain of white sand—white like a plate of salt into which Allah himself might dip his bread.' You will see that the writer has used the original as the starting point of a piece of individual creative enterprise. She captures a mood which we accept as Eastern, but her principal concern is to tell a tale in a richly personal way, keeping the narrative moving while still loading every rift with ore.

This book is a rare and rewarding experience. The illustrations are, sadly, not of the same quality. Stephen Lavis is competent, well equipped technically, but rather old-fashioned and lacking in enterprise. But a book to buy and treasure nevertheless.

Aidan Chambers

SOURCE: "Letter From England: Ever After," in *The Horn Book Magazine,* Vol. LIX, No. 3, June, 1983, pp. 339-43.

Many of [Shahrazad's] stories chime in our lives, still carry information about what it is to be human, that makes profound and entertaining sense. The problem is that they need translating from the languages of that ancient kingdom from which they first came—an Arabian place that exists now as much in fantasy as it ever did in reality.

And a new version of the tales has appeared here that makes that shift of tongue with remarkably attractive skill. Geraldine McCaughrean's *One Thousand and One Arabian Nights,* published in an extremely attractive edition in the Oxford Illustrated Classics series by Oxford University Press, manages to capture the flavor of another time and place while also making the stories sound modern and close to us. The illustrations by Stephen Lavis, some in black-and-white line and others in photo-realistic, splendidly composed and toned full-color plates, give exciting, enhancing visual pleasure.

And the style, as befits a book of stories supposedly once told to a touchy monarch, is satisfying to read aloud as well as to read silently. . . .

A pleasing volume to handle, stories full of humor, truth-to-life, plotful excitements, a cast of extraordinary—and often all too closely recognizable—characters; a world alive, peculiar to itself, yet pertinent to our own. Such is Story. Something that raw data, however well stored or retrieved, can never be—without a storyteller to give it shape and meaning and a reader or listener to enjoy the result.

📖 *THE CANTERBURY TALES* (1984)

M. Crouch

SOURCE: A review of *The Canterbury Tales,* in *The Junior Bookshelf,* Vol. 49, No. 1, February, 1985, pp. 41-2.

Ever since I read her superbly individual and eloquent versions of the Arabian Nights tales I have been looking for another book from Geraldine McCaughrean. Here it is, and it has been worth waiting for.

Ms McCaughrean approaches Chaucer without reverence but with much delight—which is just as he would have wished it. She makes no attempt to convey the poetry, but she has studied the Pilgrims closely and makes them the basis of her book. The full-length portraits in the Prologue and the casual hints dropped throughout the Tales have been thoroughly digested, so that when she intro-

duces them in the linking narrative they spring vividly from the page. She makes the tales themselves subordinate to the account of the journey to Canterbury, and that is as it should be. Instead of having a random selection of stories, we have stories closely related to their tellers. And everything is co-ordinated by the humorous and relaxed voice of Chaucer himself.

The general scheme and treatment of the book is wholly admirable. Necessarily, in such a huge undertaking, there must be criticism of detail. First, and perhaps most important, there is the question of what to do with those tales which, reflecting the characters of their narrators, are—in Professor Manly's prim words—'not fit to be read in a mixed company'. Today's children, conditioned by late-night TV, are unlikely to bat an eyelid at the Reeve's Tale and the Miller's Tale, but their parents and teachers may perhaps demand the exercise of some censorship. Ms McCaughrean does her best to find an acceptable middle way in, for example, the Reeve's Tale, but with the main admittedly pornographic point excised there is not much left, and readers may wonder what all the fuss is about. With less contentious material, such as the Pardoner's Tale, she is assured and powerful. But I wonder why she assigns the Manciple's Tale to the Magistrate (i.e. Man of Law).

The writer's lively and vigorous prose is matched on almost every page by rich and harmonious coloured drawings by Victor Ambrus on the very top of his form. Like Ms McCaughrean he has thought himself into the fourteenth century and into the tolerant and humane mind of Chaucer, and his portraits of this cross-section of society can be accepted as definitive.

Despite the opposition, which includes such redoubtable performers as Eleanor Farjeon and Ian Serraillier, this must be acknowledged as one of the very finest interpretations of Chaucer for the young. It captures most beautifully the mood of the pilgrimage, the high spirits, the smell of the countryside and the muddy road, the relationships established and developed between the disparate members of this motley crew of travellers. Surely one of the best buys of 1984 and a book which, in this handsome and durable format, will last for several generations.

Terry Jones

SOURCE: "Pilgrims' Way," in *The Times Educational Supplement,* No. 3579, February 1, 1985, p. 27.

First of all I have to declare an interest. A few years ago, I had a bash at re-telling Chaucer's *Canterbury Tales* for children and failed dismally. So the chances of my liking Geraldine McCaughrean's attempt were pretty slim—well they would be, wouldn't they? I didn't. For a start I found some of her imagery just didn't ring true—when, for example, she says of the Cook: "There were wine stains in his hair", I find myself wondering if wine really *does* stain hair, or when she describes the pilgrims as being "like a row of chessmen escaping from a chessboard", I kind of like it, but I'm not sure I really know what she means. I also found some of the dialogue a bit . . . well . . . unreal. Would the Summoner, for instance, really have said: "Open up! . . . or I'll eat the straw in your stables . . ."?

And then—predictably, I suppose—I found some of the liberties Geraldine McCaughrean has taken with Chaucer's work a bit . . . well . . . a bit of a liberty. I felt it out of character, for example, for the Poor Parson to tell a lie, and I couldn't quite reconcile myself to the summary disposal of that wonderful character, Harry Bailey's Wife, in favour of a rather cloying romance between the Host and the Wife of Bath. What is more, the freedom with which she treats the original leads her into at least one factual error where she confuses the Franklin (who is a landowner and a member of the gentry) with the Manciple (who buys provisions for an inn of court) or the Reeve (who manages a lord's estate).

On top of all this, I have a nagging doubt as to whether it's really worth trying to re-tell *The Canterbury Tales* for children in the first place. After all, by the time you've removed the sexual content from "The Miller's Tale", "The Reeve's Tale", "The Merchant's Tale" and the start

of the "Wife of Bath's Tale", you're left with pretty thin fare. When blind old January regains his sight to witness young May up in the pear tree with her smock pulled up above her waist, having it off with Damian, it's a bit tame to replace this with his finding them eating a pear—even if they're *sharing* it!

Having said all of which, I now have to report that I read Geraldine McCaughrean's **Canterbury Tales** to my two children (neither of whom, as far as I know, has ever attempted to re-tell any of Chaucer's works) and blow me down if they didn't think it was great! They laughed at all the jokes, they were riveted by the stories, and they responded with enthusiasm to the rich pageant of characters.

When I quizzed my daughter about what she liked best in the re-tellings she said: "The way it goes back to the pilgrims quarrelling after each story." And I had to agree. I think Geraldine McCaughrean's real achievement is the way she has succeeded in turning the whole pilgrimage itself into a story and has brought that far-off medieval expedition to life in a quite remarkable way. For all my carping, there is so much fun and rich detail in these pages that it would be churlish to find the book anything but delightful. For instance, I liked very much the dust

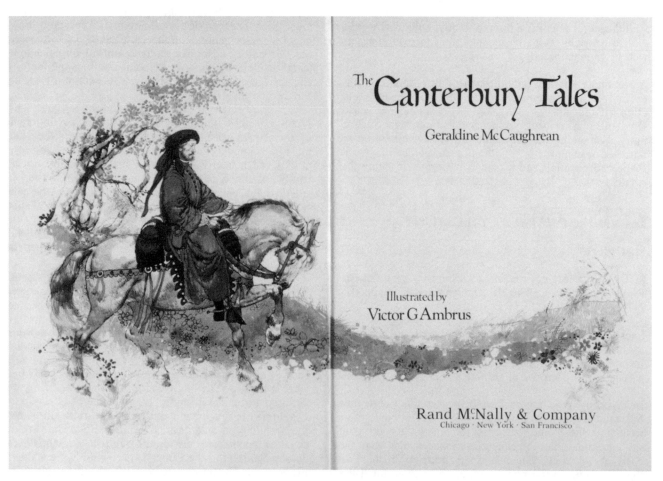

Title pages from McCaughrean's adaptation of Chaucer's classic.

storm and plague of nits that rises as the pilgrims shake their blankets after a night's sleep or the Knight's re-signed groan as his son spots a pretty barmaid: "*Another fiancée*," he murmurs.

The book itself is very handsome, with robust yet beau-tiful illustrations by Victor G. Ambrus. It is, all in all, a noble attempt at the impossible, and a book that will delight a lot of children and—who knows?—may even set some of them on the road to reading the real Chaucer.

Marcus Crouch

SOURCE: A review of *The Canterbury Tales*, in *The School Librarian*, Vol. 33, No. 3, September, 1985, p. 239.

It depends what you want. If you are looking for a mod-ern paraphrase of Chaucer, then Geraldine McCaughrean does not attempt to enter into competition with Coghill. If you need a gentle, sensitive selection from the tales for young children, you can hardly do better than Ian Ser-raillier. Geraldine McCaughrean attempts neither of these things. She applies to Chaucer the method which made her version of the **Arabian Nights** so startlingly original. That is, she saturates herself in the original until she has become part of it. Then she writes her own entirely inde-pendent book. Chaucer's poetry has vanished, but the stories and the portraits of the raffish gang of pilgrims are what, I suspect, Chaucer would have enjoyed. Ms Mc-Caughrean is a lively and eloquent writer, and above all she shares in generous measure Chaucer's gusto and his zest for life.

In this version the narrative of the pilgrimage is all im-portant. The writer makes good use of the prologues and the linking passages and does not hesitate to fill them out in order to achieve a continuous account of the journey to Canterbury. Into this story are inserted thirteen of the tales, nicely selected in order to demonstrate the range from high romance and sententious moral tale to hearty bawdiness. In deference to her presumed audience, or perhaps at the insistence of a publisher sensitive to crit-icism, she tones down some of these latter to the point where the tale loses its proper climax. Some of our tough children may be left wondering what all the fuss is about in the Reeve's Tale, and what naughtiness is left in the Merchant's Tale is contained in Victor Ambrus's seduc-tive drawings of Young May. But all in all this is a most pleasing book. Ms McCaughrean writes with a persuasive pen and readily adapts to the heroic, the romantic and the frivolous moods of her subjects. Above all, she makes us believe in the reality of the pilgrimage and of the pil-grims; each nuance of these varied characters is captured neatly and vividly in her narrative. In this she is admira-bly matched by the illustrator. Mr Ambrus is rather like Chaucer himself, and he has seldom been happier than in these strong, colourful and always dramatic drawings.

A very good book indeed. . . . I can think of few children from the upper forms of junior school to teenagers who would not find something to their liking here, and there must be plenty of teachers worthy of it.

Ruth M. McConnell

SOURCE: A review of *The Canterbury Tales*, in *School Library Journal*, Vol. 32, No. 6, February, 1986, p. 82.

These 13 rollicking interpretations take their inspiration from Chaucer but are freely adapted for young readers. Students will have to get the feel of original text else-where: the excellent *A Taste of Chaucer* (1964) by Mal-colmson, Farjeon's *Tales from Chaucer* (1948) and even the Hieatts' adapted selections from *Canterbury Tales* (1961), are long out of print. The emphasis here is on the pilgrims and their stories, and these, despite some shifts to avoid bawdiness, come off as rousingly good. In col-orful style and language, McCaughrean creatively recon-structs and adds conversation, event and detail, in keep-ing with the medieval times, to stitch the tales together. **"Death's Murderers,"** McCaughrean's version of "How the Three Found Death," is exceptionally stark and good. The collection is rounded off by having the pilgrims reach Canterbury, with a look to the return trip. A brief histor-ical note is given on the endpapers. Ambrus' handsome portrait of Chaucer gives a nod to that of the Ellesmere manuscript, but his colorful paintings showing the other pilgrims and their tales are his exuberant own. This at-tractive volume is a good introduction to medieval stories for reluctant but able junior high readers.

Hazel Rochman

SOURCE: A review of *The Canterbury Tales*, in *Booklist*, Vol. 82, No. 14, March 15, 1986, p. 1079.

In a large-size, brightly illustrated volume, McCaughrean retells Chaucer's fourteenth-century poem about a group of English pilgrims traveling to Canterbury, who pass the time by telling stories. Her lively, colloquial prose ver-sion is free and selective: she tells only 13 stories, cuts them short, sometimes too-directly interprets what Chau-cer left complex, omits the obscenity, and provides an ending to what Chaucer left unfinished. While this won't satisfy the purists, it will please children. The stories are as good as when Chaucer told (or retold) them, and McCaughrean retains the structure of the tales within a tale, using a variety of individual characters from various medieval classes. Storytellers will find material in the individual tales and in the connections between them. Ambrus' illustrations showing boisterous characters in medieval costume, often on horseback in spring land-scapes, express the tales' spirit and variety.

A LITTLE LOWER THAN THE ANGELS (1987)

Jessica Yates

SOURCE: A review of *A Little Lower Than the Angels*,

in *British Book News Children's Books,* June, 1987, p. 30.

This book is set at a key moment in the development of the English theatre, in late medieval times when the Mystery Plays, traditionally performed by local craftsmen in Guilds, began to be toured by professional travelling players around the country. This historical novel begins rather like [Rosemary] Sutcliff's *Brother Dusty-Feet,* as Gabriel, a runaway stone-mason's apprentice, is welcomed by the Master of a troupe of players, and cast as the angel who sits on God's right hand. The temptations of Pride and Greed enacted on stage are also part of the players' daily lives, as the Master develops a scheme to raise money by faking miracles whenever Gabriel is on stage. Members of the crowd are bribed to proclaim themselves cured; there's a bit of faith-healing; the money rolls in. For a time Gabriel naïvely believes he is genuinely healing the sick. Then the temptation of a gigantic fee brings the players unknowingly to a plague-stricken village.

Geraldine McCaughrean, well known for her retold myths and legends, has triumphed in her first novel in presenting the lives of ordinary people of the past, in direct, present-day language, with just a few archaisms to set the scene, and relevant historical information conveyed mainly through dialogue and Gabriel's own experience. This punchy, dramatic story could be successful with youngsters who think they don't enjoy historical fiction. Although much research must lie behind the story, it doesn't obtrude. The author concentrates directly on the players' plight: their dedication to their craft, their poverty, and the hostility they meet from local Guildsmen. The adult reader may detect something of Chaucer's world as well. I can enthusiastically recommend this book.

M. Crouch

SOURCE: A review of *A Little Lower Than the Angels,* in *The Junior Bookshelf,* Vol. 51, No. 3, June, 1987, p. 135.

I do not think that I have been alone in looking forward with confident eagerness to this book. Geraldine McCaughrean lodged her claim to be a writer to be reckoned with in brilliant, relaxed and individual versions of Chaucer and the Arabian Nights. This is her first novel.

She has hit on an unusual and promising subject. We are some time late in the Middle Ages. The old Miracle and Mystery plays put on by craftsmen in the towns are falling into disuse. In their place come the professional players, illiterate vagabonds and rogues (most of them) who trundle their pageants and wagons along the muddy roads and put on shows wherever an audience is likely to reward their efforts. The play comes literally as a miracle to Gabriel, apprentice stonemason, as he runs for his life from a brutal master. Gabriel jumps into the Mouth of Hell, and is sheltered by a playmaster who sees profit in his long golden hair and pretty looks. So Gabriel goes on the road, playing the part of an angel. There are two se-

nior players, 'God' who is an opportunist scoundrel and 'Lucifer' who is an idealist, tolerating his uncongenial role because he wants to preserve the words of the plays which are stored in his head. Then there is Izzie, Lucifer's daughter and maid of all work, drudge to every player and treated as nothing because, although she too has the words, a girl cannot play a part.

That is the situation. Drama comes when 'God' bribes an old man to feign a miraculous cure. Thereafter the fortunes of the company improve dramatically, as Gabriel's fame as a miracle-worker spreads. At first the boy believes in his powers, but this conviction fades, especially when his old master blackmails his way into the act and takes a share in the profits. The action moves to a massive climax.

Readers may fear at first that Miss McCaughrean has placed her crisis too soon. The scene is done splendidly—a performance of 'Doomsday' to an audience of plague victims—but there are still two chapters to go. Will it be anticlimax all the way? But here is a writer too wise to fall into that trap. The story moves, more slowly but still with impetus, to its golden close.

Our hopes have not been disappointed. This is a very good novel, rich in uncluttered historical detail, written with sensitive fluency, and with a gallery of memorable characters. Always highly readable, harrowing at times, it offers clear light at the end of its tunnel. For marketing purposes it comes with the label of a children's book, but it is a book without age bounds. If a criticism may be offered, although all the characters are clearly presented, the reader may find it difficult to experience a feeling of involvement with any of them, even Gabriel and the more appealing Izzie.

Anne Wood

SOURCE: A review of *A Little Lower Than the Angels,* in *Books for Your Children,* Vol. 22, No. 2, Summer, 1987, p. 19.

Gabriel lives in the middle ages and is a truly beautiful boy with golden hair and blue eyes. Apprenticed to a master mason he's cruelly treated and in despair of his life:

> 'You'll be bonded to me now, sure as a brand on a cow. You're mine you smear of lard. Mine to spit on. . . . He searched for the worst insult in his huge mental library of insults and mouthed it into Gabriel's face through bared fangs. *"Pretty boy!"'*

In despair he seeks escape through a band of travelling players where his good looks trap him into a different kind of exploitation. Dialogue and atmosphere are both superb in creating the feel of another time and place but, above all, this is a fine children's book because of the emotional power of the storytelling, unflinching and true— a remarkable achievement particularly for a first novel.

Margery Fisher

SOURCE: A review of *A Little Lower Than the Angels,* in *Growing Point,* Vol. 26, No. 2, July, 1987, pp. 4824-26.

A Little Lower than the Angels has the essential elements of a compelling narrative—appealing young characters, superbly vivid detail and an exciting plot sustained on a firm sense of the attitudes and changing social patterns of the Middle Ages. Gabriel, who is eleven, is apprenticed to a cruel stone-master and makes his escape by hiding his identity in a small group of travelling show folk whose presentation of Old Testament stories fascinates him. At first uneasy in his role as the Archangel Gabriel, an obvious one in view of his shock of silvery hair as well as his name, he succumbs to the heady excitement of acting but is gradually forced to decide which way his loyalty should go. Garvey, master of the company, plays God in the pageants but is far from lofty in mind, making money for himself by arranging supposed 'miracles' wrought by the angel-boy; meanwhile honest 'Lucre', a Frenchman who plays the Devil, holds in his memory the words of the various plays which they have never been able to write down. The superstition of the onlookers, the bitter conflict between the two men, in which Lucre's daughter Izzie is uncomfortably caught, the pressures on Gabriel to lend himself to trickery, make up a telling picture of a naive, conceited boy who comes to a more sensible view of life through danger and desperate contrivance. Young readers may find their way into the story through sympathy for Gabriel and his staunch friend Izzie or through the descriptions, never laborious and always highly coloured, of just how Gabriel's wings are made and fitted and his towering stance on the cart managed, of how the travellers live, find food, deal with opposition from an entrenched Corpus Christi town-pageant and with a terrifying contact with the Black Death. This skillfully planned and powerful tale contains a memorable panorama of a world where the tedium of poverty is alleviated by shows and wonders.

Anne Everall

SOURCE: A review of *A Little Lower Than the Angels,* in *The School Librarian,* Vol. 35, No. 4, November, 1987, p. 354.

Set some time in the Middle Ages, this story tells of a group of professionals who travel around the country performing the Mystery Plays in the hope of payment. They are led by playmaster Garvey, a complete rogue out to make a profit in any way he can. Garvey offers Gabriel, the hero of the tale, with his angelic face and long curly hair, what seems to be a miraculous escape from his cruel master. In fact, Garvey sees in Gabriel a source of profitable deceit. At one performance an old man, bribed by Garvey, claims to have been miraculously cured by 'the angel'. Gabriel believes God is working through him, a belief fostered by Garvey as more 'miracles' occur. But Gabriel's belief wavers in the face of Garvey's profit-making, and he is shattered when he finds himself play-

ing to an audience of plague victims, all clamouring for the miracle of healing.

Although the story is slow, it moves to a satisfying ending; and the language and the historical detail are rich and rewarding. The characters come alive, and the plague scene in particular is gripping. As an adult I enjoyed the book, but I wonder whether many children will stay the course without encouragement.

Nigel Andrew

SOURCE: "Raining Cats and Dogs," in *The Listener,* Vol. 118, No. 3038, November 19, 1987, pp. 39-40.

This is a lively and colourful novel set in the 14th century. The language avoids tushery (though not always anachronism), and the texture of medieval life is convincingly recreated. After a startlingly brilliant opening, the story—of a mason's apprentice who becomes a player with a touring company—rattles along through dark and light in a series of adventures which touch deeper resonances than might be expected of a tale of this kind. . . . [It] is heartening to know that children's fiction as good as this . . . is still being written. In a real world growing ever more dangerous and circumscribed, our children have need of these sustaining fictions.

Zena Sutherland

SOURCE: A review of *A Little Lower Than the Angels,* in *Bulletin of the Center for Children's Books,* Vol. 41, No. 8, April, 1988, pp. 161-62.

In a first novel from an experienced adapter and editor, McCaughrean writes a lively and informative tale of medieval England, in those days when the traveling troupes of performers of Mystery and Morality plays offered resented competition for established celebrations in towns and villages. The story concerns an apprentice, Gabriel, who is so cruelly treated that he runs away to join a band of players and becomes the focus of a belief in miracle healing. The plot has color and pace, the characters and dialogue are handled deftly, and the historical details are smoothly incorporated. The structure gives strong form to the informational aspect of a novel that marks an impressive debut.

Patricia Harrington

SOURCE: A review of *A Little Lower Than the Angels,* in *School Library Journal,* Vol. 34, No. 8, April, 1988, p. 102.

Gabriel, stonemason's apprentice, flees from a bestial master to play angel in a traveling miracle play troupe. Master Garvey stages a miracle cure hoax that has believing peasants showering the "angel" with coins and gifts; then a mob of plague victims overwhelms the company and takes their money. A winter of healing and rest results in Gabriel's conviction that he has found his profession. The main characters are vivid beings, and McCaughrean sustains a pungent, disreputable atmosphere, interwoven with values of loyalty, honor, and literacy. Somewhat easier to read, but in the tradition of Rosemary Sutcliff and Cynthia Harnett, . . . *Lower than the Angels* will illuminate the feudal era and challenge readers.

A PACK OF LIES: TWELVE STORIES IN ONE (1988)

John Clute

SOURCE: "Telling the Tale," in *The Times Literary Supplement*, No. 4469, November 25-December 1, 1988, p. 1322.

Almost immediately, the title of Geraldine McCaughrean's new book begins to work a crooked charm upon the reader, for the table of contents of *A Pack of Lies: Twelve stories in one* lists only eleven stories. The identity of that twelfth tale soon comes clear, however. It is *A Pack of Lies* itself.

In the public library of a small English town, young Ailsa begins a dull school assignment only to find her microfiche machine acting up. Several volumes of *Wisden's Cricketing Year Books* come into view, upside-down and inside-out. A strange, youngish man, loudly obsessed with cricket, appears from nowhere and beguiles her into offering him a job at her widowed mother's incompetently run antique shop. As he steps outside to wait, Ailsa's microfiche flashes a new title at her, *A Pack of Lies,* upside-down, inside-out.

The young man's name is MCC Berkshire, and he soon charms Ailsa's mother into allowing him to work at the shop for no more than food and lodging. The premises are crammed with the sort of detritus amateur bidders drag away from country auctions in the rain, but magically something begins to happen. Each time a customer enters and shows any interest at all in some object or other of bedraggled virtu, Berkshire claims to remember a tale about the piece in question, which may be an old clock, or a plate, or an umbrella-stand. Despite the fumbling embarrassment of Ailsa's mother, who has become touchingly over-apologetic since the death of her husband, he then insists on telling the tale.

Each of the eleven tales he tells is a deft and glowing invention, and they make up the bulk of *A Pack of Lies.* Each of them is delightful, well shaped, humorous and packed. But as Ailsa cannot fail to notice, something uncanny seems to be happening.

Each fable, whether or not it seems to be a true account of things, somehow manages directly to address the customer who has elicited Berkshire's mutable, coaxing attention. If that customer deserves to possess the clock or chest or desk on view, then Berkshire's tale will tickle that customer and a purchase becomes inevitable; if an unsuitable person enters the shop, Berkshire's story will be too painful for contemplation, and there will be no sale.

And just as his stories have told his customers home truths about themselves, so Berkshire's presence in the life of Ailsa and her mother teaches both of them lessons in self-reliance, humour, tolerance. In the closing pages of the book, after Berkshire has disappeared into the gloaming, it becomes quite clear to Ailsa, and to her mother, that they too were in a tale he was telling. It is only here that McCaughrean, for the first time, loses control over the complicated levels of reality she has woven together, and makes rather a shambles of her final revelations about the true Berkshire.

Fortunately, the tales he tells are almost the entirety of the enterprise. Set in the England or Asia of today, or centuries past, they are dense, luminous, and very varied. **"The Harpsichord: A story of honour and trust"** compresses into fifteen pages enough matter for a novel. **"The Lead Soldier: A story of pride"** similarly condenses a tragic life into a tough, supple anecdote. Like her prize-winning *A Little Lower Than the Angels* (1987), which could be a tale Berkshire tells, the fables bound together in *A Pack of Lies* make a strong book.

M. Crouch

SOURCE: A review of *A Pack of Lies,* in *The Junior Bookshelf*, Vol. 53, No. 1, February, 1989, pp. 37-8.

MCC Berkshire, from Reading (rhyming with breeding), is an improbable name, even for a young man whose normal wear is cricket flannels, but then Mr. Berkshire is an accomplished liar whose word is not to be relied on in any circumstances. Mr. Berkshire comes into Ailsa's life in the public library (a caricature of such institutions) and follows her home to the chaotic antiques shop of which mother is the incompetent owner. There he stays, sleeping in the bed which is part of the shop's stock, and selling goods by beguiling customers with obviously implausible stories about their origin. A pack of lies indeed!

Geraldine McCaughrean came first to notice with incomparable versions of Chaucer and the Arabian Nights in which she breathed new life into the familiar stories. From these tours de force she turned to an historical novel which won the Whitbread Award. Now she is halfway back to her beginnings in a series of brilliantly contrived pastiches strung together on a thin string of narrative. Berkshire's tales are coloured by whatever reading he has been indulging in at the time: mystery, romance, horror, twelve in all. It is all cleverly done, and Ms McCaughrean's prose bursts its self-imposed bonds very often. I couldn't help thinking all the time of the old schoolteacher's formula: 'could do better'.

From The Canterbury Tales, *adapted by Geraldine McCaughrean. Illustrated by Victor G. Ambrus.*

Valerie Caless

SOURCE: A review of *A Pack of Lies,* in *The School Librarian,* Vol. 37, No. 1, February, 1989, p. 31.

Geraldine McCaughrean has written twelve short stories, all of them fiction, all lies, entertaining lies of adventure, romance, tragedy, treachery, comedy and horror. Each is an utterly convincing example of its kind, enthralling the reader in a web of make-believe.

What raises this book from excellent to outstanding is the fiction that holds the stories together. M.C.C. Berkshire, bookworm and cricket fan, appears as if from nowhere and is taken home by gentle-hearted Ailsa. He offers to work for her mother in their run-down junk shop in return for simple board and lodging. It is he who tells the stories, each one centering on an item in the shop. The stories make the items irresistible to customers, and for the first time since her husband's death, Ailsa's mother begins to make a little money. Then, after selling the bed on which he had been sleeping, M.C.C. disappears. Ailsa, disconsolately facing the future without him and his stories, picks up a book and finds herself reading about M.C.C. and how he found his way to her shop. Who, then, is the fiction and who the liar telling it? Is Ailsa a figment of M.C.C.'s imagination or he of hers?

This is a highly entertaining book, light-hearted but thought provoking, written with skill and confidence. Children of eleven to sixteen who enjoy a 'good read' will thank anyone who makes it available to them.

Jan Mark

SOURCE: "Telling Tales," in *The Times Educational Supplement,* No. 3793, March 10, 1989, p. B13.

I took this book to read on a long-haul flight, hoping to alleviate the tedium, and wantonly shredded my boarding pass, marking particularly toothsome passages for future reference. Geraldine McCaughrean has the same throw away prodigality with a good line as Joan Aiken or Leon Garfield—don't hoard it for effect; plenty more where that came from—and shares Aiken's cheerful confidence in mixing the down-to-earth with the wildly outrageous.

The outrageous element in all this is one MCC Berkshire, a plausible stranger who wishes himself upon Ailsa Povey and her mother, owner of a failing antiques shop, and moves in on them, sleeping—indeed living—in the shop, acquiring more stock, selling less and reading compulsively in lieu of wages. The said pack of lies is made up of the stories he attaches to items he is trying to sell, or, on occasion, trying not to sell, each highly coloured and improbable—tales of murder, gluttony, passion, incipient rape et cetera, told with rollicking relish.

Not all the stories come off equally—the epic poem is a bit of a bummer, being bad Bad Verse rather than good Bad Verse (see *The Stuffed Owl:* D B Wyndham Lewis and Charles Lee) but the sheer glee of the enterprise is irresistible, culminating in the Gothic excesses of "The Bed, a story of Horrors Unspeakable", and easily encompassing low farce and genuine poignancy *en route.*

Oddly enough, the characters who fail to come wholly to life, and the ones with the best claim to be considered as "real", are Ailsa and her mother. They never quite rise above a flat fictional quality, but there may be an excellent reason for that; divulging it would be to wreck the plot, where from hang the tales. McCaughrean's literary forebears are not only Joan Aiken ("He put on his best suit and caught the train to Ballymuchtie where Gypsy Joe Padraic had a small consulting room over a fish shop") or even Leon Garfield ("The only colour about him was the university scarf which hung round his neck like the bloodstains of a murdered rainbow . . ."), but Scheherazade and Chaucer's pilgrims, retellings of whose stories comprise her earlier work. Come to think of it, the Canterbury Pilgrimage must have been the mediaeval equivalent of a 747 on a long-haul flight. *A Pack of Lies* was exactly the right travelling companion.

Stephanie Nettell

SOURCE: A review of *A Pack of Lies*, in *Books for Keeps*, No. 56, May, 1989, p. 25.

MCC Berkshire springs from nowhere (he says he comes from Reading, but significantly mispronounces it), charming Ailsa and her mother into allowing him to live in their antiques shop and their customers into buying their junk, and all with a virtuoso performance of stories—twelve of them, marvellous pastiches of different genres, horror, romance, farce, detection, tragedy, against which the real world seems powerless.

Reading Geraldine McCaughrean's *A Pack of Lies* is like playing Pass the Parcel. Each story peels away to reveal another one, the storyteller, MCC, not only casting a spell over his fellow characters but enchanting his own creator into joining them in the happy-ever-after world of his own fiction. It is an unembarrassed vindication of all escapism.

In an intriguing puzzle-ending, Ailsa and her mother realise what must be happening—that neither MCC nor they themselves can be real—so MCC's creator, a young man who escapes his pathetic, sickly self by writing, decides it is time to stop his characters getting out of hand. And then, in a marvellous last twist, he changes his mind, abandons the real world and joins them in theirs. This ending—which I really ought not to be revealing, except that it is the essence of any description of the book— might have been spelt out a little more for younger readers (and two of the judges!) who have been swept along till then by the fun and entertainment of the stories, but for teens it will be a neat surprise to tease out.

More than anything, *A Pack of Lies* is an exuberant celebration of fiction's spell, a smiling surrender to the grip of the unruly imagination, a playful introduction to the riches of style that lie waiting in books. Itself a tribute to the sheer power of story, it must be the ideal recipient of a children's fiction award.

Hazel Rochman

SOURCE: A review of *A Pack of Lies*, in *Booklist*, Vol. 85, No. 19, June 1, 1989, p. 1718.

The strange young man says he's from a place called Reading and that his name is MCC. When he moves into the shabby secondhand store run by timid English teenager Ailsa and her widowed mother, he revives their failing business by telling powerful stories about the old objects in the store and persuading potential customers to buy. Told with wit and verve, MCC's stories are mostly mock-heroic versions of popular genres, from adventure and melodrama to romance, farce, and the country-house

mystery. Every stereotype is exaggerated—vicious dwarf, country bumpkin, American tourist, panting lover. There's a wild Gothic horror spoof that mixes Dracula and Frankenstein ("Devil take me, woman, but you fire me with an insane passion") and a poem about gluttony in which the nobility eat themselves to death. Yet, however outrageous the parody, nearly all the stories have at least one strongly individualized character and unexpected moments of real sadness, especially when their connection is seen with the longings of Ailsa, her mother, and MCC. Readers will find that the entertaining fiction tells "lies" that tell the truth.

Kirkus Reviews

SOURCE: A review of *A Pack of Lies*, in *Kirkus Reviews*, Vol. LVII, No. 11, June 1, 1989, p. 839.

From the author of a fine historical novel (*A Little Lower Than the Angels*, Whitbread Award, 1987), a delightfully imaginative exploration of MacLachlan's premise that "facts and fictions are different truths."

When Ailsa brings MCC Berkshire home to be an assistant in her widowed mother's struggling antique shop, he seems at first to be more a liability than an asset—even though he eschews remuneration. But MCC proves to have an extraordinary gift: the appearance of the most casual customer—or even the man sent to disconnect the telephone for nonpayment—prompts him to tell an elaborate story tailored both to one of the objects in the shop and to the audience at hand. A dozen stories are thus generated: vigorous, full of dark ironies and dancing humor, splendid in their variety—and yet masterfully linked by the evolving portrait of the mysterious storyteller and his relationship with Ailsa and her mother.

There's a touch of magic here—magic that is adroitly fashioned by the author from the magical quality of MCC's storytelling. A fascinating, multileveled book.

SAINT GEORGE AND THE DRAGON (1989)

Brian Alderson

SOURCE: "Lives of the Saints," in *The Times Educational Supplement*, No. 3806, June 9, 1989, p. B12.

In some respects myths and legends are more conformable to treatment as picture books than are folk-tales. They are fairly precisely defined narratives, but they do not necessarily demand the same sensitive adjustment to a spoken register. They offer more scope for literary, as distinct from oral, effects, and there is thus more latitude for pictorial interpretations which will not clash with the character of the storytelling.

The potential is clearly discernible in Geraldine McCaughrean's new version of the myth of St George (involving the rescue of Sabra—not in Wordsworth's forest but on a blasted heath). McCaughrean's text for this is an exercise in controlled composition rather than brisk oral directness: "That night it left the pool, lifting its heavy haunches and heaving its scaled belly off the ground". Descriptions are graphic ("white mane scorched, white tail charred"); speech and action formally organized. In other words, the whole story stands firm, complete—if rather over-written—within its own self-imposed limits.

Such self-conscious writing calls for illustrations that will give space to the reader's own imagination. Instead. though, the publisher has seen fit to match McCaughrean's text to a piece of fashionable *nouveau* Pre-Raphaelitism. Nicki Palin has furnished a suite of double-spread water-colours which aim at a maximum of atmospheric and dramatic detail These do not always represent what is being said: the white horse comes up pale brown: a town said to be on fire in one corner appears as a holocaust. More critically though, the painstaking commitment to pseudo-medieval scene-painting subverts McCaughrean's already full-blooded text.

M. Crouch

SOURCE: A review of *Saint George and the Dragon*, in *The Junior Bookshelf*, Vol. 53, No. 4, August, 1989, pp. 159-60.

Saint George is, I think, Geraldine McCaughrean's first script for a picture-book. Hers is one of the most formidable talents at work today, but I don't think that this subject or form suits her very well. There is no room for her delicate irony and gentle humour, and she tends to underscore the drama excessively. This is nevertheless a notable book, especially for Nicki Palin's vigorous and richly coloured pictures. His dragon is unusual in form, a starkly terrifying creature who presents the grimly professional George of a challenge worthy of his talents. The combat rightly occupies the centre of the stage, but the artist has built up a clear setting for his drama. Peasants, a senile king, a pathetic princess whom terror makes ugly, are all seen consistently and drawn with much bravura.

Kirkus Reviews

SOURCE: A review of *Saint George and the Dragon*, in *Kirkus Reviews*, Vol. LVII, No. 17, September 15, 1989, p. 1406.

A straightforward retelling, with an attempt to reflect the misty historical fact (St. George may have been executed by Diocletian in 303, says an afterword) while including the dragon in all its fearsome power. The watercolor illustrations, luminous with yellow tones and hyper-realistic like a film extravaganza, are just this side of sensational in depicting the fear on unprepossessing medieval faces and the details of the battle. A down-to-earth version to compare to the elegant, courtly edition by Hodges (Caldecott Medal, 1985, text based on Spenser's *Faerie Queene*) with its outstanding illustrations by Trina Schart

Hyman, and with Grahame's whimsical, revisionist *Reluctant Dragon* (1938).

Betsy Hearne

SOURCE: A review of *Saint George and the Dragon*, in *Bulletin of the Center for Children's Books*, Vol. 43, No. 4, December, 1989, pp. 88-9.

This no-nonsense version of the St. George legend could serve elementary, junior high, and high school students as an introduction to England's patron saint. The dragon here is a rank villain whose father is Evil, whose mother is Darkness, and whose name is Wickedness. It eats dogs, sheep, and finally children until St. George arrives in time to save the princess of the medieval town under attack. The paintings do not flinch from projecting the terror of all who are threatened, from St. George's wild-eyed horse to the Princess Sabra, tied to a stake as dragon's meat after her name is chosen in the lottery to appease the creature's appetite. The red-gold cast of the art suggests blood as well as fire. The anatomical detail and facial expressions are masterfully drafted with robust action and Renaissance stylistic flourishes. Youngsters can sharpen their acumen by comparing this to Trina Schart Hyman's Caldecott-award-winning *St. George and the Dragon*. A note on the story is appended.

Ruth M. McConnell

SOURCE: A review of *Saint George and the Dragon*, in *School Library Journal*, Vol. 36, No. 3, March, 1990, p. 209.

Less literary than Spenser's adventure as retold by Hodges in *Saint George and the Dragon* (1984), McCaughrean tells the kind of crusader tale popularly told about the wandering champion who became the patron saint of England. Here, George of Lydda comes across Sabra, the king's daughter, staked out for a dragon that threatens their town. A new British illustrator pictures the setting with a golden atmosphere and a romantic surrealism that includes stone ruins and windowed manors, and ends with visual reference to modern wars as well. Townspeople wear frantic or grotesque expressions—and the dragon is seen as a huge lizard with pterodactyllike clawed wings as forelimbs, taloned hind legs, and a lobed and spiked dorsal mane. Once he subdues the dragon, this Red Cross knight does not settle down, but goes on to other dragons and other times—which the reteller ties in with her afterword. Hard to locate in print, this adventure makes a good addition to folk and dragon lore.

📖 EL CID (1989)

Kirkus Reviews

SOURCE: A review of *El Cid*, in *Kirkus Reviews*, Vol. LVII, No. 20, October 15, 1989, p. 1532.

A spirited retelling of the legends surrounding one of Spain's most revered national heroes, in a handsome new edition.

Rodrigo (or Ruy) Diaz de Bivar, who was banished by King Alfonso of Castile in about 1089, alternately served and fought against both Moors and Christians but concluded his career by capturing Valencia from the Moors in 1094 and ruling it until his death five years later. The epic *Poema de Cid* appeared in 1140; subsequent versions include Corneille's drama and (despite the publisher's claim that this is the first children's version) Sherwood's *The Tale of the Warrior Lord* (1930, o.p.). Here, McCaughrean shows herself a grand storyteller; she presents this prototypical chivalric knight in a lively narrative sparked with humor, drama, and her hero's daring trickery. Ambrus' illustrations, splendidly designed and limned, capture all the story's gusto, with vigorous characterizations and horses galloping right off the page.

There is much inherent in the story of a warrior who gloriously battled the hated infidel that might offend current sensibilities; McCaughrean meets the challenge of making the tale acceptable with partial success. Though there are careless descriptions of Moors, El Cid here respects his Islamic opponents and even their religion; he is not only a fierce warrior but a fair, generous, loving, and clever man; his wife is sturdily courageous. There is an incident with moneylenders (not actually termed Jews) that is offensively stereotypical. And yet the story itself is of historic and literary significance; ironically, to make it totally inoffensive to modern eyes would misrepresent it.

Richard Fletcher

SOURCE: "Under the Cork-oak Tree," in *The Times Educational Supplement,* No. 3828, November 10, 1989, p. 58.

The illustrations by Victor Ambrus to this re-telling of the exploits of El Cid cannot be too highly praised: strong in line and colour, bursting with vitality, faithful to the hero's 11th century in their detail. The text is rather less enthralling.

The Cid of history was a Castilian nobleman who became a soldier of fortune. He amassed retainers, treasure and fame, and ended his life as the independent ruler of Valencia which he had captured from the Moors. He died peacefully in 1099 and was buried at a monastery near his home town of Burgos by his widow. After his death a different and legendary Cid was gradually put together—the man of humble origin who rose from rags to riches, the loyal vassal of his king, the crusading paladin, the loving husband and father, the national hero, the charismatic leader whose corpse strapped to his charger Babieca led armies into battle even after death.

Geraldine McCaughrean re-hashes the legend and adds a few additional touches which anchor her version of El Cid firmly in the late 20th century. No racist he, for example. When he recruits Moors as well as Christian Spaniards into his army and his astonished hearers mutter in bewilderment, "Black faces among white?", the hero adopts one of the equine analogies of which McCaughrean presents him as so fond: "Why not? No horse judges a rider by the colour of his skin." After that, the reader is not surprised to learn that the Cid's army was "chequered as black and white as the dapple on the ground beneath the leaves of a cork-oak tree". Evidently there was nothing about the composition of the Cid's army to which the Commission for Racial Equality could take exception.

It may be pedantic to complain that grouse do not occur in Spain, but McCaughrean really should not have the Cid's wife and daughters "scowling a little into the evening sun" when they are travelling *eastward* to Valencia. Scowl they may, but like 20th-century tourists they look forward to "the pretty houses and proper sanitation" that await them there. Passages like this trivialize the story. So does the persistently overblown style with its cloying imagery. "The air was dented with Muhammadan prayers, like hammered brass." Good effort Geraldine, but you haven't quite mastered the use of simile yet.

The author could profitably have learned lessons of restraint from the earliest, grandest and most sombre treatment of the legendary Cid, the medieval Spanish epic *Poema de Mio Cid.* This is not just a matter of literary discipline. Self-indulgence is loss of dignity. The villains of the piece are the *infantes* Diego and Fernando who marry the Cid's daughters, brutally ill-treat them, and then receive their just desserts. Credible as villains in the medieval epic, they here emerge as mere loutish adolescents unworthy of any serious attention.

So the main protagonists disappoint. But some of the minor characters are very well-realized, such as the doctor who treats the dying Cid. Young readers may find the absence of introductory context a little bewildering, but after that the narrative has energy and pace. And then there are the magnificent illustrations. So it's a bit of a curate's egg of a book. One's final impressions are mixed: dappled like the ground beneath the leaves of a cork-oak tree.

Carolyn Phelan

SOURCE: A review of *El Cid,* in *Booklist,* Vol. 86, No. 8, December 15, 1989, p. 834.

Based on the twelfth-century Spanish epic poem "Poema de Cid," this prose retelling presents the heroic tale in a form and format appealing to young people. Ambrus' crisp line drawings give visual focus and vitality, while the sun-bright washes add vibrancy to the full-color artwork on alternate spreads. McCaughrean's writing keeps the episodic story simple and dramatic, making the Cid heroic without sacrificing his humanity. The only version of "El Cid" written for children, this edition is recommended for any library seeking classics of world literature retold for young people.

M. Crouch

SOURCE: A review of *El Cid,* in *The Junior Bookshelf,* Vol. 54, No. 1, February, 1990, p. 47.

It must be a problem to find suitable material for Geraldine McCaughrean's rare talents, but the story of the Cid gives scope for her sense of drama and broad action and for her strong feeling for character. All that is lacking here is humour, and even her ingenuity can find little of this quality in such a story of harsh action, treachery and stark tragedy relieved only by grandeur of soul. Ms McCaughrean draws on the many legends that have been attached to the hero as well as the more meagre historical facts, and out of them builds a strong story. Modern readers may find the Cid's unfailing loyalty to a worthless king rather hard to take, but the nobility of nature of this man of yeoman stock is nicely contrasted with the blinkered pride of the aristocrats who benefit from his deeds. The writer makes a sound point out of the tolerance of her hero, rare in any age and astonishing in the twelfth century: 'The colour of your faces means nothing to me! I see only the spirit in a man's heart, the pith in his sword arm, and the booty over his shoulder!' Ms McCaughrean is master of the heroic style, but she varies the tone of her narrative with her customary skill. The splendour of the last pages, in which the Cid makes his posthumous charge against the Moors, is the more moving for the restraint which has gone before. A timeless story of courage and integrity is here retold in words which are entirely relevant to our times.

As in her Chaucer tales, the author has support from Victor Ambrus at his most exuberant. He is perhaps a little restricted by the theme which requires from him a succession of battle scenes, and one armed and mounted warrior is much like another, whether wielding sword or scimitar. He is able, however, to point the irony of the contrast between men of action and honour and their stay-at-home masters. In alternate monochrome and dazzling colour Mr. Ambrus misses none of the passes which Ms McCaughrean sends him with such impressive accuracy.

Janet Hickman

SOURCE: A review of *El Cid,* in *Language Arts,* Vol. 67, No. 4, April, 1990, p. 427.

For advanced readers who enjoy tales of King Arthur or Robin Hood, this book opens new territory. It tells the rousing story of Spain's legendary hero, Don Rodrigo Diaz de Vivar—El Cid, a tale never before offered in English for a young audience. The presentation is attrac-

From Greek Myths, *retold by Geraldine McCaughrean. Illustrated by Emma Chichester Clark.*

tive, with oversize pages and ample illustrations, many in color, by one of England's most distinguished artists. Like most tales with medieval roots, this one offers plenty of color and excitement to be made visual. Don Rodrigo, ordered into exile following a disagreement at the King's table, takes his followers south to battle the Moors. After six years he is reunited with his wife and daughters, whose marriages lead to more adventures. El Cid dies by treachery; but even in death, tied upright on his horse, he leads one last unforgettable battle charge. This retelling has plenty of action, bloodshed, slapstick, and lively dialogue. The language is eloquent with images ("The river slipped by noiselessly, like a lost opportunity.") but briskly paced. Try reading an excerpt from the first chapter, which has both comedy and drama, to introduce this book and its hero to older intermediates.

Margery Fisher

SOURCE: A review of *El Cid,* in *Growing Point,* Vol. 29, No. 1, May, 1990, p. 5347.

Rodrigo Diaz, exiled from the court of Alonso of Castile in twelfth-century Spain, starts a career of conquest with the capture of Alcocer. The hero is seen in a brilliant flash of description as he bends to take his share of loot from the conquered city and we see under his chain-mail hood his creased linen quoif and wiry hair, his gaunt face and his beard 'grown as thick as a sheep's fleece'. A pictorial style rich in image and colour takes one through a strong account of the exploits of a romantically endowed warrior, bold to seize chances, driven by ambition, by concern for his wife and daughter and by his resolve to drive the Moors from a country to which he retains a fierce loyalty. The final scene, where the leader's dead body is tied to a war horse and sent into battle, to rout the Moorish army, is in the high epic style that makes the historical events immediate and accessible. Victor Ambrus is at his glowing best with superb scenes of warfare, with noble horses in action and with a forceful portrait of a hero noble alike in youth and in old age.

Barbara Evans

SOURCE: A review of *El Cid,* in *Voice of Youth Advocates,* Vol. 13, No. 2, June, 1990, p. 108.

The story about Spain's national hero, El Cid, was originally written in 1140 in the form of an epic poem. This oversized book is the first version written for young readers. According to this version, El Cid believes in honor, loyalty, trust, and courtesy to all; therefore people can take advantage of him. His king treats him cruelly, but El Cid takes the blame on himself and sets about making amends to his king. Young YAs may enjoy the story of this honorable, trusting hero, but it is very unlikely they'll carry such a large book around with them. It can be used as a read-along when studying the history and/or literature of Spain.

THE ORCHARD BOOK OF GREEK MYTHS
(1992; U.S. edition as *Greek Myths*)

Nicholas Tucker

SOURCE: A review of *The Orchard Book of Greek Myths,* in *The Times Educational Supplement,* No. 3983, October 30, 1992, p. 7.

Retold by Geraldine McCaughrean, these stories invite readers back into magical lands where main characters also oblige by talking in strictly contemporary tones. "Persephone darling! Time to go home", calls out Demeter. "Echo", says Hera sternly, "You've done it again!" Emotions too are immediately recognisable, with the gods shown dressing up, squabbling, lazing about and bragging just as if on a family holiday on a bad day. And on the subject of families, **"Jason and the Golden Fleece"** starts, "It's sad, but sometimes brothers hate each other." Infant readers, faced by such a stark statement of fact, may often find they can only nod in agreement.

Emma Chichester Clark's illustrations are cheerful without ever meeting the demands of these wonderful tales. Toning down the violence and eroticism is fair enough, but there is no reason to draw Helen of Troy as a wan house-wife and Narcissus as a gormless youth sporting a hair-band. Illustrating nonpareils is always difficult, but going too far in the direction of pop-eyes, false-looking beards, rosy cheeks and child-like physiques is to rob these tales of some of their grandeur. Even so, this is a welcome publication; a rich meal for the imagination in contrast to much of the junk-food offered to children on television.

M. Crouch

SOURCE: A review of *The Orchard Book of Greek Myths,* in *The Junior Bookshelf,* Vol. 57, No. 1, February, 1993, p. 22.

In addition to the unquestionable excellence of their stories, Greek myths have their share of violence, sex and black humour. To present them to very young readers, as is the aim of this collection, offers the modern writer some formidable problems. These Geraldine McCaughrean overcomes largely by ignoring them. The result is a book of enchanting and wonderful tales, just right for very small children and the attendant adult deputed to read to them, but with none of the sinister elements which make Garfield and Blishen (and even Charles Kingsley) so disturbing. The illustrations by Emma Chichester Clark are of the same kind: bright, homely and, as one might expect from this artist, often funny. Even the giants and the dragons are caricatures rather than frightening realities.

All this is intended as compliment, not criticism. Geraldine McCaughrean achieves her objective, to give the reader 'adventures and jokes, fables and fairy stories, thrills and happy endings'. They will, by their directness, stick in the memory and give the reader a sound framework on which, much later, he can hang his considered interpretation of these marvellous tales.

Pauline Long

SOURCE: A review of *The Orchard Book of Greek Myths,* in *The School Librarian,* Vol. 41, No. 1, February, 1993, p. 22.

[This book] would make a smashing present, and would be great for anyone who wants something juicy to dip into for regular bedtime reads. Each story is just long enough to be satisfying. The myths are retold in a rich narrative style, brilliant for dramatic storytelling. The famous characters preen and flatter, squabble and pose, within a narrative cleverly interwoven with rich and lively dialogue. It's not a reference text (there's no contents or index), but it could be used to enrich and enliven any staid delivery of Greek mythology. Its real purpose is to delight and entertain—and this it does in flamboyant style. Children will find that they know all about those silly gods without even realising that they have learnt something 'educationally worthwhile'.

Hazel Rochman

SOURCE: A review of *Greek Myths,* in *Booklist,* Vol. 89, No. 11, February 1, 1993, p. 982.

"There was once a king called Midas who was almost as stupid as he was greedy." Direct, robust, and gleeful, 16 epic stories of heroes and monsters, gods and warriors, are retold here in a style that's as great for reading aloud and storytelling as it is for introducing middle grade readers to the myths. Just as the narrative does, the simple watercolors on every page express the ordinariness of the characters, their silliness as well as their heroism. The monsters are appropriately gruesome (the dragon guarding the Golden Fleece "had no eyelids, it had no name, it had no pity"); the heroes (from Hercules and Perseus to Jason and Atlanta) are game to take on any dare; the journeys (whether home from Troy or down to Hades) are perilous adventures. There are no 1990s ambiguities and transformations—Penelope is waiting patiently at home for Odysseus; the Cyclops is monster, not victim—but the stories do show that Theseus is an ungrateful hero who ditches Ariadne, and that the gods themselves can be "vain, jealous, spiteful, bad-tempered—even lonely." McCaughrean, who has won several awards in Britain, lures you with the dramatic immediacy of the oral tradition: "Long ago, when fortune-tellers told the truth, there lived a very frightened man." How can you not read on?

Patricia Dooley

SOURCE: A review of *Greek Myths,* in *School Library Journal,* Vol. 39, No. 4, April, 1993, pp. 136-37.

Will this book be able to hold its own, next to the

d'Aulaires' and countless retellings? Yes, and pull well ahead of most of them. McCaughrean's style is fresh and lively, dynamic and direct. She is faithful in essentials, but not afraid to edit (the deaths of Pelias and of Orpheus, for instance, are not spelled out in gruesome detail). Most important of all, perhaps, is her subtle and intelligent interest in character and motive. What does Prometheus think about, chained to his rock? Why does Theseus abandon Ariadne? What makes Orpheus turn too soon to see Eurydice? McCaughrean's suggestions on these and similar points bridge the remote world of the Greeks, and bring human qualities to Demeter, Echo, Arachne, Midas, Heracles, Daphne, Jason, Atalanta, Perseus, Odysseus, and Helen. The text is matched by clear, rainbow-bright illustrations. Clark's watercolors are lighthearted and engaging, and a picture or decoration livens every page. Altogether, this very attractive collection is a welcome boon.

Publishers Weekly

SOURCE: A review of *Greek Myths,* in *Publishers Weekly,* Vol. 240, No. 16, April 19, 1993, p. 63.

The heroes and heroines of ancient Greece—and their evil counterparts—come to life in this excellent introduction to mythology. The stories that examine human foibles and were originally designed to explain the mysteries of life and the course of nature have formidably weathered the test of time. Readers meet the curious Pandora, ultra-strong Heracles and the lovesick musician Apollo, among others, in these 16 exciting and mystical tales. McCaughrean's retellings feature modern language and simplified plot lines and genealogical information, while retaining much of the drama of the more classical adult versions. Chichester Clark's playful watercolors are a constant reminder that myths were meant to be shared as entertainment as well as instruction. Her wide-eyed portrayal of life in Greece amuses and informs and may encourage interested fans to visit a museum or check out nonfiction on the topic. This collaboration is solid preparation for the more intricate tellings, as well as a segue into interpretation and analytical skills.

Kirkus Reviews

SOURCE: A review of *Greek Myths,* in *Kirkus Reviews,* Vol. LXI, No. 9, May 1, 1993, pp. 600-01.

The much-honored McCaughrean slyly telegraphs the philosophy behind these grand renditions in describing how Athene turns Arachne into a spider to punish the matchless weaver for her arrogance—yet Arachne's gloriously beautiful fabric depicts the gods doing "silly things . . . squabbling, lazing about, and bragging. In fact she made them look just as foolish as ordinary folk." McCaughrean is as irreverent, and as delightfully artful, in these 17 stories and epics retold in a contemporary style enlivened with snappy dialogue, whimsical descriptions, dramatic vignettes, and ingenious embroideries and explanations (Heracles gets Atlas to take the sky back because "These stars do prickle"; Polyphemus gobbled two of Odysseus's men, then "spat out their belts and sandals"). Beginning with Prometheus's creation of man and concluding with his release, McCaughrean provides enough links to give a sense of complicated community. Important particulars are intact and given in some detail (King Midas's problem with donkey's ears as well as his tactile troubles), though without the more horrendous aftermaths (Jason and Medea simply "lived together as man and wife"). A deliciously witty reminder that, as McCaughrean says, these myths "are just too good to forget." Clark's lovely, lighthearted watercolors, depicting most of the characters as foolish but appealing innocents, are generously supplied on every page. A splendid offering.

📖 *GOLD DUST* (1993)

Brian Slough

SOURCE: "Gold Fever," in *The Times Educational Supplement,* No. 4037, November 12, 1993, p. III.

This headlong narrative and the captivating characters who propel it centers around Serra Vazia, a town revitalised by rumour of gold in its bowels, initiated when the store-owning da Souza family discovers prospectors' excavations in their street. Thereafter, the plot's effrontery becomes unstoppable, its subtly orchestrated structure reinforcing the gold-hunters' obsessions. Greed triumphs over civilisation as the community is undermined, physically and morally: education stops, fixers arrive, buildings crumble.

The gold-fever offers a satirical parable on cupidity, highlighted by characters who ultimately restore the town's "air of renewal". Most heroic are the avalanche-voiced teacher, her surviving pupil Inez da Souza, and her brother, Maro. The family lodger, a militant communist, contrasts zanily with the priest who earlier succumbed to gold-grubbing in his crypt, clad in a T-shirt commemorating the Pope's visit to Rio.

Sharp observations on a kaleidoscope of topics enliven every page, often underlined by ironic humour, whether understated (Brazilian football mania) or sharper (press insensitivities).

The language is evocatively multi-layered, in throwaway phrases—bodyguards are "lumpy with weaponry"—and affluent descriptions, among which the climatic flood scene is spellbinding. The forgivably too frequent similes "provide joy enough to justify their existence". This novel is pure gold dust: not only teenagers will value it.

Jill Burridge

SOURCE: A review of *Gold Dust,* in *Books for Keeps,* No. 84, January, 1994, p. 24.

Inez and Maro live in modern-day Brazil, in a village called Serra Vazia on the edge of the rainforest. Life exists in a time warp, the juke box still plays Nat King Cole and Doris Day, until one day two local layabouts dig a hole in the main street and start excavating for gold. Soon Serra Vazia is a mish-mash of intriguing characters, strongly drawn and warmly portrayed. The close attention to detail takes you right into the heart of this community to share their sadness and laugh at their eccentricities. In their own way, everyone falls prey to the lure of wealth. Inez' ideals are undermined, her illusions shattered, but she comes to understand human nature, as she and her brother retrieve the situation with a climax that's credible, exciting and amusing.

M. Crouch

SOURCE: A review of *Gold Dust,* in *The Junior Bookshelf,* Vol. 58, No. 1, February, 1994, pp. 34-5.

Not since William Mayne in his early days has a writer had such a capacity for surprise as Geraldine McCaughrean. All we can be confident about each book is that it will be admirable—but in which way? This time she finds fun and action and zest for life in modern Brazil, the country where children are murdered in the streets because they make the place look untidy. A great subject for laughs! But Ms McCaughrean knows that laughter is another aspect of anger. Just once in this chronicle of human misery and despair does she let the comedy mask slip. After the international Press Corps moved on, seeing no more fun to be had out of gold-rush stories, the hotel in which they had stayed burned down. 'A pity that the Press had not stayed . . . If they had had to run from the Hotel d'Ouro with their clothes alight . . . it might just have increased their sensitivity to the pain of other people's comical little tragedies.'

Gold fever had passed Serra Vazia by long ago, and Inez and Maro and their parents, like their neighbours, made a precarious living in the decaying town. Inez works hard at school to please the formidable Senhora Ferretti, failed opera singer. Like every Brazilian boy Maro sees his bright future in football. Then old Enoque Furtado and his brother start digging up the road in front of the store. Gold madness is back, infecting locals and incomers alike.

The story is wonderfully inventive, consistent and hideously convincing, but I will say no more about the plot except that salvation, in so far as it comes, comes through the agency of The Baby, unnamed because Mrs. da Souza, a cautious woman, did not want to waste a name on a child who, by the law of averages, might not survive. A word must be found for the style which keeps the narrative sparkling through nearly 200 pages and the quiet social comment which never holds up the story. Here are the children at Disco Tony, Serra Vazia's nightspot: 'Candlelight from the tables lit the eyes of the cockroaches gliding suavely by to the music of *Oklahoma.*' Serra Vazia may be filthy and intolerably hot, but, at least before gold madness hits it, it has achieved social balance. It takes a visit to the city to tell Inez and Maro that they are 'black'.

' "I forgot you were," said Senhora Ferretti, and that was that.' As their town falls apart, undermined by the gold hunters and the incessant rain, its disintegration is shown in precise and vivid detail. 'The Bank Itau . . . curtsied. It spread its skirts of clinker planking and ducked down to the ground, losing its balance only at the last moment . . . Maro wished God could have seen Noah's Ark go down like that—faulty design, perhaps, or holed by shipworm.' An engrossing, funny, tragic blockbuster of a story.

N. Tucker

SOURCE: A review of *Gold Dust,* in *Books for Your Children,* Vol. 29, No. 1, Spring, 1994, p. 24.

This novel is a feat of imagination and genuinely awe-inspiring in its scope and authority. It describes the effects of a modern goldrush on a backward little town in Brazil. Forget any feeling of romantic buccaneering, what follows is closer to hell on earth.

Somehow the author conjures up a happy ending from a tale of greed, ignorance and squalor. But don't be put off; this is also a superb story about the triumph of the human spirit over almost unbearable adversity. A previous prize winner, the author surely deserves another one for this exceptional novel.

Robert Dunbar

SOURCE: A review of *Gold Dust,* in *The School Librarian,* Vol. 42, No. 2, May, 1994, pp. 72, 74.

The Brazilian town of Serra Vazia provides the setting for this extremely entertaining novel. At the heart of the story lies a consideration of the corrupting effects of greed, as we watch the town and its picturesque inhabitants succumb in their various ways to the discovery of gold on their main street. The consequences of this discovery are perceived through the eyes of brother and sister Maro and Inez, eyes which soon begin to penetrate the morality of the adult world of which, as Inez realises at one point, circumstances are making them honorary members. They rise magnificently to the demands of this changing status, being endowed with virtues—courage, perseverance and most of all, mental and physical vitality—which take their roles of hero and heroine completely credible. Of the adult characters with whom they must adjust, and readjust, their relationships, the most engaging is their schoolteacher, the redoubtable Senhora Ferretti, disappointed opera star but samba singer *extraordinaire:* the chapters which relate their journey to Marabá—'the most dangerous town since Sodom'—provide the scope for a narrative of the highest quality, characterised by wit, exuberance and a sound understanding, as articulated by Father Ignatius, the town priest, of the ties which link fiction and life.

THE ODYSSEY (1993)

Charles Causley

SOURCE: "On Translating Homer," in *The Times Educational Supplement,* No. 4037, November 12, 1993, p. II.

Slightly . . . fortissimo in tone, [this book's] springy text is bold in humour and comic allusion. Such is McCaughrean's skill that the myth, somehow, is also humanised. One has a sense that the events described, mysterious and magical though they may be, are also happening here and now. One would need a heart of stone, for example, not to be moved by McCaughrean's account of the return of Ulysses as a filthy beggar, recognised by no one but his scruffy old dog who lays its head in his lap and thumps its tail on the ground three times.

Janet Tayler

SOURCE: A review of *The Odyssey,* in *The School Librarian,* Vol. 42, No. 2, May, 1994, p. 62.

Geraldine McCaughrean has retold the adventures of Odysseus in a lively, rather tongue-in-cheek manner which is in contrast to [Rosemary Sutcliff's *Black Ships before Troy*]. Victor Ambrus's illustrations are colourful but a bit old-fashioned in style. Suitable for older readers who would prefer a humorous rendering of this Greek tale.

STORIES FROM SHAKESPEARE (1994)

M. Crouch

SOURCE: A review of *Stories from Shakespeare,* in *The Junior Bookshelf,* Vol. 59, No. 1, February, 1995, pp. 38-9.

Geraldine McCaughrean offers a direct challenge to Leon Garfield, the most recent reteller of Shakespeare's stories. She is no competitor in flamboyance. Where she scores most effectively is in plain story-telling. As she has proved many times she commands a fine narrative style, to which in this book she adds a ripe understanding of the poet's message. She does not tell the story of the play so much as a story telling Shakespeare's plot without reference to the stage. She has her own way of setting the scene and exploring the motives of the characters. Where she falls down is in her paraphrases of actual speeches from the play. Here she achieves an uneasy compromise between modern colloquial and the heightened eloquence of Elizabethan speech. The failure is underlined in the marginal quotations by which Ms McCaughrean proves her contention that 'we quote him every day without realising it'. She presumably aims her book at children who are only just coming to Shakespeare, and she gives them an excellent start, showing that the plays are great entertainment and hinting at the depths to which they can in time be explored.

The author deals here with ten plays: five tragedies, two comedies, a history and a Roman play and one philosophical late comedy. A good appetiser. A full meal would be welcome.

Additional coverage of McCaughrean's life and career is contained in the following sources published by Gale Research: *Contemporary Authors,* Vol. 117; and *Something about the Author,* Vol. 43.

David McKee

1935-

English author and illustrator of picture books.

Major works include *Elmer: The Story of a Patchwork Elephant* (1968), *123456789 Benn* (1970), *Tusk Tusk* (1978), *King Rollo and the Birthday* (1979), *I Hate My Teddy Bear* (1982), *Two Monsters* (1985).

INTRODUCTION

A highly regarded author and illustrator of inventive *pourquoi* (or "why") tales, fables, and other picture books for preschoolers and primary graders, McKee has been applauded for creating playful yet carefully crafted and thought-provoking works centering around substantive themes and subjects. In books that are distinguished by lighthearted humor, he embraces such weighty topics as war and bigotry, the need for communication and understanding, and the importance of independence and self-reliance. McKee also examines somewhat lighter subjects that are of a more temporal concern to children. His "King Rollo" books, for example, describe the childlike ruler's turmoil over making a birthday card for the queen—he fears that the others' store-bought cards may overshadow his—and his fretfulness over learning to tie his new lace-up shoes. Marcus Crouch has remarked: "The simplicity of David McKee's drawing and the innocence of his humour disguise a great deal of wisdom and craft." McKee has also created picture books that verge on the surreal, a concept which some commentators have found intriguing and others problematic. *I Hate My Teddy Bear,* for instance, depicts a squabble between two children that is set against a backdrop of odd activities, many related to the construction of a sculpture garden filled with huge carvings of disjointed hands and feet. Naomi Lewis calls the book "a brilliant foray into the surreal." *Publishers Weekly* contends, however, that "young readers will be frustrated trying to understand the full-color scenes of surrealistic doings by crowds of people, inhumanly deadpan," while Mary Butler Nickerson asks: "This is a book for children?" Other reviewers have similarly protested that McKee's wit is too mature for his audience, frequently citing *Not Now, Bernard* (1980) as an example. This story tells of a little boy completely ignored by his inattentive parents and consumed by a monster. Unmindful of their son's absence, Bernard's parents feed the monster and send him to bed at the story's end. Joy Chant wrote after sharing *Not Now, Bernard* with a group of children: "A moral tale for parents certainly; but the possible effect on a sensitive child alarmed me. Unfortunately I do not seem to know any sensitive children for my guinea pigs were obstinately undisturbed." McKee is also noted for ending many of his books with a final twist of irony: in *Tusk Tusk,* for instance, the warring black and white elephants nearly obliterate their species until a few lone

survivors escape to the woods, crossbreed, and produce grey offspring. At the conclusion of the story, however, this second generation becomes aware that some members have large ears and some have small ears. Commentators maintain that such wry touches lend added depth to McKee's message.

McKee's illustrations have been extolled for their originality and understatement. Often alternating color paintings with black-and-white drawings, the latter especially detailed, McKee also varies perspective, occasionally employing comic strip technique to dramatize a number of incidents on one page. He has been commended for his effective use of contrasting colors to highlight prominent themes and subjects, and for conveying subtle character traits that are not spelled out in the text through a careful depiction of expression and behavior.

Biographical Information

McKee worked as a cartoonist for *Punch* magazine before he published his first children's book in 1964. Although he was born in Devon, he has spent much of his adult life in Spain, France, and Italy, using these settings in the illustrations for his books. McKee has also adapted his children's titles for film and television; both the "Mr. Benn" books—tales of an ordinary little man who becomes the hero of various fantastic adventures—and the "King Rollo" stories have become highly successful animated shows, lauded for the quality of their artwork and their faithfulness to the author's whimsical plots. Nevertheless, McKee prefers the more traditional book format for his work. He likes his stories to be scrutinized at length, read and reread, and turned at various angles to fully enjoy the richness of the illustrations. McKee has also created illustrations for other children's writers, most notably Alvin Schwartz and Christine Nostlinger, and has illustrated such classics as L. Frank Baum's *The Wizard of Oz* and several of Michael Bond's *Paddington Bear* books.

Major Works

In 1967, McKee wrote *Mr. Benn, Red Knight,* in which protagonist Benn, an unassuming bank clerk, visits a costume shop. Upon donning a suit of armor, Benn finds himself in medieval times, where he valiantly aids a hunted dragon. In subsequent books, Benn proceeds to revolutionize a prison, free wild animals from hunters in Africa, and rescue a stranded circus troupe—all by means of the magical transformations afforded him each time he visits the costumier's. Also among McKee's most successful early works is *Elmer: The Story of a Patchwork Elephant,* the first of several books chronicling the adventures of this eponymous hero. In the introductory tale, Elmer learns to view his multicolored hide as special rather than shameful. Another popular McKee character, Melric the magician, made his debut in 1970 with the publication of *The Magician Who Lost His Magic,* a cautionary tale in which Melric loses his powers before realizing how much everyone in the kingdom has depended on his assistance. Wise man Kra reinstates Melric's magic, but advises him to teach the others self-sufficiency. Later titles feature Melric's struggles against Sondrak, the sorcerer intent upon usurping Melric's power and position in the court of the dependent King Ralphe. One of McKee's most appealing figures was introduced in *King Rollo and the Birthday* in 1979. Rollo, a fun-loving and lovable monarch, muddles through trials resembling those of childhood, assisted by the loyalty of his wife, his cat, a cook, and a magician.

Awards

McKee was awarded the Deutscher Jugendliteraturpreis (German Youth Literature Prize) for *Two Monsters* in 1987.

GENERAL COMMENTARY

Frances Farrer

SOURCE: "Scrambling to the Top of the Tree," in *The Times Educational Supplement,* No. 3416, December 18, 1981, p. 22.

My favourite King Rollo story goes as follows. King Rollo says he wants to climb a big tree, but everyone warns him against it. The magician says he'll dirty his hands, Cook says he'll tear his jacket, and Queen Gwen says he'll fall and hurt himself. Rollo listens patiently and starts to climb. The cat climbs with him, running up the trunk and upside-down along the branches.

All the spectators go on disapproving as Rollo climbs, falls back, and scrambles on until he reaches the top. "Here I am!" he cries, and tumbles back through the tree to the ground, where he sits grinning. "I told you that you'd dirty your hands/tear your jacket/fall and hurt yourself", they say. "But *I* said I'd climb, to the top", says the King.

King Rollo is the best known of several characters created by cartoonist David McKee, originally for children's books and now primarily for animated cartoons which are made by a small production company called King Rollo Films. Other stories are written and drawn by other artists. Victor and Maria, a bear and a little girl, have adventures rather similar to the King's. Towser is an amiable dog who does helpful things almost by accident. The feeling from them all is very positive—fantasy without sentimentality. . . .

"Everybody wants different things from children's films", says David McKee. "They want them to have morals, or to teach things, or to be full of action—by which they mean violence. Luckily what we want is often what kids want. They want magicians and dragons."

Though there are not always literally magicians and dragons, there is always the combination of imagination and pragmatism that children love. In one of the Victor and Maria films, for example, the bear Victor (who wears only a hat) goes into a gentleman's outfitters to buy a coat.

The sales assistant brings several coats and Victor tries them on, but buys a tie. This surprises the salesman (adult), but to Victor and Maria, the bear and the child, the choice is obvious and satisfactory: Victor prefers the tie. They go out, and Victor struts a little with his sartorial success.

Three people form the nucleus of King Rollo Films. David McKee is responsible for the origination, Leo Beltoft animates the films, and Clive Juster is the editor and business manager. They sail very close to the wind financially, but have turned down attractive offers from America to mass produce cartoons using their characters, because they were afraid of loss of quality.

Whether these fears were justified or not, quality has been maintained. The visual detail is often exquisite. In *The Birthday,* King Rollo, encouraged by the cook, makes a card for Queen Gwen. He scratches his head with his pen and the cat mirrors him precisely, scratching its head with its tail. The King decides on water colours, which are shown as being marbled. As he works, King Rollo tips his crown to the back of his head, for concentration.

To say that there is a conscious moral code suggests anaemia, which is not the case, but one does always find simple virtues being praised, and people and animals being helpful and friendly. Characters are encouraged to do things independently—"I won't always be here to tie your laces", says the magician to King Rollo—though when they suggest their own adventures, as in the tree story, the potential dangers are pointed out.

Showing-off tends to be discouraged. In one of the Rollo stories the King is out walking with the magician and sees a farmer eating bread. He wants to impress the farmer with the skill of the magician and so has the bread changed into all sorts of exotic food which the farmer rejects. "Please give me my bread back", he says, and in the end they do. All three share the bread. It was baked by the farmer's wife and is exceptionally good.

Success without compromise is a major achievement. David McKee and Leo Beltoft look rather puzzled by such phrases, however. "Basically we just do it because we enjoy it", they say. "There wouldn't be any point otherwise."

Audrey Laski

SOURCE: "Enjoying Life: An Interview with David McKee," in *British Book News Children's Books,* March, 1986, pp. 2-5.

I'm not sure what I expected David McKee to look like, but if I had a half-formed idea in the back of my mind of someone rather squat and chubby, like the children and monsters he draws, it was a mistake. He is tall and chunky, with the look of someone who spends time out of doors, perhaps one of Kingsley's sea-farers from *Westward Ho!,* for his voice makes it warmly clear that he is a man of Devon. His mother and brother still live in the West Country, but he describes himself as 'a gypsy . . . a vagabond', spending most of the time in Spain, but much also in France and Italy. From what he says, he has not left Devon behind, but taken it with him, 'as if, being brought up there, I'm full of it inside and can call on it whenever I want to'.

He also calls on the other places he knows. *I Hate My Teddy Bear* (which came up frequently in our conversation because of my passion for it) is set in his Spanish surroundings and peopled with family and friends; the Mr Benn stories take place in a street in Putney, and he is happily surprised that this causes no problems at all in the many foreign countries in which the films based on the stories are shown.

David McKee is one of those fortunate people who is able to live by doing what he enjoys and does supremely well; he puts it that he has never had to work since leaving Plymouth Art College, but what he means is that the work he loves is what the world wants him to do. He began by drawing cartoons for newspapers and for weeklies like *Punch,* but then the inimitable picture books began to come. *Bronto's Wings* was the first to be done, but the second to be published; published ahead of it was *Two Can Toucan,* which immediately established him as an artist with an independent vision and an individual line.

His most popular books are probably the King Rollo picture-strips, originally published as separate stories, but now available in sets of four. They have also been made into films which are shown in forty different countries. Despite his little fringe of beard, King Rollo is Everychild, doing things children like to do, supported by Queen and cat, enjoying life even when things go wrong; these are cheerful and reassuring books.

Some of McKee's individual picture books are less so. There is a disturbing message for parents in *Not Now, Bernard,* in which the child who can't get his preoccupied parents to notice the monster in the garden is eaten by it. However, it seems to be less worrying to children, who, McKee says, seem to relate first with Bernard and then with the monster. Presumably they understand instinctively, as the oblivious mother tucks the monster up, that Bernard has cheerfully become, rather than been engulfed by, this rather engagingly ugly violet-coloured beast. Here, as in several of his picture books, a wonderful new twist is put, on the last page, on the meaning of words that have been repeated many times during the story.

Still, it is a slightly equivocal ending, and this kind of mischievous playing with the idea of a happy ending is very typical of McKee's picture books. In *Two Admirals,* a book in a rather different style, with immensely detailed scenes of village life, the villagers find their days and nights made impossible by the two pompous and combative admirals who have retired there. Finally, or so the reader thinks, the inn-keeper comes up with a plan to neutralize them; life returns to normal. But McKee does not leave it there. Two retired generals decide to make the village their home: 'That was when the rest of the villagers left.' The picture of the fleeing villagers is too funny for regrets that the plan has not ultimately succeeded, but the fact remains that, having invented a happy ending, the maker has firmly undercut it (and perhaps incidentally said something sharp about the top-brass mind).

Again, his celebrated morality tale, *Tusk Tusk,* in which the aggressive black and white elephants battle until they have destroyed each other, has a hopeful ending: the grandchildren of the peaceable elephants, who have gone away into the depths of the jungle, come out all grey and live in peace; but then it has an ominous postscript; 'But recently the little ears and the big ears have been giving each other strange looks.' David McKee gently discounts the suggestion that this is bleak; he views it as a message 'to the adult that the child will be' to remember that 'we have to live with *all* the differences'. He also tells a sad and scary story about this book; apparently some teachers

From Elmer: The Story of a Patchwork Elephant, *written and illustrated by David McKee.*

have banned it as racist. Whether this is because it apportions blame equally between both colours of elephant for their wars, or because it proposes a melting-pot solution, or simply as a knee-jerk reaction to the words 'black' and 'white' is not clear; certainly it is a dotty response to a book whose overriding impulse is passionately anti-war and one that is actually no more about race than about any other divider. It is a relief to have seen it displayed in a recent exhibition of children's books for a multicultural society and to hear that a school in Nottingham has produced a stage version which its pupils have successfully taken to the Albert Hall, London.

Still, the blue and red monsters of his latest book, *Two Monsters,* which also tells a story of senseless conflict, may be safer exemplars (except that their line of invective—'You're a hairy, over-stuffed, empty-headed, boss-eyed mess!'—could lead some to suggest that they are intended as caricatures of politicians and ban the book as being unacceptably anti-Conservative or anti-Labour). Those not concerned with such matters may meanwhile enjoy the delicious visual effects David McKee obtains by setting these two brilliantly primary-coloured beasts against subtly shaded skies and rocks. He talks with great satisfaction about the developments in colour separation and printing that make such pictures possible, and pays tribute to the craftsmanship of Italian printers, who respect what they are doing in a way that is not universal. . . .

He enjoys making films of his books, but remains convinced of the value of the book as a thing in itself. Film, like music, is built on forward progression; he values in books the opportunity they give readers to stop, go back, to check information, to savour particular pleasures, to reinterpret in the light of later events, to reread. Or, as he puts it, 'If you turn a television set upside down, the goldfish falls off the top.'

It is because, unlike a television set, a book can be turned upside down, or through ninety degrees, that an artist like David McKee can play the games that make *I Hate My Teddy Bear* such a remarkable book, representing events in John's apartment-house vertically as well as horizontally so that we can watch the children come in through the front door and look into the flat along the corridor at the same time. This is probably his most audacious book, presenting a world at once realistic and surrealistic. The story-line is utterly simple: two children argue about the relative superiority of their teddy bears. But it takes place against a background of extraordinary events, particularly the passing-by of a number of enormous hands and feet, carried by workmen, suspended on ropes, trundled on carts or simply entering or leaving the picture with no visible means of support. Eventually they are silently explained by the exhibition, complete with visitors with catalogues, seen in the last picture, but no explanation can take away from their wonderful strangeness, reminiscent of Saul Steinberg's wild visions of New York roadworks.

David McKee recognizes Steinberg as one of the major influences on his work, the other being André François; both of them are draughtsmen who, like him, have seen, and want to represent, the astonishing quality of the real world, which other people so rarely notice. When he gave his mother *I Hate My Teddy Bear* to look at, she felt it opened up a new world, but almost immediately afterwards they saw a man in the forecourt of a local garage using a hose to wash down a hospital bed—exactly the sort of bizarre occurrence that the book makes commonplace. He sees adults and children sharing a certain bewilderment. 'If we see a row of nuns we feel it's strange— why are those ladies dressed the same?—adults don't know either.' He defends strongly the right of a children's picture book to be 'another art medium', and obviously approaches his work with the drives of a serious artist, though his tone is gently self-mocking: 'You start with a clean piece of paper, you make a mark on it and immediately it's wrong—you spend the rest of the time trying to put it right.'

But this concern never crowds out the other needs of the children for whom the books are first and foremost made. 'Primarily,' he says of the surreal *I Hate My Teddy Bear,* 'It's a love-story' and, of course, it is, in more than one way. Like all family members occasionally feel towards each other, John and Brenda sometimes feel like discarding Blue Teddy and Pink Teddy ruthlessly, bored with their familiarity, but then they defend their amazing qualities ("My Teddy can count backwards" . . . "So can mine") and take care to bring them home at the end. Meanwhile, the bears have reached their own understanding; it is over their heads, happily nestling together on a balcony on a basket chair that is appropriately sprouting greenery, that we at last see the great hand exhibition.

The absurdism in *I Hate My Teddy Bear* is incidental to the simple love-story; in *The Hill and the Rock* the whole story is based on an equally simple, but quite fantastic, notion. The great rock outside the Quests' little home on the top of the only hill in the neighbourhood is actually a stopper to prevent the air from rushing out of the earth, so its removal converts the hill into a deep valley. Given the initial premise, the rest of the events follow with perfect logic. Asked about the provenance of this extraordinary idea, McKee says, 'It just came.' He feels this with many of his stories: 'It's not as if you write them at all, it's as if you listen to them being told.'

This sense of being gifted, of getting gifts out of the blue, is part of the celebratory approach to life that makes McKee's work so pleasurable. 'Most of us have got more than we realize . . . I really enjoy life and I *know* I enjoy it.' And there sit his two monsters, back to back, on the mountain that was the barrier between them, which they have now reduced to rubble, chuckling, enjoying life.

TITLE COMMENTARY

📖 *BRONTO'S WINGS* (1964)

Margery Fisher

SOURCE: A review of *Bronto's Wings,* in *Growing Point,* Vol. 3, No. 2, July, 1964, p. 345.

[Here] is a composite prehistoric creature, a wistful fellow who wants to learn to fly so that he can go south with the migrating birds in winter. The eccentric illustrations are done in fine black line and are most impressive, with their geometrical patterns of clouds, falling leaves, tree-trunks, assembled birds; and there are plenty of the tiny details children like to search for in picture-books.

📖 *TWO CAN TOUCAN* (1964)

Virginia Kirkus' Service

SOURCE: A review of *Two Can Toucan,* in *Virginia Kirkus' Service,* Vol. XXXIII, No. 1, January 1, 1965, p. 2.

How the something got its something has been irresistible to tellers of tales since long before printing or Kipling setting it down *Just So.* The survivability of the folk stories and the benchmark made by Kipling in this vein depend upon imaginative detail and/or a basic humor. *Two Can Toucan* is nearly devoid of these characteristics. Maneuvering a drab, black toucan into a position to fall under color fast paints for his plumage and his bill is patently a mid-20th century gimmick, ignoring the essential "when the world was young" atmosphere on which such stories rely for their initial fascination. The illustrations make heavy use of color and are busy with ornamental detail which nevertheless provide nothing for younger eyes to discover.

Margaret F. O'Connell

SOURCE: A review of *Two Can Toucan,* in *The New York Times Book Review,* March 14, 1965, p. 30.

In *Two Can Toucan* there's a nameless, jobless black bird excluded by the other animals who seeks his fortune beyond the African jungle fringe. David McKee tells the bird's success story—finding his talent (carrying paint cans) and thereby his name—in a light, slight snippet style. His stylish illustrations in a riot of color, particularly of the paint dousing accident, are delightful.

📖 *MR. BENN, RED KNIGHT* (1967)

J. A. Cunliffe

SOURCE: A review of *Mr. Benn, Red Knight,* in *Children's Book News,* London, Vol. 3, No. 2, March-April, 1968, p. 72.

When Mr. Benn tries on a suit of armour in a little costumier's shop, he finds himself stepping into a strange world of desolate rocks. After rescuing a wronged dragon and riding him in triumph to a king's castle, he is bidden back into the costumier's shop, where he changes once more into his own sober black suit. He has had enough of adventures, for he refuses the armour and goes home to dream of other possible guises. The pictures alternate between rich colour and Steinbergian fantasies in line. Tricks are played with perspective which may be less worrying to a young child than to an adult. The book is visually stimulating, with its delicious colours and variety of textures, and text and pictures are well integrated. Children from four to six should love it, provided that the discordant ending is cut. The last two sentences assume a smug knowingness which spoils the story.

The Junior Bookshelf

SOURCE: A review of *Mr. Benn, Red Knight,* in *The Junior Bookshelf,* Vol. 32, No. 2, April, 1968, p. 95.

Mr. Benn—Red Knight is a way-out, not quite successfully integrated, picture-book. The story, of a little man of today who gets involved in a mediaeval adventure, is remarkably good. The drawings are good too, but difficult. The line drawings are finely detailed, in that crowded fashion which children so often like. Something is happening all over them. The coloured pictures are quite different; these play quite wilfully with the conventions of perspective. Interesting but confusing, but with lots of brilliant colour, for all its faults, this is a most exciting and unusual book.

Kirkus Service

SOURCE: A review of *Mr. Benn, Red Knight,* in *Kirkus Service,* Vol. XXXVI, No. 21, November 1, 1968, p. 1213.

Trying on the red armor means trying out the role of knight for Mr. Benn, who measures up: he arranges a reconciliation between the dragon replaced by a maker of matches and his employer-protector the king—who decides that his subjects should have the convenience of matches but he is entitled to "something a little different." The story within is stale and forced, the motion of assuming a new identity hardly novel and in this case triggered by expediency—Mr. Benn needs a costume for a party. Only the full-color cartoons are freshly imagined.

Gertrude B. Herman

SOURCE: A review of *Mr. Benn, Red Knight,* in *School Library Journal,* Vol. 15, No. 7, March, 1969, p. 144.

Marvelously inventive illustrations, some fine-lined and delicate, others bold and brilliantly colored, place David McKee firmly among such modern English artists as Burningham, Ambrus, Stobbs, Rose, and Wildsmith. The wordy tale of nondescript bank clerk, Mr. Benn, who while shopping for a costume to a fancy dress party finds himself transported into a medieval adventure, provides the story material for this superior picture book. Double spreads of intricately detailed line drawings alternate with double spreads of color: in a depiction of the costume shop all four walls are flattened out across two pages, while on another double spread three horizons, a castle, a forest, a river, and a procession of knights led by Mr. Benn—Red Knight mounted on the dragon are emblazoned. The masculine strength of the art work enhances the story and makes this a visual delight sure to spark the imaginations of young viewers.

☐ MARK AND THE MONOCYCLE (1968)

Margery Fisher

SOURCE: A review of *Mark and the monocycle,* in *Growing Point,* Vol. 7, No. 4, October, 1968, pp. 1196-97.

When Mark finds a piece of circus equipment in a junk shop, the owner invites him to try it but has no time to explain the braking system before Mark is away down the street, hurtling perilously through the traffic, across the sacred grass of the park, pursued by indignant townspeople. Then, halted forcibly by a blazing building, Mark uses the monocycle in the way intended—to cross a high wire—and becomes a hero. David McKee's fine scrawly technique is for the child who likes detail in pictures and is prepared to take time to examine the intricate visualising of emotion, action and background in this entertaining book.

John Coleman

SOURCE: "In the Beginning," in *New Statesman,* Vol. 76, No. 1964, November 1, 1968, pp. 596-97.

Mark and the Monocycle, told and drawn by David McKee is a splendid instance of text and pictures riding in tandem. The eponymous hero and his mount, found in a friendly antique shop, go careering through all kinds of traffic. Mark ends up cycling along a telegraph wire to bring aid to a burning building, a perfect denouement since he starts out naughty and finishes plain heroic. This well-produced book raises a further point. Every other double-page spread is uncoloured, a spiky incitement to do-it-yourself. My children yearn to get their felt pens wickedly weaving.

The Junior Bookshelf

SOURCE: A review of *Mark and the Monocycle,* in *The Junior Bookshelf,* Vol. 32, No. 6, December, 1968, pp. 357-58.

Detail . . . is the chief excellence of David McKee's *Mark and the Monocycle.* The story, in which Mark runs into all sorts of danger in his maiden ride, is of the kind which worries parents, but children will be as unruffled as Mark himself. Mr. McKee draws nice ugly people (rather as Gerald Rose does), some of whom look rather like contemporary public figures. There are in fact several touches of essentially adult humour, but plenty of the kind which children will enjoy. There is a charming page in which Mark demolishes a whole platoon of the Brigade of Guards. A jolly book, equally effective in colour and black-and-white.

Kirkus Reviews

SOURCE: A review of *Mark and the Monocycle,* in

Kirkus Reviews, Vol. XXXVII, No. 3, February 1, 1969, p. 95.

A runaway monocycle (or, U.S., unicycle) creates pandemonium, then, under control, enables Mark to pull off a life-saving stunt. The chase affords a few laughs (the sentry who cries "Who goes there," the stiff soldiers who topple in a row) but the finale—Mark riding the monocycle across a telegraph wire to a burning building—is not only impossible, it's also implausible in terms of Mark's ineptitude. Wobbly whimsey.

Doris M. Martin

SOURCE: A review of *Mark and the Monocycle,* in *School Library Journal,* Vol. 15, No. 7, March, 1969, p. 144.

Young Mark gets literally carried away while trying out an antique circus monocycle, in this drawn out, incredible, action-filled story. In trying to ride the monocycle given him by Mr. Legrand, owner of an antique shop, Mark discovers that he's unable to stop it. He speeds helplessly—but safely—through the city, attracting numerous curious onlookers, and plunges into an army parade ground where he knocks down, chain reaction-style, a line of red-uniformed soldiers. He finally jumps off the cycle across from a burning building and uses his cycling skill to ride along a telegraph wire, bring a rope to people stranded in the building, and make possible their rescue. Here, as in Mr. McKee's *Mr. Benn—Red Knight*, a small shop full of old and fascinating items, and a little shopkeeper, play major roles. The formats of both books are similar: black-and-white, delicate drawings (notably of streets and shops) alternate with spreads of big, brightly-colored, zany, cartoon-like illustrations. Though both story and art work are far more original and beautiful in *Mr. Benn—Red Knight,* those of *Mark and the Monocycle* are sufficiently amusing and well executed to invite laughter from young listeners in kindergarten and the first grade and from independently reading second graders.

Diane Farrell

SOURCE: A review of *Mark and the Monocycle,* in *The Horn Book Magazine,* Vol. XLV, No. 3, June, 1969, p. 296.

A boy who likes to poke around in an antique shop tries out an old circus monocycle which runs away with him. Mark finds himself leading a mad, merry chase across an English city, pursued by a barking dog, a shouting policeman, a reporter, a photographer, a park attendant, a crowd of people, and a troop of soldiers. A burning building diverts the crowd's attention, and Mark becomes a hero when he rides the monocycle over a telegraph wire to carry a rope to people trapped by the flames. Mark's adventure is reminiscent of the exploits of Edward Ardizzone's youthful protagonists, Tim and Paul. The illustrations, in thoroughly contemporary style, are bright, lively, and packed with detail. Especially effective are the drawings of the crowd, in which the author-artist differentiates the expression on each face.

ELMER: THE STORY OF A PATCHWORK ELEPHANT (1968; revised edition, 1989)

Kirkus Service

SOURCE: A review of *Elmer: The Story of a Patchwork Elephant,* in *Kirkus Service,* Vol. XXXVI, No. 22, November 15, 1968, p. 1281.

More vari-colored vacuity about being happy though different. Happier really, because it's Elmer who makes the other elephants laugh—especially when they don't recognize him in dye-sguise. The rains come, the patchwork reappears, and the elephants decide upon an annual tribute to Elmer—the others will pattern themselves after him (pages of polka-dotted and striped pachyderms), he will be gray like they. Ponderous.

J. A. Cunliffe

SOURCE: A review of *Elmer,* in *Children's Book News,* London, Vol. 3, No. 6, November/December, 1968, pp. 311, 313.

Elmer is a gay tale of a patchwork elephant who wanted to conform; but when he painted himself ordinary elephant-colour the herd became sad and lifeless without his jokes. A loud "BOOO" and a shower of rain restored patchwork, jokes and gaiety. Boldly coloured pictures fill each page, and there is a childlike simplicity of form—elephants cavorting, knobby trees, nursery jungle-creatures—and the colours have the jostling brilliance of a fairground. Children from about three to six will delight in it.

Eleanor Glaser

SOURCE: A review of *Elmer: The Story of a Patchwork Elephant,* in *School Library Journal,* Vol. 15, No. 5, January, 1969, p. 60.

A slight tale redeemed by big, brilliantly colored illustrations. Despite the fact that elephant Elmer's bright patchwork skin brings cheer to the other elephants in his herd, he decides that he's tired of being different. He finds a tree in the jungle with elephant-colored berries, shakes them to the ground, and rolls in their juices until he becomes a nice, typical gray. The elephants no longer recognize him; nor are they happy and cheerful as they used to be. When Elmer shouts "Boo," they realize who he is, and with their laughter show that they've appreciated his sense of humor as well as his colors. A rain storm washes away Elmer's ordinariness, the elephants declare a holiday, and Elmer adjusts to being different. The simple text and bold illustrations that parade through the book make it suitable for a read-aloud.

[*The following excerpts are from reviews of the revised edition published in 1989.*]

Liz Brooks

SOURCE: "Picturing Pets," in *The Times Literary Supplement*, No. 4501, July 7-13, 1989, p. 757.

Elmer is an elephant with a palpable inner life. McKee's style is modern and direct and he is adept at contriving striking effects with simple means. The illustrations are alive with incident from the first spread, where a herd of grey elephants fills the space in two-dimensional ranks and, with a cartoonist's economy of line, McKee imbues each with plausible character. Among an idiosyncratic host are doe-eyed, kindly trusting elephants, devious greedy ones, optimistic ones, attenuated, highly intelligent ones and crinkly old codger ones. All trunks are turned to the left, resisting the natural direction of the reading eye. But Elmer, the patchwork coloured elephant, appears on the next page turned defiantly to the right. Elmer having been introduced and his dilemma posed, the story moves straight into action, and in the turn of a page Elmer is off on an adventure in the jungle.

Picture-book elephants are massively sympathetic creatures, boisterous but gentle with a questing orality and ungainly bodies which they have not quite mastered. Perhaps it is these qualities which speak to children.

Publishers Weekly

SOURCE: A review of *Elmer*, in *Publishers Weekly*, Vol. 236, No. 10, September 8, 1989, p. 68.

Elmer the elephant is a colorful character. His heady optimism and unbridled sense of humor keep the entire community in a cheery mood. And Elmer's unusual multicolored checkerboard hide is the wonder of all the other elephants, who are characteristically gray. In spite of his sunny disposition, Elmer begins to feel conspicuous. He starts to believe the others are laughing at him because of his crazy patchwork coat. When Elmer discovers a bush in the jungle with elephant-colored berries, he shakes the bush and rolls in a berry mash until he is as gray as the others. Now no one seems to notice him; for a time he enjoys his anonymity, but after a while he begins to realize just how quiet and dull things are when he's not around. Finally the practical joker in Elmer emerges, and he soon has the whole gang laughing again. McKee's gentle humor and love of irony are in full force in this celebration of individuality and laughter. Well-designed spreads are washed with stunning color and the use of textured, painted and airbrushed surfaces contributes to the powerful visual impression.

123456789 BENN (1970)

The Times Literary Supplement

SOURCE: "Pictures With a Purpose," in *The Times Literary Supplement*, No. 3566, July 2, 1970, p. 716.

David McKee is . . . an artist who requires concentration. *123456789 Benn* is a second episode in the fantasy life of Mr. Benn, who has only to try on a suit of clothes in a little side-street shop to become involved in the life of the suit. This time, Benn chooses convict's stripes, and manages in a short visit to prison to bring hope and a sense of purpose to its gloomy inmates. Mr. McKee has an eccentric, entirely engaging trick of treating a flat piece of paper as if it were spherical; detailed, delicate Indian ink drawings take turns with gaily-coloured paintings; the draughtsmanship and the imagination are both impressive.

Publishers Weekly

SOURCE: A review of *123456789 Benn*, in *Publishers Weekly*, Vol. 198, No. 7, August 17, 1970, p. 50.

For the boy who thinks fairy tales are silly, here is a fantasy that will change his mind. This is a brilliantly illustrated story of a man who enters a prison by trying on a convict's uniform. He enters into a prison life that he changes from dismal gray and black to a kaleidoscope of bold color. The story is such inspired silliness that it could brighten the viewpoint of the most pragmatic computerizer—it could even blow his mind, *123456789 Benn* is such a good book.

The Junior Bookshelf

SOURCE: A review of *123456789 Benn*, in *The Junior Bookshelf*, Vol. 34, No. 5, October, 1970, p. 276.

David McKee's is quite a different brand of charm. The delight of his books—and few artists today give such direct and unalloyed pleasure—comes largely from his own delight in his creation. We have met Mr. Benn before. He is the man who visits a mysterious costume shop, with results at once alarming and hilarious. This time he tries on a convict costume and finds himself in gaol. This is uncommonly like the real thing—except that real criminals tend not to weep about their troubles. Mr. Benn has a few practical suggestions to make, and the inmates very quickly transform their prison. When Mr. Benn makes his way back to the charging room, via the Governor's office, he leaves behind a very colourful and gay penal institution. Mr. McKee plays entertaining games with perspective, but it is not so much these technical tricks as the shrewdness of his observation and the sweet simplicity of his humour which makes this so enchanting a book. We shall see more of Mr. Benn.

Margaret A. Dorsey

SOURCE: A review of *123456789 Benn*, in *School Library Journal*, Vol. 17, No. 2, October 15, 1970, p. 123.

In this attractive picture book, Mr. Benn returns to the costume shop he found in the author-artist's well-received

Mr. Benn—Red Knight. This time he tries on a convict's uniform and thus finds himself in a prison filled with men weeping over the inedible food and the gloomy surroundings. Mr. Benn becomes friends with convict Smasher Lagru, who describes himself as "the boss around here," and suggests that they utilize the resources of the prison paint shop and uniform shop as well as the culinary talents of some inmates to change things. They do so and now serve their time happily. The question is, of course, why they didn't think of that before. Hopefully, most children will pay less attention to the slight story than to the striking pictures—half line drawings, half dazzling full-color paintings—which are filled with action and detail in the artist's good-humored, graphic modern style. It's a feast for the eyes, if ordinary oatmeal for the ears.

Selma G. Lanes

SOURCE: A review of *123456789 Benn*, in *The New York Times Book Review*, November 8, 1970, p. 51.

Lest serious themes spell picture-book gloom, David McKee provides a surprisingly cheerful primer for prison reform in *123456789 Benn*. By means of an ingenious plot device that allows the hero to try new life roles, Mr. Benn is temporarily incarcerated. The wide-eyed reader joins him in a prison breakfast of cold coffee and burnt toast, a morning diversion of rock-crushing and a fanciful spree of cell decoration. The experience, wholly engrossing and humanizing, makes for a refreshingly novel tale.

📖 THE MAGICIAN WHO LOST HIS MAGIC (1970)

The Junior Bookshelf

SOURCE: A review of *The Magician Who Lost His Magic*, in *The Junior Bookshelf*, Vol. 34, No. 6, December, 1970, p. 345.

[David McKee] is a sophisticated artist and humorist. He draws complicated pictures, in colour and line, which are packed with relevant and very funny detail. Melric, whose magic runs out, goes through a number of awkward and hilarious adventures before getting a recharge. He returns just in time to save the king from defeat. A good spell is called for, and Melric rises to the occasion, turning all the enemy soldiers into black cats. The castle dogs complete the rout. This is not vintage McKee but good fun for all that.

Gabrielle Maunder

SOURCE: A review of *The Magician Who Lost His Magic*, in *The School Librarian*, Vol. 18, No. 4, December, 1970, p. 502.

David Mckee has two great gifts which will be familiar to those who have seen his former books—*Two-can Toucan, Elmer,* and the books about Mr Benn; these are his ability to tell a ridiculous story with an absolutely straight face, and the other his talent to make each spread interesting by the way in which he divides it into sections.

In this story of a magician who over-indulges his fellow countrymen with magic help with their daily chores, his work is well up to standard. The delightful chaos which befalls the population when Melric's magic is taken from him, and they find themselves thrown back on their own resources is witty and ideal for the young of four and up, though humour in the illustration will give it a place on the shelves of a much older child.

Kevin Crossley-Holland

SOURCE: A review of *The Magician Who Lost His Magic,* in *The Spectator,* Vol. 225, No. 7432, December 5, 1970, p. xv.

A magician loses his powers, travels, learns the lesson that magic must be put to sensible ends, and regains them. The pictures are a hive of activity but both they and the text are far too earthy. No sense of strangeness, or of wonder.

Mary B. Mason

SOURCE: A review of *The Magician Who Lost His Magic,* in *School Library Journal,* Vol. 17, No. 4, December 15, 1970, pp. 36-7.

"Melric was the king's magician . . . If the King wanted to swim, Melric made the sun come out." But one day his magic fails, and all the people of the kingdom are totally helpless, so dependent had they been on Melric. In an effort to regain his power, Melric visits a witch, a wizard, and the wise man, Kra. The latter restores his magic, but warns Melric he will lose it if he does not use it judiciously and teach the people to help themselves. Returning to the castle which is under attack, Melric changes the invaders into cats and sets the dogs on them, announces that "'In the future you must manage without me'" and that "'Magic will only be used on very special occasions'"—and even undertakes to learn how to make his own bed. This effectively told story is complemented by alternating black-and-white pen sketches and color illustrations characterized by expressive, comic detail. The well-designed book has an uncluttered, balanced look, and will be useful for storytelling.

📖 THE MAN WHO WAS GOING TO MIND THE HOUSE: A NORWEGIAN FOLK-TALE (1972)

The Times Literary Supplement

SOURCE: "As Old as the Hills," in *The Times Literary Supplement,* No. 3692, December 8, 1972, p. 1498.

A Norwegian folk-tale, the old favourite about the farmer

and his wife who exchanged roles, is retold and illustrated by David McKee in *The Man who was Going to Mind the House,* a story that looks suspiciously like an early attempt to promote the feminine mystique. The mind-boggling disasters that Ulrik brings upon himself as house-minder make you think that he could not have been much use as a farmer either. The story is told with pace and wit and Mr McKee's bright, dramatic illustrations make good use of comic-strip technique.

Gabrielle Maunder

SOURCE: A review of *The Man Who Was Going to Mind the House,* in *The School Librarian,* Vol. 21, No. 1, March, 1973, p. 285.

[Always] good for a belly-laugh is David McKee's humour, completely and reassuringly of this world. His story of the original male chauvinist pig, confident in his opinion that a wife's life is ease and comfort, and then left to discover for himself its trials, is delicious. The simplicity of line, the clarity of the colours in the drawings showing the dreadful sequence of domestic disaster are splendid and, what is more, partner accurately the text, vital in books for children who depend upon illustrations to follow the story.

The Junior Bookshelf

SOURCE: A review of *The Man Who Was Going to Mind the House,* in *The Junior Bookshelf,* Vol. 37, No. 2, April, 1973, p. 102.

A Norwegian version of the well-known folk-tale. There is very little text and the story is sometimes told by a series of pictures in sequence. The usual disasters which bewilder the man who thinks he can keep house, offer an opportunity for dramatic and amusing illustrations of the kind which is so effective by this artist. In nearly every picture, the hero's unchildlike son appears to disconcert his clumsy parent, a species of devastating comment on his ineptness.

From the point of view of reading aloud, this version cannot compare with Wanda Gag's *Gone is Gone,* but the illustrations are larger and more suited to a visual age perhaps.

Zena Sutherland

SOURCE: A review of *The Man Who Was Going to Mind the House,* in *Bulletin of the Center for Children's Books,* Vol. 27, No. 1, September, 1973, p. 13.

Stiffly executed but colorful pictures illustrate an adequate retelling of the Norwegian folktale about a man who changes places with his wife for a day. Convinced that he will have a day of ease while his wife toils in the field, the man goes from one domestic catastrophe to another: any moral or lesson is implicit, since the story ends abruptly when the wife comes home to find no dinner, the cow hanging over the edge of the roof, and her husband falling headfirst down the chimney into a pot of porridge. First published in England, the story is dependent on the exaggeration of a stretched situation and the action in illustration for its minimal appeal; it has little of

From The Magician and the Petnapping, *written and illustrated by David McKee.*

the narrative quality of most folktales and even less of the cadence of oral tradition when read aloud.

📖 *SIX MEN* (1972)

The Times Literary Supplement

SOURCE: "Whispers Down the Wastepipe, Fables for Our Times," in *The Times Literary Supplement,* No. 3692, December 8, 1972, pp. 1494-95.

Mr McKee is not afraid to point a moral, and the one here comes across loud and clear—get yourself an army and a war is bound to follow. Or the story can be read simply as the recurring history of man: the book starts with six men who set out in search of a place where they can live and work in peace, and it ends in much the same way, but between the beginning and the end comes any amount of tyranny and bloodshed. Mr McKee's scratchy black drawings, reminiscent sometimes of cave paintings and sometimes of the Bayeux tapestry, offer plenty of interesting detail to the eye.

📖 *LORD REX: THE LION WHO WISHED* (1973)

Kirkus Reviews

SOURCE: A review of *Lord Rex: The Lion Who Wished,* in *Kirkus Reviews,* Vol. XLI, No. 22, November 15, 1973, p. 1259.

Lord Rex, the lion who "always wanted things to be different from the way they were," just happens all in one day to run into a magic butterfly, elephant, tropical bird, kangaroo, and giraffe, so that each time he says "I wish I could have wings/ a trunk/ a tail/ hind legs/ a neck like yours"—it's done. Of course when he then sees his freakish reflection in the pond he's happy to note that there is also a magic lion standing by to change him back. It's an old story and McKee makes no notable improvements, but the moral is easily grasped (if not articulated) at this level and the bouncy, glowing cartoons—of Rex in a fanciful jungle looping the loop with his jazzy butterfly wings (never mind that one upside-down sky glide owes a lot to Snoopy), displaying his splendid feathered tail, or arching that ungainly neck—cater to a preschooler's sense of the ridiculous.

Publishers Weekly

SOURCE: A review of *Lord Rex: The Lion Who Wished,* in *Publishers Weekly,* Vol. 204, No. 22, November 26, 1973, pp. 37-8.

Another tale with the urgent message: Be yourself, this one features pictures which are hilariously persuasive. The lion wishes for the wings of a butterfly, an elephant's trunk, a giraffe's neck, the great tail of a bird and all his

wishes are granted. Then he catches sight of himself in a pond and—yuck!—wishes instantly to be a plain lion again. The young reader will love the illustrations, showing the gradual disintegration of a noble animal, and will be relieved at the end.

Alice Ehlert

SOURCE: A review of *Lord Rex: The Lion Who Wished,* in *School Library Journal,* Vol. 20, No. 6, February, 1974, p. 54.

Lord Rex the lion is always wishing he were different. One day he meets a succession of animals who have the power to grant his desires, so Rex ends up with the wings of a butterfly, the trunk of an elephant, the tail of a bird, the legs of a kangaroo, and the neck of a giraffe. A glance into a pool of water makes him realize how ridiculous he looks. Fortunately Lord Rex is allowed one more wish which he uses wisely albeit predictably to return to his original form. The colorful, childlike pictures are more entertaining than the overly familiar story, but Charles Dougherty's *Wisher* tells the same tale much more effectively.

📖 *THE MAGICIAN AND THE SORCERER* (1974)

Margery Fisher

SOURCE: A review of *The Magician and the Sorcerer,* in *Growing Point,* Vol. 13, No. 3, September, 1974, p. 2461.

Melric the King's magician, confronted by Sondrak, a sorcerer visiting the court whose ambitions are secret and dangerous, overcomes him because he follows the advice of the local wise man and is mindful of "the power of laughter". David McKee shows his usual virtuosity in the variety of his graphic devices, from split-level interiors packed with incident to dramatically simple scenes (as when the Sorcerer repels a flight of arrows by magic). Fresh, lively colour; caricatured faces; a pointed narrative in pictures and text.

The Times Literary Supplement

SOURCE: "Enticing Ingredients," in *The Times Literary Supplement,* No. 3785, September 20, 1974, p. 1011.

Incidental detail is an important part of David McKee's work. . . . In his new book, **The Magician and the Sorcerer,** the illustrations offer all kinds of comic detail to delight the mind and eye, whether in vast set pieces, like the banquet scene, or in the rapidly moving comic-strip sequences which are vital to the action. The story is another thriller, about the confrontation between Melric the good magician and Sondrak the power-mad sorcerer, whom Melric defeats by making people laugh at him.

David McKee's television series, **Mr Benn,** demonstrates, like **The Magician and the Sorcerer,** that this author is particularly drawn to characters who are wary of popular enthusiasms and opinions and rely on humour and common sense to show them the way out of their problems.

R. Baines

SOURCE: A review of *The Magician and the Sorcerer,* in *The Junior Bookshelf,* Vol. 38, No. 5, October, 1974, pp. 273-74.

The king knows a simple definition of the duties of a court magician: he should give his royal master more and more power. Melric, the magician, doubts the wisdom of doing this, so a sorcerer, Sondrak, is auditioned for Melric's job. The true magician discovers that Sondrak's magic is evil, and that he can be defeated by the power of laughter. A puddle magically turns into ice beneath the sorcerer's feet and the watching crowd is roused to mocking merriment as Sondrak slithers and slides.

David McKee works as a cartoonist, and his illustrations for his story are lively and full of incident. The characters are cheerfully, not distastefully, ugly.

This is a satisfactory book but I am not convinced that it justifies its author's apparent anticipation of numerous sequels.

Josephine Carr

SOURCE: A review of *The Magician and the Sorcerer,* in *School Library Journal,* Vol. 21, No. 4, December 15, 1974, p. 38.

A court magician-in-residence must work some hocus-pocus in order to drive out an ambitious, evil sorcerer. After consulting his sister the witch, Melric follows her advice and uses laughter to mortify his adversary. Despite funny watercolor cross-sections of palace life that young children will love to pore over, the lame story falls flat.

Edward Hudson

SOURCE: A review of *The Magician and the Sorcerer,* in *Children's Book Review,* Vol. IV, No. 4, Winter, 1974-75, p. 145.

David McKee is a man full of ideas and with a sense of humour which enables him to convert them into words and pictures which will appeal to young children. This is his second story about Melric the magician and it involves an adversary, Sondrak the sorcerer, who seeks the King's favour by promising him more power. How Melric overcomes Sondrak with the power of laughter and the help of Kra, 'the wise man, who lives on top of a

mountain', makes an enjoyable story, but it is the illustrations, many of them painted with the detail of the old *Babar* tradition, which will appeal most to six to eight-year-olds. If David McKee intends to follow this second adventure with others and to develop his main character he could produce a series as popular as *Pugwash* or *Noggin the Nog.*

📖 ***THE DAY THE TIDE WENT OUT . . . AND OUT . . . AND OUT . . . AND OUT . . . AND OUT . . . AND OUT (1975)***

Kirkus Reviews

SOURCE: A review of *The Day the Tide Went Out . . . And Out . . . And Out . . . ,* in *Kirkus Reviews,* Vol. XLIV, No. 5, March 1, 1976, pp. 252-53.

McKee's jungle animals, who look like stuffed toys, spend their time making sand castles on the beach—and on the back of the beachkeeper, an odd creature who, you'll soon discern, needs only the castle/hump to be a camel. And that of course is what he does become on the day that the tide goes out for good and he can no longer wash off the sand, as was his custom. As for the other, pyramid-shaped castles on the beach, they become tourist attractions after the animals retreat to the jungle; "people . . . look at them and wonder how they were built." But McKee's few grains of inspiration just never pack down, and what might have come off as a passable joke on the camel is buried here under those larger cones of sand, which resemble neither pyramids, castles nor natural configurations.

Children's Book Review Service

SOURCE: A review of *The Day the Tide Went Out . . . And Out . . . And Out . . . And Out . . . And Out . . . And Out,* in *Children's Book Review Service,* Vol. 4, No. 10, May, 1976, p. 83.

The illustrations in this book are bright, whimsical, and intriguing. The story line is clear enough for a four year old to follow, yet an eight year old's interest would be held. This book gives a folk-tale explanation of why animals are in jungles, how the camel got his hump, where pyramids and deserts come from. Questions requiring factual answers are apt to be stimulated. Although the animals never talk, the narrative description and illustration easily communicate the animals' feelings to the reader. A good story to read aloud.

Helen Gregory

SOURCE: A review of *The Day the Tide Went Out . . . And Out . . . And Out . . . ,* in *School Library Journal,* Vol. 22, No. 9, May, 1976, p. 52.

A triple pourquoi story: how the desert came to be, how the pyramids were built, and how the camel got his hump.

Once, when "the tide went in and out endlessly," the jungle animals built sand castles on the beach, which the beachkeeper flattened. The animals would tease the beachkeeper by building a sand castle on his back while he slept, in order to make him chase them. Instead, when he'd wake, he'd lie down by the sea and wait for the tide to wash it off. But one day, the jungle animals made a bargain with the tide to stay out. The simple and direct text balanced with large, clear, and glowing watercolors outlined in ink by the author-illustrator of *Lord Rex: the Lion Who Wished* (1973) make this perfect for story hour.

THE MAGICIAN AND THE PETNAPPING (1976)

Joan E. Bezrudczyk

SOURCE: A review of *The Magician and the Petnapping,* in *School Library Journal,* Vol. 23, No. 7, March, 1977, pp. 133-34.

Melric the magician gives the king a pet troon (a cuddly pink beastie) which becomes his inseparable companion. A group of disgruntled citizens complain that their pets are missing, but it's not until his pet troon is also stolen that the king orders Melric to solve the petnapping or else lose his position. By turning himself into an animal Melric is able to return the villagers' pets and foil the evil sorcerer, Sondrak, who planned to take over Melric's job. This whimsical, fast-paced story, illustrated with humorous full-color cartoon-style illustrations, has great appeal and is suitable for individual or group reading.

Barbara Elleman

SOURCE: A review of *The Magician and the Petnapping,* in *Booklist,* Vol. 73, No. 17, May 1, 1977, p. 1354.

It is only when his own pet, a pink troon, is "petnapped" that the king calls in Melric, his magician, to solve the mystery of the kingdom's disappearing pets. Melric and his cousin, Guz the wizard, discover that the troublemaker is Sondrak the sorcerer, who plots to get Melric's job. Refusing to be outwitted, Melric and Guz concoct some hocus-pocus of their own and the animals cause such earsplitting din that Sondrak releases the spell and with a gasp, disappears. McKee creates a marvelous menagerie of kooky animals and characters in a gay array of colors, topped off by the hot-pink troon and skillfully melded into a funny story which promises a span of joyous investigation.

TWO ADMIRALS (1977)

Kirkus Reviews

SOURCE: A review of *Two Admirals,* in *Kirkus Reviews,* Vol. XLV, No. 20, October 15, 1977, p. 1095.

McKee's two admirals, both of them famous and boastful, arrive separately in a peaceful village and so disrupt it with their childish, noisy, and/or dangerous competitions (who can make a cow jump higher, who can run across the road more often) that half the population moves away. The innkeeper finally settles them down by offering a prize to the admiral who can keep the peace longest—but if this is leading up to some kind of home truth McKee deliberately blows it by introducing two famous generals whose arrival drives out the other half of the town's population. Till then the pages have teemed with McKee's primitivist villagers, who are more grotesque than his usual cartoon figures—all those gaping, tonsilbaring shouts—but the visual din is as pointless as the story.

Marjorie Lewis

SOURCE: A review of *Two Admirals,* in *School Library Journal,* Vol. 24, No. 4, December, 1977, p. 45.

Two admirals drive the inhabitants of a small English town to distraction with their nonsensical contests: who can fall down stairs without crying; who can make a cow jump higher; who can run across a road more often. The problem is solved when they are given a clever challenge: which one can keep the peace longest. The villagers breathe a collective sigh of relief—until two generals arrive. At that point, the entire village picks up and leaves. McKee is a talented artist, but the busy full-color illustrations fail to generate the needed focus and excitement that might bring his cardboard story to life.

Margaret M. Nichols

SOURCE: A review of *Two Admirals,* in *Children's Book Review Service,* Vol. 6, No. 6, Winter, 1978, p. 52.

The illustrations in this book are busy, but they are not of the same caliber as Richard Scarry's. Small children will not be attracted to this book. It is *Punch* humor, suitable for adults, but not for pre-schoolers. The ending of the book implies that bullies can win and get their way, not a concept to be recommended to children.

TUSK TUSK (1978)

Carolyn O'Grady

SOURCE: "Paradise Lost and Found," in *The Times Educational Supplement,* No. 3285, June 23, 1978, p. 21.

In *Tusk Tusk* David McKee makes little attempt to characterize his elephants; they are symbols, but it does not matter. In this simple moral tale, a first lesson in tolerance, we are told how once the black elephants hated all the white elephants. They fought each other to the death leaving the world apparently unpopulated until the peace-loving elephants, who had fled into the forest, emerged to a happier existence. However, "recently the little ears and big ears have been giving each other strange looks." The illustrations are exceptionally ingenious: trunks become guns, revolvers and hands to point an accusing finger. The colours are especially lovely—reminiscent of candy floss, sherbert and Brighton rock: a paradise lost or found depending on your age.

Elaine Moss

SOURCE: "Going to the Pictures," in *The Times Literary Supplement,* No. 3991, September 29, 1978, p. 1087.

Tusk Tusk by David McKee is a humorous treatment of race antagonism and its cure. "Once all elephants in the world were black or white. They loved all creatures but hated each other." Like Michael Foreman, David McKee can use humour and his considerable talents as an artist to make young people think about current issues. Militant black-and-white elephants gun for each other with their trunks—while peaceable black-and-white elephants go deep into the jungle, their progeny emerging grey.

Publishers Weekly

SOURCE: A review of *Tusk Tusk,* in *Publishers Weekly,* Vol. 214, No. 25, December 25, 1978, p. 59.

McKee's seriocomic fable is illustrated by fine paintings in full color and designed to tickle little ones while conveying a warning. Once upon a time, all the elephants in the world were either ebony black or glaring white. Except for a few pacifists who escaped, all the elephants perished in battles between black and white. That's why we have only gray pachyderms today, descendants of the survivors. All have been living together in peace and love since the great war. But one day, elephants with big ears began looking suspiciously at those with little ears. . . . Adult fans of James Thurber will be reminded of his classic, *The Last Flower,* but McKee uses the theme in a different and striking way.

Ruth M. McConnell

SOURCE: A review of *Tusk Tusk,* in *School Library Journal,* Vol. 26, No. 5, January, 1980, p. 59.

A well-intentioned parable against intolerance is conveyed in simple text and bold cartoons by the British illustrator of the more sophisticated *Mr. Benn: Red Knight* (1968). The world's elephants, seen as all black or all white, hate one another and fight to the death—except for the peace loving ones who flee to the stylized maze of jungle. Their descendants emerge as peaceful—and gray. "But," the book ends, "recently the little ears and the big ears have been giving each other strange looks," while small birds (their memories longer than the elephants' it seems) clutch their heads in "here we go again" poses. The moral is muddied as a final cameo shows elephants with medium

ears clasping trunks ("I'll love you when you're more like me" for tots?), while the ironic caption of *"Viva la différence"* under the opening cameo of a pachyderm-punch-out will also be lost on small fry. Clever in concept, McKee's symbolic beasts are monstrosities with humanoid stances and faces, their trunks portrayed as perches for butterflies, as hands to whisper behind, as fists, or as silhouettes of fingers triggering pistols.

Publishers Weekly

SOURCE: A review of *Tusk Tusk,* in *Publishers Weekly,* Vol. 237, No. 15, April 13, 1990, pp. 63-4.

Two bands of elephants, one black and one white, "loved all creatures, but they hated each other." Each group keeps to its own side of the jungle, until a war breaks out between them, and the peace-loving elephants from both sides take cover in the jungle. After a bitter battle, all the elephants lay dead; no elephants are seen for many years. One day the descendants of the peace-lovers emerge: "They were grey." The book ends on an ironic note as members of the new grey breed notice that they fall into two groups once again, each with differently shaped ears. The stylized renderings of the elephants and their environs make this straightforward book about prejudice easier to digest in an allegorical sense; the story becomes both accessible and illuminating. In clear, bold illustrations that celebrate shape and color, McKee incorporates several witty touches: the elephants' trunks become weapons, the "darkest jungle" is portrayed as a giant maze. Although the book stands on its own merit, it might also offer an excellent point of departure for discussion between parent and child.

THE MAGICIAN AND THE BALLOON (1978; republished as *Melric and the Balloon,* 1988)

M. Crouch

SOURCE: A review of *The Magician and the Balloon,* in *The Junior Bookshelf,* Vol. 43, No. 2, April, 1979, p. 98.

If you want proof that the ideal illustrator of a picture book is the author, then David McKee provides it. He has written a neat and amusing story, but his pictures extend it enormously, giving it a setting and all sorts of subsidiary action for which there is barely a hint in the text. Melric the magician saves the country from the king's benevolent tidy-mindedness, or at least he wins time by fooling the king most agreeably. (He confuses the royal map-maker by altering the shape of a single island every day, thereby postponing indefinitely the completion of the master-plan.) It was all unnecessary, as it happens; all the king wanted was the fun of making plans for change: he never intended them to be carried out. Every one of Mr. McKee's double-spreads is bustling with activity, much of it very funny. There is material here for a hundred stories, and the reader can write them for himself.

Frances Ball

SOURCE: A review of *The Magician and the Balloon,* in *The School Librarian,* Vol. 30, No. 3, September, 1982, p. 223.

Here is another book from David McKee's 'Melric the Magician' series. At one level the story describes how Melric tricks the king into doing what he wants. The king is very much a child dressed in a crown. He combines the advantages of royal position and childlike enthusiasm. Melric keeps him under control. Within that story is a hint that it is unwise to meddle in other people's lives.

Text and illustrations appear on the pages in varied arrangements. There is a pleasant contrast between the busy pictures of the opening pages, where the king's subjects go about their business, and the long strips of sky, where we see Melric travelling in his balloon. The combination of clear, humorous pictures and simple but subtle text works well.

Moira Small

SOURCE: A review of *Melric and the Balloon,* in *Books for Keeps,* No. 52, September, 1988, p. 9.

Another funny and warmhearted book from David McKee. Children who know Melric will always want to know what he's up to . . . and will enjoy meeting Kra the wise man and Mertel the witch, who is so domesticated! In this story the Royal Balloon is to the fore as the King plans changes to his kingdom . . . until Melric grows alarmed and convinces him that everything's all right just as it is.

Introduce Melric to a child today and you'll both be delighted. There's much to look at and plenty to consider in this thoughtful tale.

BIG GAME BENN (1979)

Margery Fisher

SOURCE: A review of *Big Game Benn,* in *Growing Point,* Vol. 18, No. 4, November, 1979, pp. 3607-08.

Revisiting the shop of magic clothes, adventurous Mr. Benn finds himself, suitably attired, whisked off to Africa as leader of a hunting party where, by a series of stratagems, he saves snake, monkeys, giraffe, hippo and even elephant from the guns. The providential visit of a camera-salesman to the camp completes a comic statement about conservation in which the message is lightened by the author's subtly teasing colour-range and odd perspectives and the offhand brilliance with which he suggests a jungle atmosphere.

The Junior Bookshelf

SOURCE: A review of *Big Game Benn,* in *The Junior Bookshelf,* Vol. 44, No. 2, April, 1980, p. 63.

Benn visits his special costume shop, dons a hunter's outfit and steps through a magic door into the jungle. Posing as a guide to a group who are intent on shooting the animals, he thwarts their killing by appealing to their vanity—the biggest for the greatest. With the help of a herd of shaking elephants, he persuades the hunters to change their guns for cameras.

A pleasant fantasy, it is brightly and amusingly illustrated, the packed vegetation of the jungle being particularly well represented; whimsical full-page line drawings alternate with the striking colour pictures.

KING ROLLO AND THE BIRTHDAY; KING ROLLO AND THE BREAD; KING ROLLO AND THE NEW SHOES (1979)

Ursula Robertshaw

SOURCE: A review of *King Rollo and the Birthday* and others, in *The Illustrated London News,* Vol. 267, No. 6977, December, 1979, p. 141.

David McKee's **King Rollo** books are of small format (about 4 by 5 inches) to appeal to small people—they would be ideal for the Christmas stocking or for the tree for a three- to five-year-old. Brightly illustrated, the three new volumes in the series tell of Rollo's battle to do up his own shoelaces, of his making a birthday card for Queen Gwen, and of his kindly meant but misdirected attempts to change a peasant's loaf into various more exotic foods. The words used in the minimal text are not, I am glad to say, restricted to "the-cat-sat-on-the-mat" type of vocabulary: the author clearly feels it is never too early to learn to spell magician, delicious or spaghetti.

Cliff Moon

SOURCE: A review of *King Rollo and the New Shoes* and others, in *The School Librarian,* Vol. 28, No. 1, March, 1980, pp. 31-2.

Little books for little hands are always popular. These are typical McKee flights of fancy, comprising pictures with a short caption under each. Because the captions match up well with the illustrations the stories are suitable for young children who have just started to read; and the picture sequences are simple enough to be used as picture story books with 'non-readers'. The stories are about a fat king and his personal magician in familiar domestic dilemmas like attempting to tie shoe-laces and paint a birthday card.

Denise M. Wilms

SOURCE: A review of *King Rollo and the Birthday* and others, in *Booklist,* Vol. 76, No. 15, April 1, 1980, p. 1129.

These three small books are child sized, centered, and

packaged; each tells a brief episode involving King Rollo, a child-king possessed of an appropriately ingenuous quality. In **King Rollo and the Birthday,** the little king takes his cook's advice and paints a homemade birthday card for Queen Gwen even though he finds it hard to be imaginative and draw well. Still, it turns out to be Gwen's favorite, and the only one that's not a duplicate. In **King Rollo and the Bread,** Rollo and his magician try to razzle dazzle a peasant by changing his hearty loaf into chocolate cake, spaghetti, ice cream, etc. The peasant remains unmoved however, and keeps wanting his homemade bread. In the end they all share it happily and agree it's delicious. **King Rollo and the New Shoes** is perhaps the most strikingly childlike in dealing with Rollo's getting new lace-up shoes and learning to tie them. The illustrations are full-color cartoons with light lines and good humor to match the text. With their box casing, the books will be eye-catchers for borrowers or owners.

Kirkus Reviews

SOURCE: A review of *King Rollo and the Birthday* and others, in *Kirkus Reviews,* Vol. XLVIII, No. 12, June 15, 1980, p. 777.

Three diminutive (4 1/8 x 5 1/4) volumes, bound in paper over boards, and enclosed in a slipcase: three teeny-tiny stories of some slight, raffish charm and varying amounts of substance—varying, that is, from almost none to as much as one might expect (except perhaps from Sendak), given the format. The least of the lot is **King Rollo and the Birthday,** wherein the King—who, though bearded, is unquestionably a child (one of the series' charms)—is prevailed upon to send Queen Gwen a birthday card of his own inexpert making; and since everyone else sends her the store card he had first selected, his is indeed "different" and "special." The one that's continuously engaging is **King Rollo and the Bread.** Here, the king and the magician—one of a stock company that includes a bossy cook—meet a farmer who has for lunch only a loaf of bread; and, it turns out, wants only that loaf of bread. King Rollo has the magician turn it first into roast chicken, then into chocolate cake, then spaghetti, then ice cream; but each time the farmer begs for his bread back. And finally, of course, King Rollo and the magician share the bread with him. "Your magician is clever," says the farmer; "So is your wife," says the king. **King Rollo and the New Shoes** casts the king more obviously as a child: his new shoes—and he already has, in a dandy picture, "lots and lots"—are different because they have laces. So the magician, scorning to use magic ("A waste"), shows him how to loop and tie them; and after some to-do, he does. Memorable these are not, but they are diverting.

Bessie Condos Egan

SOURCE: A review of *King Rollo and the Birthday* and others, in *School Library Journal,* Vol. 26, No. 16, August, 1980, p. 54.

A British trilogy about King Rollo and his adventures—learning to tie his own shoes, creating a birthday card, eating bread. The text is short, with enough humor and action to retain readers' interest. Double-page illustrations, similar to Jack Kent in style, are engaging and colorful and capture the spirit of each story. Format is small and reminiscent of Beatrix Potter and binding is weak; books are packaged in a slipcase but can be catalogued and circulated independently. A good series for lower elementary age beginning readers and good bedtime fare to share with pre-schoolers, King Rollo is bound to be a hit with American audiences.

THE MAGICIAN AND THE DRAGON (1979; republished as *Melric and the Dragon,* 1987)

The Junior Bookshelf

SOURCE: A review of *The Magician and the Dragon,* in *The Junior Bookshelf,* Vol. 43, No. 6, December, 1979, pp. 318-19.

If you have any doubt about the advantage of the picture book artist being his own author, look at **The Magician and the Dragon.** David McKee's pictures do not need to depend on hints in the text. They go their own way, weaving delicate and humorous fantasies around the plain, simple but highly idiosyncratic story. We have been in this happy country before, ruled over by a youthful and impulsive king who is kept on the right lines—but only just—by Melric the Magician. When reports come in of an invasion by fierce dragons the king orders his over-fed army into action. Melric does a private investigation of his own to discover that the invasion is by a single small dragon who likes above all chocolate cake—so does the army! Melric puts this charming creature where he will be least likely to come to harm, in the king's castle, while the army tries out its courage on all sorts of dragons—toys, pictures, kites, a pub sign, even a pantomime dragon. The king orders his soldiers back to headquarters, where there is plenty of chocolate cake for everyone, including the dragon. The pictures are crammed with excellent jokes.

Jill Bennett

SOURCE: A review of *The Magician and the Dragon,* in *The School Librarian,* Vol. 34, No. 3, September, 1986, p. 240.

When a plague of dragons is reported the king decides that the ideal way to get his overfed army (who are somewhat too fond of chocolate cake) fit again is to send them on a dragon hunt. But real dragons are, it seems, hard to find, especially when the only true dragon is helped to hide by Melric, the court magician. Not an easy read, but McKee's illustrative style is instantly accessible, providing numerous lovely visual jokes for those attempting the text themselves, as well as for younger listeners.

From I Hate My Teddy Bear, *written and illustrated by David McKee.*

Connie M. Hornyak

SOURCE: A review of *The Magician and the Dragon,* in *School Library Journal,* Vol. 33, No. 4, December, 1986, pp. 92-3.

A humorous but confusing tale about a kingdom supposedly under the attack of several dreadful dragons. The king's "too fat" and not-too-smart soldiers bravely set off to fight the intruders. Meanwhile, Melric, the court magician, locates and befriends a young homeless dragon and hides the creature. The soldiers attack everything but the real dragon, including dragon paintings and dragon toys—believing that they are risking their lives fighting and conquering dragons. Upon retreat to the castle, the king and the soldiers find the dragon playing with Melric, and the king adopts the dragon as the army mascot. The idea is clever, but its execution is stifled by awkward phrasing, gaps in the storyline, and a few made-up words. Even Kra's advice is confusing—it is given to Melric in a riddle that probably will not be deciphered by children. The double-page watercolor spreads do little to complement the accompanying text since they are too crowded and without a line of focus. Other pages have illustrations blocked out in comic-strip style, but not all have the pictures going in the same sequential direction. There's no magic in this one.

Liz Waterland

SOURCE: A review of *Melric and the Dragon,* in *Books for Keeps,* No. 49, March, 1988, p. 17.

At first, the children's reaction to the sight of this book was delight. They immediately recognised David McKee's style of illustration and, since they very much like King Rollo, were all ready to welcome this. However, Melric is a quite different cauldron of spells from the childlike and simple King and the point of this story was simply lost on them. This is not to say that it isn't an excellent book . . . I enjoyed it very much, and so would many an older child. It is wasted to some extent on very young children.

In order to 'get' the story, you need to understand a page like this:

'Did you hear about the little boy who left his toys all

over his room? When his mother came in she said, "There are toys everywhere."

"Not everywhere," said the boy. "There are none in the toy cupboard."

"Thank you, Kra," said Melric. Now he knew where to hide the dragon.'

My children just couldn't understand the joke and it spoils a story to have to explain to totally uncomprehending faces why it is supposed to be funny!

We did enjoy the pictures, though, and several children tried hard with reading the book because they love dragons. But I should have waited for another year or two.

📖 *NOT NOW, BERNARD* (1980)

Carolyn O'Grady

SOURCE: "Horrors," in *The Times Educational Supplement*, No. 3340, June 20, 1980, p. 44.

What adults fear and what frightens children are two quite different things.

A lot of adults, I'm sure, will hate David McKee's *Not Now, Bernard.* Kids love it. "Not now, Bernard" is the unseeing retort that follows on everything that Bernard says or does, even his warning that there's a monster outside. The monster eats Bernard and is tamed by the stream of "Not now, Bernards" and the busy indifference of the parents.

A book in which the main child character is eaten, never to reappear, and in which the parents are portrayed as coldly indifferent is unlikely to be popular with adults. But even very young children see the joke and apparently couldn't care a jot about poor Bernard, transferring their affections immediately to the lovable gruesome monster.

Joy Chant

SOURCE: "Winning Pictures and Moral Tales," in *The Times Literary Supplement*, No. 4034, July 18, 1980, p. 809.

[In *Not Now, Bernard* the] pictures are as vivid and vigorous as any David McKee has produced; it is the story that worried me. "Not Now, Bernard" is the answer this little boy gets whenever he speaks to his parents, who throughout the book *never* look at him: even the information that there is a monster in the garden waiting to eat him is insufficient to make his mother vary her response, or even turn round. The only one to take notice of Bernard is the monster: who eats him. After this he attempts

to terrify Bernard's parents, but gets only that bored "Not now, Bernard". In fact he goes to bed without having his imposture noticed. The last page shows him, much disconcerted, saying "But I'm a monster!"; while mother, reaching in to turn off the light, replies . . . you've guessed it. A moral tale for parents certainly; but the possible effect on a sensitive child alarmed me. Unfortunately I do not seem to know any sensitive children for my guinea-pigs were obstinately undisturbed.

Aidan Warlow

SOURCE: A review of *Not Now, Bernard*, in *The School Librarian*, Vol. 28, No. 3, September, 1980, p. 252.

Not now, Bernard is . . . a clever joke for grown-ups, with only limited appeal for children: Bernard is eaten by a monster, the monster moves into Bernard's house, and the mother feeds him his tea and sends him to bed without noticing any change in the membership of the family. As a satirical comment on neglectful parents, it works. As a picture book for infants, it doesn't.

Publishers Weekly

SOURCE: A review of *Not Now, Bernard*, in *Publishers Weekly*, Vol. 219, No. 14, April 3, 1981, p. 74.

In almost painfully bright colors, McKee's paintings are strikingly modern, suited to the cruel caricature of family life that is the heart of his story. "Hello, Dad," little Bernard says, but "Not now, Bernard," is the answer as the father tries to drive a nail into a wall. Bernard's mother is also too busy to even turn around and look when Bernard says "hello," or when he reports a monster in the garden. So the monster eats Bernard up and goes into his house. Trying to get the parents' attention, the monster gets the same phrase that the boy had heard all his short life: "Not now, Bernard." The mother feeds and sends it off to bed without seeing it. And that's the end of a bizarre, negative picture book that should be for grownups. 'Taint funny, McKee.

Joan W. Blos

SOURCE: A review of *Not Now, Bernard*, in *School Library Journal*, Vol. 27, No. 9, May, 1981, p. 58.

A British import and surely one of the strangest books published recently on either side of the Atlantic. In the opening pages, a small boy who has been totally ignored by his parents goes out to the garden where he is eaten by (becomes?) a monster. Even when the monster bites the father's finger, the parents seem oblivious of the change that has occurred. Dinner is set out before the TV. The monster eats. The monster goes to bed. The colors used are very bright. The style is that of the cartoon. It is all very deadpan and very odd. "'Not now, Bernard.'"

📖 *BIG TOP BENN* (1980)

Linda Yeatman

SOURCE: A review of *Big Top Benn,* in *British Book News,* Autumn, 1980, p. 14.

Mr Benn is a well-known, well-established book and television personality. He always visits a special shop, tries on a suit of clothes in the changing room and walks out into a world that fits his costume. This time he dresses up as a clown and finds himself in a circus drama. His creator, David McKee, should be congratulated on producing yet another attractive Mr Benn book. The story is simple, but full of happenings, and the artwork has a great deal to offer in detail, interesting perspectives and bright colours, and is over all an extension to the text in the best possible way.

The Junior Bookshelf

SOURCE: A review of *Big Top Benn,* in *The Junior Bookshelf,* Vol. 45, No. 1, February, 1981, p. 12.

When visiting the magic costume shop, Mr. Benn, who is a familiar character on children's TV, is given a clown's suit complete with red nose and comic car. As he drives along he encounters an entire circus, held up by a landslide of rocks. Fortunately Mr. Benn manages to enlist the help of a friend from a former adventure, Smasher Lagru, a convict with notable rock-smashing abilities. Smasher's prowess as he clears the road wins him the offer of permanent employment as a strong man. Next there is a bridge to be built, but at last the circus reaches its destination and gives a show. Entering the magician's booth takes Mr. Benn back to the magic shop and brings his adventure to an end.

This book contains a generous amount of story and alternating black and white sketches and coloured pictures, all illustrations displaying unusual notions of perspective.

📖 *THE MAGICIAN AND DOUBLE TROUBLE* (1981)

The Junior Bookshelf

SOURCE: A review of *The Magician and Double Trouble,* in *The Junior Bookshelf,* Vol. 46, No. 4, August, 1982, p. 134.

Medieval magic is at its most confusing as King's Magician Melric is accused by the villagers of making mischief. With the help of sister Mertel and cousin Guz, and the advice of wise man Kra, Melric realizes that his arch enemy Sorcerer Sondrak has upset the king and stolen Melric's job, and created havoc in the village by taking on Melric's appearance. So Melric turns the table on Sondrak. . . .

A sturdy picture book, the brightly coloured illustrations are a riot of detail, with dozens of lively strip cartoon characters—village and town houses full of occupants "doing their thing"—action insets for the villagers' complaints. The easy script is almost unnecessary, but it does help to clarify some of the pictures, and it adds humour to the situations.

📖 *I HATE MY TEDDY BEAR* (1982)

Naomi Lewis

SOURCE: "Once Upon a Line," in *The Times Educational Supplement,* No. 3464, November 19, 1982, p. 32.

[A] most remarkable book . . . [is] David McKee's *I Hate My Teddy Bear,* a brilliant foray into the surreal—or far more likely, a demonstration of the real: that the centre of any happening is never where we think. While their mothers meet for tea and confidences (at once arousing our interest), Brenda and John are sent outside with their "hated" teddy bears which they leave under a tree. But trying to outboast each other about their teddies' achievement ("Mine can count, backwards." "Mine can fly") they discover a fondness for the uncomplaining toys. Meanwhile, all round, as in daily urban-suburban life, scenes from any number of novels are glimpsed. Workmen stagger along under the weight of a huge sculptured hand. Another follows—a disturbing, menacing item. Nobody looks. A woman winds a ball of wool—but where's the other end? Turn a few pages—no, don't. Brenda and John don't care; indeed, any under-eight readers will see just what they choose to see. Adults (or story-writers looking for plots) may get a bonus, though.

Books for Your Children

SOURCE: A review of *I Hate My Teddy Bear,* in *Books for Your Children,* Vol. 17, No. 3, Autumn/Winter, 1982, p. 16.

Another elegant eccentric book from David McKee who has a genius of understatement both in his words and pictures which enter into the young child's own world and appeals to their own particular sense of humour. Whilst Brenda and John play and squabble in a mundane way as children do, the most extraordinary events are taking place as a background to the pictures. David McKee will be remembered for his little *King Rollo* books and television cartoons, and this latest book has the same visual impact and liveliness.

Margery Fisher

SOURCE: A review of *I Hate My Teddy Bear,* in *Growing Point,* Vol. 21, No. 5, January, 1983, p. 4016.

Caught in parental compulsion, Brenda and John refuse to play amicably and extend their enmity to their bears, which are abandoned and later picked up casually, demonstrating all the time the happiest of alliances. The brief text, mainly conversation, is expanded in pictures in which the children's boasting escalates against a surreal background where adults move slowly under heavy loads of gigantic hands for a sculpture exhibition. Visual incongruity here, as with Anthony Browne's books, adds a bizarre understory which isolates the children and communicates its own disquieting humour in a shrewd commentary on childhood in particular and humanity in general.

Gabrielle Maunder

SOURCE: A review of *I Hate My Teddy Bear,* in *The School Librarian,* Vol. 31, No. 1, March, 1983, p. 30.

I have been devoted [to David McKee] since . . . *8, 9, Benn.* This book's title, *I hate my teddy bear,* is a challenge in itself, and the book is fascinating for more than one reason. Firstly, the title is an oblique one and not descriptive of the contents; secondly, the pictures carry several more stories than the text tells; and thirdly, the text itself works on two levels. I know it sounds tricky, and it is, which makes it exactly right for children over a wide range of competence.

Karen Stang Hanley

SOURCE: A review of *I Hate My Teddy Bear,* in *Booklist,* Vol. 80, No. 15, April 1, 1984, pp. 1117-18.

Two children, sent outside to play while their mothers chat, agree that they hate their teddy bears but subsequently get into a heated debate about the talents of each bear. "'My teddy can talk,' said John. 'So can mine,' said Brenda," and on it goes, with the two insisting that their bears can count (backwards and forwards), sing, and fly. Later, while John and Brenda are having tea, the teddies themselves carry on a more amiable dialogue: "'I didn't know you could sing,' said Blue Teddy. 'Oh yes,' said Pink Teddy. 'But I can't fly.' 'Neither can I,' said Blue Teddy." Each sentence of these humorously parallel conversations is set against a bizarre backdrop of unexplained, largely unexplainable detail in surrealistic, pastel-toned watercolor paintings. A woman is doing a headstand in the park while a palmist tells a person's fortune and a sad-eyed man strolls in the foreground; in the next scene, a gentleman studying what may be a treasure map holds on to the end of a string that takes the eye across the page to where a woman is winding it in a neat ball. Sharp-eyed, agile-minded viewers will enjoy establishing connections between the pages, the most obvious being the giant hands and feet throughout, which all come to rest in an extraordinary sculpture garden. The meager, though clever, story line and rather self-conscious artwork may be more puzzling than appealing to most. Certainly not to everyone's taste, but a singular challenge for youngsters with a proclivity for the uncommon; especially recommended for artistically gifted children.

Publishers Weekly

SOURCE: A review of *I Hate My Teddy Bear,* in *Publishers Weekly,* Vol. 225, No. 22, June 1, 1984, p. 64.

From Two Monsters, *written and illustrated by David McKee.*

McKee's latest exemplifies certain picture books that seem to be meant for grownups rather than for children. The story, blithe and simple, is no problem. John and Brenda take their teddy bears out to play while their mothers visit. The friends insist that they hate their stuffed toys, then argue nonstop about whose is better and can do more fancy tricks. When the mothers call John and Brenda in at teatime, the bears privately agree that they are equally talented, winding up the tale on a perky note. But young readers will be frustrated, trying to understand the full-color scenes of surrealistic doings by crowds of people, inhumanly deadpan—in the building and outside in the heart of a metropolis. There seems to be no reason, except extra self-indulgence, for one picture that's half upside down.

Mary Butler Nickerson

SOURCE: A review of *I Hate My Teddy Bear,* in *School Library Journal,* Vol. 30, No. 2, August, 1984, p. 62.

First, the text, which is below the large square sherbet-colored pictures: Brenda and her mother visit John and his mother, and the two children are sent outside with their teddy bears. Brenda and John claim to hate their teddy bears but exchange a number of boasts about what they can do. When the children are called back in for tea, the bears comment on the boasts. Then there are the pictures, which have virtually nothing to do with the text and are disturbing on several levels. In each picture there is at least a portion of an enormous sculpted hand or foot being transported. The final illustration shows all the giant pieces mounted as statues, but they are hardly less grotesque for being explained, and in several of the illustrations are truly menacing as they seem to reach for the children. The children are generally oblivious to these disconnected appendages and are also oblivious to the very strange people and events around them. Although activity is portrayed (people spying, dancing, knitting, painting), it is surreal, unexplained and gratuitous and overwhelmed by the preponderance of isolated sad-faced people who sit and stare. The sense of dislocation and desolation is strong. This is a book for children?

Elaine Moss

SOURCE: A review of *I Hate My Teddy Bear,* in *Picture Books for Young People 9-13,* edited by Nancy Chambers, revised edition, Thimble Press, 1985, p. 13.

Make of this surrealist picture book what you wish, but don't miss it so long as you don't mind not being sure what it's all about. Because what it's all about is fantasy games: the kind the two children play with their teddy bears, and the teddy bears play with their children; and the fantasy-provoking half-stories that we adults also become involved in as we go about our daily business (walking in the park, for instance, where vast sculptured feet and arms are being carried around for an art exhibition?; and palmistry, photography, conjuring). As Russell

Hoban said of this book, it 'will help any child to get a grip on the ungraspable'.

KING ROLLO'S PLAYROOM AND OTHER STORIES (1983)

Naomi Lewis

SOURCE: "Feather, Fur and Fantasy," in *The Times Educational Supplement,* No. 3492, June 3, 1983, p. 44.

[Zany] as they may seem, the King Rollo books have more in them than you would think. ***King Rollo's Playroom*** by David McKee—the larger format is new (now four square pictures to a page)—contains four fine new picture stories. They are, as before, at once witty and childlike: something for glancing adults as well as for two to five year olds. Rollo is of course not so much a king being a child as a child playing at kings—therefore, even, the moral hint now and then. Cook, Magician and Cat make characteristic (loony, yet slightly admonitory) appearances. Don't wait to enter the glorious Rollo world if you're four or less.

THE HILL AND THE ROCK (1984)

The Junior Bookshelf

SOURCE: A review of *The Hill and the Rock,* in *The Junior Bookshelf,* Vol. 48, No. 3, June, 1984, p. 118.

Mr. Quest arrives in this book by bicycle, which must be a challenge since the family home is atop an extraordinarily steep hill. As this is the only hill in the area people come from far and wide to visit: the one drawback is a huge rock standing outside the kitchen window. Mrs. Quest keeps on complaining about it, and one day her husband pushes the rock away down the hill. Unfortunately the effect is disastrous. Air escapes from the hole where the rock was, and the distinctive hill subsides.

The amusing story of Mr. and Mrs. Quest's reactions is illustrated in a series of detailed and brightly coloured cartoon style pictures, sometimes one and sometimes several to a page. The text, which conveys a remarkably convincing impression of ordinary domestic life attempting to adapt to a bizarre set of circumstances, is printed in blocks beneath each set of pictures.

Jonni Moore

SOURCE: A review of *The Hill and the Rock,* in *School Library Journal,* Vol. 32, No. 1, September, 1985, p. 121.

Despite living atop the only hill around and hosting constant admirers of the panorama, Mrs. Quest feels disgruntled. The reason: her view from the kitchen window is partially obscured by a huge rock. But when Mr. Quest dislodges the rock, the hill deflates until the Quests find themselves living deep in a valley. Visitors no longer find their habitat unique and even worse, the rock rolls downhill, completely blocking the window. Painting a landscape on the rock solves the scenic problem, delighting Mrs. Quest, and with the rock back in place the hill reinflates. Illustrations in a brightly colored primitive yet expressive style humorously supplement the imaginative theme, but the drollness of the whole will be lost on the intended age group.

KING ROLLO'S LETTER AND OTHER STORIES (1984)

Books for Keeps

SOURCE: A review of *King Rollo's Letter and Other Stories,* in *Books for Keeps,* No. 40, September, 1986, p. 22.

Four self-standing stories about the likeable, absent-minded King, popular from the TV versions of his exploits. Given the attraction of the characters (Queen Gwen is my favourite—a super invention in one-upwomanship) and the talent of McKee, it's a pity that this doesn't quite succeed.

Is it because the pattern of TV stories is different—quicker, more immediate than storyreading? Do they need the cumulative action and surprise that's missing in this foursquare, static format? I'll video one of the TV versions, then get the kids to tell me about the differences as I don't want those who queue in the bookshop for *Not Now, Bernard* to be disappointed.

TWO MONSTERS (1985)

Books for Keeps

SOURCE: A review of *Two Monsters,* in *Books for Keeps,* No. 35, November, 1985, p. 21.

The latest of David McKee's fables for our time. Two monsters (one red, one blue), who live on either side of the mountain and never meet, find they disagree. From hurling verbal abuse they move to hurling rocks and verbal abuse and bigger rocks. As they stand face to face on a flattened landscape they suddenly find they agree after all. 'Pity about the mountain.' The message is unashamed and inescapable; the artist/author's line and language as funny and inventive as ever.

William Henry Holmes

SOURCE: A review of *Two Monsters,* in *The Listener,* Vol. 114, No. 2934, November 7, 1985, p. 32.

The contemporary master of the children's parable is David McKee, whose King Rollo books make all sorts of moral points with deft, gentle wit. His *Tusk Tusk,* about a fight to the death between two elephant tribes, is a classic story

of destruction and rebirth. On a much smaller scale, and with far less variety in the illustrations, his latest story, *Two Monsters* is a similarly potent lesson. The red monster and the blue monster live on opposite sides of a mountain; they chat happily enough through a hole in the mountain until a sudden row at sunset about whether day is departing or night is arriving. The insults fly hard and fast, and so do rocks hurled over the mountain—which eventually demolish the mountain altogether. 'Incredible. There's night arriving. You were right . . . ' 'That was rather fun . . . pity about the mountain.' And the chubby little chaps bask in the fading light on the pile of stones. A book about barriers, real and imaginary, and how to get rid of them.

Kirkus Reviews

SOURCE: A review of *Two Monsters,* in *Kirkus Reviews,* Vol. LIV, No. 4, February 15, 1986, p. 304.

McKee's picture book about two monsters who disagree cleverly shows children how much better it is to communicate with each other.

McKee, author and film animator, has created two monsters who are appealing in their shortsightedness. The blue monster lives on the west side of a mountain, and the red monster lives on the east side. They talk to each other through a hole in the mountain, but all they do is disagree. One says the day is departing; the other says no, the night is arriving. One says the night is leaving and the other disagrees, claiming that the day is arriving. They call each other names—"You hairy, long-nosed nincompoop!"; "You're a stupid old wind-filled prune!"; "And you are a bowlegged, soggy cornflake!"—and then start throwing stones at each other. Soon, their rock-hurling results in smashing down the mountain, and they see each other for the very first time. And, finally, they can see each other's viewpoints: they end up enjoying watching the sunset together.

McKee's goofy-looking monsters and their creative insults make this an engaging little story.

Nancy A. Gifford

SOURCE: A review of *Two Monsters,* in *School Library Journal,* Vol. 32, No. 9, May, 1986, p. 81.

An amusing story of developing friendship that shows the futility of arguing and brutality. Two monsters live on opposite sides of a mountain—one of them is round and blue with a crew cut and large teeth, and the other is round and red with spikes on his head and a pointed tail. Neither monster can see the other, but the blue on the west side can see the sun departing and the red on the east sees the night arriving. One day their differing viewpoints cause a fight and name-calling between them. The name-calling leads to rock throwing, then boulder throwing. With each throw a little bit more of the mountain top is knocked off until the mountain is smashed flat and the monsters see each other. They also see the same view of the sky and sit down to watch the sunset together. This is a story that can be used as a funny monster story and accepted at face value or as a vehicle for discussion about friendship. Illustrations are colorful, bold and simple. The monsters stay the same color throughout, but the mountain changes constantly to reflect the colors of the sunrise and sunset, ending in a warm pinkish-purple with the two new friends sitting together.

The Junior Bookshelf

SOURCE: A review of *Two Monsters,* in *The Junior Bookshelf,* Vol. 50, No. 4, August, 1986, p. 142.

Anyone who enjoyed David McKee's **Not Now Bernard** cannot fail to appreciate the delights of his latest book. Two monsters, who begin by speaking to each other only through a hole in the mountain end, after a mountain-shattering argument, sitting together to watch dusk close over the chaos. I lent my copy to an infant teacher whose five and six year old class laughed hilariously as the insults between the two monsters became more and more outrageous (they particularly enjoyed the "bandy-legged, soggy cornflake"!). David McKee's bold use of colour is superb for individual or for classroom use and should ensure that the book—taken with or without moral messages—is one young children will ask to hear again and again.

Jill Bennett

SOURCE: A review of *Two Monsters,* in *Books for Keeps,* No. 52, September, 1988, p. 25.

One of the bonuses of using picture books with learner readers is that they are not so anxious to 'get on to the next book' that they never have time, or indeed wish, to return to a book they have already read. Many books are read over and over and those that can be read on several levels are especially valuable. David McKee's **Two Monsters** certainly can; this fable has two monsters (one red and one blue) living on opposite sides of a mountain and having opposing views on dawn and dusk. Inevitably conflict results and the two hurl first abuse and then missiles at one another. The size and ferocity of both increase until the mountain is levelled and then the pair come to see each other's viewpoint. Such insults as 'And you're a bandy-legged, soggy cornflake' delight young readers; older readers may see the whole thing as a political statement; in between, there is great potential for discussion and all will enjoy the deftness of McKee's touch.

📖 KING ROLLO'S AUTUMN; KING ROLLO'S SPRING; KING ROLLO'S SUMMER; KING ROLLO'S WINTER (1986)

Annette Curtis Klause

SOURCE: A review of *King Rollo's Autumn* and *King Rollo's Summer,* in *School Library Journal,* Vol. 34, No. 7, March, 1988, pp. 170-71.

In these appealing, brightly colored board books, a child-like king rolls, bounces, waves, and prances through his small world, always with a sense of true delight and discovery. In . . . *Autumn,* the king is astonished that the leaves fall from the trees. After the court magician assures him that magic is not needed, the queen shows him how to enjoy this very natural event. In . . . *Summer,* King Rollo finds a familiar way to cool off. Attractive two-page spreads, containing only one line of text per page, show comfortably tubby people. Illustrations are done in a cartoon style in ink and watercolor. Although these books have more story than many board books, their gentle, understated humor and clear presentation make them simple enough to be enjoyed by most toddlers *and* their parents.

Moira Small

SOURCE: A review of *King Rollo's Autumn* and others, in *Books for Keeps,* No. 52, September, 1988, p. 6.

Four sensitively written little books featuring the characters in King Rollo's household. Full of fun and simple detail, the stories tell about each season and its peculiarities through the freshness of David McKee's approach, using his King Rollo character whom he shows as curious and innocent but who is informed by the cook, the wizard and the queen.

The simple storyline and the clear, attractive pictures make these an excellent first series for very young children finding out about their world. Highly recommended.

📖 THE SAD STORY OF VERONICA WHO PLAYED THE VIOLIN (1987)

Chris Powling

SOURCE: A review of *The Sad Story of Veronica Who Played the Violin,* in *Books for Keeps,* No. 44, May, 1987, p. 29.

[The] success of **Veronica** depends on the ending—as blatant a violation of readerly expectation as I've come across in a long time. It had me laughing out loud. So will most readers, I guess, as they follow the career of a little girl with a musical talent so tear-jerking, it can charm the most savage of beasts. That is, until . . . well, try it for yourself. As with all the best McKee, every stroke—verbal or visual—is a masterly celebration of the *droll.*

Jan Dalley

SOURCE: "Animal Magic," in *The Times Literary Supplement,* No. 4395, June 26, 1987, p. 700.

Veronica, a child prodigy, goes to the jungle to find adventure. Her beautifully sad playing has always reduced everyone to tears. Miraculously, when she plays in the jungle the animals laugh and dance; her music now has the power to make everyone happy. But disaster looms, in the guise of a hungry old lion. A visual exuberance, a witty blend of realism and fantasy (his animals are india-rubber cuddly, his humans grotesque) make David McKee's story curiously memorable.

Margery Fisher

SOURCE: A review of *The Sad Story of Veronica Who Played the Violin,* in *Growing Point,* Vol. 26, No. 2, July, 1987, p. 4835.

The sub-title proclaims that this is 'an explanation of why the streets are not full of happy dancing people'. Veronica's playing is bad enough to empty the streets, certainly, and her fame is clearly not a matter of flattery; however, she has hopes of being a success in the African safari park where her belaboured strings set the animals dancing—until a deaf lion eats her up and the rest lapse into tears. Jazzy pictures emphasise the irony in a tale which should either discourage young amateurs or set them devotedly to extra practising. However one reads the story, David McKee's idiosyncratic scenes and comic characters are a delight.

The Junior Bookshelf

SOURCE: A review of *The Sad Story of Veronica Who Played the Violin,* in *The Junior Bookshelf,* Vol. 51, No. 5, October, 1987, pp. 214-15.

No one does a funny picture-story better than David McKee. Here he introduces a musical genius whose beautiful playing reduces audiences everywhere to tears. Seeking adventure she goes on musical safari into the jungle, guarded by three 'fearless hunters', and tries her art on the wild animals. For once she brings not tears but joy and they all dance—at least, nearly all! The last lovely joke is masterly in its unexpectedness. As always with this fine artist, lots of mini-plots proceed in parallel with the main action, and every detail of the drawings is richly relevant. Surely television will not pass this one by.

Gabrielle Maunder

SOURCE: A review of *The Sad Story of Veronica Who Played the Violin,* in *The School Librarian,* Vol. 35, No. 4, November, 1987, pp. 323-24.

David McKee's new book—how nice to see him still pulling out such marvellous plums after all this time—is utterly enchanting, full of the visual wit and ingenuity that marked books like *. . . 7-8-9-Benn,* but with a more essential text. Indeed it is in the text that one can most clearly trace McKee's development, for he now has a deliciously ironic style. It was there in *Not now, Bernard,*

but here it is more prominent, and this is crucially a book to read—and then look at the pictures. Awful Veronica is totally single-minded about wanting to play the violin, to the despair of her teachers (one of whom moves to China) and the entire neighbourhood. For the first half of the story, everyone is shown weeping, but I will leave you to work your way through the book in order to understand the subtitle: 'being an explanation of why the streets are not full of happy dancing people'. (I am a bit bothered by David McKee though. Does he want *all* his child characters eaten . . . ?)

Heather Noble

SOURCE: A review of *The Sad Story of Veronica Who Played the Violin,* in *Books for Your Children,* Vol. 22, No. 3, Autumn/Winter, 1987, p. 7.

Tears flood the pages of this wryly tragic story of Veronica who wanted to play the violin. Her determination survives the less than encouraging responses of violin teachers and distraught neighbour who moan and wail through her perpetual practising until eventually their tears overflow because her music is so beautiful rather than so bad. Such talent is designed for stardom but our hardy heroine soon tires of fame and throws the exploiting record moguls aside in favour of the jungle and adventure. What happens next cannot be disclosed without spoiling the experience of a tremendous joke of a book. As always David McKee's expressive pictures enlarge on the ironic understatement of the text and he is certainly at his best in this laugh aloud tale teasingly subtitled 'Being an explanation of why the streets are not full of happy dancing people.'

Liz Waterland

SOURCE: A review of *The Sad Story of Veronica Who Played the Violin,* in *Books for Keeps,* No. 55, March, 1989, p. 17.

I must admit to liking David McKee's work best when he is at his most simple. ***Not Now, Bernard*** and the King Rollo stories manage to suggest such a lot in so little that they seem to me to be masterpieces of storytelling. ***Veronica*** seems to lack something by comparison. The somewhat longer and more complex story doesn't leave the same scope for speculation and debate.

Having said that, however, we did enjoy the story of how Veronica learnt to play the violin and her sad end as a meal for a lion, a deaf lion at that, thus explaining why 'the streets are not full of happy, dancing people'.

Sue Williams

SOURCE: A review of *The Sad Story of Veronica Who Played the Violin,* in *Books for Your Children,* Vol. 24, No. 1, Spring, 1989, p. 11.

From The Sad Story of Veronica Who Played the Violin, *written and illustrated by David McKee.*

This story will appeal to all children who have ever learned to play an instrument (or heard anyone practicing!) There are jokes on every page and wonderful illustrations with lots of unusual viewpoints in them and much to look at and discuss. Veronica's violin playing makes everyone cry. She develops it into a career and is discovered and becomes famous. This allows her to visit Africa. Here she has the opportunity of playing to the animals and finds that she can make them happy and keen to dance. Sadly she comes to an untimely end which is why the book is subtitled "an explanation of why the streets are not full of happy dancing people"—subtle stuff for 6 year olds.

Publishers Weekly

SOURCE: A review of *The Sad Story of Veronica Who Played the Violin,* in *Publishers Weekly,* Vol. 238, No. 44, October 4, 1991, p. 88.

For optimists who wonder "why the streets are not full of happy dancing people," McKee's darkly comic tale offers some explanation. When Veronica begins violin lessons, the neighbors and even her teachers weep at the girl's sour notes. After she masters her instrument, however, she continues to bring her audience to tears with her sweet songs. Her adventurous soul leads her to abandon a concert career and journey to the "deepest darkest jungle," where her music has an opposite effect and sets the animals to dancing—until one fierce lion ruins the party. McKee's (*Who's a Clever Baby?;* the King Rollo series) busy illustrations depict an array of unusual perspectives and minute details that urge close inspection (alligator and cheetah couples moving cheek-to-cheek are not to be missed). The text's sudden, startling finish teeters on the absurd, but finally provokes more thoughtful consideration of Veronica's circumstances than laughs.

THE MAGICIAN'S APPRENTICE (1987)

Jill Bennett

SOURCE: A review of *The Magician's Apprentice,* in *British Book News Children's Books,* September, 1987, p. 14.

The Magician's Apprentice [is David McKee's] latest addition to the 'Magician' series. The magic ingredient present in King Rollo and some of the earlier Magician titles has eluded him here. The story of how apprentice Rydar rescues King Ralphe from the power of Sorcerer Sondrak is, in the words of one young critic, 'dead boring,' and even McKee's normally captivating illustrations fail to redeem this disappointing book.

📖 *SNOW WOMAN* (1987)

Patt Triggs

SOURCE: A review of *Snow Woman,* in *Books for Keeps,* No. 47, November, 1987, p. 4.

The war between the sexes is fought out in the pictures that hang on the walls of a very eighties household. Rupert makes a snowman ('"You mean snowperson," said his father.'). Kate makes a snow woman ('"That's a good girl," said her mother.'). And something odd happens. Or perhaps it's not so odd after all. An original and multi-layered book which will intrigue older readers especially.

Kirkus Reviews

SOURCE: A review of *Snow Woman,* in *Kirkus Reviews,* Vol. LVI, No. 2, January 15, 1988, p. 125.

Kate and Rupert are the same size and identically dressed. When Rupert says, "We're going to build a snowman," his father pauses from vacuuming to reply, "You mean a snowperson." But when Kate announces, "I'm going to build a snow woman," her mother (who has the shortest hair in the family and is busy hanging pictures) says, "That's a good girl"—but Rupert says, "Nobody builds a snow woman." Two snow people are built, however, and apparently depart during the night, pleased to find that they are of different sexes.

McKee's simple, repetitive text makes its point with deadpan humor; his cheerfully colored, cartoonlike illustrations are full of hilariously detailed artifacts and possessions that depict or refer to sex roles and relationships. There's a lot here that will appeal especially to adults, but the kids should have fun with it, too.

Publishers Weekly

SOURCE: A review of *Snow Woman,* in *Publishers Weekly,* Vol. 233, No. 2, January 15, 1988, p. 95.

McKee brings his avant-garde views on the question of gender to playtime. When Rupert says he's building a snowman, his father corrects him: "You mean a snow person." And when Kate says she's building a snow-woman, her mother agrees with the terminology. The snowpeople are up, side by side, fully dressed. But, by morning, the snow couple have vanished, clothes and all. The kids resign themselves to building a snowbear instead—not a man bear or a lady bear, but "just a bear." There are several points of view to be argued here, but

most everyone will agree that there is more to life than simple male/female categorizations. It is McKee's superb humor—conveyed almost solely in the illustrations—rather than his intentionally ambiguous ending—that wins the day, particularly a series of hilariously inventive and often absurd framed pictures on the walls.

Carolyn Caywood

SOURCE: A review of *Snow Woman,* in *School Library Journal,* Vol. 35, No. 1, September, 1988, p. 169.

A boy and a girl build a snowman and a snow woman despite their parents' confusing messages that the boy should be non-sexist and create a snowperson but the girl should affirm her gender with a snow woman. The snow people disappear in the night, clothes and all, and the children decide to build a snow bear instead. This simple story is pictured in bright watercolor outlined in ink. The children look and dress enough alike to be twins but the parents are a cartoon-like exaggeration of militant feminist and liberated male. Bosomy father vacuums and cooks in an apron while crew-cut mother sets down her drill and puts on a leather motorcycle jacket to take pictures of the snow people. Nevertheless, they seem a happy family, so it isn't entirely clear whether McKee is mocking their lifestyle. *But,* in the background of every indoor scene is artwork that hammers on the theme of female domination and sexuality as a battleground. The overall effect is somewhere between Thurber's *The War Between Men and Women* and a Jules Feiffer cartoon. In the *New Yorker,* this might be thought-provoking. On the picture book shelves it is confusing and possibly frightening.

📖 *WHO'S A CLEVER BABY THEN?* (1988; U.S. edition as *Who's a Clever Baby?*)

Kirkus Reviews

SOURCE: A review of *Who's a Clever Baby?,* in *Kirkus Reviews,* Vol. LVII, No. 2, January 15, 1989, p. 126.

As in David Lloyd's *Duck* (1988), the baby here persists, in spite of Grandma's best efforts, in calling all animals by the same name—in this case, "dog." But McKee offers a less affectionate rendition of this early power struggle than Lloyd did, who depicted it as an important, misunderstood learning process. As they tour their neighborhood, Grandma gets more and more frantic in her attempts to cajole: "See the statue? See strong Samson silently struggling with Simon, the serious stone lion. Say 'lion,' Baby." Combined with the cartoonlike illustrations showing a dumpy, middle-aged grandma and her self-possessed grandchild, these alliterative tirades hold some humor, especially as they lead up to Baby's mischievous triumph: finally confronted with a dog, he says "Cat." But since there's no real development of the idea here, the book goes on too long. An acceptable additional story.

Publishers Weekly

SOURCE: A review of *Who's a Clever Baby?,* in *Publishers Weekly,* Vol. 235, No. 8, February 24, 1989, p. 230.

Grandma's pride in her bouncing baby grandchild is tested when she is called on to babysit. Grandma turns herself inside out trying to get baby to repeat a few simple words. "What terrible teeth Trevor the television tiger has. Say 'Tiger,' Baby," implores Grandma. "Dog," says Baby. "Dog" it turns out, is the only thing Baby can say and it doesn't matter what kind of verbal virtuosity Grandma manufactures, the response from Baby is always "Dog." Grandma, determined to prove her grandchild is clever, spies a dog. "Such a darling dog, Baby. . . . say 'dog,' Baby." The obstinate child replies, "Cat." McKee's colorfully textural illustrations are, as usual, loaded with interesting background vignettes: a rather staid older couple give each other sample licks of their ice cream cones; a child slips a mechanical duck into a pond filled with real ducks. Although the story is singular in its direction (some readers may be reminded of David Lloyd's *Duck*) and has a somewhat predictable outcome, Grandma's alliterative frenzies are fascinating and readers will find Baby's manipulative stubbornness vastly amusing.

The Junior Bookshelf

SOURCE: A review of *Who's a Clever Baby Then?,* in *The Junior Bookshelf,* Vol. 53, No. 4, August, 1989, p. 163.

The simplicity of David McKee's drawing and the innocence of his humour disguise a great deal of wisdom and craft. The repetitive text of *Who's a Clever Baby Then?* seems easy until one looks closely at its use of alliteration. As for the drawing it is child-like but certainly not childish. David McKee plays brilliant tricks with perspective, and every inch of his pictures is packed with shrewd, relevant and very funny details. As for the story, Baby drives Grandma to the brink with his perversity; even when at the end she thinks she has trapped him he still has an unexpected card to play. His face is a wonderfully expressive bladder of lard.

Janet Hickman

SOURCE: A review of *Who's a Clever Baby?,* in *Language Arts,* Vol. 66, No. 5, September, 1989, pp. 566-67.

Grandma's efforts to get her "clever baby" to say "cat" and "tiger" and "fish" and "teddy" all bring the same response: "'Dog,' said Baby." Anyone who has ever urged a toddler to name names will appreciate Grandma's persistence and Baby's eventual success with "cat"—just when she finally wants him to say "dog." The illustrations are busy with droll figures and off-balance perspectives that call for a second look and a smile. Grandma's facial expressions are an eloquent counterpoint to her

cheerful conversational patter. For listeners, alliterative phrases invite repetition, and the predictable refrain of "Dog" is a natural point for chiming in. While this book might be used to generate serious discussion about language, I vote for simply enjoying it.

Lori A. Janeck

SOURCE: A review of *Who's a Clever Baby?,* in *School Library Journal,* Vol. 35, No. 13, September, 1989, p. 230.

This unoriginal story suffers from a stilted, redundant text and jarring illustrations. The slight plot has Grandma (who looks more like a chubby sister) trying to get baby to name different animals. Baby's only answer is "dog" until he is asked to say "dog." Then he switches his reply to "cat." Grandma's exasperation and Baby's final smile are reminiscent of Diane Paterson's *Smile for Auntie* (1976). The illustrations are not without humor, but they are done from such strange perspectives that the total effect is unpleasant. At times people who are supposedly upright are shown standing, lying sideways, and walking upside down. Rosemary Wells' *Max's First Word* (1979) is simpler, funnier, and far more effective.

THE MONSTER AND THE TEDDY BEAR (1989)

Susan Perren

SOURCE: A review of *The Monster and the Teddy Bear,* in *Quill and Quire,* Vol. 56, No. 3, March, 1990, p. 23.

British children's book author David McKee has a large following in his homeland. His books *Not Now, Bernard, Who's a Clever Baby Then?,* and others are notable for their "off-the-wall" quality. McKee's books are slightly savage; they abound with voracious monsters and depict a world in which children and adults inhabit different spheres. Adults appear remote and self-interested, and children live within themselves in a densely and fantastically populated universe of their own construction. His newest book, *The Monster and the Teddy Bear,* is no exception.

Angela is disappointed with her present of a teddy bear. She does not want something warm and cuddly; she wants a "big and strong and exciting" monster. Later that night when a monster appears at her bedroom window her wish is fulfilled. McKee's monster, a highly developed squiggle like the rest of his characters, is a loathsome creature, slime-green, covered in carbuncles, with enormous fangs and livid eyes. Angela finds him both exciting and repellent. She watches him with horror as he goes on a rampage in the kitchen, stuffing himself with food and doing other monstrous things.

The situation is saved when Angela's once-reviled Teddy begins to grow and to growl. Teddy drags the monster into the garden and, whirling him round and round his head, hurls him into the stratosphere from which he will never return. All these scenes are punctuated by shouts of "Angela, be quiet!" from the oblivious baby-sitter as she turns up the volume on the TV.

This book will appeal to children and adults who can appreciate and revel in its orgiastic craziness. It will be disliked by others because of these same qualities, and by those who will suspect this is a book that undermines the sovereignty of adulthood.

William Feaver

SOURCE: "Monster Mania," in *The Times Educational Supplement,* No. 3848, March 30, 1990, p. B11.

The Monster and the Teddy Bear by David McKee contrasts the domestic teddy bear and the ravenous monster of untamed Nature. Angela thinks she prefers monsters, but her Heathcliff proves impossible to handle and after a difficult evening, during which the babysitter just sits in front of the telly and does nothing to help, she learns that uncontrollable urges are best eliminated. Better the teddy you know than feelings that could land you in deep trouble. McKee shows, of course, that monsters are far more interesting than dumb, button-eyed teddies.

Ann G. Hay

SOURCE: A review of *The Monster and the Teddy Bear,* in *The School Librarian,* Vol. 38, No. 2, May, 1990, p. 60.

This is a moral little story. Angela, on receiving the gift of a teddy, rejects it because she prefers monsters. That night a monster arrives, and together it and Angela do 'monstrous things'. These turn out to be destructive and not much fun, and Angela is delighted when Teddy comes to the rescue and throws the monster out. The large bright illustrations are in tune with the story, and have a child-like lack of perspective, but could be a little frightening for a sensitive child, as could the idea of a trusted adult (in this case, the babysitter) failing to deal with an out-of-hand situation. However, most five-year-olds sharing this with parents as a bedtime story should find it fun.

📖 *ANNABELLE PIG AND THE TRAVELLERS [AND] BENJAMIN PIG AND THE APPLE THIEVES* (1990)

Margery Fisher

SOURCE: A review of *Annabelle Pig and the Travellers* and *Benjamin Pig and the Apple Thieves,* in *Growing Point,* Vol. 29, No. 6, March, 1991, p. 5489.

Two front covers, two separate stories, a gimmick supported by the artist's free and easy caricatures in strip form, cheery in colour and engagingly odd in shapes and perspective. Annabelle's home on the crossroads attracts plenty of traveller's tales which eventually inspire her to set off, only to find the much-praised ruins and mansions are closed, while the popular 'rest-house' proves to be none other than her own home. Benjamin's routing of greedy trespassers in his orchard is equally lively in action and in the strong sense of personality in Benjamin and his wife. Humour is nicely adjusted here to young listener/readers.

Judith Sharman

SOURCE: A review of *Annabelle Pig and the Travellers* and *Benjamin Pig and the Apple Thieves,* in *Books for Keeps,* No. 70, September, 1991, p. 9.

David McKee at his best with two witty stories ideal for fledgeling readers or to read aloud. Benjamin Pig manages to con the apple thieves into picking his apples for him before they're forced to retreat, victims to a clever 'sting', and Annabelle discovers that home is where her heart is. Two familiar themes, yet David McKee offers them to us with freshness and verve that keeps the reader and listener spellbound from cover to flip-over cover!

📖 *ELMER AGAIN* (1991)

Carol Hill

SOURCE: A review of *Elmer Again,* in *The School Librarian,* Vol. 39, No. 3, August, 1991, p. 102.

A big welcome back to Elmer the patchwork elephant. This time Elmer is bored and a bored elephant is liable to get up to all sorts of tricks. Happily Elmer's trick is to paint all the elephants to look like him—bright, colourful patchwork. Just to open this book is to be confronted with a kaleidoscope of shape and colour. The language is interesting and the reader will enjoy reading this book aloud as there is plenty of mystery and excitement in the story. There is some complication in the plot and it is likely that a second or third telling will be necessary to fully appreciate the narrative; but this book is so delightful that it will be read again and again.

📖 *ZEBRA'S HICCUPS* (1991)

Lolly Robinson

SOURCE: A review of *Zebra's Hiccups,* in *The Horn Book Guide,* Vol. IV, No. 2, Fall, 1993, pp. 267-68.

When dignified Zebra gets the hiccups, the animals suggest cures that Zebra thinks are too silly. But when the hiccups cause his stripes to shift, he tries everything. In the process, he gains a sense of humor. Boldly colored collage paintings depicting animals with appropriately silly expressions should delight children, and all will appreciate the amusing text—"HIC" replaces key words throughout.

📖 THE SCHOOLBUS COMES AT EIGHT O'CLOCK (1993)

The Junior Bookshelf

SOURCE: A review of *The Schoolbus Comes at Eight O'Clock,* in *The Junior Bookshelf,* Vol. 58, No. 2, April, 1994, p. 48.

David McKee has his own view of reality. The Giles family have problems about time, mostly arising from the fact that they have no clock in the house. What need? 'Here comes the school bus so we know it's eight o'clock.' The trouble comes when Mr. Giles abandons his principles and buys a clock, and then another, and another. . . . Ultimately a compromise is found. Just one clock, and that silent, its hands at eight o'clock. It will always be right for the school bus and bedtime. This crazy family is composed of very normal (by McKee standards) people. The words are moderately good, the pictures funny and very beautiful too. As always David McKee finds an original theme which is precisely suited to his very personal view of a zany world, one which is vastly preferable to the real thing.

Irene Babsky

SOURCE: A review of *The School Bus Comes at Eight O'clock,* in *The School Librarian,* Vol. 42, No. 2, May, 1994, p. 56.

The family manage quite well without one until Mother decides that a clock would be rather nice. They then embark on a period of confusion as they worry whether their clock is correct. In an effort to check its accuracy, they buy more clocks and are woken through the night by an orchestra of chimes, strikes and cuckoos. In the end, they rationalise the problem down to one, stopped clock!

A beautifully conceived, written and illustrated picture book by an acknowledged master of the genre. An engrossing storyline enhanced by some simple yet stimulating ideas about time make this a must for children who appreciate a good story told with gentle humour. It will not be long before the concepts about time which are embedded in the story are recognised by infant teachers and they take this to their hearts as one of those marvellous stories that instruct as well as entertain. A must.

Publishers Weekly

SOURCE: A review of *The School Bus Comes at Eight O'Clock,* in *Publishers Weekly,* Vol. 241, No. 21, May 23, 1994, p. 87.

Although [this] narrative is slightly short on zing, there's appeal to spare in the richly textured pastel spreads. The tale opens on Jennifer and Eric Gilbert's first day of school. As the title indicates, the school bus comes at eight, but the children aren't quite sure when to look for it—their parents don't own so much as a sundial. Mr. and Mrs. Gilbert buy a rickety grandfather clock to remedy the situation, then add a backup in case the first ticker fails; although the hourly chimes keep them awake at night, they collect two more clocks before reverting to their original ways. This agreeable story is not for technophobes alone: the clocks and the opening of school demonstrate the importance of schedules (perhaps this is why, when the grandfather clock stops permanently at eight, the Gilberts keep it as a reminder of the a.m. bus and p.m. bedtime). Philosophical considerations aside, McKee's slightly smeary, blocky compositions—which retain their brightness despite an unusually heavy application of color—warrant a good look.

📖 ELMER'S COLOURS; ELMER'S DAY; ELMER'S FRIENDS; ELMER'S WEATHER (1994)

S. M. Ashburner

SOURCE: A review of *Elmer's Day* and *Elmer's Colours,* in *The Junior Bookshelf,* Vol. 58, No. 6, December, 1994, p. 204.

The simple adventures of Elmer, a patchwork elephant, are related in these board books for the very young child.

In ***Elmer's Day*** the author takes the elephant through a typical day with suggested activities. In ***Elmer's Colours*** the young child is introduced to colours: of Elmer's scarf, food and surroundings.

There is gentle humour in the observation of the elephant. The vocabulary is simple and key phrases are repeated to familiarise the child who is learning to talk, with the language. The pictures are bright and direct, with expression and movement. There are contrasting colours on each page; these add to the interest and the development of the story.

Linda Wicher

SOURCE: A review of *Elmer's Colors* and others, in *School Library Journal,* Vol. 41, No. 1, January, 1995, p. 90.

These books feature a colorful patchwork elephant in their title subjects. Elmer's winsome personality shines through as he romps with a variety of wild animals from all over the world—polar bears and leopards, elephants and kangaroos—in this jungle fantasyland. ***Elmer's Friends,*** the most sophisticated of the four, leaves readers with the message that we can be different and still get along. The other texts are fairly generic, according to the concept depicted; most of the illustrations, done in bold, textured paints, are appealing and will encourage responses from toddlers. Solid choices for the board-book set.

Additional coverage of McKee's life and career is contained in the following sources published by Gale Research: *Contemporary Authors,* Vol. 137; *Major Authors and Illustrators for Children and Young Adults*; and *Something about the Author,* Vol. 70.

Gary Soto

1952-

Hispanic-American author of fiction, nonfiction, poetry, and picture books.

Major works include *Baseball in April and Other Stories* (1990), *Taking Sides* (1991), *Neighborhood Odes* (1992), *Local News* (1993), *Jesse* (1994).

INTRODUCTION

Considered among the most distinguished Chicano poets and a major contributor to American literature for the poems, memoirs, and essays he directs to an adult audience, Soto is also celebrated for the poetry and stories he has written for middle graders and young adults. Praised for his originality and sensitivity as well as for his virtuosity as a literary stylist, he is credited with providing both adult and child readers with illuminating portrayals of Hispanic culture, while underscoring the universality of the experiences and feelings of his subjects. Soto explores the particulars of daily life, ordinary events and emotions represented in a manner that reveals their intrinsic mystery and wonder; he is often lauded for his insight and perceptiveness as well as for his ability to describe new ways of looking at the familiar. Much of his poetry and prose is autobiographical or rooted in the community life of Fresno, California, Soto's birthplace and home through his adolescence. His works for both children and adults address such themes as prejudice and class consciousness, and Soto also describes the poverty, fear, and isolation faced by Hispanic Americans. However, his books are considered distinguished for emphasizing the spirit of the Chicano people along with their loyalty, unity, and strong family ties. Both his poetry and prose are often acknowledged for Soto's rounded characterizations and strong narrative sense. In addition, Soto is noted for his distinctive vision, positive view of life, nondidactic approach, and use of humor; he is also commended for the directness, vibrant images, and spare language of his poetic style and for his lyrical prose, which is characterized by realistic dialogue and use of whimsical simile and metaphor.

In his adult poetry and essays, several volumes of which have been adopted by young adults, Soto has consistently drawn on his childhood and adolescence in Fresno, demonstrating what Suzanne Gurley calls a "seemingly total recall of his youth." In fact, one of Soto's most frequent subjects is his exploration of the child's imagination. When he began writing specifically for young people, Soto continued to mine his knowledge of both the Latino community and the young, creating works that are credited for combining cultural authenticity with keen observations about the universality of growing up. In much of his work for children and young adults, Soto shows both the joy and pain of daily life; as the young people he profiles

attempt to gain maturity and self-awareness, Soto describes their hopes and dreams as well as the results of their experiences, which range from embarassment to triumph. Although he includes instances of prejudice, injustice, and resignation in his chronicles, Soto is acknowledged for describing his characters with dignity, stressing their love, determination, and zest for life in an affectionate, wryly humorous manner. Soto is consistently praised for his understanding of and compassion for his audience; in addition, he is commended for encouraging Chicano children to develop pride in their heritage while demonstrating to them that life is full of exciting possibilities. Noted for the immediacy and clarity of his writing for children and young people, Soto often inserts Spanish words and phrases in his poems and stories; several of his works include glossaries of the terms, a feature that receives a mixed reception. However, most critics consider Soto a significant recent contributor to juvenile literature, a poet whose works are considered accessible introductions to the genre, and a storyteller whose novels and short stories successfully capture the varied experiences of the young with subtlety and charm. "Soto views life as a gift," writes Pamela L. Shelton, "and his talent for expression is his gift to his readers."

Biographical Information

Born and raised in Fresno, in the center of the agriculture-based San Joaquin Valley, Soto grew up in what he calls "pretty much an illiterate family. We didn't have books, and no one encouraged us to read. So my wanting to write poetry was sort of a fluke." Although his parents were born in America, their Mexican heritage became an integral part of Soto's early life. As a child, Soto worked as a migrant laborer, as did the rest of his family. After his father was killed in a work-related accident when Soto was five, he moved with his family to a Mexican American community on the outskirts of the city; memories of his childhood in the barrio, as well as the social concerns which manifested themselves there, later became the basis for much of his literature. After graduating from high school, Soto enrolled at Fresno City College, where he discovered *The New American Poetry*, a collection of poems edited by Donald Allen. Soto recalled, "I thought, This is terrific: I'd like to do something like this. So I proceeded to write my own poetry, first alone, with no one's help, and then moving on to take classes at [California State, Fresno] and meeting other writers." Initially influenced by such writers as Gregory Corso, Kenneth Koch, Edward Field, and Philip Levine, who instructed him in creative writing, Soto was later inspired by such figures as Theodore Roethke, Gabriel Garcia Marquez, E. L. Doctorow, Pablo Neruda, and Nathanael West. After graduating from college in 1974, Soto began graduate school in creative writing at the University of California, Irvine, and married Carolyn Oda, the daughter of Japanese American farmers; while still in graduate school, he began publishing his poetry in such periodicals as the *American Poetry Review*, the *Nation*, and the *New Yorker*. After receiving his master's degree, Soto became writer-in-residence at San Diego State University and a lecturer in Chicano studies at the University of California, Berkeley; in 1977, he became an associate professor in both the Chicano studies and English departments at UC, Berkeley, where he has been a senior lecturer since 1992.

In 1977, Soto published his first volume of poetry, *The Elements of San Joaquin*, which presents a grim view of the violence and pain of the barrio while allowing occasional hopeful and affirmative images. After publishing three more well-received volumes of poetry, Soto published his first book of prose, *Living Up the Street: Narrative Recollections* (1985), which was also the first of his books to become popular with young adults. In this work, which according to Mary Ellen Quinn describes "how one smart and lively kid confronts life, explores possibilities, solves problems," Soto writes about his experiences from boyhood through marriage in twenty-one impressionistic vignettes. In his next prose collection, *Small Faces* (1986), Soto continues his exploration of his past and present as he recalls his life from adolescence through fatherhood. Subsequently, Soto has published concurrent volumes of adult poetry and essays—one of which, *A Summer Life* (1990), describes his childhood and adolescence in Fresno and is admired by young people—as well as children's literature; he is also the editor of a collection of reminiscences about growing up in California and a volume of recent Chicano fiction. In addition, Soto has recently produced two short films, "The Bike" and "The Pool Party," for Spanish-speaking children; the latter is based on one of his stories for middle graders.

Major Works

With the publication of *Baseball in April and Other Stories*, a collection of eleven short stories about Latino young people in a contemporary barrio, Soto is considered to have made an impressive foray into juvenile literature. Profiling an individual character as the focus of each story, he shows these boys and girls in the process of becoming teenagers and also reflects their increasing Americanization; a companion volume, *Local News*, features significant moments in the lives of thirteen adolescents. Soto's first young adult novel, *Taking Sides*, describes how eighth grader Lincoln Mendoza adjusts to moving from the Mission District of San Francisco to the wealthier Anglo suburb of Sycamore, California; faced with playing in a basketball game between his current school and his former team, Linc learns to make peace with himself by integrating the old and the new. In *Pacific Crossing* (1992), Linc goes to Japan on a summer exchange program, sharing his own customs while learning to appreciate those of his host country; Osbelia Juarez Rocha calls the novel "a truly multicultural experience." With *The Pool Party* (1993), a story directed to middle graders, Soto introduces Rudy Herrera, a working-class Hispanic boy who receives an invitation to a rich girl's party and enjoys unexpected success; its sequel, *Boys at Work* (1995), involves Rudy and his best friend Alex in humorous money-making schemes after they break a portable CD player belonging to the neighborhood tough guy. With *Jesse*, a young adult novel set in the late 1960s, Soto created a work praised for effectively presenting the lives of Hispanic Californians during a time of dramatic social and cultural change. Sixteen-year-old Jesse has left both school and home, which he has escaped to avoid his drunken stepfather; living with his older brother, he struggles with poverty, learns about discrimination, and finally discovers himself as an artist; "Like Soto," notes Cathryn M. Mercier, "Jesse has the voice of a poet." Soto is also the author of such works as *Crazy Weekend* (1994) and *Summer on Wheels* (1995), comic novels for young adults that describe the rollicking adventures of blood brothers Hector and Mando, two teens from East Los Angeles; *A Fire in My Hands: A Book of Poems* (1991), a collection of autobiographical poems that Soto prefaces with individual introductions to the events he describes and the poetic process he uses in each poem; and *Too Many Tamales* (1993), a humorous picture book set at Christmas. In this story, Maria loses Mama's ring when it falls into the dough being used to make the tamales for Christmas dinner; after she and her cousins eat two dozen tamales to find the ring, it turns up in a surprising place. Betsy Hearne notes that *Too Many Tamales* is "rendered so acutely that everyone who has lost something precious will respond," and *Kirkus Reviews* says that it "should become a staple on the holiday menu."

Awards

Baseball in April received the John and Patricia Beatty Award in 1991, the Reading Magic Award from *Parenting Magazine* in 1992, and the George G. Stone Award in 1993; it was also named a Best Book for Young Adults by the American Library Association in 1990. *Neighborhood Odes* received the Hungry Mind Award in 1993. With John Kelly, Soto received the Andrew Carnegie Medal for video for his short film "The Pool Party." Soto has also been the recipient of many awards, prizes, and fellowships for his contributions to adult literature; with his second poetry collection, *The Tale of Sunlight* (1978), Soto became the first Hispanic American to be nominated for the Pulitzer Prize.

AUTHOR'S COMMENTARY

Gary Soto

SOURCE: "Author for a Day: Glitter and Rainbows," in *The Reading Teacher,* Vol. 46, No. 3, November, 1992, pp. 200-02.

After the 1990 publication of ***Baseball in April,*** my first book for young readers, I began to get invitations to come and wear the cocked hat of Author for a Day, especially at schools where Mexican-American children warmed almost every chair. I felt good, if not wholly excited, because I wanted to know the readers I'd heard from—Raquel, Dulce, Armando, Fortino, and Joel the Gangster—the *chavalitos* who wrote me the sweet letters that rained glitter and contained crayoned rainbows on lined paper. The letters arrived like clouds from schools in Fresno, Porterville, Sanger, Huron, Shafter—no-nonsense schools in the San Joaquin Valley. At one such school, for instance, the vice principal had to weigh quite heavily his decision to bring Gary Soto as Author for a Day or buy three footballs. He went for the footballs, and perhaps he had a winning year. I'll never know.

I was in love with my readers, brown faces shadowing my own characters with names like their own. I could see them turning the page, a fistful of sunflower seeds in their laps. And now I could see them upfront. I had done many book signings but was never so happy as when a little girl came up and, hands pressed together sweetly, said, "I want to be a writer, too." I gave her a free book and bit my tongue when I started to say, "Sweetie, don't do that to yourself. Go into engineering."

A year later a second young adult book came out, ***Taking Sides,*** which had on the cover a boy going up for a basketball lay-up. Like my first book, whose cover had boys in a pick-up truck wearing baseball caps, it hinted at a sports story. So, when I went to Shafter, my young readers assumed that I had played minor league ball and given pro basketball a try. They were surprised at my average

height, the gray marching through my hair, and my arms that were not strong enough to move the podium without the help of the librarian. Nevertheless, during recess, they expected me to play baseball with them. Teams were made up, and with 15 on each side, the field was clotted with more kids than dandelions. There were 3 second basemen, for instance, and I was one of them, a tiny glove dangling from the end of my wimpy arm. Luckily, the one pop-up that drifted my way I was able to catch. I was all teeth, happy that I hadn't disappointed them. I popped my fist in my glove and yelled, *"Orale!"*

But before recess ended, just as I was getting into the game and chattering louder than any of them, I managed to misjudge a grounder that popped against my chest. In a panic, I gathered the ball quickly and let it fly from my hand to first base. It sailed like a dirty bird, scattering three girls watching from the sidelines. And one of the girls was my best customer—she had bought two books.

Later, after two more periods of creative reading and goofy stories. I, Author for a Day, was led out to play basketball. For the first time in my life, I was chosen first. After all, hadn't I written a basketball book?

Following two feeble shots the kids caught on that I was no good. In one drive toward the hoop, when I was open and beckoning for the ball, my teammate looked me straight in the eyes, and I could see that she wanted to pass me the ball but knew better. She feigned a pass to me but shot it to a small kid with unlaced shoes. Right there, with black on my palms and twin moons of sweat under my arms, I understood my position from their eyes: a good writer but what a hack on the court.

On another more serious school visit, I was asked by a teacher to meet with a parent whose son had run away from home several days before. I met the tearful mother in the hallway, and we walked onto the school yard. Just as I started trying to comfort her with some inept words, we spotted the boy on the far end of the school grounds. When we started walking toward him, he vanished, continuing the emotional game of tag that so upset his teachers and parents. I suggested that we get into my car and look for him, the town being very small. Surely we could find him. We drove up and down the streets, the mother telling me repeatedly that everything was OK at home, he was not being beaten, he was eating enough, the town was a hell hole but he was much loved. We drove until the mother stopped talking, and it was clear to both of us that the town was not small enough to find a boy who doesn't want to be found.

The peak of these surrealistic author days occurred at Huron Elementary, where they held, among other festivities, a school contest to draw Gary Soto's face. This occurred on the evening of the Gary Soto Parade in which approximately 800 celebrants marched—800 from a town of only 4,000!

We were celebrating the première of my little film **"The Bike,"** which featured actors from Huron, a town that, except for three families, is entirely Mexican or Mexican American. The cafeteria was noisy. There were small babies, big babies, school children, sweethearts, vendors, grandparents, and the mayor proclaiming good wishes to *raza!*

The film also featured my uncle, "El Shorty," a foundry worker for 20 years. He was asked to judge the Gary Soto portraits. We walked along one side of the cafeteria chuckling at the 100-plus portraits. Uncle Shorty kept saying *"Qué feo,"* meaning, "how ugly" I was. My uncle was laughing. I was laughing. The portraits showed me with big teeth, crooked glasses, spiky hair, big ears, square head—all the body parts of a happy-go-lucky Frankenstein. The pictures were full of love and enough talent to suggest that the human features, lopsided as they were, added up to me.

Ribbons were awarded to the winners. A bicycle was auctioned off. Speeches were given and children half-listened with nachos in their mouths.

Finally the movie was shown to applause and laughter, not entirely because it was funny (it is), but because they recognized their friends in the film. When the lights came on, I was shocked to see the paper cups, staggered chairs, puddles of soda, candy wrappers, sweaters and jackets, and popcorn like snow on the cafeteria floor—the calamity of a town entertaining itself as best it could.

I was surprised when children tugged at my sleeve and held up their wrists, asking for autographs. I played along, wondering if Woody Allen would run from such attention. I signed my name on their wrists and grew weary.

Later, as Author for a Day, I had to stack chairs and collect my wits in order to later be funny at the cast party in my honor. I received my check and then gave back some of it by picking up the dinner tab.

The letters still arrive, still like clouds. When I open them, glitter rains on my table, and the first-grade rainbows fill my eyes with something like love.

TITLE COMMENTARY

📖 *LIVING UP THE STREET: NARRATIVE RECOLLECTIONS* (1985)

Publishers Weekly

SOURCE: A review of *Living Up the Street: Narrative Recollections,* in *Publishers Weekly,* Vol. 228, No. 4, July 26, 1985, p. 165.

Poet Soto's recollections of growing up in Fresno, Calif., form the basis of his first book of prose, which won the 1985 Before Columbus Foundation American Book Award. He writes here of the typical trials of boyhood—fighting at school, trying out for the baseball team, discovering girls—as well as some less common problems. As a Mexican living in the U.S., Soto experienced prejudice; his father's death forced his mother to work and to leave her children alone all day; because his family was poor, Soto and his siblings had to labor at such jobs as picking grapes and cotton. By book's end, Soto has married and has become a poet. His style here is casual, his images repetitive. Each of the recollections seems to be leading up to something profound, only to stop just short of it. Consequently, the narrative leaves the reader with nothing but a jumbled impression.

Mary Ellen Quinn

SOURCE: A review of *Living Up the Street: Narrative Recollections,* in *Booklist,* Vol. 81, No. 22, August, 1985, p. 1629.

Poet Gary Soto's first prose work is a pleasure to read. In an impressionistic series of vignettes, he re-creates the experience of growing up Mexican American in Fresno, spending one's time with kids whose parents are consumed by backbreaking efforts to make ends meet, always comparing one's own family with the families in "Leave It to Beaver" and "Father Knows Best." The lack of money is a theme that persists throughout the book and plagues Soto even into his marriage and his initial literary success. Although Soto is not sentimental about the impoverished lives of almost everyone he knew, his book is seldom grim. Instead, it is an often very funny and absolutely convincing look at how one smart and lively kid confronts life, explores possibilities, solves problems. This marvelous work received an American Book Award from the Before Columbus Foundation.

Geoffrey Dunn

SOURCE: A review of *Living Up the Street: Narrative Recollections,* in *San Francisco Review of Books,* Summer, 1986, p. 11.

In the nine years since Berkeley poet Gary Soto burst onto the American literary scene with his award-winning ***The Elements of San Joaquin,*** he has continuously culled his Mexican-American youth in Fresno, California, for poetic imagery and vision. . . .

In his latest volume, ***Living Up the Street,*** Soto has changed literary forms, though he returns once again to the dusty fields and industrial alleyways of his Fresno childhood. The twenty-one autobiographical short stories (or, more accurately, vignettes) assembled here recall with amazing detail the day-to-day traumas, tragedies and occasional triumphs of growing up brown in the American Southwest.

Living Up the Street begins with Soto as a precocious, streetwise five-year-old, "polite as only Mexicans can be polite," though with a "streak of viciousness" which Soto defines simply as "being mean." His neighborhood is full of Mexican kids like himself, most of whose parents are employed in the sweltering vineyards of the San Joaquin Valley or in the dreary confines of the Sun-Maid Raisin factory.

Soto posits implicitly in these recollections that the incandescent anger of his youth was the inevitable, perhaps even rational, response to the often violent social setting into which he was thrust by birth. In a passage that is delicately charming, yet distressing as well, Soto recounts his response to being called a "dirty Mexican" by a white playmate. "I looked at my feet and was embarrassed, then mad," he writes. "I approached him slowly in spite of my brother's warnings that the kid was bigger and older. When I threw the bottle and missed, he swung his stick and my nose exploded blood for several feet. Frightened, though not crying, I ran home . . . and dabbed at my face and T-shirt, poked mercurochrome at the tear that bubbled, and then lay on the couch, swallowing blood as I slowly grew faint and sleepy."

In **"Father,"** the book's most poignant vignette, Soto reminisces about a warm summer's day on which he was taught by his father how to water a lawn. "Standing over me," writes Soto, "he took the hose and placed his thumb over the opening so that the water streamed out hissing and showed silver in the dusk. I tried it and the water hissed silver as I pointed the hose to a square patch of dirt that I soaked but was careful not to puddle."

The next day his father suffered a neck injury at work. Two days later he was dead: "A week after that, Rick, Debra, and I were playing in an unfinished bedroom with a can of marbles Mother had given us. Behind the closed door we rolled the marbles so that they banged against the baseboard and jumped into the air. We separated, each to a corner, where we swept them viciously with our arms—the clatter of the marbles hitting the walls so loud that I could not hear the things in my heart."

Soto's poetic prose goes right to the core of the Chicano experience (and, in many ways, to all ethnic experiences) in the United States during the past quarter century. His continual references to the vast chasm between his own reality and the "Father Knows Best" imagery of American television brought back a truckload of memories—and anxieties—from my own Italian-Catholic childhood.

I was particularly struck by Soto's painful description of a so-called beauty contest sponsored by an after-school recreation program. The contest, according the the program director, was to determine which "little kid was the best looking." Soto, then nine, was too old for the competition, so he entered his younger brother, Jimmy.

At the contest, Soto remembers, he was "awed by the blond and fair skinned kids in good clothes. They looked beautiful, I thought, with their cheeks flushed red from the morning heat." The Mexican kids had already developed a sense of inferiority about their looks—their dark skin, their eyes, their hair—so that they were certain they would lose.

And they were right. "A little girl with curlicues" received the crown, and the inferiorities, along with the resentments, became even more imbedded. Soto, already accustomed to such defeats, responded angrily to the decision; his little brother ran away quietly to play on the swings.

Such little incidents, insignificant as they may seem from the distance of the suburbs, constitute a terrible psychological tragedy taking place daily in the ghettos, barrios, and labor camps of this country, and Soto is absolutely brilliant in placing them under the magnifying glass of his literary perceptions. While ***Living Up the Street*** may not hold up to the very best of Soto's poetry, it is certainly a formidable work by one of America's more gifted and sensitive writers.

Rosie Peasley

SOURCE: A review of *Living Up the Street: Narrative Recollections,* in *Voice of Youth Advocates,* Vol. 15, No. 4, October, 1992, p. 232.

These autobiographical recollections of a childhood in the Fresno of the 1950s and 60s tell a poignant story of growing up in the barrio. Soto captures the essence of long hot summers in the central valley of California, of an aimless childhood of looking for, and avoiding, trouble, of warring relationships with siblings, parents, friends and acquaintances. Poverty, boredom, fear, exhilaration, and the constant struggle to survive, and escape, the fate of many impoverished Mexican-American youths are all portrayed in simple, singing descriptions that often leave room for the reader's imagination to fill in the personal responses which allow for Soto to develop into the well-known author he has become. His images will remain in the mind's eye of readers long after they have closed this slim volume.

SMALL FACES (1986)

Raymond A. Paredes

SOURCE: A review of *Small Faces,* in *Rocky Mountain Review of Language and Literature,* Vol. 41, Nos. 1-2, 1987, pp. 124-28.

The most successful Mexican American prose often assumes briefer, less expansive forms in which the focus is relatively narrow and the subject matter rises out of the author's own experiences. Gary Soto's second volume of "narrative recollections," ***Small Faces,*** manifests precisely these qualities. As its title suggests, Soto's volume is as modest as [Lionel] Garcia's [*Leaving Home*] is ambitious, and it is a measure of Soto's skill that he so effectively invigorates and sharpens our understanding of the commonplace.

Small Faces very much resembles Soto's four volumes of poetry and earlier collection of autobiographical sketches, *Living Up the Street.* Soto continues to regard American materialism and notions of success with great skepticism and guilt; he remembers almost hauntingly the Mexican Americans, Asians, and "Okies" of his childhood who struggled, far removed from public concern, against long odds. Soto delivers his observations with his characteristic knack for the whimsical simile or metaphor. In *Small Faces,* days pass "white as clouds," Soto's wife rests her head on his shoulder "like a tired moon," and a jacket Soto's mother gives him as a boy is "the color of day-old guacamole."

In all his work, Soto establishes his acute sense of ethnicity and, simultaneously, his belief that certain emotions, values, and experiences transcend ethnic boundaries and allegiances. *Small Faces* opens with a sketch entitled **"Like Mexicans"** in which Soto recalls a bit of "good" advice from both his mother and grandmother: "Marry a Mexican." Dutifully, the adolescent Soto embarks on his quest for the proper "brown girl in a white dress," only to find himself—to his great surprise—in love with a Japanese American. Soto goes with his fiancee, Carolyn, to

From Neighborhood Odes, *written by Gary Soto. Illustrated by David Diaz.*

meet her parents and is relieved to discover that "these people are just like Mexicans. . . . Poor people." But not long after a plate of *sushi,* Soto reevaluates: Carolyn's people "were like Mexicans, only different."

Together, Soto's ethnic and class consciousness constitute an essential part of his literary sensibility. His recollections, from childhood to his current position as a Berkeley professor, are punctuated by flashes of endured bigotry and his awareness that in the United States to be "Mexican" generally means to be poor. *Small Faces* abounds with images of the poor. In one sketch, Soto imagines himself as a hobo; in another, he ponders the words of a hitchhiking soldier: "The poorer you get, the more people think you look dead. And dead people don't need a damn thing." Soto occasionally romanticizes poverty, but more frequently, he simply acknowledges the human dignity of the poor and expresses his kinship with them.

Against the injustice and cruelty of the outside world, Soto retreats into the pleasures of family life. As he depicts them, the roles are wholly conventional. We see Carolyn as a wife and mother should be, stable and dependable and, consequently, utterly reassuring—the perfect complement to Soto's admitted volatility. Soto reveals hardly anything about her life away from home. His daughter, Mariko, is very much the bright, charming child but as a girl, something of a mystery to her father. It is perhaps too much to say that Soto's portrayals of his wife and daughter are offensive but it is significant that his imagination, so finely tuned in other circumstances to the diversity and nuance of behavior, should perform unremarkably here.

Suzanne Curley

SOURCE: "A Better Place to Live," in *Los Angeles Times Book Review,* August 15, 1993, p. 8.

"And so I went, in my guacamole-colored jacket," writes Gary Soto in *Small Faces.* "So embarrassed, so hurt, I couldn't even do my homework. I received Cs on quizzes, and forgot the state capitals and the rivers of South America, our friendly neighbor. Even the girls who had been friendly blew away like loose flowers. . . . I blame that jacket for those bad years."

Soto's memory of how his mother sent him, "bitter as a penny," to junior high wearing a cheap and hideous green jacket, is typical of the author's seemingly total recall of his youth. Soto writes wonderfully well, making this slim collection of brief essays—like much of his other work, about growing up poor and Mexican-American in Fresno—a delight from beginning to end.

Gloria Treadwell Pipkin

SOURCE: A review of *Small Faces,* in *English Journal,* Vol. 83, No. 3, March, 1994, p. 92.

The publisher has billed the pieces in this collection as stories, suggesting that they are fiction, but a more accurate description might be *memoir*. Each piece represents Soto's reminiscences and his attempts to make meaning of the events of daily life, past and present. Particularly strong are the selections that deal with poverty and class differences, such as **"June,"** Soto's recollection of a high-school rival who "smiled the perfect teeth of magazines" while he was "among the lessers she never saw." Although the reminiscences lack the high drama that adolescents favor, the poetic language, brilliant details, and distinct voice make them suitable for mini-lessons as well as for serious independent readers.

BASEBALL IN APRIL AND OTHER STORIES (1990)

Hazel Rochman

SOURCE: A review of *Baseball in April and Other Stories,* in *Booklist,* Vol. 86, No. 13, March 1, 1990, p. 1349.

Like the Latino young people in these 11 short stories, poet Soto grew up in Fresno, California, and he writes with affectionate ease about a world too seldom represented in children's books. He captures the vitality of language and culture and the closeness of community. He's also open about the conflicts of immigration—among generations and within the individual. Several stories will make funny read-alouds: in **"Seventh Grade"** Victor pretends he can speak French and then tries to bluff his way out by making appropriate French noises ("Frenchie oh wewe gee in September"). **"La Bamba"** finds Manuel covering his confusion by spouting the latest scientific jargon from magazines, while Gilbert (a polite fifth-grader who does his homework) dreams of being the Karate Kid. Soto's message isn't always upbeat, and he doesn't ignore the sadness of prejudice and self-rejection; for example, Veronica thinks her dark Barbie doll is false and wants the blond, blue-eyed version. Not all the stories are as resonant as these, but the characters are warmly individualized, and they will make young people everywhere smile with wry recognition.

Kirkus Reviews

SOURCE: A review of *Baseball in April and Other Stories,* in *Kirkus Reviews,* Vol. LVIII, No. 6, March 15, 1990, p. 431.

Eleven affectionate glimpses of young people, most of them Hispanic, amid the trials and triumphs of daily life in their California neighborhoods.

Coping with small adversities is the common theme here. Veronica's cherished new Barbie doll has lost its head, but she lovingly carries it to bed anyway. Alfonso nervously prepares to go riding with a girl and his bike chain breaks. As Manuel is lip-synching "La Bamba" for the talent show, the record sticks. In the title story, Michael and his younger brother Jesse find an alternative when they fail—again—to make Little League. Lupe's shyness melts when she discovers that she can beat anyone, girl or boy, at marbles. Though some of these episodes seem to trail off, their humor is unforced, and the characters (ranging from middle-graders to adults) are drawn with realism and sympathy. Soto salts the natural-sounding dialogue with Spanish words and phrases (a vocabulary list is given at the end), and binds the stories together with webs of close family ties.

Roger Sutton

SOURCE: A review of *Baseball in April and Other Stories,* in *Bulletin of the Center for Children's Books,* Vol. 43, No. 8, April, 1990, p. 199.

Eleven short stories, told with tenderness, optimism, and wry humor, portray the lives of Mexican-American children in Fresno, heart of California's Central Valley. While the cultural context is authentic, the characters are all school-story ordinary and recognizable: a girl dismayed at the destruction of her Barbie doll ("'Darn it,' she hissed. 'Her head's gone'"); a boy who wants to be *The Karate Kid;* another boy whose lip-synching to a (skipping) record of "La Bamba" turns from humiliation to triumph. Chicano children and parents will be pleased to find a book that admits larger possibilities than the stereotype of the noble-but-destitute farmworker; kids of all cultures will feel like part of this neighborhood.

Roberto Gonzalez Echevarria

SOURCE: "Growing Up North of the Border," in *The New York Times Book Review,* May 20, 1990, p. 45.

Gary Soto's sensitive and economical short stories center on Mexican-American boys and girls becoming teen-agers. They are set in homogeneous lower-middle-class Hispanic neighborhoods in California. At the same time the young people are turning into adolescents, their milieu is becoming progressively Americanized, largely through the pervasive influence of the media. The overall theme of the book is thus individual and social change being provoked by strong outside forces. The boys and girls are transforming themselves awkwardly into facsimiles of adults; the world of adults is turning into an anxious copy of the Anglo world.

Mr. Soto, who was born and raised in Fresno, Calif., teaches Chicano studies and English at the University of California, Berkeley. Because he stays within the teenagers' universe in *Baseball in April,* he manages to convey all the social change and stress without bathos or didacticism. In fact, his stories are moving, yet humorous and entertaining. The best are also quite subtle.

In **"Two Dreamers,"** Luis, Hector's grandfather, is inspired by some advertisements to plot a real estate deal that will make him rich, so he can return to the Mexican town of Jalapa in triumph. But to make phone calls, he needs Hector as interpreter—a common situation in immigrants' homes. Hector, both skeptical and embarrassed, demurs. At the same time he is fascinated by Luis's knowledge and his memories of Mexico ("his hometown with its clip-clop of horse and donkey hooves"). As Hector grows older, the situation is reversed. With his command of English, Hector is now a probe into the future, and into the alien yet alluring world that surrounds him. The story is about this swap of roles. It is very revealing that the contrast of generations skips the father, a figure generally absent in this collection. Luis and 2nd Hector better embody the generational differences. The grandfather is unwaveringly Mexican; Hector is on his way to becoming something still undefined, but certainly not Mexican anymore.

The title story is a poignant tale about compromise and resignation. Michael and Jesse practice hard to make the Little League. At the tryout, nervously watched by other boys' fathers (obviously Anglo and middle-class), they both fail. But they join an independent team, the Hobos, run by Manuel, a fatherly man who coaches with affection and compassion. The team does not do very well, and neither do Jesse and Michael, who are not very good. The Hobos disband slowly, as the boys lose interest in baseball. April is over. What was a consuming interest is suddenly left behind, like so many other things. Life can and will go on without baseball—a somewhat melancholy lesson.

The same air of resignation prevails in other stories, like "Barbie," where Veronica finally gets the doll she wants, only to have it lose its head. This story has a lurking sexual subtext that gives it a more serious and compelling tone than the others, though everything is very understated. The best by far is "The Karate Kid," which has a quixotic theme. Gilbert Sanchez, who is delicate and sensitive, is overwhelmed by the movie *The Karate Kid*. He assumes the persona of his movie hero and challenges his tormentor at school, Pete the Heat, who beats him up unmercifully. Gilbert begs his mother to pay for karate classes. She gives in and he attends a school run by a Mr. Lopez, who is something of an impostor. After a few months, Gilbert feels ready for his second sally. The Heat demolishes him again before all his friends. Gilbert gives up karate gleefully for fiction—that is, for "super-hero comic books; they were more real than karate. And they didn't hurt."

Baseball in April is more than literature for teenagers. The stories give a bittersweet account of reconciliation to the givens of self and life while growing up that will be recognized as authentic by all.

Lynda Brill Comerford

SOURCE: A review of *Baseball in April and Other Stories*, in *Los Angeles Times Book Review*, May 27, 1990, p. 8.

Readers who think of Gary Soto primarily as a poet will be pleasantly surprised to discover that this first volume of young-adult stories offers the same unadorned expression and concrete imagery that have characterized his previous works. . . .

Although the stories in *Baseball in April* are contemporary, their subject matter may well have been influenced by Soto's own childhood in California's San Joaquin Valley. In a down-to-earth manner, Soto presents everyday life as it exists in the streets, homes and schools of poor Mexican-American communities located in the Central Valley. His heroes and heroines are the children of practical-minded laborers who have little extra money to spend on their families' growing needs.

Without attempting to moralize, Soto reveals the pain of having to do without. Yet rather than focus on despair, he concentrates on the hopes and dreams of young people struggling to find a place for themselves in the world.

Desire and determination are perhaps best exemplified in the title story. Here, a boy's resilient spirit allows him to cope with disheartening realities. Although he is not as good at baseball as is his older brother Michael, 9-year-old Jesse loves the sport and is excited about the prospect of trying out for Little League. Neither of the brothers makes the team, but after recovering from the disappointment, the two join a group of neighborhood players who are being coached by the fatherly Billy Reeves.

The team has no uniforms, few good players and continually loses games to the Red Caps, the only other team in the league. Even though other players become discouraged and drift off to pursue other interests, Jesse continues to show up for practice and never loses his enthusiasm for baseball.

The rich texture of Soto's writing stems from his ability to convey a mixture of deeply felt emotions through economical language. Moments of disappointment are balanced with experiences of gratification, joy and warmth.

In the story, "Mother and Daughter," the humiliation that Yollie feels in having to wear an old dress to a dance is followed by exhilaration when she wins the attention of an attractive young man. Eventually, she is allowed to purchase a new blouse, skirt and shoes for an upcoming date. In "Barbie," the frustration that Veronica experiences in owning less-than-perfect dolls is tempered by her more deeply rooted affection, revealed when the little girl carries her two broken Barbies lovingly to bed.

Many of Soto's selections portray a longing to rise above the crowd; the need children feel to be recognized for special talents. Characters' attempts to emulate idols— movie celebrities and rock stars—is sometimes humorous and often poignant. The stories, "La Bamba," "The Karate Kid" and "The Marble Champ" reveal that accomplishing greatness goes beyond creating a new, flashy image; rather, it is the product of very hard work, and is sometimes accompanied by physical or emotional pain.

Family unity is another theme that emerges throughout the collection. Although several stories touch on sibling rivalry and general rebelliousness against the older generation, loyalties to brothers, sisters, parents and grandparents are strongly emphasized.

The opening story, **"Two Dreamers,"** unveils a close relationship between 9-year-old Hector and his immigrant grandfather as the two discuss a scheme to get rich. The coming-of-age story, **"Growing Up,"** presented at the end of the volume, shows the strength of family ties as it explores how an independent 10th-grader comes to realize how much she really cares for her parents, younger sister and brothers.

All of Soto's stories have a strong Latino flavor derived from precise descriptions of home environments and true-to-life dialect; yet the experiences and emotions of characters are universal. If less-sophisticated readers miss some of the subtler messages of the stories, they will find characters with whom they can identity, and will not fail to be moved by the book's more tender moments. For readers unfamiliar with Chicano slang, there is a helpful glossary of Spanish words and phrases.

With tremendous success, Soto transfers to prose his poetic skills of crystallizing a moment and revealing many layers of meaning through ordinary events. His sensitivity to young people's concerns and his ability to portray the world as it is perceived by children is nothing less than remarkable.

Susan Stan

SOURCE: A review of *Baseball in April and Other Stories,* in *The Five Owls,* Vol. IV, No. 6, July/August, 1990, p. 115.

Baseball in April and Other Stories by Gary Soto will be picked up by many potential readers simply because of its title and pleasing jacket illustration, as the publishers surely intended when they chose the name of the collection. All of the stories are set in a contemporary Mexican-American neighborhood in Fresno, California, but the characters in each story vary. In **"Baseball in April,"** two young boys try out for the Little League team for the third summer in a row; when they fail to receive a call, they content themselves with playing for the Hobos until the team peters out for lack of interest. **"Seventh Grade"** is the story of Victor, who likes Teresa and tries to impress her by raising his hand when his teacher asks if anyone knows French. He's put on the spot when his teacher addresses him in French. Soto also writes about girls, such as Veronica, who wants a Barbie doll, and Maria, a tenth-grader testing her independence. These stories reflect Soto's experiences growing up in a Mexican-American family and portray strong, positive family relationships. His writing style is spare, and the Spanish words and phrases scattered throughout the descriptions and characters' conversations are defined on a page at the end of the book.

Margaret A. Bush

SOURCE: A review of *Baseball in April and Other Stories,* in *The Horn Book Magazine,* Vol. LXVI, No. 4, July/August, 1990, pp. 458-59.

Gary Soto is an astute observer of the desires, fears, and foibles of children and teenagers going about the business of daily living. Take Fausto, who longs for a guitar, "to sweat out his songs and prance around the stage; to make money and dress weird." A dog that has strayed from a wealthier neighborhood a few blocks away provides inspiration; Fausto returns Roger to his owners, telling them that their pet was found near the freeway. A cheerfully proffered reward of twenty dollars would buy a second-hand guitar, but the success of his fraudulent scheme weighs heavily on Fausto until he deposits the guilt-laden money in the collection plate at church. Ultimately he becomes the proud owner of his grandfather's old bass *guitarron.* Lupe Medrano, "a shy girl who spoke in whispers," has a razor-sharp mind but no athletic prowess whatsoever until grim determination makes her a marbles champ. Not all of the featured characters are winners. Gilbert suffers through the charade of phony karate classes, afraid to quit and admit that he has wasted his mother's money; tenth-grader Maria declines to go on a boring family vacation only to find that staying home is lonely and that her family has had the astonishing nerve to have fun in her absence. The character portrayals are gentle, and the tone is quiet and somewhat bittersweet. Respect for family is a consistent value throughout the eleven vignettes. Set in central California, the tales all feature Mexican-American families and a liberal sprinkling of Spanish words and phrases, which are defined in a concluding glossary. Potentially an awkward contrivance, these borrowed bits flow naturally, in the manner of speech of many bilingual speakers who shift back and forth. Apart from the flavor imparted by names and terminology, the stories reflect more universally on the experiences and yearnings of a particular economic rather than ethnic group. This illumination of the everyday will strike chords of recognition in readers of all ages.

Kevin Kenny

SOURCE: A review of *Baseball in April and Other Stories,* in *Voice of Youth Advocates,* Vol. 13, No. 3, August, 1990, p. 163.

Alfonso pushes on his crooked teeth with his thumb in a desperate attempt at in-home orthodontia. Jesse allows himself to be hit by a pitch because he knows it's his only ticket to first base. Yollie's evening at the dance becomes a humiliating nightmare when rain ravages her recently dyed dress. Maria can't stand the thought of another boring family vacation, yet can't stop worrying about them when they leave. These and the other characters in this work all share a Latino background. More significantly, the characters share with all YAs the passions, the mercurial emotions, and the seemingly endless struggle that is youth.

Soto's book is a charming collection of 11 short stories, each of which gets at the heart of some aspect of growing up. The insecurities, the embarrassments, the triumphs, the inequities of it all are chronicled with wit and charm. Soto's characters ring true and his knowledge of, and affection for, their shared Mexican-American heritage is obvious and infectious. A glossary of the Spanish words and phrases which flavor the dialogue is included with the collection although contextual definitions are regularly provided. . . .

A decent balance between male and female protagonists results in a work, which, in addition to being accessible to average readers, has something to offer to all.

📖 *A SUMMER LIFE* (1990)

Kirkus Reviews

SOURCE: A review of *A Summer Life,* in *Kirkus Reviews,* Vol. LVIII, No. 9, May 1, 1990, p. 639.

A 126-page collection of rich, lyrical essays on growing up poor in Fresno, Cal., during the 1950's and 60's—altogether, less memorable for their content than their wistful tone and evocative imagery.

As the title indicates, these vignettes by Soto, a leading Chicano poet, are set in the summers of his youth. While some of his "memoirs" obviously contain invention (they start at age four and continue into his teens), the details he uses to flesh them out—the sights, sounds, smells; the objects, gadgets, and discarded trinkets that fascinate a child—re-create a realistic, immediate world. Certain images recur throughout Soto's days of play and discovery: red ants; dirty sneakers; bottle caps, often pressed into heat-softened asphalt; fruit—usually juicy and dripping down his chin and arm. His family is incidental to his play and neighborhood wanderings. His mother goes "out" frequently and is most often found in the kitchen. His uncle, home from the military, has a tattoo and owns a plaster Buddha that young Soto drags outdoors to play with. There is a barely recalled stepfather who drinks and changes channels when the Beatles appear on Ed Sullivan. His two brothers and little sister are at times coconspirators, at other times combatants in his adventures and childish mishaps. Once in a while, Soto's descriptions are jarring: "The sun, yellow as a tooth . . ." But more often, he writes with charming sensitivity: "We walked for a good mile, each of us dragging a sled of loneliness"; or, "After the rain, puddles marked the world's dents."

Plotless mood pieces—sometimes requiring patience but frequently rewarding with rich nuggets and gentle surprises.

Publishers Weekly

SOURCE: A review of *A Summer Life,* in *Publishers Weekly,* Vol. 237, No. 23, June 8, 1990, pp. 40-1.

Poet Soto here offers 39 brief essays about his years from age five to 17 in and around Fresno, Calif. In supple, evocative language he remembers quietly euphoric summer days spent in the shade of fruit trees, when the taps he fastened to his shoes—"kicking up the engine of sparks that lived beneath my soles"—were enough to keep him amused, and when an imaginary brake prevented the boy from speeding out of control. A favorite theme is childish fantasy, whether the rumor of a giant who "lived nearby" or a breeze that "moved a hat-sized tumbleweed," and, without saying a word on the subject, Soto suggests the rich implications of imagination for the future writer. It is mostly his fondness for place that buoys memory up, with the sights, tastes and feelings of home and earth revealed in carefully chosen yet seemingly casual details: "I ate like a squirrel with a burst of jaw motion"; "Grandmother sipped coffee and tore jelly-red sweetness from a footprint-sized Danish." Soto the realist does not neglect his boyhood mischief, and his sly sense of humor is exercised throughout.

William Gargan

SOURCE: A review of *A Summer Life,* in *Library Journal,* Vol. 115, No. 12, July, 1990, p. 97.

Like some of Soto's earlier work, these autobiographical sketches deal with growing up in Fresno during the late 1950s and early 1960s. Each vignette focuses on one particular object or incident, but all the action is filtered through the changing consciousness of the young narrator. Soto's carefully wrought prose achieves a rich poetic texture as images and symbols, repeated from story to story, adumbrate and reinforce each other. Soto is generally known as a Chicano poet, but these stories transcend ethnic and regional interests. They are small but perfect slices of childhood and adolescent life that should have a wide appeal.

Ernesto Trejo

SOURCE: "Memories of a Fresno Boyhood," in *Los Angeles Times Book Review,* August 5, 1990, pp. 1, 9.

Life in this book is not always easy, but most of the time it is fun. And recalled in a prose that bristles with energy, it is never dull.

Presented as a series of "snapshots" that shed light on particulars (**"The Buddha," "The Grandfather," "The Taps," "The Shirt,"** etc.) these 39 brief essays make up a compelling biography of the author's early childhood growing up Chicano in California's Central Valley. Much like in his earlier book, ***Living Up the Street*** (1985), Soto holds the past up to memory's probing flashlight, turns it around ever so carefully, and finds in the smallest of incidents the occasion for literature. Of course, the small turns out to be not so small after all; it's life played out before our eyes.

More than with William Saroyan, another author who wrote about growing up in Fresno, we find correspondences with Follain and Gorki: It's not so much the kid having a hell of a time growing up; this is rather the work of an adult intelligence dealing with time. Always the world is out there, just about to close in on the lives of the characters who breathe in these recollections.

Soto has been, from his first book of poetry, *The Elements of San Joaquin,* to this *A Summer Life,* a writer of careful, intense attention to language. This style, described as "poetic," is simply the stuff that good writing, both poetry and prose, is made of: the direct vision of the world.

And what a vibrant world. Helping Uncle Shorty, just back from the Korean War, collect copper from abandoned machinery in the neighborhood, the young boy, probably 4 years old, notices "the flakes of egg shells, nails, broken bottles, bottle caps pressed into asphalt, grass along fences, sleeping cats, boards, shattered snail shells, liquid-eyed jays, pot holes, black ants, red ants, jaw-lantern insects with blue eyes, half-eaten fruit, ripped shoes, buttons, metal slugs, cracks in the earth, leather thongs, ripped magazines—everything except copper." Though unwilling to yield its copper treasures, the world parades before the attentive eyes of this child.

The 39 short essays in this collection are built around objects, events, and persons or animals. But the subject in question usually is a point of departure or a point of arrival, a talisman holding anecdote and meditation together, an emblem of a larger meaning.

For example, in **"The Rhino,"** the author at 4 years old, after seeing a billboard with the picture of a rhinoceros in front of a tire factory, mistakenly believes that car tires are made of rhino hide. He later gathers enough courage to ask his father if this is true. Father and Uncle explain to him that this is not so, and that "rubber drops from trees into buckets."

But in the meantime, the child has noticed, remembered and described a monumental carnage around him: We eat cows, pigs' feet, bacon (with the happy faces of pigs grinning from the wrappers), and drink goats' milk from cans and cows' milk from cartons decorated with the picture of Hopalong Cassidy, whose horse has no feet. His and his father's shoes are made from hide; Father's belt came from an alligator; Mother and her pillow, a "restrained cloud of feathers," contributed to the demise of chickens; a rabbit had to give up one of its feet for her key chain; the Molinas stir bony pigeons in pots of boiling water.

Later, Father and Uncle watch two boxers hurt each other on television. Dogs and cats lie splattered on the road. Broken pigeons are found on the grills of cars.

Something has happened here. By the end of the essay,

the accumulated horror and fear, the realization that we live surrounded by death, renders the rhino a plausible sacrificial victim on the altar of our comfort and survival, the point being that if rubber could not be obtained from rubber trees or petrochemicals, we would not hesitate to slaughter rhinos (or any other animal) and turn them into tires.

However, preaching or pontificating is the last thing that the reader will find in this brilliant collection. Soto has honed down his artistry to the point where language (a slight description, a character sketch, a passing thought) conveys a vision of the world. He goes for the little particulars, the telling facts. The dull sociologist, or social psychologist, who studies the Chicano Experience will despair at Soto's way of describing what they might consider trivial, unnecessary matters instead of thoroughly examining and solving the problems of barrio existence.

Here is an excerpt from **"The Weather":** "Wind was one thing, frost another. I walked on hard lawns and looked back, happy that my shoe prints were visible, that a dog would stop and sniff them. I followed bike tracks and got nowhere. I followed clouds as well, the heavy machinery of rain that did more than keep me inside. It made my brother and me fight a lot, made my mother sit at the table stirring black-black coffee, the worry of bills resting on a sharp elbow." Instead of describing the child's mood and worries, Soto gives us here, as well as in the rest of the book, what is authentic literature.

The book is divided into three sections and roughly follows a chronological order. In the first section, the father plays a prominent role in the mythology of the child and the memory of the adult. In the second section, the subject is late childhood, the mood introspective, the focus on the immediate family. Finally, in the third section, we see the author entering the world of adolescence, a world larger and more bitter, as it now includes the dreaded stepfather, a character who, though briefly sketched, will linger in the reader's mind for a long time.

Events in these recollections usually happen during the long summer days. Most of the time the vision, though clouded by doubt and discovery of harsh realities, is celebratory; the child is enthralled and amazed at his own existence. In **"The Guardian Angel,"** he exclaims, "I loved my life, and loved playing and eating the same meal over and over and even the loneliness of a thirteen-year-old in jeans bursting with love."

A Summer Life as a whole is a joyous book. After reading the last page, which speaks so eloquently to anyone who pays attention to his childhood or who enjoys literature, we can identify with these words:

"The tennies lay like struck animals on the side of the road. But they are warm and soft, as they let off the steam of a full day."

TAKING SIDES (1991)

Kirkus Reviews

SOURCE: A review of *Taking Sides,* in *Kirkus Reviews,* Vol. LIX, No. 18, September 15, 1991, p. 1228.

Lincoln Mendoza, 12, has felt in limbo ever since moving from San Francisco's Mission District barrio to neat, tree-lined Sycamore—a feeling exacerbated by a game his basketball team is going to play against his former team. Various forces work on Lincoln's fragile sense of identity: he senses that his coach has it in for him because he's Mexican-American; he has trouble accepting his mother's white boyfriend; and he's accused by his main man from the barrio of going "soft" living among whites. Sorting through these internal and external prejudices, Lincoln comes to realize that life isn't a matter of taking sides but of integrating the new with the old.

Soto (***Baseball in April,*** 1990) creates a believable, compelling picture of the stress that racial prejudice places on minority children. He respects the intelligence of his readers, sparing dramatics and allowing them to read between the lines of his quiet yet powerful scenes and bringing the racial issue closer to home for a mainstream readership: the Mendozas are now suburban and middle class and could be anyone's neighbors. There's a tad too much Spanish (it becomes tiresome to read Spanish followed by its translation), and the glossary of Spanish terms should point out that Mexican idioms are included. Nonetheless, a fine, useful contribution.

Deborah Stevenson

SOURCE: A review of *Taking Sides,* in *Bulletin of the Center for Children's Books,* Vol. 45, No. 3, November, 1991, pp. 75-6.

Lincoln Mendoza is suffering from new-kidness and culture shock: he and his mother have moved from the Mission District barrio in San Francisco to the affluent, mostly-white suburb of Sycamore after their apartment was burglarized. Lincoln is a "star basketball player, tall but not thin. . . . His stomach was muscle, his legs were muscle," and he's troubled by the thought of playing for his new school against his old friends. Although the writing is understated to the point of dryness, there are some nice moments, such as Lincoln's "date" with Monica (a one-on-one Sunday basketball game), and the day-to-day junior-high life rings true: "She's *real* cute. Do you have any more Corn Nuts?" Complications such as Linc's mother's white boyfriend, the new coach's racism, and the burglary attempt on the Mendozas' new house, are smoothly incorporated. This also provides an interesting look at youngsters one generation beyond bitter poverty, with both Lincoln and Monica recalling their parents' "boring" stories of agricultural work. As a basketball-and-life story it's less powerful than [Bruce Brooks's] *Moves Make the Man,* but it's an easily readable story of an individual and likable boy adjusting to new ground.

From Neighborhood Odes, *written by Gary Soto. Illustrated by David Diaz.*

Bruce Anne Shook

SOURCE: A review of *Taking Sides,* in *School Library Journal,* Vol. 37, No. 11, November, 1991, p. 124.

This light but appealing story deals with cultural differences, moving, and basketball. Eighth-grader Lincoln Mendoza and his mother have just moved from a San Francisco barrio to a wealthy, predominantly white suburb. He misses his Hispanic friends, the noise, camaraderie, and even the dirt and fights in his old neighborhood. Having made first-string on the basketball team, he finds that the coach dislikes him for no good reason. Plot development hinges on an upcoming game between his new school and the old one. As the big day approaches, Lincoln cannot decide which team he wants to win. He's not sure where he truly belongs, but the game helps to clarify this for him. Readers will easily understand the boy's dilemma. The conflicts of old vs. new and Hispanic vs. white culture are clearly delineated. So is the fact that the differences are not as great as they first appear. Lincoln is a typical adolescent: energetic, likable, moody at times, but adaptable. Other characters are less finely drawn. The coach is the stereotypical obnoxious jock. Lincoln's divorced mother works hard and tries to be a good parent. Her boyfriend Roy is a minor player but he helps Lincoln to deal with his problems. Because of its subject matter and its clear, straightforward prose, the book will be especially good for reluctant readers. A glossary of Spanish words appears at the end of the book.

Sherry Hoy

SOURCE: A review of *Taking Sides,* in *Voice of Youth Advocates,* Vol. 14, No. 5, December, 1991, p. 318.

Fourteen year old Lincoln Mendoza has moved with his mother (his parents divorced when he was seven) from the Mission District barrio of San Francisco to Sycamore, a white suburb. His old junior high is in the same basketball league as his new school. He is having enough problems fitting in, how can he do his best against his old teammates without feeling like a traitor? When he hurts his knee and ends up benched for most of the game (his new coach has a prejudice problem), the decision seems made for him. Lincoln does end up playing, he does his best, but it's not enough to close the gap caused by poor coaching.

The story is slow moving, even the game sequence plods. There are Spanish terms and phrases riddling the text. Most are followed by the same thought rephrased in English, plus there is a partial list of translations in the back. (The notable absence is the translation for pendejo—asshole). If you know Spanish, the rephrasing is annoying, if you don't, having to look them up or not noticing the list in the back until the end is also annoying. For a limited audience.

Carolyn Phelan

SOURCE: A review of *Taking Sides,* in *Booklist,* Vol. 88, No. 7, December 1, 1991, p. 690.

Moving from his inner-city San Francisco neighborhood to a middle-class suburb 10 miles away, Lincoln Mendoza finds conflict without and conflict within. He has a lot to put up with: basketball injuries, an unsympathetic (and slightly crazed) coach, and misunderstandings with his old buddy from Franklin Junior High and his new girlfriend at Columbus Junior High. However, Lincoln does find an unexpected ally in his mother's boyfriend. When Franklin plays Columbus in basketball, Linc becomes his own man at last and resolves in some measure the problems that have troubled him. Linc's cool appraisal of the differences and similarities between his two communities makes for interesting reading, but the book's universality springs from the essential realism of the boy's hopes, fears, and disquieting moments. While the use of Spanish words within the text (some translated in context, others requiring a flip back to the glossary) is a mixed blessing, the novel itself is well constructed, well written, and believable.

A FIRE IN MY HANDS: A BOOK OF POEMS (1991)

Betsy Hearne

SOURCE: A review of *A Fire in My Hands: A Book of Poems,* in *Bulletin of the Center for Children's Books,* Vol. 45, No. 6, February, 1992, p. 170.

Twenty-three poems, eight of which are reprinted from Soto's book *Black Hair* and the rest from other sources, get brief, italicized introductions that may disarm teenagers who are ill at ease with poetry and who think they need explanations. Soto's informal free verse should do the rest, since the narrative flow makes them accessible, and the common subjects—from baseball to buddies—carry inherent appeal. While the language is consciously and unmusically plain, the strong visual imagery will stay with young readers as it has with the adults for whom the poetry was originally intended. [James M.] Cardillo's pen-and-ink drawings are competent if uninventive, and the concluding question-and-answer segment is mildly informative.

Barbara Chatton

SOURCE: A review of *A Fire in My Hands: A Book of Poems,* in *School Library Journal,* Vol. 38, No. 3, March, 1992, p. 264.

A collection of 23 free-verse poems, each prefaced with a comment on how it came to be written. All reflect Soto's own experiences of growing up as a Mexican American in California, and, later, as the father of a young child. The poems, about everyday activities and events, are similar to Paul Janeczko's work in *Brickyard Summer.* In the brief foreword and a question-and-answer section in the back of the book, Soto explains how he came to write poetry and why he writes as he does. Like the selections and comments by a number of contributors in Janeczko's *The Place My Words Are Looking For,* Soto's poems and thoughts provide gentle encouragement to young people who are seeking to express themselves through the use of language.

Maeve Visser Knoth

SOURCE: A review of *A Fire in My Hands: A Book of Poems,* in *The Horn Book Magazine,* Vol. LXVIII, No. 2, March/April, 1992, p. 216.

Gary Soto's collection of twenty-three poems reflects the Hispanic culture of California's Central Valley. The simple poems of childhood, adolescence, and adulthood are about ordinary events and emotions made remarkable by Soto's skilled use of words and images. **"How to Sell Things"** describes a young boy's experience knocking on doors selling oranges two for a dime. Other poems talk about a first date, hitchhiking, and feeding birds. Each poem is prefaced with a short explanation of the poem's origin, which young readers and writers will find particularly helpful in understanding where poetry comes from. Soto includes a foreword and a friendly "question and answer" section to discuss his poetry. He states that "the task is always the same—to get the language right so that the subject of the poem will live." This additional material will be very useful for adults working with young people.

Eleanor Klopp

SOURCE: A review of *A Fire in My Hands: A Book of Poems,* in *Voice of Youth Advocates,* Vol. 15, No. 1, April, 1992, p. 64.

First, why this book is a 5Q: Soto has the universality of a true poet. Though the poems are of boyhood and young manhood in California, they will appeal to the young of both sexes and all areas. His free verse reads smoothly and often lyrically. His figures of speech are vivid and true to life: "Torn pieces of paper / Scuttling like roaches, a burst at a time." Each poem is preceded by a two to four sentence "anecdote" elucidating its source or inspiration. . . .

However, all of the 23 poems are reprints from Soto's earlier works. Eight of them deal with his relationship with his little daughter, not perhaps of great interest to YAs, especially younger ones. The only original parts are the Foreword (2 1/2 pages), in which he describes how he came to be a poet; the anecdotes; and the final "Questions and Answers about Poetry" (four pages), such as "Where do your poems come from?" "When do you write?" "Why don't your poems rhyme?" Both Foreword and Questions and Answers may well be of interest to aspiring poets. Soto's is indeed a refreshing voice, but think carefully before buying, especially if you already have some of his books.

Hazel Rochman

SOURCE: A review of *A Fire in My Hands: A Book of Poems,* in *Booklist,* Vol. 88, No. 15, April 1, 1992, pp. 1437-38.

This small, illustrated volume will attract poetry readers and writers, not so much for the 23 poems, as for its candid, personal, undogmatic "advice to young poets." Few of these poems have the depth of Soto's adult collection **Home Course in Religion,** which is mainly about growing up poor, Catholic, and Mexican-American, and about friendship, dating, and fatherhood. Some of the best poems here—like **"Oranges"** and **"Finding a Lucky Number"**—have been anthologized in Janeczko's YA collections. But Soto's casual foreword, his questions and answers about poetry, and his brief autobiographical anecdotes with each poem emphasize that poetry keeps alive "the small moments" and finds meaning in "commonplace everyday things." While not denying that poetry can be difficult, he makes us want to pay attention.

NEIGHBORHOOD ODES (1992)

Publishers Weekly

SOURCE: A review of *Neighborhood Odes,* in *Publishers Weekly,* Vol. 239, No. 15, March 23, 1992, p. 74.

The Hispanic neighborhood in Soto's 21 poems is brought sharply into focus by the care with which he records images of everyday life: the music of an ice cream vendor's truck, the top of a refrigerator where old bread lies in plastic, dust released into the air when a boy strums a guitar. The diverse voices include that of a 12-year-old girl "with hair that sings / like jump ropes" and a fourth-grade boy whose new teeth create the "racket / Of chicharron / Being devoured. . . ." The vocabulary sprinkled with Spanish (there is a glossary at the back of the book) remains consistent, as does the form of the poems, which fall in long vertical columns with short lines. The tight clumps of language reproduce the quality of rapid and playful conversation. Affectionate without being overly sentimental, the collection provides a good introduction to contemporary poetry as well as a fine homage to a Chicano community.

Reneé Steinberg

SOURCE: A review of *Neighborhood Odes,* in *School Library Journal,* Vol. 38, No. 5, May, 1992, p. 128.

The rewards of well-chosen words that create vivid, sensitive images await readers of this collection of poems. Through Soto's keen eyes, they see, and will be convinced, that there is poetry in everything. The odes celebrate weddings, the anticipation of fireworks, pets, grandparents, tortillas, and the library. Although Soto is dealing with a Chicano neighborhood, the poetry has a universal appeal. A minor drawback is that the Spanish words are not translated on the page, but in a glossary; to consult it interrupts the reading. Still, children will surely recognize the joy, love, fear, excitement, and adventure Soto brings to life. It is the same sensitivity and clarity found in **Baseball in April,** his collection of short stories. [David Diaz's] black-and-white illustrations blend well with the astute verbal imagery. Each selection is an expression of joy and wonder at life's daily pleasures and mysteries.

Kirkus Reviews

SOURCE: A review of *Neighborhood Odes,* in *Kirkus Reviews,* Vol. LX, No. 9, May 1, 1992, pp. 616-17.

The memories and experiences of Hispanic children are celebrated in a collection of short-lined poems from the author of **Baseball in April** (1990). With the one exception of the deliciously shivery **"Ode to La Llorona"** (a weeping ghost), the mood ranges from tired happiness to downright exuberance. A girl boasts that she doesn't have to pay for *raspados* (snow-cones) because her father drives the ice-cream truck; Pablo goes to bed without a bath because "he wants to be / Like his shoes, / A little dirty"; a child eats a spoonful of ground chile pepper from the *molcajete* (mortar), to his huge regret; others fondly recall picnics, a wedding, the library, running through the sprinkler, and similar pleasures of a California neighborhood. . . . Soto's language leans slightly toward the formal (as befits an ode) and is sprinkled with Spanish words, clear in context but also translated in a glossary.

Ellen Fader

SOURCE: A review of *Neighborhood Odes,* in *The Horn Book Magazine,* Vol. LXVIII, No. 3, May/June, 1992, pp. 352-53.

Twenty-one poems, all odes, celebrate life in a Hispanic neighborhood. Other than the small details of daily life—peoples' names or the foods they eat—these poems could be about any neighborhood. With humor, sensitivity, and insight, Soto explores the lives of children: having a dog or cat; lifting weights; enjoying a Sunday visit to the park for a family cookout; and experiencing the exhilaration, on a steamy day, of dashing through a lawn sprinkler, only to suffer the pain of a bee sting. Librarians will be intrigued by **"Ode to My Library,"** in which a child delights in his research on the Incas and the Aztecs—"our family of people"—and fantasizes about showing "*mis abuelitos* [my grandparents] . . . / The thirty books I devoured / In the summer read-a-thon." Some of the poems, such as **"Ode to a Day in the Country,"** offer startling new ways of thinking about common things; it is a paean to sheep: "We love sheep. / We love the fatness / of wool, the itch / Of something warm to wear. / So man tugs on a sock, / And this is sheep. . . . / So child slips on a hat, / And this is sheep. / We're closer to the country / Than we think." David Diaz's contemporary black-and-white illustrations, which often resemble cut paper, effortlessly capture the varied moods—happiness, fear, longing, shame, and greed—of this remarkable collection. With a glossary of thirty Spanish words and phrases.

Carrie Eldridge

SOURCE: A review of *Neighborhood Odes,* in *Voice of Youth Advocates,* Vol. 15, No. 3, August, 1992, p. 195.

Take a walk through an Hispanic neighborhood in these 21 poems by Soto. Each ode highlights the small joys of neighborhood life and evokes images familiar to young people. In **"Ode to Pablo's Tennis Shoes"** "He loves his shoes / Cloth like a sail, / Rubber like / A lifeboat on rough sea. / Pablo is tired, / Sinking into the mattress. / His eyes sting from / Grass and long words in books. / He needs eight hours of sleep / To cool his shoes, / The tongues hanging / Out, exhausted." In **"Ode to Pomegranate,"** rich images bring to mind scenes from my own childhood: "The pomegranate / Bursts a seam / And the jewels / Wink a red message." This is accessible poetry, written in free verse in plain language, but filled with

images that will pull in young readers. Teachers may want to use them for the classroom and assign students to write odes to their own neighborhoods. A glossary of Spanish words will help readers unfamiliar with the language.

Osbelia Juárez Rocha

SOURCE: A review of *Neighborhood Odes,* in *MultiCultural Review,* Vol. 1, No. 4, October, 1992, pp. 82-3.

Soto recalls his childhood in a neighborhood in Fresno, California, in this collection of 21 truly exuberant poems offering an authentic view of the day-to-day events in Hispanic neighborhoods, or *barrios,* in the southwestern region of the United States. Written in English with a few Spanish terms dispersed throughout, the refreshing lyrics will particularly inspire Hispanic readers who readily identify with the topics (such as *la llorona, la tortilla, la piñata, el gitarrón, el molcajete,* and *los chicharrones*) which are unique to his culture. Both Hispanic and non-Hispanic readers will be able to identify with topics such as "the snowcone" (*la raspada*) and "my dog" (*mi perro*) for which the Spanish term is used in the ode's title but which are not distinctively Hispanic topics and with topics such as "the library" and "fireworks" for which the English term is used in the title. Non-Hispanic readers who yearn to learn about the United States' fastest-growing minority group will certainly benefit from this entertaining book.

In **"Ode to *La Tortilla,"*** the *tortillas* are cleverly described as "flutes when rolled" and eaten with butter. In **"Ode to *Los Chicharrones,"*** the fried pork rinds are said to be "shaped like trumpets" and their "music is a crunch on the back molars." **"La Llorona"** cries out for her children, "Normaaaa, Marioooo, Carlooooos." The occasional mixture of Spanish and English terms to convey a thought ("I love *mi gato, porque* I found him on the fender of an abandoned car.") makes Hispanic readers feel at ease: It seems as if the poet is speaking face-to-face with the readers.

Soto's depiction of his childhood encourages Hispanic children to develop a sense of pride in their cultural heritage since his poetry collection is free of stereotypes and racial biases. At the same time, non-Hispanic children are provided with an objective, realistic representation of Hispanic culture, including its folklore (**"La Llorona"**).

THE SKIRT (1992)

Publishers Weekly

SOURCE: A review of *The Skirt,* in *Publishers Weekly,* Vol. 239, No. 38, August 24, 1992, p. 80.

Miata is proud of her family's Mexican heritage. Lately, she has been practicing with her folklorico dance troupe for a performance, and she has even brought her costume to school to show her classmates. But on the Friday before the show Miata forgets her decorative skirt on the school bus. Afraid to tell her parents about her mistake, the girl enlists her friend Ana in a bit of derring-do to retrieve the garment. Soto's light tale offers a pleasant blend of family ties, friendship and ethnic pride. Readers will be introduced to a few words, foods and customs that may be new to them, but will also relate to Miata's true-to-life, universal experiences and relationships. Though her problems are far from grave, and her actions not so dangerous, some moralists may be concerned that Miata never tells her parents what she's done. However, she does express some guilt and comes across as a spunky and imaginative heroine who tries to take responsibility for her own actions. This short novel should find its most appreciative audience at the lower end of the intended age range.

Ann Welton

SOURCE: A review of *The Skirt,* in *School Library Journal,* Vol. 38, No. 9, September, 1992, p. 255.

Miata Ramirez has a problem that will strike a chord with many children: she forgets things. This particular Friday afternoon, she has left her *folklórico* skirt on the school bus, and she is supposed to dance in it on Sunday. She sees no alternative but to break into the bus and retrieve it. So, dragging along her shy friend, Ana, that is exactly what she does. This is a light, engaging narrative that successfully combines information on Hispanic culture with familiar and recognizable childhood themes. The San Joaquin Valley, California, setting is realistically drawn, and the closeness of Miata's family is reassuring. A fine read-aloud and discussion starter, this story blends cultural differences with human similarities to create both interest and understanding.

Betsy Hearne

SOURCE: A review of *The Skirt,* in *Bulletin of the Center for Children's Books,* Vol. 46, No. 2, October, 1992, p. 55.

Children's anxiety about losing something precious is certainly common enough to form the basis of a cogent story in which a nine-year-old girl leaves behind, one Friday afternoon on the school bus, a Mexican *folklórico* skirt that belonged to her mother as a child. Miata is supposed to perform in the skirt Sunday morning, so the intervening time is tense with her efforts to hide the loss and retrieve the skirt, a feat she manages just in time for a rather ironic surprise ending. This is light, easy reading, the dialogue natural and the Mexican-American cultural setting unaffected. Miata's family and friends are typical without becoming stereotypical, offering readers a cast and situation with which to identify, whatever their own ethnic origins.

Kirkus Reviews

SOURCE: A review of *The Skirt,* in *Kirkus Reviews,* Vol. LX, No. 19, October 1, 1992, p. 1261.

Again, fourth-grader Miata Ramirez has lost something. This time it's her mother's *folklórico* skirt, saved from her childhood in Mexico. Miata's costume for the church dance performance is now on board a school bus, locked up for the weekend. Unable to face her mother's scolding, Miata breaks into the bus and retrieves the garment, only to find out later that her mother has bought a new skirt as a surprise. Sorry that the old skirt may not be worn again, Miata dons both on her special day. As in previous books (**Baseball in April,** 1990; **Taking Sides,** 1991), Soto shows a mainstream audience that the lives of middle-class Hispanics resemble their own. Ultimately, however, the story is unsatisfying: Miata rescues the old skirt to avoid a lecture, not because the garment embodies a sense of time, culture, or tradition for her. A mixed showing from a talented author.

Nancy Vasilakis

SOURCE: A review of *The Skirt,* in *The Horn Book Magazine,* Vol. LXVIII, No. 6, November/December, 1992, pp. 720-21.

An unpretentious story for readers new to chapter books presents a cheery snapshot of a Mexican-American family from the San Joaquin Valley in California, recently arrived in the suburbs. The events of the narrative concern Miata's attempts to retrieve from her schoolbus the *folklorico* skirt she left behind. Once worn by her mother as a child in Mexico, the skirt will be needed by Miata for her dance troupe's performance after church on Sunday. She enlists the help of her best friend, Ana, and with the unexpected assistance of Rudolfo—whose teasing was one of the reasons for Miata's forgetfulness in the first place— they sneak into the school parking lot. After a few close calls, they reclaim the garment. A surprise twist at the end has Mama proudly presenting her daughter with a new skirt on the day of the performance. In a fitting symbolic gesture Miata decides to wear both—the old one under the new. There is just enough suspense in the spare story line to hold the attention of younger readers, and the scattering of Spanish words that appear in the text— primarily the names of foods—can be understood in context. This glimpse into the life of the Ramirezes offers yet another view of the American family.

Isabel Schon

SOURCE: A review of *The Skirt,* in *Journal of Youth Services in Libraries,* Vol. 7, No. 4, Summer, 1994, p. 426.

Miata Ramirez, a fourth-grader, is anxious and worried when she forgets her mother's folklórico skirt on the school bus as she needs to wear it in a dance performance. With help from her best friend, Ana, she finally gets it back and is relieved that she doesn't have to tell her parents about her loss. Miata's loving and supportive Mexican American family is warmly depicted in this light-hearted story in which children do all the things children are not supposed to do, such as lock themselves out of their houses, climb trees, and play with matches. It is also wonderful to read about a Mexican American family that enjoys its food, language, and background and is happy in its new home in Southern California. In addition, Miata's verve will please all readers.

📖 PACIFIC CROSSING (1992)

Kirkus Reviews

SOURCE: A review of *Pacific Crossing,* in *Kirkus Reviews,* Vol. LX, No. 18, September 15, 1992, p. 1194.

Lincoln Mendoza makes new friends when he flies to Japan as part of a summer exchange program. Soto smoothes Lincoln's path: the money is easily raised; the Chicano teenager is intelligent, eager to please; and he adapts easily to life on a small Japanese farm (it reminds him of the migrant labor stories his relatives tell) and to practicing a martial art, embracing Japanese customs, and sharing his own with his friendly temporary family. Soto salts the text with Spanish and Japanese terms, defined in context and in glossaries at the end. A pleasant, easygoing story about sharing cultures, like David Klass's *Breakaway Run* (1987) but without the complication of a stressful family situation.

John Philbrook

SOURCE: A review of *Pacific Crossing,* in *School Library Journal,* Vol. 38, No. 11, November, 1992, pp. 124-25.

Mexican-Americans Lincoln and Tony, both 14, are chosen as exchange students for a summer in Japan. They reside with different families and the focus is on Lincoln, with Tony appearing only when a sounding board is needed. The boys prepare a botched Mexican meal for their hosts, and Lincoln saves his host family's father's life by driving, unlicensed, to a hospital. Other than these episodes, little happens in what is essentially a novel of manners contrasting cultural mores. The writing is very good, often elegant, and the point of view is in keeping with a 14-year-old. The text contains many words and phrases in Spanish and Japanese, set off in italics and defined in separate glossaries. Unfortunately, this becomes distracting and often vexing, slowing down an already uneventful narrative. Readers will wonder just what is the *lingua franca* between the boys and their hosts. All of the Japanese exhibit a complete mastery of English, a nearly universal proficiency that is never explained. Though not without interest, the story is too languid and linguistically confusing to hold the attention of this age group.

Stephanie Zvirin

SOURCE: A review of *Pacific Crossing,* in *Booklist,* Vol. 89, No. 5, November 1, 1992, p. 505.

In this sequel to *Taking Sides* Soto writes about open minds, not closed ones, as he turns once more to multicultural themes. Lincoln Mendoza, now happily out of the suburbs, is selected for a summer exchange program to Japan, where he will continue the martial arts training he began in San Francisco. Lincoln discovers that Mr. and Mrs. Ono and their son, Mitsuo—his host family—are congenial guardians and as eager to learn about the U.S. and his Mexican American heritage as 14-year-old Lincoln is to learn about Japan. Their cultural collisions are affable and gently humorous, as when Lincoln, who's not a good cook, prepares frijoles for his "family," and when he visits the *sento,* a men's public bath, for the first time. The episodic plot is not particularly dramatic, except for one incident, when Lincoln, who can't drive, must rush an ailing Mr. Ono to the hospital. It's the language that seems to punch things up: Soto uses a heroic combination of contemporary American slang ("fresh," "bad") and Spanish and Japanese terms likely to have readers making good use of the book's two glossaries. Yet the strange word mix works more often than not; the story, though slight, is warm and winning; and its setting is strikingly authentic.

Ellen Fader

SOURCE: A review of *Pacific Crossing,* in *The Horn Book Magazine,* Vol. LXVIII, No. 6, November/December, 1992, pp. 725-26.

Lincoln Mendoza and Tony Contreras, best friends and almost-eighth graders from the barrio in San Francisco, are recommended for a summer-exchange program in Japan because of their mutual interest in the Japanese martial art of *shorinji kempo.* After a tediously long airplane trip, they find themselves welcomed by their respective families in Atami, a little farming town three hours outside of Tokyo. Lincoln achieves all the goals he sets for himself for his six weeks in Japan: he learns some Japanese, practices *kempo,* and develops a warm relationship with his host family—especially with the son, Mitsuo. While he expects to encounter many differences between the two countries, he quickly discovers that many things, such as playing baseball and telling jokes, are shared. His hardest task is trying to refine his own thinking and explain to his hosts what it is like to be Mexican-American. Lincoln finds himself fighting back tears when he says his final good-byes to the Ono family. Readers will be attracted to this steadily paced sequel to *Taking Sides* which is filled with authentic details about life in present-day Japan. The novel highlights the truisms that people are the same all over the world and that friends can be found anywhere, if one makes the effort. Soto's graceful integration of many Spanish and Japanese words and phrases into his writing renders the two appended glossaries almost superfluous.

Roger Sutton

SOURCE: A review of *Pacific Crossing,* in *Bulletin of the Center for Children's Books,* Vol. 46, No. 4, December, 1992, pp. 122-23.

Somewhat fortuitously, Lincoln and Tony, introduced in *Taking Sides,* find themselves winging across the ocean to Japan, courtesy of a summer student exchange program. This isn't so much a novel as it is a series of episodes that lightheartedly explore the culture clash between Lincoln's Mexican-American heritage and the customs of his Japanese host family. "Mitsuo tilted his head curiously and asked, 'What is "tortilla"? And that other word—"freeholies"?'" Mitsuo is the son in Lincoln's Japanese family, and Soto effectively uses the friendship between the two fourteen-year-olds to explore cultural currencies (the author seems only intermittently to remember that Tony, Lincoln's best friend, is also staying in the same town). Like Lincoln, most readers will discover here a Japan different from samurai (or electronic Tokyo) stereotypes: Mitsuo's family lives in a small farming town and dresses in Western clothes; Lincoln's *sensei* (martial arts teacher) is a woman. Attempts at action, such as a Keystone Cops chase through Tokyo, are sketchy and silly; the book works best in the small moments of family banter. Lincoln and Mitsuo hope for a reunion in San Francisco, a situation that would make a pleasing sequel.

Osbelia Juárez Rocha

SOURCE: A review of *Pacific Crossing,* in *MultiCultural Review,* Vol. 2, No. 2, June, 1993, pp. 76, 78.

Pacific Crossing is a cleverly crafted, entertaining anecdote that acquaints the reader with the Japanese and Mexican-American cultures. Juxtaposing humor with insight, this prolific author presents a spectacular story which compels its audience to continue reading, chapter after chapter. A sensational celebration of Japanese and Mexican-American customs via a realistic fiction anecdote, *Pacific Crossing* exhibits a powerful, action-filled plot and strong characterization.

Lincoln Mendoza and his *Barrio* buddy, Tony Contreras, travel from San Francisco to Japan as exchange students. Envisioning Japan as a country that concentrates solely on the automobile industry and martial arts, Lincoln is prepared to devote all of his time to martial arts. To his astonishment, Japan proves to be a country of diversity as Lincoln discovers commuter trains, baseball, joking, farming, history, and tradition. Lincoln has difficulty explaining what it means to be both Mexican and American. But enlightening his Buddhist friend, Mitsuo, to the sacrament of confession is exceptionally difficult for the Catholic *Chicano.* After a few adventures with Mitsuo, the teenager from his host family, Lincoln decides that his Japanese brother is as great a friend as Tony.

The narrative is accompanied by glossaries titled "Spanish Words and Phrases" and "Japanese Words and Phrases." Defining all Spanish and Japanese terms used in the text, Soto allows his audience to fully appreciate the story by providing effortless reading. Diacritical marks are included in each glossary. A pronunciation key for each word or phrase in the glossaries would have been helpful, since targeted readers will not necessarily be fluent in English, Spanish, *and* Japanese. While the absence of pronunciation keys does not detract from the story's effectiveness, it leaves doubt in the reader's mind regarding correct pronunciation.

The cover's watercolor illustration features Lincoln in his *gi* (martial arts uniform). While the painting will appeal to most boys, it will also attract many girls. Unlike other stories in which the narrator and his closest friends are males, this tale will appeal to both boys and girls through its focus on Japanese and Mexican-American cultures. A truly multicultural experience, *Pacific Crossing* has much to offer its readers.

📖 *LOCAL NEWS* (1993)

Kirkus Reviews

SOURCE: A review of *Local News,* in *Kirkus Reviews,* Vol. LXI, No. 7, April 1, 1993, p. 464.

The author of *Baseball in April* (1990) offers 13 more domestic reversals of fortune. Javier snaps a picture of Angel in the shower and threatens **"Blackmail"**; Alex's **"First Job"** turns into disaster when he accidentally sets a neighbor's fence afire; Robert almost botches his one line in **"The School Play"** (about the Donner party); Jose challenges new classmate Estela to a game of racquetball—which he's never played—and is wiped out; flying is not the peak experience Araceli expects when she signs up for a **"Nickel-a-Pound Plane Ride,"** etc. As always, Soto shows that the concerns and triumphs of Latino children are no different from anyone's, and though he respects his characters, their misadventures are treated with a light touch—vignetters rather than life-changing incidents. Also as usual, the narrative is sprinkled with Spanish words and idioms, defined at the back—excellent flavoring but, for many, extra work.

Publishers Weekly

SOURCE: A review of *Local News,* in *Publishers Weekly,* Vol. 240, No. 15, April 12, 1993, p. 64.

Once again, the author of *Taking Sides* and *Pacific Crossing* creates a vibrant tapestry of Chicano American neighborhoods in this newest collection of stories highlighting small yet significant moments in the lives of 13 adolescents. Soto's sharp ear for contemporary lingo and keen insights into teenagers' minds bring life to such characters as Philip Quintana, self-proclaimed mechanic; quarreling brothers Angel and Weasel; and lovesick José, who tries to win a girl's notice by pretending to be a racquetball champ. Conflicts may vary, yet in almost all of the selections determination, loyalty and a general zest for life are acutely depicted. Mexican terms and expressions (defined in a glossary) add particular spice and believability. Catching the infectious spirit of these slice-of-life stories, readers will have no trouble staying involved—they may pause only long enough to reflect on the subtle ironies that emerge at piquant moments.

Carolyn Phelan

SOURCE: A review of *Local News,* in *Booklist,* Vol. 89, No. 16, April 15, 1993, p. 1516.

Soto's latest collection includes 13 short stories about young people in a Hispanic neighborhood—at home, at school, at the mall. One vivid tale concerns a girl who takes her sweet kitten to school to protect it from the feline bully at home, only to find her little darling mauling a mouse on the playground. Another shows the desperation and awkwardness of a girl who's lost her "boyfriend's" Raiders jacket. Another is about a boy whose extortionist of an older brother takes a picture of him in the shower and threatens to show it to the girls at school. Varied in tone, the stories show the humor of growing up as well as the anguish. Their appeal extends beyond ethnic boundaries. Spanish teachers and Latino / Latina kids may see the inclusion of Spanish words within the text as a plus, but readers who don't know the language will find all that flipping back to the glossary a bit tiresome. Still, Soto's one of the better short story writers for this age group, plunging readers into each new situation with immediacy and conviction.

Dona Weisman

SOURCE: A review of *Local News,* in *School Library Journal,* Vol. 39, No. 5, May, 1993, pp. 128, 130.

Much as he did in **Baseball in April,** Soto uses his ability to see the story in everyday experiences and to create ordinary, yet distinctly individual and credible characters to charm readers into another world. He uses his poetic writing style and the Spanish of the Mexican-American community in the San Diego area to create 13 new stories for this book. The appended list of terms and phrases will be useful to readers unfamiliar with the language, although many of the terms used are not included in the list. The book will be as popular as a collection of stories about young people as it will be useful for starting discussions regarding sibling rivalry, self-image, growing up, cultures, or writing styles.

Ellen Fader

SOURCE: A review of *Local News,* in *The Horn Book Magazine,* Vol. LXIX, No. 4, July/August, 1993, p. 460.

In a companion book to **Baseball in April,** Gary Soto again captures nuances in the everyday lives of boys and

From Too Many Tamales, *written by Gary Soto. Illustrated by Ed Martinez.*

girls growing up in a Mexican-American neighborhood. In this second book of short stories we share in their embarrassments (Angel's mean older brother photographs him in the shower and bribes him with the results); their disappointments (Araceli's longed-for airplane flight turns out not to be the fun that she anticipated); and their joys (Robert's delivery of his one line in the school play at the end of sixth-grade earns his teacher's praise). These stories resonate with integrity, verve, and compassion. Although the protagonists vary in age, the vignettes have a consistent quality in the demands they place upon the reader; teachers will appreciate that each story possesses several levels of meaning. Another first-rate collection from a perceptive and sensitive chronicler of ordinary life.

Caroline S. McKinney

SOURCE: A review of *Local News,* in *Voice of Youth Advocates,* Vol. 16, No. 3, August, 1993, p. 158.

Soto's latest collection of short stories may be his very best work to date. This gifted writer has produced poetry, essays, recollections, and an award winning short story collection, ***Baseball in April*** for young adults. Now he has given us another journey into a Mexican-American community in California with his little volume entitled, ***Local News.*** Within this neighborhood we find young teens encountering all kinds of daily events, problems, and decisions as they work to gain maturity and understanding. These characters have ambitions, dreams, and aspirations that are often lofty and sometimes small, yet significant. They strive to accomplish daily tasks, and major goals. They are humorous, imaginative, clever, insightful, creative and very, very real.

What makes this collection particularly appealing is that in spite of the title, these people touch universal concerns and themes. Like Wilder's *Our Town,* this setting provides a backdrop for human questions and concerns. The ordinary events of his young characters are both products of this special neighborhood and representations of a larger universal community. The first story, **"Blackmail,"** describes the relationship between Angel, a fourth grader, and his older brother Weasel. Weasel takes a picture of Angel in the shower, and threatens to take it to school to show to his friends unless Angel can come up with twenty dollars. This is the ultimate nightmare to any young person, and the reader is torn between great pity for Angel and the desire to laugh out loud at the predicament. This is a story that teachers will love to read to their classes, and the liberal scattering of Spanish words and phrases enhances the story without being a distraction. The flavor of the community is generously given by the use of the Spanish terms, and a glossary is provided in the event that the reader is unable to determine the meaning from the context.

From Angel and Weasel, to 6th grader Robert Suarez trying to remember his lines for the school play, to Lorena Malvaez who believes she has lost her boyfriend's favor-

ite Raiders' jacket, each character has a unique and often poignant story. Each story is a little treasure of human experience skillfully drawn with poetic sensitivity. The characters and their families have a dignity that warms the reader and makes us hope that Soto will tell us more— soon.

Miriam Martinez and Marcia F. Nash

SOURCE: A review of *Local News,* in *Language Arts,* Vol. 71, No. 2, February, 1994, p. 138.

Local news can be absorbing; certainly this is the case in Gary Soto's latest book. The news is about young people who are involved in the ordinary ups and downs of life. There is Angel, whose brother snaps his picture in the shower and proceeds to blackmail him with the photo, and 13-year-old Alma, who dresses like a football player for trick-or-treating, only to find herself stopping off at the home of a friend who is giving a girl/boy party. Blanca, determined to show her family she can stay up alone to see in the New Year, inadvertently locks herself out of the house. Also featured in the news is Nacho, whose resolve to help save the world by becoming a vegetarian begins to falter in the face of meat. Soto's pithy dialogue and engaging narrative makes readers feel very much a part of the Mexican American neighborhood about which he writes.

THE POOL PARTY (1993)

Susan F. Marcus

SOURCE: A review of *The Pool Party,* in *School Library Journal,* Vol. 39, No. 6, June, 1993, p. 112.

Rudy is an average kid from a nice family. In his young life, between the time he receives an invitation to a rich girl's pool party and his subsequent social success there, various episodes occur that will entertain readers with their humor and assure them with their familiarity. In one scene, Rudy astonishes the mother of his hostess by overdoing it on the small talk his father has advised him to employ. In another episode, a sense of relief at the boys' close call is inevitable when, thinking they're performing a good deed, they help two men steal a Mercedes. A few elements make this story special: the poetic perfection Soto exhibits both in description and in authentic dialogue and the immersion of readers into the bosom of a loving, hard-working Mexican-American family.

Publishers Weekly

SOURCE: A review of *The Pool Party,* in *Publishers Weekly,* Vol. 240, No. 23, June 7, 1993, pp. 70-1.

As he did in ***The Skirt,*** Soto again portrays a working-class Mexican American family. When Rudy Herrera is invited to a pool party by a wealthy classmate, he muses about what it will be like and tries to come up with an appropriate gift for his hostess. Rudy's relatives offer plenty of advice on how to make small talk and his father stresses that Rudy be proud of his heritage and his family—no matter what. In the days leading up to the big event Rudy and his friend Alex get into a few scrapes, but the pool toy that they finally find ends up being the hit of the party. This time out Soto delivers a quick read, liberally flavored with slapstick humor and sprinkled with a few stereotypical situations (the boys hitch a ride with two guys who have stolen a car, for example). The novel, however, lacks the flashes of emotional intensity found in the author's other works. Nonetheless, Rudy's eccentric grandfather, self-conscious teenage sister and other colorful characters, along with snippets of Spanish, lend authenticity to this breezy slice of Hispanic life.

Kirkus Reviews

SOURCE: A review of *The Pool Party,* in *Kirkus Reviews,* Vol. LXI, No. 12, June 15, 1993, p. 792.

The Herreras are living in a Fresno, California, barrio when Tiffany Perez, one of the richest kids in school, invites Rudy Herrera to a pool party. His whole family helps him get ready: Grandfather ("El Shorty") advises that a pool party is "when a bunch of guys get together and shoot pool"; older sister Estela urges an improvement in manners lest Rudy embarrass the whole family; his father finds a huge inner tube to take along and tries to teach Rudy how to make small talk; but when the big day comes, the boy's main concern is having a good time. This Latino family has an exemplary warmth and dignity; no matter how often Grandfather tells the same stories, they listen politely; and they all pitch in when Father needs help with his gardening jobs. "Work is honorable," Grandfather asserts as he shows hands "rough as bark." Mexican-American colloquialisms sprinkled throughout the dialogue (and nicely defined by the context—no glossary this time) give it an authentic, playful tone. Engaging, gently humorous—with plenty of realistic full-page drawings and a jacket that's sure to attract readers.

📖 *TOO MANY TAMALES* (1993)

Publishers Weekly

SOURCE: A review of *Too Many Tamales,* in *Publishers Weekly,* Vol. 240, No. 33, August 16, 1993, p. 103.

Snow is falling, preparations for a family feast are underway and the air is thick with excitement. Maria is making tamales, kneading the *masa* and feeling grown-up. All she wants is a chance to wear her mother's diamond ring, which sparkles temptingly on the kitchen counter. When her mother steps away, Maria seizes her opportunity and dons the ring, then carries on with her work. Only later, when the tamales are cooled and a circle of cousins gathered, does Maria remember the diamond. She and the cousins search every tamale—with their teeth. Of course

the ring turns out to be safely on Mom's finger. Soto, noted for such fiction as *Baseball in April,* confers some pleasing touches—a tear on Maria's finger resembles a diamond; he allows the celebrants a Hispanic identity without making it the main focus of the text—but overall the plot is too sentimental (and owes a major debt to an *I Love Lucy* episode). [Ed] Martinez's sensuous oil paintings in deep earth tones conjure up a sense of family unity and the warmth of holidays. The children's expressions are deftly rendered—especially when they are faced with a second batch of tamales.

Kirkus Reviews

SOURCE: A review of *Too Many Tamales,* in *Kirkus Reviews,* Vol. LXI, No. 17, September 1, 1993, p. 1152.

The whole family is coming for Christmas, so Maria and her parents are busy making tamales—Maria helps Mom knead the *masa,* and her father puts them in the pot to boil. While they're working, Maria secretly tries on Mom's diamond ring, then forgets about it until she's playing with her cousins. Since it's not on her thumb she's sure it's in a tamale, so the four cousins consume all 24 (with some difficulty) in hopes of finding it. No luck—the ring's on Mom's finger, after all. In this family, there's no scolding: Aunt Rosa says, "It looks like we all have to cook up another batch," and so they do, three generations laughing and working together. Soto's simple text is charmingly direct; he skips explanations, letting characters reveal themselves by what they do. . . . This one should become a staple on the holiday menu.

Hazel Rochman

SOURCE: A review of *Too Many Tamales,* in *Booklist,* Vol. 90, No. 2, September 15, 1993, p. 151.

More than the usual feel-good holiday celebration of ethnic pride, this warm picture book about a Latina child at Christmas is rooted in cultural tradition and in the physicalness of happy family life, with echoes of universal fairy tale. It's also a very funny story, full of delicious surprise. The handsome, realistic oil paintings, in rich shades of brown, red, and purple, are filled with light, evoking the togetherness of an extended family, and making you notice individual expression and gesture. Maria is happily kneading the *masa,* helping her mother and father make tamales. When her mother takes off her diamond ring, Maria can't resist secretly slipping it onto her finger. The ring falls off into the sticky dough, but it's only after the 24 tamales have been cooked and her cousins, grandparents, and aunt and uncle have arrived for the festivities that Maria suddenly realizes the ring is lost. She begs her cousins for help, and the four kids doggedly, secretly, eat up all the tamales, searching for the ring. In one unforgettable painting, the queasy kids focus on the youngest child's extended stomach: "I think I swallowed something hard," he says. Tearful Maria finally owns up to her mother, but the ring is found, everything is cheerfully resolved, and the whole family moves to the kitchen to cook up another batch of tamales—despite the protesting groans of the stuffed children. Gary Soto is an accomplished poet and adult writer, and his children's stories are widely popular. His first entry into the picture book genre is a joyful success.

Betsy Hearne

SOURCE: A review of *Too Many Tamales,* in *Bulletin of the Center for Children's Books,* Vol. 47, No. 2, October, 1993, p. 59.

A Christmas story, Latino story, and child-appealing story all rolled into one starts with Maria and her mother preparing for a family gathering by making tamales together: "Maria happily kneaded the *masa.* She felt grown-up, wearing her mother's apron. Her mom had even let her wear lipstick and perfume. If only I could wear Mom's ring, she thought to herself." A classic setup! When Mom leaves the room, Maria tries the ring on, kneads the dough, forgets the ring, and remembers too late—after the tamales are cooked and the ring is missing from her finger. The only solution is to gather all the cousins and make them eat every tamale. What they get is not the ring, but stomachaches all around. When Maria confesses, she sees the ring gleaming securely on the hand of her mother, who had rescued it from the dough, and is gently teased out of her chagrin by Aunt Rosa, who starts another batch of tamales. This is a mini-drama rendered so acutely that everyone who has lost something precious will respond, from young viewers to erstwhile children now reading the story aloud to their own charges. The deeply colored paintings, though somewhat posed, intensify the emotional tenor with realistic portraits and thickly textured domestic interiors that serve as dark backdrop to the expressive central character. Soto inflects the narrative with details that incline unpretentiously toward the lyrical without interrupting or overextending the story (as Maria kneads the second batch of dough, "a leftover tear fell from her eyelashes into the bowl and for just a second rested on her finger, sparkling like a jewel"). Vividly traditional but more subtle than the overused piñata scenario, this Christmas crowd-pleaser will serve up a nice balance for Anglo holiday lore.

Jane Marino

SOURCE: A review of *Too Many Tamales,* in *School Library Journal,* Vol. 39, No. 10, October, 1993, p. 48.

A warm family story that combines glowing art with a well-written text to tell of a girl's dilemma on Christmas Eve. While helping make tamales, Maria takes advantage of her mother's brief absence to answer the phone, and tries on her diamond ring. Hours later, when the tamales are made and her relatives have arrived, she realizes that she doesn't remember putting the ring back. Fearing it is in one of the tamales, she employs a real child's attitude toward problem solving and enlists her cousins' aid in eating all of the treats in hopes of finding it. When they are all gone and all tummys are full to the breaking point, and the ring still has not been found, Maria must confess. All ends well, however, thanks to her mother's keen eyes and wisdom as well as the understanding guests who pitch in to make more tamales. Martinez's expressive oil paintings capture the full range of Maria's emotions and her family's reactions. . . . Well worth a year-round place on the shelves.

Ellen Fader

SOURCE: A review of *Too Many Tamales,* in *The Horn Book Magazine,* Vol. LXIX, No. 6, November/December, 1993, p. 727.

Maria is excited to be old enough to help her parents make tamales for Christmas dinner. Wanting to appear as grown-up as possible, she decides to try on the sparkling diamond ring that her mother has placed on the kitchen counter. Hours later, when all the relatives have arrived for Christmas Eve and Maria and her cousins are playing in her room, she remembers the ring. Convinced that it fell off her finger while she was kneading the *masa,* or cornmeal, and is now hidden in one of the tamales, she and her three cousins eat all twenty-four of the increasingly less delicious tamales. Her youngest cousin Danny thinks he may have swallowed the ring, and Maria goes to her mother to confess. But the ring, coated with a few flecks of cornmeal, sits safely on her mother's hand. Maria's punishment, in the forgiving spirit of Christmas, is not very harsh: she must make a new batch of tamales. Her Aunt Rosa teases her: "'Hey, *niña,* it's not so bad. Everyone knows that the second batch of tamales always tastes better than the first, right?'" The cousins, with their achingly full stomachs, "let off a groan the size of twenty-four tamales." Illustrated with rich, glowing oil paintings that reinforce the warmth of a loving family, this book offers a nonreligious glimpse into the celebration of Christmas in one affluent Hispanic household.

CRAZY WEEKEND (1994)

Publishers Weekly

SOURCE: A review of *Crazy Weekend,* in *Publishers Weekly,* Vol. 241, No. 5, January 31, 1994, p. 90.

In this winning combination of a thriller and a comedy, Hector and his "carnal" (Spanish for blood brother), Mando, two realistically represented teens from East L.A., are first excited and then scared when they and Hector's Uncle Julio become the only witnesses to a robbery. Soto (*Baseball in April and Other Stories; Pacific Crossing*) comically contrasts the adolescent wit and energy of these teens (when the two go with Julio on a dinner date, Hector notices that "All evening [Julio] had complimented Vicky with such comments as . . . 'I like the buttons on your dress,' and 'You're a tidy woman'—small talk that made Hector wonder how his uncle ever got girlfriends") with the slowness and spaciness of the robbers (as they look around for a car to steal, Huey "Crybaby" Walker suggests, "Let's get another American car," to which Freddie Bork responds, "Yeah, I like what GM's doing"). The boy's language is a lively and often musical mixture of English and Spanish, and a glossary provides readers with translations of words that may be unfamiliar. An entertaining novel, especially for contemporaries of these hip, likable protagonists.

Kirkus Reviews

SOURCE: A review of *Crazy Weekend,* in *Kirkus Reviews,* Vol. LXII, No. 3, February 1, 1994, p. 150.

Seventh-graders Hector and Mando are spending a weekend with Hector's uncle in Fresno, California. No sooner is the visit underway than the boys run into trouble: Uncle Julio, shooting aerial farm photographs, accidently snaps a crime in progress. Hector and Mando mouth off to a local newspaper about their role in obtaining this evidence and get their names in print along with enough details of the heist to make the robbers nervous. Huey and Freddie, who are comic-book bad guys, are only slightly more dimensional than Julio and his love interest, Vicky. In fact, all the adults are goofy, including chiropractor Dr. Femur; and there are too many points of view, too many lapses in storytelling in quest of easy laughs, too many tics in the unexpectedly graceless writing. *Not* in evidence are such hallmarks of Soto's short stories as low-key humor, fully fleshed-out characters, and defining situations, incisively handled. The weekend may have been crazy; the book is just plain clumsy.

Tom S. Hurlburt

SOURCE: A review of *Crazy Weekend,* in *School Library Journal,* Vol. 40, No. 3, March, 1994, p. 224.

Best friends Hector and Mando, seventh graders from East L. A., spend a weekend with Hector's uncle in Fresno. Uncle Julio, a photographer, takes the boys on an aerial shoot and, by chance, photographs an armored car hold-up. After the local paper features the boys in an article concerning the heist, the robbers pledge to teach them a lesson. A couple of brief encounters come to a head when the crooks try to break into Uncle Julio's apartment. This climactic scene is a cross between *Home Alone* and Hitchcock's *Rear Window,* as the two friends continually foil the break-in attempts and eventually subdue and capture the bad guys. Soto's adept character development brings to life the witty, streetwise boys; the bumbling thugs; and the disheveled but well-meaning Julio. Humor is interjected on each page but is seldom forced, and while the ending may be a bit much, it works. As is a number of other books by this talented author, Spanish words and phrases are sprinkled throughout and a glossary is appended. A fast-moving, light read.

Karen Williams

SOURCE: "Lands Real and Imagined," in *The Christian Science Monitor,* May 6, 1994, pp. 12-13.

When Hector and his friend Mando, two seventh-grade *vatos* (guys) from East Los Angeles, visit Uncle Julio, a photographer in Fresno, Calif., they have more excitement than they ever imagined. In *Crazy Weekend,* Gary Soto creates a rollicking adventure of wise-cracking good guys and accident-prone bad guys. On a photo shoot in a rented Cessna, the boys and Julio witness and photograph an armored-car heist. When the robbers find out, the weekend becomes a chase-filled time of nonstop action.

Adults may roll their eyes at the boys' antics in the last chapters, but kids will applaud dumping marbles and squirting salad dressing—and revel in the crime-doesn't-pay outcome. Soto works many Spanish phrases into conversations and provides a glossary for the uninitiated.

Elizabeth Bush

SOURCE: A review of *Crazy Weekend,* in *Bulletin of the Center for Children's Books,* Vol. 47, No. 11, July/August, 1994, p. 374.

Hector and Mando escape the boredom of an East L.A. February by spending a few days in Fresno with Hector's hospitable young uncle. Tío Julio, a freelance photographer who ekes a living from aerial vanity shots of prosperous farm spreads, takes the boys along on a shoot. Accidentally capturing frames of an armored car robbery, Julio scents the possibility of earning extra cash by selling the story to the press. Our junior high heroes are carried away by their sudden chance at fame and blurt out too much information to their charming newspaper interviewer. When thugs Freddie Bork and Huey "Crybaby" Walker identify the witnesses, the comic chase is on. The boys ultimately foil their foes in a scene abounding with boobytraps and pratfalls, sure to appeal to *Home Alone* fans. The contrast between the boys' warmly realistic relationship with Uncle Julio and the slapstick portrayal of the bumbling criminals makes the tone somewhat uneven. Dialogue is peppered with Spanish phrases, and although a comprehensive glossary is appended, some readers may become impatient with frequent flipping to the back pages. Still, this should satisfy the young adolescent who wants something kind of funny, pretty exciting, and not too long.

Journal of Reading

SOURCE: A review of *Crazy Weekend,* in *Journal of Reading,* Vol. 38, No. 1, September, 1994, p. 72.

Mando and Hector go to Fresno to visit Uncle Julio. When Uncle Julio meets them at the train station, the boys are whisked away to a job he must complete, taking an aerial photo of a local farm. While flying, they photograph a broken down armored truck and two suspicious men. When they read about a robbery in the paper the next morning, Uncle Julio takes his photograph to the local newspaper, where Hector and Mando are interviewed. When an article about them appears and the two bungling robbers see it, the comedy of errors gets frantic.

Gary Soto does a wonderful job of capturing the essence of the Hispanic boys in this novel, not only because of the Spanish sprinkled in the dialog but also because of the mannerisms and speech of the characters. Readers will laugh out loud as the boys catch robbers who are not only inept but comical, reminiscent of the stumbling villains in the *Home Alone* movies.

JESSE (1994)

Cathryn M. Mercier

SOURCE: A review of *Jesse*, in *The Five Owls*, Vol. IX, No. 3, January/February, 1995, p. 64.

In this vivid, muscular portrait, the title character emerges as a complex, winning young man. Jesse narrates his story and fills it with descriptions of his family, his friends, and his surroundings. Without simplifying causal relationships, he shares his dislike for his drinking stepfather and the displacement he feels at home, and he explores the genuine affection he feels for his mother despite her inability to recognize his ambitions to break free of limiting Mexican-American expectations. At sixteen, Jesse has left high school and moved away from home "because it was scary there." What Jesse fears most is that he, too, will slip unwittingly into the life of dissatisfaction and unhappiness he witnesses at home. Jesse's remarkable insight enables him to understand the source of his stepfather's disenchantment, but only escape can alleviate Jesse's discomfort and diminish some of his fear. Jesse's new situation does not offer ease as he and his brother struggle for money and food; it does bring satisfying self-sufficiency and curious, even entertaining, neighbors.

Jesse searches within his close Mexican-American community for connection. He respects and loves his brother and housemate Abel; however, when Abel becomes interested in women, Jesse feels cast out. Jesse fantasizes about Lupe and Minerva, two girls with whom he could foster an association, but his poverty holds him back. At the community college where he studies art, Jesse finds approval and affirmation for his work. The campus Mechistas actively recruit Jesse for participation in protests against conditions and wages for Chicano field workers. Jesse's own back-breaking work on weekends to make rent money by harvesting grapes, cantaloupes, and other seasonal produce and traveling dusty roads on crowded labor buses for meager earnings make him an ideal protester, but he enjoys hanging out with the group less because of political commitment and more because he likes the feeling of being wanted.

Jesse wants to be understood as an individual, with personal hopes, dreams, and talents, with independent likes and preferences. He struggles to pursue his American dream of becoming an artist, and he knows first-hand the societal oppression of Mexican-Americans. The novel's conclusion finds Jesse at his most lonely: Abel is gone, drafted to serve in Vietnam, and someone else inhabits their apartment while Jesse lives alone in the shed. After consideration, Jesse dismisses the romantic image of enlisting to reunite and fight side-by-side with his brother and opts instead to stay in school, paying for it in the only way open to him, as a laborer in "the fields running for miles with cantaloupes like heads, all faceless in the merciless sun."

Gary Soto places Jesse's story in Fresno, California, and realizes that setting with details of clarity and precision. He describes the world through Jesse's eyes: an inhospitable place, cracked, curled, callous. Soto's choice of a first-person narrator establishes an unequivocal authority because Jesse's direct, quiet (almost sotto voce), understated storytelling claims the story. Like Soto, Jesse has the voice of a poet, bending words into evocative images. Jesse sees humor and fun in his world even as he sees its despair. The Vietnam War and labor revolts establish the temporal setting of the novel and serve as tense influences which shape Jesse's life.

Soto's *Jesse* wins readers not only because they admire and like Jesse and not only because they, too, feel heartbroken as Jesse gains painful awareness about the world, but because with Jesse they come to question how the crooked world gets set straight.

Ellen Fader

SOURCE: A review of *Jesse*, in *The Horn Book Magazine*, Vol. LXXI, No. 2, March/April, 1995, pp. 201-02.

In an attempt to escape the drunken stepfather who dominates his household, seventeen-year-old Jesse leaves home to live with his older brother, Abel. Both attend Fresno City College and look forward to lives better than those of many other Mexican Americans in their community. Both struggle with ever-present poverty and discover that race limits their ability to find employment. They often earn spending money by working in the fields picking melons or cotton. Jesse is a serious sort of person, regularly occupied with thoughts of God and the role religion plays in his life. Proud of his increasing talent as an artist, Jesse experiences intense disappointment when his mother fails to understand and appreciate one of his drawings. He wrestles with jealousy when Abel finds a girlfriend, and agonizes over his own shyness as he tries to connect with a young woman who has captured his attention. The novel takes place in 1968 against the backdrop of the Vietnam War, and Soto includes various historical details that evoke that turbulent time, such as the brothers' fear of receiving draft notices, and Jesse's participation in Caesar Chavez's farm workers' movement that attempted to improve working conditions for farm laborers. Just as

Soto tenderly captures Jesse's tentative forays into adulthood, so he paints a more universal picture of the lives of Mexican Americans in central California in a time of cultural and political change. A moving, engrossing novel that contains strands of both humor and despair.

📖 ***SUMMER ON WHEELS* (1995)**

Susan Knorr

SOURCE: A review of *Summer on Wheels,* in *School Library Journal,* Vol. 41, No. 4, April, 1995, p. 136.

Hector and Mando, 13-year-old friends introduced in ***Crazy Weekend,*** return in this story that follows them as they bike from their homes in East Los Angeles to visit Hector's relatives throughout the city. Along the way, Hector earns $100 for appearing in a TV commercial and is rewarded for being the one-millionth attendee at a Dodgers' game. The boys teach bookish cousin Bently how to wrestle, ride a bike, and be more like them; make friends with a spoiled rich girl who challenges them to contests in every sport imaginable, including a paint-ball war; and nearly get mugged until Mando realizes that one of the thugs is his cousin. At their last stop, they get drafted into painting a library mural, which inspires them to paint a rendition of their adventure on Hector's garage. Although the paint-ball episode is a bit overlong, the plot is rollicking, with some dream-come-true aspects, touches of reality, and humor, emphasized by the boys' banter and enhanced by a sprinkling of Spanish words and phrases. Soto's descriptions make the journey vivid and, throughout the boys' scuffles and escapades, they maintain a deep respect for their elders, a love of family, and a healthy curiosity about life. A glossary of Spanish words and phrases is appended, although there is no pronunciation guide.

Maura Bresnahan

SOURCE: A review of *Summer on Wheels,* in *Voice of Youth Advocates,* Vol. 18, No. 1, April, 1995, pp. 27-8.

Bicycles and summer vacation spell freedom for Hector and Mando two pre-teens from East Los Angeles. The two friends first appeared in Soto's ***Crazy Weekend,*** where they helped catch a couple of crooks. In ***Summer on Wheels*** the boys' adventures expand as they bike through Greater LA staying with Hector's far-flung relatives on the way to their final destination—the beach at Santa Monica. Readers will quickly become caught up in the boys' many schemes and escapades which occur with humorous regularity. They have barely left their neighborhood when Hector lands the starring role in a Band-Aid (Soto is obsessed with brand names) commercial because he convinces an exasperated director he can act. As the boys travel through various LA enclaves their worries about a long, boring summer are replaced with memories of performing back-up rap music in a recording studio, watching the Dodgers from a luxury box at Dodger Stadium, playing paintball in an abandoned warehouse, and painting a mural that promotes the power of reading. Throughout their odyssey Hector and Mando make new friends and reestablish ties with relatives not seen for quite some time. In a larger sense Hector's trip has also healed some wounds that had estranged his mother's family. As the novel ends, the boys, proud of what they accomplished on their journey, paint a mural on Hector's parents' garage to commemorate their summer on wheels.

Soto has created two wonderfully believable friends in Hector and Mando. They are typical boys on the cusp of adolescence, still more interested in food and things grotesque than girls. The boys' speech, which is spattered with Spanish expressions that are defined in the glossary at the back, mimics the conversations carried on every day by boys who know each other inside out. This urban slice of life focuses on the positives found in inner city neighborhoods and on the carefree summer adventures that shape us all, no matter our socioeconomic background. Encourage your readers to take a sedentary spin with ***Summer On Wheels.*** Highly recommended.

📖 ***BOYS AT WORK* (1995)**

Rosie Peasley

SOURCE: A review of *Boys at Work,* in *School Library Journal,* Vol. 41, No. 6, June, 1995, p. 113.

Soto once again tells a story of Mexican-American youngsters growing up in the heat of California's Central Valley. When Rudy Herrera accidentally breaks the neighborhood tough guy's Discman, he and his best friend, Alex, are desperate to earn enough money to replace the expensive item before the bully returns to town and destroys them. One crazy money-making scheme after another fails with humorous and not totally unexpected results. Sprinkled with Spanish and teen-specific expressions ("homeboy," "raza-style"), the dialogue is contemporary and realistic. Soto's strength lies in the depth, warmth, and humor of his characters. Especially memorable are Rudy's grandfather, who loves to tell stories of his youth that he thinks relate to Rudy's current problem, and Mrs. Estrada, an elderly neighbor with 13 cats. With its universal growing-up themes of bully-fear, friendship, and family relationships, ***Boys at Work*** is a reader-friendly addition.

Additional coverage of Soto's life and career is contained in the following sources published by Gale Research: *Authors and Artists for Young Adults,* **Vol. 10;** *Contemporary Authors,* **Vol. 125;** *Contemporary Literary Criticism,* **Vols. 32, 80;** *Dictionary of Literary Biography,* **Vol. 82;** *Hispanic Literature Criticism; Hispanic Writers;* **and** *Something about the Author,* **Vol. 80.**

CUMULATIVE INDEXES

How to Use This Index

The main reference

> Baum, L(yman) Frank
> 1856-1919 .... **15**

lists all author entries in this and previous volumes of *Children's Literature Review*.

The cross-references

> See also CA 103; 108; DLB 22; JRDA;
> MAICYA; MTCW; SATA 18; TCLC 7

list all author entries in the following Gale biographical and literary sources:

AAYA = *Authors & Artists for Young Adults*
AITN = *Authors in the News*
BLC = *Black Literature Criticism*
BW = *Black Writers*
CA = *Contemporary Authors*
CAAS = *Contemporary Authors Autobiography Series*
CABS = *Contemporary Authors Bibliographical Series*
CANR = *Contemporary Authors New Revision Series*
CAP = *Contemporary Authors Permanent Series*
CDALB = *Concise Dictionary of American Literary Biography*
CLC = *Contemporary Literary Criticism*
CLR = *Children's Literature Review*
CMLC = *Classical and Medieval Literature Criticism*
DA = *DISCovering Authors*
DC = *Drama Criticism*
DLB = *Dictionary of Literary Biography*
DLBD = *Dictionary of Literary Biography Documentary Series*
DLBY = *Dictionary of Literary Biography Yearbook*
HW = *Hispanic Writers*
JRDA = *Junior DISCovering Authors*
LC = *Literature Criticism from 1400 to 1800*
MAICYA = *Major Authors and Illustrators for Children and Young Adults*
MTCW = *Major 20th-Century Writers*
NCLC = *Nineteenth-Century Literature Criticism*
PC = *Poetry Criticism*
SAAS = *Something about the Author Autobiography Series*
SATA = *Something about the Author*
SSC = *Short Story Criticism*
TCLC = *Twentieth-Century Literary Criticism*
WLC = *World Literature Criticism, 1500 to the Present*
YABC = *Yesterday's Authors of Books for Children*

CUMULATIVE INDEX TO AUTHORS

Author Index

CUMULATIVE INDEX TO NATIONALITIES

Nationality Index

CUMULATIVE INDEX TO TITLES

Title Index

Title Index

Title Index

Title Index

Title Index

Title Index

ISBN 0-8103-9285-2